WATERLOO

c

Also by Paul O'Keeffe

A Genius for Failure: The Life of Benjamin Robert Haydon
Gaudier-Brzeska: An Absolute Case of Genius
Some Sort of Genius: A Life of Wyndham Lewis

WATERLOO

The Aftermath

PAUL O'KEEFFE

THE BODLEY HEAD
London

Published by The Bodley Head 2014

2 4 6 8 10 9 7 5 3 1

Copyright © Paul O'Keeffe 2014

Paul O'Keeffe has asserted his right under the Copyright, Designs
and Patents Act 1988 to be identified as the author of this work

First published in Great Britain in 2014 by
The Bodley Head
20 Vauxhall Bridge Road,
London SW1V 2SA

A Penguin Random House Company

www.bodleyhead.co.uk
www.vintage-books.co.uk

global.penguinrandomhouse.com

A CIP catalogue record for this book
is available from the British Library

ISBN 9781847921826

Penguin Random House supports the Forest Stewardship Council®
(FSC®), the leading international forest-certification organisation. Our books
carrying the FSC label are printed on FSC®-certified paper. FSC is the only
forest-certification scheme supported by the leading environmental
organisations, including Greenpeace. Our paper procurement policy
can be found at www.randomhouse.co.uk/environment

Typeset in Sabon LT Std by Palimpsest Book Production Limited,
Falkirk, Stirlingshire
Printed and bound in Great Britain by Clays Ltd, St Ives plc

For Will Sulkin

CONTENTS

Mayer

Galemart
Annogart
Galemart

Cse du Loup

Bas Ransbeeck

Waterlo
Barriere

Ransbeeck

Piec

Joly Bois

Roussu

de Vieux Amis

Verd Coucou

Dernierment

Ohain

Mesnil

Mont St Jean

Barriere
Braine

Mont St Jean

Jean lin

Lasne

le Culte

la Haye

Papelotte

Frischermont

la Haye Sainte

Smohen

Houyoumont

Aywiers

Reu

la Belle Alliance

Plancenoit

Mon Plaisir

Marausart

Rossomme

Sauvager

Barriere

Maison du Roy

Vieux Manans

Courtelet

Croisant

Caillon

Ste Gertrude

los Flamans

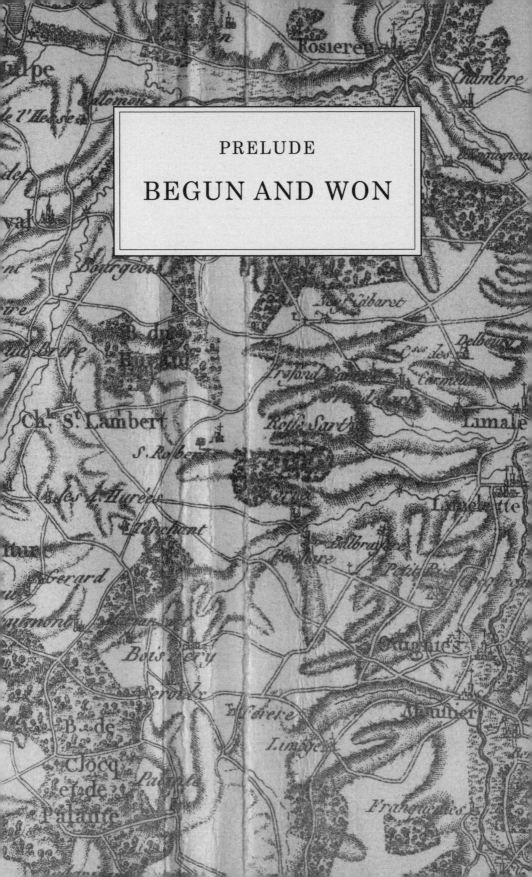

PRELUDE
BEGUN AND WON

MARSHAL Grouchy would insist until the end of his life that a dispatch he received on 18 June 1815 – a dispatch written at one o'clock in the afternoon and which did not reach him until five – had declared the battle won: '*en ce moment la Bataille est gagnée*'. What Napoleon's chief of staff, Marshal Soult, had in fact written was: '*en ce moment la Bataille est engagée*' – that the battle had begun.

'A battle!' the Emperor had said to his staff the evening before in a farmhouse on the road from Charleroi to Brussels. 'Do you know what a battle is? There are empires, kingdoms, the world or its end between a battle won and a battle lost!'[1] The same might have been said of a battle begun and a battle won. But there was little more than a transposition of characters between *engagée* and *gagnée*.

Misinterpretation aside, Grouchy would also insist on the physical impossibility of his complying with the order contained in an already four-hours-old dispatch: that he was not to lose an instant in manoeuvring more than 30,000 men and nearly a hundred cannon across six miles of 'difficult wooded country, cut by ravines',[2] in time to support the Emperor's right flank against an approaching Prussian army. Whether begun or won – *engagée* or *gagnée* – at one o'clock, the battle of Waterloo was not to be materially affected by any action Marshal Grouchy would or could have taken at five.

*

Three days earlier, Bonaparte had launched a pre-emptive campaign against the coalition of enemies massing in Belgium to threaten his restoration as Emperor of France. At dawn on 15 June, when his Armée du Nord crossed the Belgian frontier and marched towards the river Sambre, two hostile armies lay ahead. At Charleroi, and eastwards as far as Liège, were the four corps of Marshal Blücher's Prussian army; north of Charleroi and to the west was the polyglot conglomeration of Britons, Brunswickers, Dutch, Hanoverians, Nassauers and Walloons constituting the I and II Corps, the Cavalry Corps and the Reserve of the Anglo-Allied army commanded by the Duke of Wellington. Napoleon had calculated that, while each of these armies could be beaten separately, their combined forces would constitute an insurmountable obstacle to his principal objective: the capture of Brussels. His strategy was to keep them apart. The road from Nivelles in the west to Namur in the east – the only serviceable, cobbled route across the region, and the vital axis of communication and reinforcement linking the coalition armies – was to be seized at two points. Marshal Ney, Prince de la Moscowa, commanding the French left wing of 25,000 men and forty-four guns, was ordered to capture the junction of this road with that running north from Charleroi to Brussels. The four roads radiating from the crossing gave the place its name: Les Quatre Bras. It would be defended by Wellington's hastily mustered I Corps and Reserve. Meanwhile, the French right wing, commanded by the Emperor himself and numbering nearly 60,000 men and 216 guns, advanced on Blücher's headquarters at Sombreffe, six miles from Quatre Bras along the Nivelles–Namur road.

By the afternoon of 16 June, battle was joined between the French and Prussians on a four-mile-wide front from Tongenelle and Sombreffe to Saint-Amand and Wagnelée, with the village of

Ligny at its centre, while six miles to the east, Ney's forces struggled to break through Wellington's position in front of Quatre Bras. The outcome of each battle was dependent upon that of the other. If the Emperor succeeded in disposing quickly of Blücher's army, he would come to Ney's assistance against Wellington and sweep in triumph to Brussels; if Ney succeeded in disposing of Wellington's army first, he was to attack Blücher's right flank and assist the Emperor in destroying the Prussian army; however, if Wellington was able to defeat Ney at Quatre Bras, he had promised to come to Blücher's assistance and together they would drive the Emperor and his forces back across the Belgian border.

*

Everybody remembered the guns on 16 June. Sound travelled far in the still, hot air: a formidable spike of high pressure building to a storm.

'There they go shaking their blankets again,' one old soldier muttered at Enghien, just over twenty-five miles west of Quatre Bras and Ligny, as his comrades of the 52nd Light Infantry Regiment were cooking their beef ration. 'The sound of a distant cannonade', another veteran wrote later, 'is not unlike that arising from the shaking of a carpet or a blanket.'[3]

Twenty-five miles to the north, Henri de Merode, Belgian nobleman and philosopher, reading on a hilltop close to his ancestral home, Château d'Everberg, east of Brussels, did not at first hear the gunfire, but his studies were disturbed by an unmistakable and continuous tremor underfoot. Kneeling and pressing his ear to the ground, he could clearly distinguish explosions.[4]

They could also hear the guns of Ligny and Quatre Bras in the streets of Antwerp, fifty miles north. Magdalene – for less than three months the young bride of Wellington's acting Quartermaster General, Sir William Howe De Lancey – had left Brussels eight hours before the fighting started. Antwerp was 'a very strongly fortified town', her husband had assured her, 'and likewise having the sea to escape by, if necessary, it was by far the safest place' for her. Wishing to spare his wife the anxiety of hearing the conflicting rumours inevitable at such times, Sir William had made her promise 'to believe no reports' and she had obediently instructed her maid not to communicate any. Under no prohibition from her mistress to listen, however, Emma waited outside their lodgings, terrified by all the latest hearsay: the French had won; the French were at that moment looting Brussels; the French were on their way to ransack Antwerp. Lady De Lancey meanwhile remained in her room with the windows closed to shut out the sound of firing. But she could still hear 'a rolling like the sea at a distance'.[5]

Ten miles to the west of the fighting, somewhere between Braine-le-Comte and Nivelles, Captain Alexander Mercer was leading his troop of Royal Horse Artillery through a forest when he 'became sensible of a dull, sullen sound that filled the air, somewhat resembling that of a distant water-mill, or still more distant thunder'. As he emerged from the trees, the sound became more distinct and, to an artillery officer especially, 'no longer questionable – heavy firing of cannon and musketry, which could now be distinguished from each other plainly. We could also hear the musketry in volleys and independent firing.' Above another forest on the horizon, 'volumes of grey smoke arose'.[6]

Mercer's 'G' Troop consisted of five nine-pounder guns and one heavy 5½-inch howitzer, nine ammunition wagons, a mobile forge, a curricle cart, a baggage wagon and a carriage loaded with spare wheels for the guns and other vehicles. One hundred and twenty draught horses were required to pull all this equipment. Then there were horses for the officers, staff sergeants, collar makers, a farrier, a surgeon, and eight horses for each of six mounted detachments. Counting spare horses, there were 226 animals overall. Guns, wagons and horses were tended by a total personnel of 193, including three shoeing smiths, a wheeler, eighty gunners and eighty-four drivers. 'Perhaps at this time a troop of horse-artillery', Mercer observed, 'was the completest thing in the army . . . a perfect whole.'[7] The complex whole that was 'G' Troop rumbled on to join the guns at Quatre Bras.

In the borrowed Château Walcheuse at Laeken, three miles north of Brussels, Lady Caroline Capel, née Paget, sister to Lord Uxbridge, commander of the Anglo-Allied cavalry, could also hear the gunfire. 'To an English Ear unaccustomed to such things,' she wrote to her mother, 'the Cannonading of a Real Battle is Awful beyond description.' Eight months pregnant, she had not attended Lady Richmond's ball the evening before, but her husband and two of their daughters, Georgiana and Maria – 'Georgy' and 'Muzzy' – had been there, and the juxtaposition of frivolity with a deadly artillery barrage was startling: 'to have one's friends walk out of one's Drawing Room into Action, which has literally been the case on this occasion, is a sensation far beyond description'. At about two o'clock she had first heard 'the distant Cannonading which approached for some time, and awful as it was – every breath was hushed to listen the better – [she did not] think any one of the party [at Château Walcheuse] felt a sensation of fear'. It was 'Anxiety', rather, for the previous evening's dancing partners that 'predominated over every other feeling'.[8]

At Brussels, twenty-five miles closer to the battlefields than Lady De Lancey and three miles closer than Lady Capel, the gunfire was louder still. The English novelist Fanny Burney – Madame d'Arblay by marriage to a French officer loyal to the exiled Louis XVIII – also 'passed [the day] in hearing the cannon'.[9]

Edward Heeley, a fourteen-year-old groom on the staff of Sir George Scovell, wrote that the sound 'came through the air like a quantity of heavy muffled balls tumbling down a long wooden stairs – or perhaps more like a rolling ball, and causing it now and then to hop about on the head of a big drum'.[10]

Elizabeth Ord recalled her brother and stepfather departing for a dinner engagement near the Park – on the eastern edge of the city – and 'soon after a very heavy [firing] began'.[11] Having left his stepdaughter, Thomas Creevey – former Whig MP for the rotten borough of Thetford and awaiting a change in his political fortunes while he cooled his heels abroad following a conviction

for libel – estimated that it was between four and five o'clock
that he and Charles Ord heard the sound of cannon. Arriving at
their destination, they 'found everybody on the rampart listening
to it. In the course of the evening the rampart was crowded with
people listening, and the sound became perfectly distinct and
regular.'[12]

Charlotte Waldie, with her sister and brother, drawn from their
rooms in the Hotel de Flandres by the sound, were in the formal
gardens of the Park itself. Like Madame d'Arblay, Creevey and
the Ords, Miss Waldie and her family were part of the disparate
British expatriate population of Brussels, made a community in
the comforting democracy of crisis:

> One common interest bound together all ranks and conditions of
> men – all other considerations were forgotten – all distinctions
> were levelled – all common forms thrown aside and neglected, –
> ladies accosted men they had never seen before with eager questions;
> no preface – no apology – no ceremony was thought of – strangers
> conversed together like friends – all ranks of people addressed each
> other without hesitation – every body seeking – every body giving
> information – and English reserve seemed no longer to exist.[13]

Madame d'Arblay devised a means of opening conversation with
total strangers: 'by asking them the way to some part of Brussels
of which I was nearly certain they had never heard; & on their
English "I don't know" I hailed them as Countrymen: I then gave
them my good wishes, with an eulogium of the Duke of Wellington,
& we were Friends immediately: & the little they could tell was
communicated with pleasure'. Even the domestic barriers for maintaining privacy seemed removed: 'All the people of Brussels lived
in the streets. Doors seemed of no use, for they were never shut.
The Individuals, when they re-entered their houses, only resided at
the Windows: so that the whole population of the City seemed
constantly in Public view.'[14] Everyone had watched the troops march
south that morning, and by mid-afternoon they were listening,
fascinated, to the sounds of a battle no one had expected so soon.

Lieutenant Basil Jackson was still in Brussels when he first heard 'the booming of distant guns' about two o'clock, and 'the cannonade soon became almost continuous, seeming very near'.[15] Feeling it to be his 'only . . . proper course to endeavour to join head-quarters', his 'boyish ardour' aroused by 'the roar of the cannon', he mounted his horse and galloped towards the action. About seven miles south of the city, having fallen into the company of an elderly colonel and riding at a more sedate pace, Jackson became disorientated by the sound: 'traversing the forest of Soignes, the cannonade was so loud as to lead us to believe that the battle was raging within very few miles of us, probably near Waterloo. On emerging, however, from its glades, the firing seemed to be more distant than we had supposed.'

The same strange fluctuations of sound confused those listening in the Park and on the Brussels ramparts. No one could be sure how far away the fighting was, nor how far off the threat of marauding French hordes, should the city's defenders fail. 'Some people said it was only six, some that it was ten, and some that it was twenty miles off.' Some, to settle the matter, had gone out in carriages or on horseback several miles along the road the army had taken, and all had come back 'in perfect ignorance of the real circumstances of the case'. Reports based on that ignorance nonetheless circulated constantly among the listening crowds: that the allies had 'obtained a complete victory, and the French [had] left *twenty thousand dead* upon the field'; that conversely 'our troops were literally cut to pieces and that the French were advancing on Brussels'. Then a man returned who, riding further than the rest, professed to have actually seen a battle. He reported that the French had fought the Prussians and that 'old Blücher had given the rascals a complete beating'. No sooner had that news allayed the anxieties of the crowd than another man arrived advising everyone 'to set off instantly' for Antwerp if they wished to escape, because 'certain intelligence had been received "that the French had won . . . and that our army was retreating in the utmost confusion"'. Miss Waldie bridled: 'such a report', she declared, 'deserved only to be treated with contempt; and that it must be false, for that the English would never retreat *in confusion'* from anything. At this the gentleman 'seemed a little ashamed of himself', she thought.

The wounded began to arrive late in the afternoon. Among the first to impress the populace was a Brunswicker whose arm had been amputated on the field. 'He rode straight and stark upon his horse, the bloody clouts about his stump, pale as death but upright, with a remarkable stern expression of feature, as if loth to lose his revenge.'[16] The predominant black of the Brunswick division's uniform, relieved by a silvered death's-head badge on the shako, was said to have been worn in mourning for their commander-in-chief's father, killed fighting the French at the battle of Iena in 1806. The death in turn of their commander-in-chief, at Quatre Bras, gave the 'Black Brunswickers' further cause to mourn and avenge. Miss Waldie observed other casualties: 'Waggon loads of Prussians . . . Belgic soldiers, covered with dust and blood, and faint with fatigue and pain [coming] on foot into the town . . . and soon, very soon, they arrived in numbers. At every jolt of the slow waggons upon the rough pavement, we seemed to feel the excruciating pain which they must suffer.'[17]

*

The sun was setting as Captain Mercer and his troop of Royal Horse Artillery passed through Nivelles, about seven miles from Quatre Bras:

All was confusion, agitation, and movement. The danger was impending, explosion after explosion, startling from their vicinity, and the clattering peals of musketry . . . The whole population . . . was in the streets, doors and windows all wide open, whilst the inmates of the houses, male and female, stood huddled together in little groups like frightened sheep . . . In a sort of square . . . a few soldiers, with the air of citizens (probably a municipal guard), were drawn up in line, looking anxiously about them at the numerous bleeding figures [entering town from the east]. Some were staggering along unaided . . . others supported between two comrades, their

faces deadly pale, and knees yielding at every step . . . Priests were
running to and fro, hastening to assist at the last moments of a
dying man . . . There were women, too, mingling in this scene of
agitation. Ladies, fair delicate ladies, stood . . . at the doors of
several handsome houses, their hands folded before them . . . whilst
ever and anon they would move their lips as if in prayer.[18]

On a hill beyond the town, many more citizens stood, straining
their eyes to see the fighting.

In Brussels, the distant roar of cannon continued, and in the
stillness of the evening air it actually seemed to grow louder and
nearer, causing fresh disquiet to the people on the ramparts, who
feared that the battle was moving in their direction. Then, at
about half past nine, the sound became fainter and gradually died
away.

*

Having ridden all day, the men of 'G' Troop arrived at Quatre
Bras, their horses 'stumbling from time to time over the corpses
of the slain, which they were too tired to step over'. By then the
gunfire they had listened to for the previous ten miles had slackened. The last cannon rounds that flew over their heads and the
occasional shell exploding nearby, Mercer noted ruefully, 'were
sufficient to enable us to say we had been *in* the battle . . . just
too late to be useful'.[19] In two days' time, the members of 'G'
Troop would be more than compensated for missing the action.

Returning to her hotel after nightfall, Miss Waldie heard reas-
suring news from Sir Neil Campbell, who had it from Sir George
Scovell, who had left the field at half past five, that 'all was well';
that although greatly outnumbered, the Anglo-Allied army 'had
not yielded an inch of ground . . . and . . . were still fighting in
the fullest confidence of success'.[20] Only one contingent had
disgraced itself. A regiment of 'raw Belgic troops' had run 'like
sheep'[21] from the enemy, but Miss Waldie felt satisfaction that
they had 'almost to a man' been slaughtered by the very troops

they had not dared to fight. 'The fate of cowards is unpitied,' she reflected.[22] Later, around midnight, Major Hamilton, 'his face black with smoke and gunpowder & his mouth so parched he could hardly speak',[23] reported to Creevey and Miss Ord that 'our Army . . . had beat the French, but as not a man of the Cavalry had arrived on the ground, no advantage could be taken of it'.[24] Hostilities had been postponed. 'Tomorrow the engagement will most probably be renewed,' Campbell told Miss Waldie, 'and I hope it will prove decisive.'[25]

*

Neither battle had proved decisive so far. Dogged Prussian resistance at Ligny did not allow Napoleon to comprehensively destroy Blücher's army without reinforcement from Ney, nor was the Emperor able to offer his marshal help at Quatre Bras. Meanwhile, Wellington's initially weak defensive position, although sufficiently strengthened throughout the afternoon to prevent the French from breaking through, did not permit him to send the aid he had promised to Blücher.

The outcome at Quatre Bras might have been different had not Ney's offensive been compromised by the loss of his I Corps. Twenty-one thousand men under the command of Lieutenant General Jean-Baptiste Drouet, Comte d'Erlon – comprising one cavalry and four infantry divisions, six artillery batteries and five companies of engineers – had remained at Gosselies, a position roughly equidistant from Quatre Bras and Ligny, ready to be called upon by Ney or the Emperor as required. At five o'clock, Ney was about to order those fresh troops into action and push forward to the crossroads when he was informed by d'Erlon's chief of staff, General Delcambre, that they were already marching away to attack the Prussian right flank at Ligny. The order for this manoeuvre had come directly from the Emperor, and Ney was neither consulted nor notified until after it had been put into effect. Nettled by the slight, and convinced that a decisive victory could still be secured at Quatre Bras, Ney sent Delcambre to recall the I Corps. Meanwhile, d'Erlon had led his men in the wrong direction, and instead of advancing on Ligny was causing panic further south among troops of the French III Corps, who feared that the unidentified force approaching their rear signalled an outflanking action by the enemy. Then, at about six o'clock, before the hapless I Corps could make any contribution at Ligny – other than to add to the confusion – General Delcambre caught up with d'Erlon and presented him with Ney's countermanding order to return to the attack on Quatre Bras. Leaving just two divisions behind to move on Ligny – insufficient to make any strategic difference to the battle – d'Erlon turned his main force around and marched them back the way they had come. It was nine o'clock when they arrived south of Quatre Bras, and darkness had brought hostilities in that sector to an end. The I Corps had not fired a single shot.

Meanwhile, in a desperate attempt at the breakthrough he had striven for all afternoon, Ney launched a brigade of nearly 800 heavy cavalry on a suicidal charge into the very heart of Wellington's army. Lieutenant General Kellermann, Comte de Valmy, led his 8th and 11th Cuirassiers to glory. Resplendent in thigh boots and shining steel breastplates, with two feet of black horsehair streaming from the brass crests of their helmets, they hacked their way through the 69th South Lincolnshire Regiment and scattered the 33rd Yorkshires, before being raked by musketry and nine-pounder gunfire from the fields and farm buildings to left and right, leaving the approach to the crossroads 'literally macadamised . . . with the carcasses of the Cuirassiers and their horses'.[26] Many gained their objective, if only momentarily, and French cavalry hooves rattled on the cobbles of the Nivelles–Namur road for the first time that day. Then a point-blank barrage of musket fire, round shot and canister fragments ripped through them from three sides, and the vanguard of Kellermann's elite collapsed in a welter of slaughtered horseflesh, perforated steel and mangled humanity. The survivors turned and hurtled back down the carnage-strewn route to the French lines, duty done, glory won and the brigade depleted by more than a third.

At eight o'clock in the evening, the Duke of Wellington – his army reinforced, now outnumbering Ney's by two to one – judged it prudent to advance, and by nightfall the Anglo-Allied positions were approximately where they had been when the fighting started at two o'clock. It had been 'a day without result', according to a French aide-de-camp, 'a drawn battle'.[27] Wellington had lost 4,800 men, Ney 4,140.

The day had not been without result for Napoleon's right wing: between 20,000 and 25,000 Prussians had been killed or wounded or had deserted, at the expense of between 10,000 and 12,000 French.

The Prussian chief of staff, Graf von Gneisenau, called the struggle for Ligny and its neighbouring village of Saint-Amand 'one of the most obstinate recorded in history'.[28] It was an obstinacy born of grudge. The Prussians had suffered too many defeats and humiliations at the hands of the French during the previous decade to meet them on any other terms than that of the most intense ferocity. 'As if overcome by personal hatred, man battled against man . . . as if every individual had met his deadliest enemy and rejoiced at the long-awaited opportunity.'[29] The same commitment was apparent on the opposing side, where French troops could be rallied by history in the same way as the Prussians: 'Soldiers, are you not ashamed', General de La Bédoyère demanded at one crisis in the battle, 'to fall back before these same men whom you have beaten so many times, who begged for mercy while throwing their weapons at your feet at Austerlitz, Iena and Friedland? Attack, and you will see them once more flee and recognise you as their conquerors!'[30] Again they attacked and again fell back and attacked again. Saint-Amand was taken and retaken several times in the course of that broiling hot day.

'Never so cold as in Russia,' a French veteran recalled, 'never so hot as at Ligny.'[31] The natural heat of the day, combined with the man-made conflagration, turned Ligny into a flaming crucible. Napoleon's tactic was to draw the enemy into its own destruction, to sap its strength, exhaust its reserves, until it was too weak to attack or resist. It was a tactic that required monstrous sacrifice of his own forces. Like air sucked into a furnace, troops from both armies poured down the narrow smoke-filled streets, blazing buildings to either side. Intense heat exacerbated the very aspect of savagery, thirst causing men to foam at the mouth as though rabid.[32] The town was so closely packed that the only combat possible was hand to hand, 'with clubbed muskets and bayonets . . . The French plunged their bayonets in the chests of those already falling from their wounds; the Prussians . . . killed everyone that fell into their hands.'[33] A French captain of grena-diers wrote: 'This was not a battle, this was a butchery.'[34] When the Imperial Guard, held in reserve throughout the day, finally attacked at half past eight in the evening, Lieutenant General François Roguet sent them into Ligny with a warning: 'the first man to bring me a Prussian prisoner will be shot'.[35] There was to be no quarter. The streets were by this time so thickly covered with dead that the grenadiers advanced without once treading on firm ground. Passage of the horse-drawn artillery and ammu-nition wagons inflicted further injury to corpses that writhed and jerked under the crushing wheels as though galvanised into renewed, agonised life.[36]

Ligny was taken and the Prussian army defeated, but, despite the slaughter, not annihilated. Blücher was able to retreat, regroup and finally tip the balance towards Napoleon's defeat forty-eight hours later.

On the morning of Saturday 17 June, Wellington received news that the Prussian army was withdrawing north towards Wavre. With no support to be expected from Blücher, his own position at Quatre Bras was unsustainable, and he ordered his forces to march northwards – along a route roughly parallel to that of the Prussians – and await the main French army on the ridge of Mont-Saint-Jean.

*

Very early that same Saturday morning, a Scottish gentleman drove a gig out of Brussels down the Charleroi road to view the previous day's battlefield. On the way he passed two unattended English ladies returning on horseback, 'in agonies of grief'.[37] Having reached Quatre Bras and paid his respects to the field, in particular to the high proportion of tartan-clad slain, the gentleman turned his gig and began the journey back to Brussels. After a couple of miles, he was disconcerted, on looking behind, to find the entire Anglo-Allied army at his heels. He was soon overtaken and his progress along the choked-up road slowed to the pace of the retreating host.

Progress slowed further as it began to rain, the oven heat of 16 June breaking into a cataclysmic storm on the afternoon of the 17th.

'G' Troop was still at Quatre Bras, under orders to 'remain in the rear with [Lord Uxbridge's] cavalry, to cover the retreat'[38] of the main army. It was a risky position but it allowed Captain Mercer to fulfil a cherished ambition. 'I had often longed to see Napoleon,' he recalled:

Now I saw him, and there was a degree of sublimity in the interview rarely equalled. The sky had become overcast since the morning, and at this moment presented a most extraordinary appearance. Large isolated masses of thundercloud, of the deepest, almost inky black, their lower edges hard and strongly defined, lagging down, as if momentarily about to burst, hung suspended over us, involving our position and everything on it in deep and gloomy obscurity; whilst the distant hill lately occupied by the French army still lay bathed in brilliant sunshine.

It was then that he saw Bonaparte, 'a single horseman, immediately followed by several others . . . their dark figures thrown forward in strong relief from the illuminated distance, making them appear much nearer to us than they really were'.[39] As Mercer watched, the horseman and his entourage were joined by squadrons of cavalry and a troop of horse artillery.

'Fire!' roared Lord Uxbridge. 'Fire!'

The guns of 'G' Troop fired.

Had a lucky shot killed the Emperor that day, the village of
Waterloo might not have been memorialised by battle on the day
following: stations, streets, terraces and squares in towns and
cities around the world would have found other names. But
Mercer's guns had no such transformative impact upon history.
And yet, as though in reply to the howitzer and nine-pounders,
the natural storm detonated: 'an awful clap of thunder, and lightning . . . almost blinded us, while the rain came down as if a
water-spout had broken over us . . . Flash succeeded flash, and
the peals of thunder were long and tremendous.' The French
artillery began firing, 'as if in mockery of the elements, [sending]
forth their feebler glare and scarcely audible reports – their cavalry
dashing on at a headlong pace, adding their shouts to the uproar'.
Meanwhile, having fired its single volley, 'G' Troop was retreating
through the driving rain. 'Make haste! – make haste!' Lord
Uxbridge urged them on. 'For God's sake, gallop, or you will be
taken.'[40]

Sergeant Morris of the 73rd Regiment of Foot was on high
ground as the storm hit:

The sky suddenly darkened; and . . . we appeared to be enveloped
in clouds, densely charged with the electric fluid. The rain descended
literally in torrents . . . Our journey hitherto had been up hills, and
now we had some very steep ground to descend; and the rapidly
accumulating water came down with such inconceivable force, that
it was with the utmost difficulty we could keep our feet.[41]

Ahead, the roads were churned to quagmire and 'in some places
more like canals than anything else'.[42] The army 'waded through
mud and water to the knees'.[43] Lieutenant Pattison of the 33rd
Regiment of Foot remembered 'such torrents of rain, and . . .
such vivid lightning, accompanied with such tremendous peals of
thunder, that, though long in a tropical climate, I never beheld
or heard the like before'.[44] From the lowest rank of Pattison's
regiment, Private George Hemingway struggled to give his mother
an account of it: 'and if ever it rained or ever people was exposed

to the bad weather since the memory of man the poor fellows was that day and the whole of that night and marched that most of our road was fast to the knees in mud which caused a great [number of] prisoners and others killed'.[45]

The rain continued to fall when the army reached what would be the site of the following day's battlefield. 'We had to pass the night without tents or covering of any kind save our cloaks, many of us suffering from undressed wounds,'[46] wrote a lieutenant of the 42nd Foot. Another officer described his bivouac 'in a newly ploughed field, in no part of which could a person stand in one place, for many minutes, without sinking to the knees in water and clay'.[47] There was but one consolation as the rain sheeted down on them: they knew 'the enemy were in the same plight'.[48] And so they were. 'Never so cold as in Russia,' the French veteran of the 1812 campaign would tell his grandson, 'never so hot as at Ligny, never so wet as on the eve of Waterloo.'[49]

It took the Scottish gentleman until nightfall to reach Brussels, where he immediately began making preparations to leave. Many other civilians had the same idea, and transport was at a premium; '100 Napoleons',* it was said, 'were offered in vain for a pair of horses to go to Antwerp . . . and numbers set off on foot, and embarked in boats upon the canal'.[50] All that day periodic panics had swept the city as news arrived that the army defending Brussels was in retreat. Miss Waldie had been roused from bed at six o'clock in the morning by cries of '*Les Français sont ici! Les Français sont ici!*' and a 'troop of Belgic cavalry, galloping from the army, at the most furious rate, through the Place Royale, as if the French were at their heels'. For Miss Waldie – making her own arrangements to leave that day – it was always the native 'Belgic' troops who were foremost in any panic. More arrived around noon: infantry running, cavalrymen 'cutting their horses with their sabres' to make them gallop faster.[51]

The governor general of the Belgian provinces, Baron de

---

* 100 napoleons was the equivalent of eight guineas. The napoleon was a gold coin worth 20 francs which, at the exchange rates of the time, amounted to 16 shillings.

Capellen, had tried to allay anxiety with the first of a series of hearty proclamations, issued at seven o'clock that morning. An officer had returned from the advanced posts bringing news that 'all was going well' and that the 'false alarm [was] without foundation'. The governor general himself had 'made no preparations to depart', and he reassured the frightened populace: 'Our armies will renew the attack of the enemy today.' Another proclamation was issued half an hour later with the heartening news that the Duke of Wellington 'was preparing to attack the French army, which was retiring'.[52]

About four o'clock, Creevey had been told by someone who had met a man 'just returned from Head Quarters' that 'things were looking very ill'. This third-hand intelligence was confirmed during dinner by the rumble of baggage wagons and the movement of troops north, not south. 'Everything came *down* the Rue de Namur, nothing went up.' The former member for Thetford went outside and spoke to some soldiers, 'who all looked gloomy and told [him] things were looking but badly when they came away'. That night Major Hamilton, Creevey's most authoritative source of information, 'was graver than usual [and gave] his opinion that a most infernal battle for Bruxelles would be fought the next day'.[53]

On the Sunday morning, the Scottish gentleman was fortunate to secure places on a canal boat for himself and his ailing wife. From the water they could see the congested chaos of exodus by road:

> When horses fell, the waggon wheels crushed the rider; baggage was thrown off and carried away by the peasants to be cut open and plundered. Great sums of money were in this way lost; and clothes and other property spread over the fields . . . The persons crushed in the flight . . . were thrown into the ditches . . . The confusion was dreadful, yet no one had seen a single Frenchman.[54]

Miss Waldie and her family had been on the same road the day before, having persuaded a coachman to take them to Antwerp. She reported that 'the canal . . . was covered with boats . . . and

vessels of every description, and presented a scene of tumult and
confusion scarcely inferior to that upon land'.[55]

During that late morning of 18 June, those remaining in
Brussels again heard the guns, but considerably closer and louder
than those they had heard on the sixteenth: 'one uninterrupted
peal of thunder in their ears for ten hours'. Henri de Merode
had set out to walk the ten miles from Everberg to Brussels.
Several times he encountered the human debris of Ligny and
Quatre Bras still limping north, but as he approached the city
he could hear the artillery fire of a much larger conflict, 'one
that would decide the fate, if not of Europe, then at least of
France and Belgium'. Arriving at his town house, he again felt
the tremors of forty-eight hours previously, this time strong
enough to shatter window panes. After Mass, he collected jewel-
lery and loose gemstones from the house to take back to
Everberg, determined that if he could not get his family out of
the country, then at least they might find shelter further east in
Louvain.[56]

Madame d'Arblay, writing to her husband, was incoherent:
'Since I have *heard* – *since I HEAR* the cannon! Oh mon ami!
– one line! *One word!* – *Daily!* Daily! – For the present awful
moment!' That morning she had gone with her friends Mr and
Mrs Boyd and their eighteen-year-old daughter to take a canal
boat for Antwerp, only to learn that it had been requisitioned by
the military authorities: 'seized for some wounded officers, & we
could get no other'.[57] Returning, disappointed, to the city centre,
they heard what Merode had heard: the Emperor's opening
cannonade accompanying the first French assault on Hougoumont:
'The dread reverberation became louder & louder . . . Every shot
tolled to our imaginations the Death of myriads . . . the destruction & devastation so near us.' They were also aware of the
ramifications of the sound. Rumours circulated that Bonaparte
had encouraged his troops with the promise of three days'
unrestricted pillage of Brussels when the city was taken: 'The
probability that, if all attempt at escape should prove abortive we
might be personally involved in the carnage, gave us sensations

too awful for verbal expressions; we could only gaze, & tremble; listen & shudder.'[58]

By a curious acoustic anomaly not everyone in Brussels could hear the guns from Waterloo. Elizabeth Ord, who had on 16 June heard so clearly 'for several hours . . . a cannonade, the concussion of which on the Air . . . felt as it was close at hand',[59] made no mention of hearing gunfire more than twelve miles closer on the 18th. She and her sister Anne, she recalled, 'during the morning . . . tried to flatter ourselves that as we heard nothing of a very distinct firing perhaps nothing very material was going on'.[60] Their stepfather Mr Creevey, who walked some way along the road towards Waterloo around three o'clock in the afternoon, 'heard no firing' and thought 'all this was well'.[61] It was also said that although the guns of 16 June could be clearly heard in Antwerp, those of the 18th could not. And yet at Ghent, temporary refuge of Louis XVIII and his court – as far to the north-west as Antwerp was to the north – the royalist historian François de Chateaubriand, sharing His Majesty's exile, was walking in the country beyond the city gates when he heard 'a dull rumble . . . now short, now long, at irregular intervals; sometimes . . . perceptible as a tremor of the air, so distant that it communicated itself to the ground over those vast plains'.[62]

The guns at Waterloo could be heard sixty miles away to the east at Herve. They were heard a hundred miles to the south-west at Amiens. The gunfire was heard 'by many hundreds of the inhabitants' at Montreuil, 120 miles west, and described as 'resembling the distant rolling of thunder'.[63] It was even heard 150 miles away in Ramsgate. The *Kentish Gazette* reported: 'A heavy and incessant firing was heard from this coast on Sunday evening in the direction of Dunkirk.'[64] And yet, less than ten miles northwest of the battle, the 6,000 men of Sir Charles Colville's division stationed at Halle, securing Wellington's route to Ostend should the day be lost, 'never heard the firing or anything about the action at Waterloo, till the morning of the 19th'.[65]

But Grouchy heard. Just after half past eleven at a notary's house in Walhain, fifteen miles to the east, he was called outside to the garden from his breakfast strawberries. Several of his staff officers were already there, listening to the distant cannonade.

'I believe we should march to the guns,' said General Gérard after a few moments. Commander of the IV Corps, Gérard had expected to be awarded the baton of a marshal of France before Grouchy and had difficulty concealing his contempt for the man promoted above him.

Some officers knelt, ears to the ground, ascertaining the distance and direction of the gunfire, but this undignified posture became unnecessary as the volume increased, the earth trembled underfoot, and clouds of smoke appeared on the western horizon. A local peasant employed as a guide told them that the sound and smoke came from Mont-Saint-Jean and that they could get there in four or five hours' march. It was 'on the edge of the forest of Soignes', Grouchy's host, the notary, added. 'The distance from here is about three leagues and a half.'

'We must march to the guns!' Gérard said again.

General Valazé agreed: 'We must march toward the guns!'

Marquis Emanuel de Grouchy, newest marshal of France, his star-encrusted blue baton just a fortnight old, had been given command of the right wing – almost a third of the army – comprising about 28,000 infantry, 5,000 cavalry and ninety-six pieces of ordnance. He was, by his own admission, 'vexed' at being given advice by his subordinates, and particularly in the presence of civilians.

He had received the Emperor's orders the day before: he was to pursue Prince Blücher's Prussians retreating from the battle of Ligny, and prevent them from manoeuvring westwards to join Wellington's Anglo-Allied army, in retreat from Quatre Bras. Wellington's force was all that then separated the French from Brussels and could be beaten so long as it was not reinforced by the Prussians. While Napoleon's main army attacked Wellington's, therefore, Grouchy was to be the sword in Blücher's back, '*l'epée dans les reins*', as the Emperor put it: a rapier to the kidneys.[66]

'I am not in the least surprised at the engagement that is now taking place,' Grouchy told his officers, restoring his authority in front of the notary and the peasant. 'But if the Emperor had wished me to take part in it, he would not have sent me away from him, at the very moment that he was himself bearing down upon the English.' He also argued that the roads would be so waterlogged by the recent rains that progress would be sluggish at best and his army 'would not arrive on the field of battle in time to be of any use'.

'Monsieur le Maréchal,' insisted Gérard, 'it is your duty to march to the guns.'

'My duty', snapped Grouchy, 'is to execute the Emperor's orders, which direct me to follow the Prussians; I would be disobeying his commands were I to follow your advice.'

It was then that a message arrived from General Exelmans, commanding the advance guard of the I Cavalry Corps: a large Prussian force had been sighted at Wavre, eight miles to the north. Convinced that this was the main army he had been following since the previous day, Grouchy mounted his horse, feeling entirely justified in continuing the pursuit.

Gérard tried again: 'If you do not wish to march toward the forest of Soignes with all your troops, allow me, at any rate, to do so with my army corps and General Vallin's cavalry. I am certain of arriving, and arriving in time to be useful.'

'No,' came the reply, 'it would be an unpardonable error to divide my troops; unable to give one another support, they would be exposed to annihilation by forces two or three times greater.'

As Grouchy rode north to join Exelmans, he was unaware that only a rearguard of 15,000 Prussians and thirty-five guns – the III Korps only of Blücher's army – awaited him at Wavre, and that the I, II and IV Korps, comprising 75,000 men and over 250 guns, were already marching west from Wavre to Waterloo.

*

Three miles outside Ghent, in the early afternoon of 18 June, Chateaubriand was leaning against a poplar tree at the corner of a hop field, a southerly wind carrying the distinct sound of

artillery, when he saw a courier approaching. Stepping out into
the middle of the road, he stopped the horseman and questioned
him. He had come from the Duc de Berry at Aalst, halfway
between Brussels and Ghent. 'Bonaparte entered Brussels yesterday
after a bloody fight. Battle was due to be re-joined today. The
allies are thought to have suffered a decisive defeat, and the
order for retreat has been given.' The courier rode on towards
Ghent. Chateaubriand followed, his country walk ruined. At one
stage he was overtaken by a carriage bearing a merchant and
his family who confirmed the courier's story. They were closing
the city gates as he arrived, 'some inadequately armed civilians
and a few soldiers from the army depot . . . standing guard'.[67]
Panic was spreading. An emergency council meeting was called
for that evening at Louis XVIII's temporary residence, the Hotel
d'Hane Steenhyse. A wagon containing the crown jewels was
harnessed to a team of horses and made ready for a hasty departure should that prove necessary.

Meanwhile, a holiday atmosphere prevailed as Mr Creevey
took a stroll: 'the Sunday population of Brussels being all out in
the suburbs [beyond] the Porte Namur, sitting about tables
drinking beer and smoking and making merry'. Back in the city
by four o'clock, Creevey was dressing for dinner when his stepdaughter ran in. 'For God's sake, Mr Creevey, come into the
drawing room to my mother immediately. *The French are in the
town.*'

Having calmed his wife, Creevey went outside and discovered it to have been another false alarm, 'occasioned by the
flight of a German regiment of cavalry [the Hanoverian
Cumberland Hassars] who had quitted the field of battle,
galloping through the forest of Soignes, entering the Porte
Namur, and going full speed down the Rue de Namur and thro'
the Place Royale, crying out the French were at their heels. The
confusion and mischief occasioned by these fellows on the road
were incredible.'[68]

Young Edward Heeley encountered the Cumberland Hussars
in another part of town: 'about 50 of the[m] . . . coming at full

gallop, crying out "*Franceuse, Franceuse*, the French, the French"'.
The horsemanship of the female camp followers who fled with
their men made a particular impression on the stable lad. 'They
were well mounted, riding astride on men's saddles, they had on
boots and trousers like dragoons, and wore a gown over all, with
small round bonnets on their heads . . . these women were
amongst the first retreating party who entered Brussels screaming
all the way as they came. They rode well, for their horses' feet
made the fire fly out of the pavement . . . they galloped on straight
forward and if the Devil had been in the way, they would have
went over him.' The origin of this stampede lay back along the
road from Waterloo. 'The confusion may be better imagined than
described', Heeley explained:

> only fancy the quantity of baggage that follows a regiment of
> soldiers in England, say 600 or 700 men, and then fancy
> the baggage, hospital wagons, ammunition carts and wagons,
> officers' baggage animals, etc., etc., belonging to an army of 70,000
> men, besides the roads full of soldiers advancing, and wounded
> leaving the field, every road leading to the field crammed up with
> all the above requisites for the army, and then all in a moment
> the word comes like wildfire, crying 'the British are beaten, retreat,
> retreat'. The whole of this mass wheels round immediately and
> begins to gallop but of course cannot proceed, for at about every
> thirty or forty yards a concussion takes place, and there they all
> are down together. At one spot on the road above twenty horses
> were killed, and of course the men shared the same fate.

It was estimated that 'above a thousand men and horses were
killed in this unfortunate affair'.[69]

*

Towards four o'clock, Grouchy received a dispatch from Marshal
Soult. It had been written at ten o'clock that morning but not
sent until a quarter past eleven – at about the time Grouchy was

enjoying his breakfast in the notary's house at Walhain. He was ordered, in the Emperor's name, to march on Wavre in pursuit of the Prussians, and in so doing manoeuvre closer to Napoleon's forces, which were, at the time of writing, 'about to attack the English Army . . . at Waterloo near the forest of Soignes'.[70] Grouchy 'congratulated himself on having so well fulfilled the instructions of the Emperor . . . instead of listening to General Gérard's advice'.[71] And he wrote to another of his staff – General Berthezène – who had anxiously reported sighting Prussian troops marching west: 'Let the General's mind be at rest, we are on the right road. I have heard from the Emperor, and he commands me to march on Wavre.'

An hour or so later he was there, directing operations against the heavily fortified Prussian positions along the river Dyle. The main focus of attack was the suburb of Wavre on the east bank and the two bridges connecting it with the rest of the town.

Exelmans' dragoons were deployed downriver to the village of Basse-Wavre, and a battalion under General Lefol was ordered to attempt a crossing of the bridge defended by the fortified mill at Bierges upstream. At about five o'clock, Grouchy received a second dispatch from the battle thundering to the west. Like the first, it had arrived several hours after the time written at the bottom of the paper: one o'clock in the afternoon. Again Marshal Soult assured Grouchy that his 'movement . . . to Wavre agrees with His Majesty's arrangements'. But the Emperor's chief of staff was more emphatic than in his previous communication, and more explicit as to Grouchy's wider responsibilities:

The Emperor requests me to tell you that you must keep manoeuvring in our direction, and seek to draw nearer to the army, so as to be able to join us before any [enemy] corps places itself between us. I do not indicate to you any special direction. It is for you to ascertain the point where we are, to act accordingly, and to keep up our communications, and to see that you are constantly in a position to fall upon and annihilate, any of the enemy's troops which might try to molest our right.

There then followed that contentious portion of the dispatch informing him that the fighting was in progress but which Grouchy misread as news of a French victory: 'At the moment the Battle is engaged on the line of Waterloo in front of the forest of Soignes. The centre of the army is at Mont St Jean, therefore manoeuvre to join our Right.'

Grouchy showed the paper to his chief of staff, General Sénécal, and together they studied the word that could have been either *engagée* or *gagnée*. Sénécal would later provide written testimony in support of his commanding officer: 'This dispatch, written in very fine characters and almost illegible, we took great pains to decipher . . . and we thought we read that the battle was won on the line of Waterloo. The marshal closely questioned the officer bearing the dispatch, but he was so drunk as to be incapable of further clarification.'[72] However, the dispatch contained a post-script suggesting that the battle was very far from won. At the Emperor's command post on the ridge of Rossomme – the highest position south of an inn called La Belle Alliance – a message taken from a captured Prussian officer had provided Soult with disturbing intelligence. The letter was addressed to the Duke of Wellington and had come from General von Bülow, commander of the Prussian IV Korps. As telescopes were raised to the distant north-eastern skyline, Napoleon, Soult and the general staff could see the tiny black specks that some took to be trees, some to be troops in position, but most recognised as troops on the march. Before sending his one o'clock dispatch to Grouchy, Soult scribbled at the bottom of the page: 'PS A letter which has just been intercepted tells us that General Bülow is to attack our right flank. We believe we can perceive this corps on the heights of Chapelle-Saint-Lambert. Therefore do not lose an instant to draw nearer to us and to join us and crush Bülow, whom you will catch *en flagrant délit*.'

Generations of Bonapartists and military historians have condemned Grouchy for failing to take into account the urgency of this second dispatch, for his earlier refusal to 'march to the guns', and for thereby effectively losing his Emperor the battle.

Grouchy did however comply with the spirit of Napoleon's orders, even though by that time in the afternoon he must have known that the tactical situation could no longer be the same as when Soult had written. Nevertheless, as instructed, he manoeuvred towards the Emperor's right, but with only half of his forces. After all, he had been told that the battle was won. He sent his aide-de-camp, Vicomte de Pontbellanger, to Lieutenant General Pajol, commander of the I Cavalry Corps, with an order to cross the river Dyle three miles upstream of Wavre, and capture Limale. This village was on a direct route to Chapelle-Saint-Lambert four miles west, where the enemy troops threatening the main army's right flank had been sighted. The III Corps and a division of cavalry were to remain on the right bank of the rain-swollen Dyle, facing impregnable Prussian positions at Wavre, while Gérard's IV Corps was to march south to assist Pajol in occupying Limale.

'Never was the Emperor so great!' Intoxicated by the misreading of a single word, Pontbellanger spoke as though he had actually witnessed the triumph. 'The battle is won,' he told Pajol as he delivered Grouchy's orders, 'and only cavalry is needed to complete the rout!'[73]

Not all Grouchy's staff had such confidence either in his military judgement or in his competence. General Exelmans, commander of the II Cavalry Corps, is said to have threatened to 'blow that bastard's brains out'.[74] The hot-headed Gérard – shortly before receiving a Prussian musket ball to the chest – anticipated two centuries of blame that would be heaped on Grouchy's head, when he shouted at him: 'If we're fucked, it's your fault!'[75]

Later, Gérard having been carried gravely wounded from the field, his command was taken by Grouchy who personally led two infantry divisions of the IV Corps to join Pajol's troops at Limale.

*

In Antwerp that Sunday, Miss Waldie waited in the rain for news. Anxious crowds thronged the place de Maire, 'one compact mass

of umbrellas'[76] when seen from the hotel windows above. At last
they learned the worst:

> Between nine and ten in the evening, some wounded British officers
> arrived on horseback from the field, bringing the dreadful news
> that the battle was lost, and that Brussels was actually in the
> possession of the French! This was corroborated by fugitives from
> Brussels, who affirmed they had seen the French in the town; and
> one gentleman declared he had been pursued by them, half way
> to Malinés . . . later accounts tended to confirm these disastrous
> tidings, and Antwerp was filled with consternation and dismay.[77]

Many who had already fled from Brussels considered Antwerp
no longer safe and continued to flee northwards into Holland.

If Magdalene De Lancey's maid had suggested flight that Sunday
evening, her mistress would have answered as she had done the
day before: 'Well, Emma, you know that if the French were firing
at this house, I would not move till I was ordered; but you have
no such duty, therefore go if you like. I dare say any of the families will let you join them.' Emma stayed with her mistress. Lady
De Lancey left no detailed impressions of Antwerp on the day
of the battle. Indeed, if she had spent it as she had spent Friday
– in her room with the windows closed against the sound of
firing – there would have been little to report. At midnight on
the Saturday she had received a short note from her husband,
written the previous evening, just after the battle of Quatre Bras.
He was safe, he told her, and in great spirits: 'They had given
the French a tremendous beating.' Her only other source of reliable information was Captain Mitchell of the Quartermaster
General's department, who reported that 'the last effort was to
be made' on Sunday. The euphoria occasioned by her husband's
letter faded. The fighting, she wrote:

> had continued so much longer than I had expected already that I
> began to find it difficult to keep up my spirits, though I was
> infatuated enough to think it quite impossible that he could be

hurt . . . I might be uneasy at the length of the separation, or anxious to hear from him; but the possibility of his being wounded never glanced into my mind, till I was told he was killed.[78]

Sometime between ten and eleven o'clock on Sunday night, Major Hamilton arrived in Brussels. Slightly wounded in the head and foot, he had walked the twelve miles from the battlefield, leading the more seriously injured Major General Barnes on a horse which had two musket balls in its flank. When they left the field, at about five o'clock, he told Mr Creevey, 'his impression was . . . the battle was lost, that the Prussians had not come, and that all was over or nearly so'. Creevey's family went to bed, his stepdaughters Elizabeth and Anne 'never taking off their clothes, and all expecting the French every moment'.[79]

Madame d'Arblay was staying with the Boyd family, who had also gone to bed fully dressed in preparation for the worst. She, however, because of 'excessive inquietude', was prevented from sleeping and wrote to her husband, recounting the fluctuating rumours of the day:

All at first was ill . . . The news then changed, & in the Evening, I was assured Lord Wellington & M[arshal] Blücher united had gained a complete victory . . . But now, the last news of all, tells us the Enemy is working at turning the right wing of Lord Wellington, who is in great danger, & that Brussels is threatened with being taken to-morrow morning . . .[80]

Hamilton had promised Creevey and his stepdaughters that, if they wished to leave Brussels, he would find a carriage and send a guard with them. 'He did not think [the French would] do more than plunder us,' wrote Elizabeth, 'but we must think whether we could stand the fright.'[81]

The Boyds and Madame d'Arblay did not need to think long about the matter and had already determined to start early in the morning to secure places on a canal boat to Antwerp that had been denied them the previous morning.

Lady Caroline Capel, at the Château Walcheuse, had decided her family would be safer taking the opposite course: '[that] if everything failed, to get back into Brussels'. The house was in the middle of a wood, isolated from neighbours and assistance, and the threat of 'a party of French stragglers coming up, was not to be borne'.[82]

*

At seven o'clock in the evening, Lieutenant General Pajol, with two cavalry divisions, one infantry division and three artillery batteries, crossed the river Dyle without difficulty. The Limale bridge – unlike those downstream at Bierges and Wavre – had been neither destroyed nor barricaded by the Prussians. Limale itself was captured with equal ease, and by the time Grouchy arrived with two infantry divisions of the IV Corps at about nine o'clock, the Prussians had retreated to the high ground north of the town. In the fading light Grouchy ordered his troops up the steep slope to the plateau, where confused fighting continued late into the night. The Prussians launched a near-blind bayonet charge in the dark, wading through man-high corn in some places, stumbling over clumps of heather in others. Unable to maintain order and contact, the first wave of troops was overtaken by the second, which was supposed to support them. It became difficult to distinguish friend from foe in the gloom, enemy skirmishers and cavalry as likely to be encountered from the rear as from the front. At one stage of this melee, a Prussian battalion blundered into a sunken road under heavy fire from the French. Concealed by darkness, and just below the level of the enemy's gun barrels, the infantry survived uninjured, French musket balls passing overhead and rattling harmlessly among their raised bayonets. Dismounted officers were also spared, but those on horseback were hit without exception, among them the regimental and battalion commanders, both wounded, and the battalion's adjutant killed.

Meanwhile, in front of Wavre, battle was joined with a fierce obstinacy recalling the attack and defence of Ligny two days earlier. General Vandamme's III Corps made thirteen separate attacks against the barricaded bridges, each one driven back by musket volleys from the loopholes cut into every house wall facing the river. Sometimes the Prussians succeeded not only in repelling the attacks but in reaching the French positions across the Dyle, before being driven back in their turn. Around eleven o'clock the fighting ended and both sides prepared to renew hostilities in the morning. Parts of Wavre burned through the night.

*

Six miles to the west, the disintegration of Napoleon's Armée du Nord on that evening of 18 June had taken just an hour and a half as the main Prussian army arrived from Wavre in sufficient numbers to turn the tide of battle against him. At around seven o'clock, 4,600 troops from the I Korps, commanded by Generallieutenant von Zieten, began to flood on to the battleground from the north-east, through the fortified farms of Smohain, La Haye and Papelotte, and the chateau of Frichermont. The Prussian arrivals strengthened Wellington's left wing, allowing him to re-inforce his dangerously depleted centre in time to meet the Emperor's main attack.

To the east and south-east, a ferocious struggle had been in progress since about half past four between the French VI Corps and a Prussian force three times its size. Generallieutenant Graf Bülow von Dennewitz's IV Korps poured men, lead, fire and iron into the village of Plancenoit, bleeding the French of their reserves as the Prussian reserves had been bled by the French during the infernal battle for Ligny. To retain this vital position on his vulnerable right flank and prevent encirclement from the rear, by seven o'clock Napoleon had already thrown all eight battalions of his Imperial Young Guard into the carnage. Nearly 4,300 strong as they advanced, they were reduced – dead, wounded and missing – to fewer than 600. As the Young Guard's fragments were beaten back, two battalions of the Old Guard were sent in. Numbering little more than a thousand, they were dispatched under personal orders from the Emperor – the Old Guard did not march at any lesser bidding – and were to lose no time stopping to fire and reload their muskets: 'Do not fire a shot,' Napoleon instructed them, 'but fall on the enemy with the bayonet.'[83] These elite troops would normally have been kept in reserve until a final push to certain victory. Their deployment at Plancenoit against overwhelming enemy numbers indicated the recklessness of desperation. Bülow had been even more profligate with his forces and, overall, lost a greater number of men to the savage street fighting at Plancenoit than did the French. He had, however, considerably more men to spare.

Meanwhile, the Emperor prepared to launch his last hope – another eight Guard battalions, five of the Middle Guard supported by three of the Old – towards the north-west, against Wellington's centre. To raise morale, he had attempted to deceive his troops into believing that the cannon fire they could hear in the east came not from the Prussian guns but from those of Grouchy's long-awaited reinforcements. General de La Bédoyère brought the treacherous news to Marshal Ney, who instructed his own aide-de-camp to communicate it to the ranks. '*Voilà Grouchy!*' shouted Colonel Levavasseur, galloping along the lines of waiting troops, his hat raised on the tip of his sabre: 'Here is Grouchy! *Vive l'Empereur!*' And the Guard responded: '*Vive l'Empereur! En avant! En avant!*'[84]

Their advance up the sloping ground between Hougoumont and La Haye Sainte towards Wellington's newly strengthened positions on the ridge began soon after 7.30. Within twenty minutes, the hitherto invincible Imperial Guard – the 'bulwark of the Army'[85] – had broken under murderous salvoes of canister shot and rapid musket fire. Of 2,900 men, some 2,200 fell, either 'killed or mutilated', as a sergeant of the 1st Grenadiers observed, 'for all the wounds were most serious'.[86] The trauma of this unprecedented catastrophe coincided with von Zieten's Prussians breaking through the French I Corps in front of Papelotte.

The debacle began. There were cries of 'Sauve qui peut!' translating literally as 'Save who can', loosely as 'Every man for himself'. There were cries of 'Trahison!' – and they had reason to think themselves betrayed. 'Voilà Grouchy!' they had been told, and their victory assured. There were cries also of 'La Garde recule!' This unthinkable news, that the indomitable Guard had retreated, spread and 'augmented the disorder', a French artillery officer remembered. 'The crowd became terrified; no description can do it justice.'[87] Lieutenant Martin of the 45th Infantry Regiment was caught up in the melee: 'Everyone was fleeing as fast and far as possible. I did the same as everyone else . . . Panic had seized the entire army. There was nothing more than a confused mass of infantry soldiers, cavalry and guns that rushed, all mixed together, across the plain like an unstoppable torrent.'[88]

Driven by Wellington's lines advancing from their ridge and by von Zieten's I Korps sweeping down from Papelotte at an oblique angle to the Brussels–Charleroi road, the torrent flowed, undifferentiated by rank or regiment, in the direction of the border, France and safety. The remnants of a Middle Guard battalion close to Hougoumont tried desperately to conduct an orderly retreat. Depleted by concentrations of round shot, shell and canister from 500 men to a hundred, an infantry square of three ranks was battered into a triangle of just two before finally breaking up completely. Three Old Guard battalions – unused in the main attack – also maintained discipline for a time, retreating in square, surrounded by the horde of frantic humanity, 'as rocks in a raging sea'.

And so the French army collapsed under pressure, first from two sides, then from a third as – at around 8.30 – Plancenoit fell to the Prussians. When the last defenders were driven out of its streets and blazing ruins, between 5,000 and 6,000 corpses from both armies were left behind. As 400 or so survivors of the 15th Prussian Infantry Regiment's fusilier battalion emerged from undergrowth on the southern outskirts of the village, they could see, across a broad expanse of wheat, the road ahead streaming with fugitives. Crossing the field, the fusiliers came under inadvertent fire from Wellington's guns off to their right. The Prussian gunners, for their part, are said to have hesitated from firing on the road because, as night fell, it was becoming increasingly difficult to distinguish friend from foe, pursuer from pursued.[89]

*

Six miles to the east, on the plateau above Limale, the Prussians had withdrawn from their chaotic nocturnal attack to bivouac along the edge of the forest of Rixensart. The French waited out the night close enough to the enemy lines to hear conversation, the routine challenge and response of sentries, the moans of wounded and dying. The vigil was tense, punctuated by the occasional crackle of musketry from either side as targets presented themselves in the moonlight.

Generallieutenant von Thielemann, commanding the Prussian III Korps, received an unconfirmed report during the night that Napoleon's army had been defeated.[90] At the same time, Grouchy was comforted by his contrary but equally unsubstantiated conviction of a French victory. From his headquarters at a farm called La Bourse, he wrote to General Vandamme with orders to join him on the heights above Limale, leaving only as many of the III Corps opposite Wavre as were necessary to hold those positions. Grouchy intended attacking the Prussians at dawn, joining his Emperor as instructed and pressing on to Brussels.

It was approaching midnight. No gunfire had been heard from the west for several hours.

*

Four and a half thousand miles away, on the other side of the Atlantic Ocean, events were proceeding with a dramatic irony only possible in an age without electronic communication.

On 12 June 1815, the day Bonaparte left Paris for the Belgian border to do battle with his enemies, a French schooner was approaching the Caribbean Leeward Islands. The *Agile* had sailed from the port of Rochefort on 9 May carrying dispatches from Napoleon's Minister of Marine, Admiral le Duc Decrès, to the French colonial governors of Martinique and Guadeloupe, bringing news of the Emperor's escape from Elba and urging them to renew their allegiance to the restored imperial dynasty.* Among these papers was incidental advice on the subject of flags: to avoid unwelcome interference from vessels hostile to the Emperor, for the time being French ships were to continue flying the Royal Standard of Louis XVIII and his Bourbon forebears – a white flag signifying purity – rather than the revolutionary tricolour.

The two main islands of the Guadeloupe archipelago, Basse-Terre to the west and Grande-Terre to the east, are separated by a very narrow sea channel. Despite her white flag, the *Agile* was intercepted by two British ships – a brig and a cruiser – as she approached the harbour of Sainte-Françoise on the eastern island. The French vessel was boarded and escorted to the flagship *Venerable*, anchored off Les Saintes, the small cluster of islands ten miles south of Basse-Terre, recently seized for their strategic importance by the British. Aboard HMS *Venerable*, Rear Admiral Durham deliberated how best to deal with the situation.

In addition to Les Saintes, the Royal Navy had also occupied the island of Martinique – at its governor's invitation – to preserve the colony for the French King in this time of crisis and prevent its 'being thrown into a state of revolutionary convulsion'[91] by news of Bonaparte's return to power. Durham suspected that the dispatches carried by the *Agile* – dispatches bearing Napoleon's seal – 'would produce a Pandora's Box effect', exacerbating unrest on Guadeloupe, its people notably sympathetic to Bonaparte and already inflamed by the occupation of Martinique and Les Saintes by the hated English. Having no authority, as yet, to attack French

* Both colonies, captured by the British in 1809–10, had been restored to France the previous year under the terms of the Treaty of Vienna.

shipping travelling under any flag, and therefore unable to seize the dispatches by force, Admiral Durham could at least stop them reaching Guadeloupe and gave orders for the *Agile* to be escorted to Martinique instead.

Then he changed his mind.

It was later claimed, by Colonel Boyer de Peyreleau, second in command to the governor of Guadeloupe and chief instigator of its uprising, that Durham was 'hungry for a pretext to take over the colony', and had even been heard to say that 'since the English had not been able to occupy it on the same basis as Martinique, they would have it at any price'.[92] If that price entailed creating a pretext for invasion by allowing Bonapartist dispatches to fan the flames of insurrection, then so be it. Whatever the truth of this allegation, having first directed the *Agile* towards Martinique, Durham pursued and caught up with the schooner in the Dominican Channel and pointedly allowed her captain to deliver the 'Pandora's Box' of dispatches wherever he wished.

And so, on the morning of 15 June, the day that Napoleon's army crossed the Sambre and captured Charleroi, firing the first shots of his last campaign, the *Agile* dropped anchor in Basse-Terre harbour on Guadeloupe's eastern island. Lieutenant Forsan was rowed ashore, a tricolour cockade in his hat, carrying the dispatches and a parcel of French newspapers. On the quayside, he was greeted by the harbourmaster and distributed copies of the *Moniteur Universel*, containing the months-old news from France, among the waiting crowd. Excitement grew as the newspapers were scanned and the rumours circulated by previous visiting ships confirmed in hard print: of the Emperor's return from exile; of his landing at Antibes; of his triumphant arrival at the Tuileries on 20 March; of the King's flight to Ghent on the 19th. As Forsan crossed the town on his way to Government House the crowd following him swelled until, by the time he was admitted to the governor's presence, over 4,000 waited outside, avid for further news and sensation.

Having taken delivery of the dispatches, Rear Admiral Durand, Comte de Linois, governor of Guadeloupe, prevaricated. He had

known of events in France since the end of April. A letter from
the French ambassador in London had informed him then of
Napoleon's return and had ordered him to maintain control of
Guadeloupe in the exiled King's name. Linois had written in reply
'protesting his fidelity and devotion to His Majesty'.[93] This letter
would be submitted as evidence at his court martial, alongside
further evidence that he had subsequently betrayed that fidelity
and devotion to his King.

Linois must have known he would eventually receive orders
from the new administration, but that did not make him better
prepared for the arrival of Admiral Decrès' dispatches. Their
conflicting claim on his fidelity and devotion paralysed him. He
gathered his officials to discuss the best course of action. They
stared at Napoleon's seal. All knew that, apart from their symbolic
importance, the actual content of the dispatches was an irrele-
vance. But in breaking the seal, the governor would acknowledge
the usurping power's authority and be thereby guilty of an act
of treason. Linois decided to leave the seal intact and to send the
dispatches, at the earliest opportunity, to London, for the French
ambassador there to deal with.

While the port of Basse-Terre was Guadeloupe's administrative capital, Pointe-à-Pitre, on its eastern island, had the greater
population. It was also the centre of what military strength the
colony possessed. Two thousand men of the 62nd Infantry
Regiment and the 6th Regiment of Artillery were garrisoned
there, as well as 4,000 National Guards. At Pointe-à-Pitre, the
governor's second in command, Colonel Boyer, held sway. It
was from here that the rumour spread, throwing both islands
into a state of agitation, that the Basse-Terre administration
intended following the example of Martinique in surrendering
the colony to the English. It was at Pointe-à-Pitre that the insurrection began.

Late on the Sunday morning of 18 June, the day that the
Emperor's guns roared across a shallow Belgian valley to begin
the battle he could not afford to lose, a tricolour was hoisted in
Pointe-à-Pitre's place des Armes. Captain Fromentin, Boyer's

adjutant, addressed his men. Waving his hand at the flag that he said had 'never been conquered', Fromentin spoke of its 'fixing for ever the destinies of France'.[94] Meanwhile, on the western island, Colonel Boyer himself had roused the garrison at Beausoleil by confirming the prevailing rumour of imminent invasion. He read aloud to the troops a letter intercepted from M. Vaucresson, chief naval commissar, saying that 'the English will descend on the island in order to bring the *canaille* to reason'.[95]

From Beausoleil, Boyer sent Captain Desrivières and two companies of grenadiers to Government House in Basse-Terre. At six o'clock in the morning, Linois was preparing to attend Mass with his family when Desrivières burst into his quarters and addressed him in terms that only a man with a drawn sabre in his hand and a body of troops at his back could make convincing: 'You are my prisoner, all resistance is useless.'[96] In the name of Colonel Boyer, 'commander of the island of Guadeloupe',[97] the captain ordered Linois to surrender the dispatches delivered by the *Agile*. When he refused, the governor was placed under house arrest. Mass had to be deferred for the Linois family that day.

Boyer arrived at half past nine and asked for the dispatches in a less belligerent manner than his captain had done. Linois replied that he no longer had any objection to the dispatches being opened because, rather than betray his oath of loyalty to the King, he intended renouncing his duties as governor and demanded that a ship be found to take him off the island the following day. That night, he was visited by a delegation of citizens, who pleaded with him to remain. A letter arrived from Colonel Boyer: he was reluctantly prepared to take on the authority the governor was surrendering, but he implored him to reconsider. By the following morning, Linois had decided to resume his duties and join the revolution. Later, on trial for his life, he would explain his reasoning:

The more I saw of the dangers of remaining head of the colony, the more it seemed that it would be cowardly of me to abandon it. I knew that if the King recovered his throne, I would be called to give an account of my conduct. I also knew that if Bonaparte remained in power, he would never forgive me for refusing to read his dispatches and I would be banished for ever from my beloved country.[98]

Later that morning, surrounded by the civil and military authorities of the colony, he greeted two British naval officers sent ashore by Admiral Durham, whose flagship lay at anchor in the harbour. The previous day, HMS *Venerable*'s lookouts had sighted the tricolour flag flying at Pointe-à-Pitre, and Durham wished to know if there was any assistance His Britannic Majesty's Royal Navy could offer to the governor.

'We are now all of one mind here,' Linois told the Englishmen, and pointed at the blue, white and red ribbon in his hat: 'You see this cockade, we will defend it to the death.'

The officers returned to their ship, having no orders, for the moment, to attack these or any other colours.

The governor was 'radiant', declaring this to be 'one of the most beautiful days of his life'.[99] He ordered the tricolour raised on the roof of Government House and a twenty-one-gun salute marked the occasion. Having foregone Mass the previous morning, he attended church, sang a solemn *Te Deum* in thanksgiving and issued a decree that a *Te Deum* be sung in every parish of the colony on the Sunday following. He published a proclamation:

Soldiers, National Guards, inhabitants of Guadeloupe, reports have already brought us news of the return to France of Napoleon. In his triumphal march from the Gulf of Juan to the Tuileries, not a drop of blood has been spilt, not a single act of violence committed: the love of the people, the enthusiasm of the army were all that was needed.

Today there is not a single part of France where the tricolour flag does not fly, and where the love of the nation is not unanimously supporting the Sovereign restored to it with so great acclaim.

The ministerial dispatches which we received by the *Agile* from the French government leave no doubt that we should rally, on this great occasion, to the government's will for the re-establishment of the Imperial dynasty. Let us swear this vow, colonists and servicemen, and let all wear the tricolour cockade that twenty-five years of glory have made illustrious. Let us never separate ourselves from the great family and let us merit the glorious title of true Frenchmen.

Citizens of Guadeloupe and soldiers, I count on your loyalty and your generosity, to work with me towards maintaining the order and peace of the colony, and to reverently respect the people, and public and private property; let us banish from our hearts and from our thoughts all sentiments of hatred and recrimination.

All individuals who disturb the public order will be severely punished. *Vive l'Empereur.*[100]

As the governor signed his proclamation, on 19 June 1815, the Imperial Army was retreating across the Belgian border, a beaten rabble. Just over fifty days later, the flag waving above Linois' head from the roof of Government House, Basse-Terre, Guadeloupe, would be among the last tricolours struck in the wars against Napoleon.

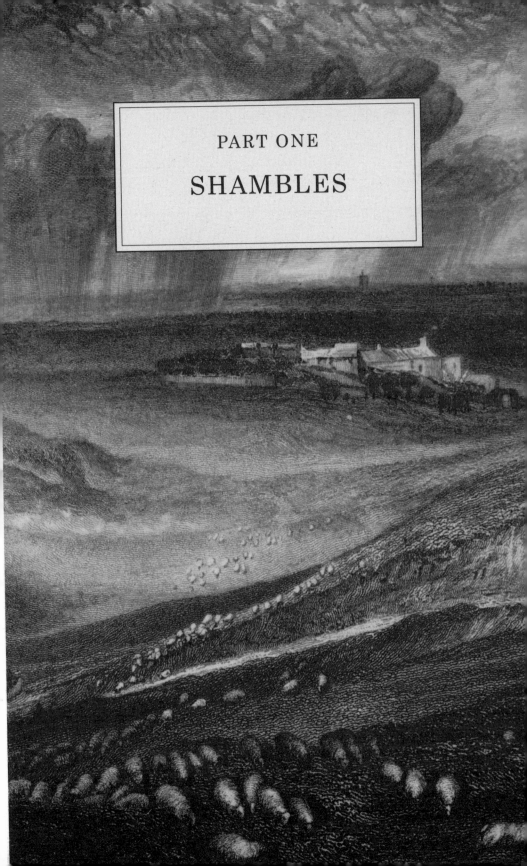

PART ONE
SHAMBLES

I

TWELVE o'clock, and with a gibbous moon waxing to full, Sunday
18 June passed into Monday. Captain Mercer woke to a slaughter
ground rendered perversely beautiful by the night. He saw 'pale
wan faces [of the dead] upturned to the moon's cold beams, which
caps and breastplates, and a thousand other things reflected back
in brilliant pencils of light from as many different points'. It was
'a thrilling sensation', this serene contemplation after the day's
tumult. All was 'calm and still', and to Mercer, whose eardrums
had been pounded to deafness by eleven hours of artillery fire,
eerily silent. The landscape of carnage, observed through the
silvered filter of moonlight, appeared as artificial as a theatrical
setting, a scene of fascination for the curious spectator:

> Here and there some poor wretch, sitting up amidst the countless
> dead, busied himself in endeavours to staunch the flowing stream
> with which his life was fast ebbing away . . . From time to time
> a figure would half raise itself from the ground, and then, with a
> despairing groan, fall back again. Others, slowly and painfully
> rising . . . would stagger away with uncertain steps across the field
> in search of succour. Many of these I followed with my gaze until
> lost in the obscurity of distance; but many . . . after staggering a
> few paces, would sink again to the ground, probably to rise no
> more. It was heartrending – and yet I gazed![1]

Gazed and did nothing. Gazed and *could* do nothing.

Standing in the moonlight, Mercer cut a truly 'bloody figure'. The blood was not his own, but a result of gruesome collateral damage. He had been chatting with Lieutenant Breton during the battle, Breton's horse standing at right angles to Mercer's. Bending out from his saddle to hear what Breton was shouting to him above the roar of the enemy's guns, Mercer casually rested an elbow between the ears of his colleague's animal and felt its muzzle press against his thigh. At that moment a round shot crashed through the horse's head, and as the skull exploded, a warm swill of blood and brain matter splashed up Mercer's chest and gushed down into his lap, drenching him to the skin. This was the third horse killed under Lieutenant Breton that day, and for Mercer, one of three miraculously narrow escapes, making him 'feel in full force the goodness of Him who protected . . . among so many dangers'.[2] But, unable to change his clothes or wash for twenty-four hours afterwards, the congealing blood would fuse the saturated fabric of his overall trousers – clotted to the stiffness of board – on to the tender flesh of his groin. The resultant chafing cut him severely between anus and scrotum, an injury that would cause him intermittent torment for years to come and, more immediately, oblige him to ride 'side-saddle fashion' to Paris, 'except on very urgent occasions'.[3]

But for that night Mercer believed himself unscathed as he contemplated the terrible achievement of the day before. Each of his guns had expended nearly 700 rounds over the course of the battle, and in the latter stages, 'G' Troop had withstood and repelled three French cavalry charges with salvoes of canister shot. The tin casings containing shot disintegrated when fired, and hundreds of 3½-ounce iron balls fanned wide from the six gun barrels, raking through the front rank of men and horses. Discharged into the dense mass of cavalry from less than twenty yards, the effect of canister shot was cumulative devastation. Fallen victims of the first salvo hindered the oncoming rank behind, who were demolished in turn by the next salvo, and so on, piling the carnage higher and higher. 'G' Troop's position would have been protected, had a fourth cavalry attack been attempted, by an impassable bulwark of mangled dead left by the previous three. 'The heap of slaughter was far greater in front of our Battery than on any other part of the Field,' wrote Mercer, 'so much so that Colonel Sir Augustus Frazer told me two days afterwards . . . that in riding over the French Position he could distinctly see where G Troop had stood from the dark pile of bodies in front of it, which was such as even to form a remarkable feature in the Field.'[4] He was clearly proud of his troop's contribution to the topography. But similar 'heaps of slaughter' were to be seen in front of other gun batteries along Wellington's front line. Brigade Major Harry Smith noticed one, to the right of La Haye Sainte: 'French Cuirassiers were literally piled on each other; many soldiers not wounded lying under their horses; others, fearfully wounded, occasionally with their horses struggling upon their wounded bodies. The sight was sickening, and I had no means or power to assist them.'[5] Smith, like Mercer, could only gaze, storing the sight for future memoirs.

*

Sergeant Thomas Morris of the 73rd Regiment of Foot slept for the first part of the night, despite the bedlam din of the injured. 'The cries and shrieks of the poor creatures would have been dreadful . . . if we could have heard them; but the continued discharges of the artillery during the battle had so affected the drums of the ears, that we could scarcely hear anything for two or three days afterwards but the roaring of cannon.' It was the torment of thirst that woke him about midnight, and he picked his way among the sleeping, the dead and wounded, by the light of the moon, in search of water:

Passing where a horse was lying dead on its side, and a man sitting upright with his back against the horse's body, I thought I heard the man call to me . . . I went towards him, and placing my left hand on his shoulder, attempted to lift him up with my right; my

hand, however, passed through his body, and I then saw that both
he and his horse had been killed by a cannon-ball.[6]

He returned, shaken, to rouse his brother for company, and
together they plundered the water canteen of a sleeping comrade,
rather than encounter further horrors in searching the wider field.

Seasoned troops, although accustomed to the violent trade of
nineteenth-century warfare, and despite having participated in so
titanic a bloodbath, could yet feel superstitious dread at such
sights. A victorious army would normally expect to advance, in
pursuit of the enemy, leaving the corpse-strewn battlefield behind
them. But at Waterloo, the pursuit had been undertaken by
comparatively fresh Prussian troops, while the exhausted Anglo-
Allied army bivouacked where they halted, and were forced to
spend the night in the middle of the vast shambles they had
helped to create.

Captain Mercer, 'after standing all day amongst all these horrors
. . . felt no squeamishness about sleeping amongst them'. But the
other men of 'G' Troop bedded down as far away as possible
from the heaps of dead in front of their guns, 'the neighbourhood
of which, they said, was too horrible to think of sleeping there'.[7]
Even so, some found their rest disturbed by Driver Crammond,
and his would be the first corpse hurriedly buried in that vicinity
the following morning.

'And why particularly Driver Crammond?' Mercer asked his
sergeant.

'Because he looks frightful, sir', came the reply, 'many of us
have not had a wink of sleep for him.' Driver Crammond had
perished when a round shot took away most of his head. Only
the face remained, still attached to what was left of his neck:
'The men said they had been prevented from sleeping by seeing
his eyes fixed on them all night; and thus this one dreadful object
had superseded all the other horrors by which they were
surrounded.'[8]

From the particular to the general, it was a spectacle without
parallel. 'The number of the dead was far greater than I had seen

on any former battle field,' wrote Sergeant Robertson of the
Gordon Highlanders, 92nd Regiment of Foot. 'The bodies were
not scattered over the ground, but were lying in heaps – men and
horses mixed promiscuously together.'[9] For another veteran,
Jonathan Leach of the 95th Rifles, the scene defied description:

> It was not the first of the kind on which I had looked; but the
> frightful carnage of men and horses lying in so comparatively
> small a compass . . . produced such an impression on the mind
> as every writer who has attempted to bring it home to . . . those
> who were not eye-witnesses of . . . this huge charnel-house . . .
> has failed to effect. I relinquish it, therefore, as a hopeless
> undertaking.[10]

Death on such a scale could be numbing. 'I looked on with
less concern, I must say . . . than I have felt at an accident, when
in quarters,' wrote Private Thomas Howell of the 71st Highland
Light Infantry. 'I have been sad at the burial of a comrade who
died of sickness in hospital and followed him almost in tears; yet
have I seen, after a battle, fifty men put into the same trench,
and comrades amongst them, almost with indifference. I looked
over the field of Waterloo as a matter of course, a matter of small
concern.'[11] According to Sergeant Morris, 'It was supposed there
were about forty thousand dead bodies of men, and ten thousand
horses.'[12] Forty thousand dead *and wounded* would be closer to
the mark, but that was a conservative figure. Another commentator placed an estimate at the upper extreme, prose heightened
characteristically in his *Correct Narrative of the Late Sanguinary
Conflict*. 'In one short day,' Lieutenant General Scott declared,
'60,000 persons were in the vigour and pride of youth, made
mute for ever, and their souls gone to that bourn, whence no
traveller returns.'[13] The true figure lay somewhere between.

The Anglo-Allied army's dead and wounded numbered roughly
15,000, those of the Prussian army 7,000, while the French losses
are impossible to quantify with any accuracy. The Armée du
Nord's strength along the ridge of La Belle Alliance on the morning

of 18 June was 77,500. A week later, the remains of the army were mustered at Laon, numbering 30,844. Of the 46,656 difference between these two figures – counted as 'losses' – it is not known how many deserted and returned to their homes, how many were killed by Prussian lance and sabre during the murderous pursuit in the days after the battle, and how many were left dead and wounded on the field of Waterloo itself. The lower estimate of French battlefield losses has been put at fewer than 22,000; the upper at 31,000.[14]

The battle of Waterloo was remarkable, however, less for the number of casualties than for the congestion of slaughter. At Leipzig in October 1813, about 92,000 had been killed and wounded. But the battle of Leipzig was fought by 600,000 troops over a period of three days and along a twenty-one-mile front. At Waterloo, the opposing armies occupied an area measuring two and a half miles from one ridge to the other, by three miles from east to west, and the actual fighting was confined to a front just two miles long. This meant that for little more than ten hours, some 200,000 men, 60,000 horses and 537 guns were in action on a piece of land measuring five square miles.* Differing levels of ground, the prevailing fog of cannon smoke and the limitations of human eyesight meant that no individual viewpoint could possibly encompass the entire field. However, based on his partial observation, Lieutenant John Hamilton of the 2nd Line Battalion, King's German Legion, hazarded a surprisingly accurate figure for the average ratio of troops to area of ground: 'In my view there were at least 20,000 Infantry occupying a space of half an English mile.'[15]

While estimates of the combined human casualties, dead and wounded, sustained by the Anglo-Allied, Prussian and French armies range from 42,000 to 53,000, there are similarly imprecise statistics for the number of horses killed and injured – or else

---

* Michael Crumplin has calculated that the mean average of casualties suffered by Wellington's army per mile of front during the single day of fighting at Waterloo was 2,291; as compared with an average of 234 British casualties per mile of front over the 120 days of the first battle of the Somme in 1916 (see Crumplin, *Men of Steel*, p.80).

injured then killed as a mercy. One source gives the combined number of dead horses from the armies of Wellington and Blücher as 2,610, and estimates that the toll of the French mounts 'must have been nearly double that'.[16] The butchery of these beasts, however computed, was prodigious. Because a horse offered a larger target than a man, it was clearly more vulnerable to indiscriminate firing. And when an infantry square was attacked by cavalry, the defenders' musketry was deliberately aimed at the horses as the most effective means of bringing their riders down.

After the battle, wounded horses became a menace to the injured. 'Hundreds of these fine creatures were . . . galloping over the plain, kicking and plunging, apparently mad with pain, whilst the poor wounded wretches who . . . could not get out of the way . . . tried to shrink back to escape from them, but in vain.'[17] A visiting coachman two days after the action recalled 'that it was more shocking to see the wounded horses than the wounded men, because, poor things, they had no will of their own or knowledge why they were thus tormented'. Another eyewitness spoke of 'horses running about on three legs and bleeding to death'.[18] Frederick Hope Pattison of the 33rd Infantry described one such creature: 'standing at a considerable distance from me. I went towards him [and] found the poor animal on three legs – one of his fore-legs having been taken off near the shoulder by a cannon-ball. His sufferings seemed terrible [and] I only regretted I had not a pistol by which I might have put an end to his anguish!'[19] It was also noted that many wounded animals 'were seen herding together with sympathetic feelings'.[20]

Captain Mercer calculated that of the 226 horses he had brought to the battle, more than 140 were dead or maimed at the end of it, strewn among the carcasses of French cavalry mounts brought down at point-blank range by his own nine-pounders and howitzer:

Some lay on the ground with their entrails hanging out, and yet they lived. These would occasionally attempt to rise . . . quickly falling back again, would lift their poor heads, and turning a wistful gaze at their side, lie quietly down again, to repeat the same until strength no longer remained, and then, their eyes gently closing, one short convulsive struggle closed their sufferings.

Another observer described how 'Some of the horses, as they lay on the field, having recovered from the first agony of their wounds, began eating the grass about them, – thus surrounding themselves with a circle of bare ground, the narrow extent of which demonstrated their weakness.'[21] The plight of one represented thousands: both hind legs shot away, 'there he sat the long night through on his tail, looking about, as if in expectation of coming aid, sending forth, from time to time, long and protracted melancholy neighing'. Yet Mercer was incapable of ordering the creature shot. 'Blood enough I had seen shed . . . and sickened at the thought of shedding more.'[22] The following day, at three o'clock in the afternoon, as 'G' Troop moved off south with the rest of the army to consolidate their victory on French territory, Mercer would notice the mutilated horse again. Since no one else had thought fit to put a musket ball through the animal's brain, 'there . . . he still sat . . . neighing after us, as if reproaching our desertion of him in the hour of need'.[23]

*

The first order of the day on the morning of 19 June, for soldiers who expected to be on the march within hours, was 'to cook with as much haste as they possibly could'.[24] While men foraged for firewood, a freak accident resulted in two of the last, and most spectacular, casualties of the battle. Armed with billhooks, Private Rouse of the 40th Infantry and a rifleman from the 95th were hacking up the wooden lid of an abandoned French ammunition wagon when a spark, struck from a nail by one of their tools, ignited the powder inside. The explosion and fireball blew them twenty or thirty feet into the air and burnt off every stitch of clothing – Rouse, it was said, retaining just a single shoe. John Kincaid of the Rifles saw the blackened bodies hit the ground:

On falling . . . though lying on their backs or bellies, some extraordinary effort of nature, caused by the agony of the moment, made them spring from that position, five or six times, repeatedly, to an extraordinary height, just as a fish does when thrown on the ground after being caught; it appeared . . . that of five or six springs made by the two bodies in that manner, that the highest exceeded the height of a man, and the lowest was not less than three or four feet. It was so unlike a scene in real life that it was impossible to witness it without forgetting, for a moment, the horror of their situation.[25]

Both men were still able to speak, and Private Rouse to swear. Repeatedly cursing his own stupidity, he damned his eyes for a fool. His eyes, Sergeant Lawrence pointed out, 'happened, as it was, to be both gone'. The charred men were able to walk, with help, but soon died, Rouse in a Brussels hospital some days later, 'raving mad'.[26]

Following this distraction, fires were lit, meat cooked and eaten. The steel breastplates of dead cuirassiers served as both makeshift braising pans and dining chairs.

*

Staff Officer Basil Jackson's horse had been shot in the lower belly, the musket ball passing between skin and ribs for a distance of eighteen inches. The parts around the wound were swollen but the animal did not seem in pain, and by two o'clock in the morning, Jackson was able to ride him across the battlefield:

What desolation unfolded itself as the light increased! Every vestige of crops had disappeared, the ground looking like a vast fallow, strewn with the wrecks of a mighty army – nay, I may say armies; for, if the presence around of an abundance of cannon, muskets, and other *debris*, together with the bodies of the fallen, attested the utter ruin of the French, I had but to look across the wide valley to [see] that Wellington could have no very imposing army left.

Approaching La Belle Alliance, he found the sunken section of road leading up to the French position completely blocked, 'Guns and tumbrils packed and wedged together, and, indeed, pitched topsy-turvy one upon another, many having evidently rolled down the banks, some ten feet high; the space occupied by this confused mass was about fifty yards . . . I counted twenty guns.' Writing some sixty years later – in an age of steam travel – Jackson likened it 'to the appearance which a railway presents after a tremendous smash'.[27] More wreckage was to be found behind the Anglo-Allied lines on the narrow road to Brussels through the forest of Soignes. It was here that the great crash of baggage wagons had occurred during the battle, when an order to move back was misinterpreted and caused a stampede:

> The road . . . completely confined on either side by trees . . . was soon choked up; those behind attempted to get past those before . . . panic-struck people forcing their way over every obstacle, with the desperation of fear, – and a complete scuffle ensued, which might really be called a battle burlesqued, in which numbers of horses were killed, and some lives lost . . . The road was covered with broken and overturned waggons – heaps of abandoned baggage – dead horses, and terrified people. In some places, horses, waggons and all, were driven over high banks by the road side, in order to clear a passage.[28]

The miscellany of warfare became a litany common to all the recollections of those crossing the field in the days following the battle. Riding on a captured horse bearing the brand of the French Imperial Guard, Captain Harry Ross-Lewin of the 32nd Infantry recorded the detritus: 'broken gun-carriages, caps, helmets, cuirasses, arms . . . harness, accoutrements, pieces of battered uniforms, knapsacks, letters, and cards, that strewed abundantly in all directions, and the crops levelled by the trampling of infantry and cavalry in the strife, plainly marked the extent of the field'.[29] He noticed particularly the profusion of drums, because the French drummers customarily marched at the head of an infantry advance and consequently were among the first to fall. Riding through the ranks of the Anglo-Allied dead, he was surprised by 'the postures into which some of the men had thrown themselves in their last agonies'. One soldier of a Highland regiment looked like a frozen pugilist, 'lying on his back, with his arms firmly bent in an exact boxing attitude'. Nearby was an Enniskillen Dragoon 'whose hands were joined and elevated above his breast, as if he had expired in the act of prayer'.[30] Assistant Commissary General Tupper-Carey took the left fork at Mont-Saint-Jean instead of the right and found he was riding not towards Nivelles but across the battlefield. Near La Haye Sainte, he saw the remains of men 'who had fallen on the road [and] been trampled on by horses and wheels of artillery, into a mass of blood, flesh and clothes, hardly to be distinguished one from the other'. On either side dead Frenchmen lay in heaps, large bearskin caps of the Imperial Guard 'thrown away in the struggle, strewed the ground [and] many dead cuirassiers, still with their cuirasses on'.[31] Horses had difficulty keeping their footing on parts of the road that were 'literally paved with steel, the cuirasses . . . so numerous, shining and glittering in the midday June sun, making it quite dazzling to the eyesight'.[32]

*

On the morning of the 19th, fatigue parties were sent, 'as many as could be spared . . . to carry the wounded to the roadside, or any other convenient place where the wagons could be brought to convey them to hospital'.[33] But Sergeant Robertson and his comrades of the 92nd Highlanders had no sooner started than their work was interrupted by the order to march, and at seven o'clock they took to the road south, dead and wounded to right and left. 'No one could speak, so awestruck were we with the horrid spectacle,' Robertson recalled:

Here lay French and British in all the agonies of death, many of them calling on us to shoot them and put an end to their sufferings; while others were calling on us to come back, and not leave them exposed to the inclemency of the weather, to breathe their last in a land of strangers, with no friendly hand to comfort them and close their eyes in death.[34]

Captain Mercer and his men were similarly importuned as they brought water to the wounded. The French were particularly vehement. 'Many begged me to kill them at once,' he recalled, 'since they would a thousand times rather die by the hand of a soldier than be left at the mercy of those villainous Belgic peasants . . . "*Ah, Monsieur, tuez moi donc! Tuez moi, pour l'amour de Dieu!*" . . . It was in vain I assured them carts would be sent to pick them all up . . . They looked on us as brother soldiers, and knew we were too honourable to harm them: "But the moment you go, those vile peasants will first insult, and then cruelly murder us."'[35]

II

SUNRISE on 19 June had been at a quarter to four, and by its gathering light the local people could be seen prowling the field to loot. William Tomkinson of the 16th Light Dragoons saw one peasant pulling the boots off a soldier of the Guard not yet dead. Tomkinson 'made the fellow desist' by thrashing him with the flat of a sword, 'and attempted to teach him we did not allow such proceedings'.[1] But civilian looters, though despised, were generally tolerated. Plunder might even be regarded as due compensation for wrecked farm buildings and spoiled crops. 'If the peasants in the neighbourhood of Waterloo suffered great alarm, and considerable damage,' one publication pointed out, 'it must be acknowledged they have had peculiar and ample means of indemnification.' The tangled wreckage of the abandoned baggage trains provided easy pickings. 'Many of our officers, and some but ill able to afford such a loss, were in this manner deprived of all their clothes and baggage, at the moment of their advance into the territories of France.'[2] Some looters had been at work for much of the night, while others, 'reckless of their own lives, in their anxiety to be the first on the ground', had even ventured on to the field before the battle was over. Charles O'Neil, of the 28th Infantry, lying wounded in the arm and leg, claimed to have seen one woman carrying a baby:

She stooped to take a gold watch from the pocket of an officer. As she raised herself, a shell struck the child, as it lay sleeping in her arms, and severed its little body completely in two. The shock struck the mother to the ground; but, soon recovering herself, she sat up, gazed a moment upon the disfigured remains of her child, and, apparently unmoved, continued her fiendish work.[3]

The bodies of officers were the most sought after, for the gold in their purses, for pocket watches and for expensive uniform accessories: 'epaulets and lace from the clothes, and decorations of honour smeared with blood'. Thousands of buttons, belt buckles and badges were filched that would be hawked to tourists for years to come. Strange choices of booty were made: 'unable to carry off a sufficient number of heavy firelocks found in the field, you saw the women, laden with the ramrods, thinking them more valuable, and these were collected into piles'. Captain Mercer watched one group 'fairly staggering under the enormous load of clothes, &c., they had collected. Some had firearms, swords, &c., and many had large bunches of crosses and decorations; all seemed in high glee, and professed unbounded hatred of the French.'[4] As the number of pillagers increased with the dawn, haste and competition made the hunt ruthless: 'fingers and ears were cut off for the rings [even though] some of these poor wretches were then alive'. It was believed they did not scruple at murder: 'knocking out the brains of those who were disabled . . . to rob them of what they might have about them'.[5]

The frenetic search produced a characteristic feature of the battlefield that would be commented on by visitors for months afterwards – a widespread litter of paper: 'the quantities of letters and blank sheets of dirty writing paper were so great that they literally whitened the surface of the earth'.[6] One tourist likened it to 'the rubbish of a stationer's shop'.[7] Charlotte Waldie, who visited the field a month after the battle, saw 'French novels and German testaments – scattered music belonging to the bands – packs of cards, and innumerable papers of every description, thrown out of the pockets of the dead, by those who had pillaged them'.[8] One patriot noticed the 'characteristic distinction' between the respective piety and worldliness of friend and foe: 'while the debris on the allied ground showed leaves of Bibles and prayer-books, we saw numbers of playing-cards on the French'.[9] Another made the similar observation that 'in the pockets of the dead German soldiers . . . several bibles were found, – and in those of the slaughtered French, many of the loose pamphlets and collections of songs which are vended in the Palais Royal'.[10] Levity was not the sole preserve of the French, however, and 'a coarsely printed book of Scotch songs'[11] was taken away by one gentleman, while another preserved a page from an English joke book entitled *The Care Killer*.*

The most commonplace item was the *livret militaire*, or account book, carried by every French soldier. It contained 'the state of his pay and equipments . . . the occasions on which he served and distinguished himself, and the punishments, if any, which he had incurred . . . and a list of the duties of the private soldier, amongst which is that of knowing how to dress his victuals, and particularly to make good soup'.[12] Walter Scott would take home with him to Abbotsford a *livret militaire* that had belonged to a man named Mallet of the 8th Regiment, who had served since 1791. Another visitor found one 'much defaced with blood, of a French soldier, lately a conscript'.[13]

Then there were 'French love-letters, and letters from mothers to sons, and from children to parents; all, all these, and a thousand-fold more . . . were scattered about in every direction'. Miss Waldie observed that 'amongst the thousands that we examined, it was . . . remarkable, that we found only one English

---

* See John Scott, *Journal of a Tour*, p.47. The author is not to be confused with that of *Paris Revisited in 1815*, editor of the *Champion*. 'John Scott of Gala' was an intimate friend and kinsman of Walter Scott. The 'jest book' he found on the battlefield was probably *Davenport's Care Killer: being an entertaining selection of whimsical adventures, laughable tales, bon mots, and other devilish good things Extracted from the most celebrated authors in prose and verse* (London: printed and sold by J[oshua] Davenport . . . and sold by the Booksellers in town and country, 1802).

letter. It was from a soldier's wife to her husband.'[14] Another was picked up by the Reverend Mr James Rudge, who toured the area a few days after the battle. It had been written on 17 June to a girl in the north of England. The soldier told her that he had been in the fighting at Quatre Bras the day before, but 'had been so fortunate as to escape without a single wound'. He was expecting to fight again the following day and 'hoped that Boney might be taken, and an end put to the war'. Then he would return, 'and be happy with [her], for the remainder of his days'. The letter had been addressed but not sealed, and the good Mr Rudge wrote to the young person concerned, enclosing her fiancé's last message, with an account of the place where he had found it.[15]

Worthless paper discarded, pockets emptied of cash and valuables, finally the clothes were taken. It was a common procedure during wars of the time. 'Nothing . . . has ever astonished me more, than the celerity with which these body-strippers execute their task,' wrote an infantry subaltern after an earlier battle. 'A man falls by your side and the very next moment, if you chance to look round, he is naked as he was when he came into the world, without your being able so much as to guess by whom his garments have been taken.'[16] At Waterloo, Lieutenant Colonel Currie of the 90th Foot suffered this degradation in death. A friend was with him when he fell and came to recover the body the following morning. 'He was stripped, and with difficulty distinguished from those around him.'[17] In an age before military dog-tags, the dead could be identified only by uniform and possessions. Without these it was often impossible to differentiate subaltern from colonel, English from French, friend from foe. It was said that 'by nine o'clock, on the Monday morning, the peasantry had stripped the whole of the dead who were lying naked in heaps', and that a gentleman who visited the field at that time 'only saw one English officer who had any clothes left on'.[18] The Duke of Richmond, who paid his first of many visits to the field on the Wednesday morning, claimed that the stripping of the bodies was 'performed by the fair sex'.

The most valuable articles of dress to the looters were 'the shoes and stockings', and these were taken first. Curiously, the peasants could find no use for the long, thick woollen socks worn by the Scottish regiments, and consequently the corpses of Highlanders were seen in large numbers naked apart from 'their plaid stockings'.[19] Such anomalies aside, all reports agreed on the efficiency of the plunder. 'The bodies of the slain were stripped in an incredibly short time', Jackson recalled, and so routine was the practice that if a body was not stripped, the occasion was noted. When Colonel Ompteda of the King's German Legion was found dead by the hedge alongside La Haye Sainte, his corpse 'was plundered, but fully clothed', the singed bullet hole in his coat collar showing that the weapon had been near or touching his neck, in the press of fighting, when it was fired.[20]

Even naked, a cadaver had one final valuable commodity to offer. It was a commodity sought by a particularly enterprising breed of scavenger. A man by the name of Butler, encountered near the Franco-Spanish border in 1814, towards the close of the Peninsular campaign, was a typical specialist. 'Oh, Sir, only let there be a battle and there'll be no want of teeth,' he said. 'I'll draw them as fast as the men are knocked down!' Taken back to England and set in hippopotamus ivory by London dentists, the strong, healthy incisors of war dead would allow the toothless rich to smile again, for a price. A former 'resurrectionist', or body snatcher, Butler claimed to have collected teeth from the Spanish battlefields that made him a clear profit of £300. He was not the first 'to make the Peninsula the scene, or the Duke's achievements the means of such lucre',[21] nor would he be the last. Jack Harnett, another resurrectionist, brought home £700 worth of teeth from just one such expedition. He prospered and 'died comparatively rich, leaving nearly £6,000 to his family'.[22] To disguise their activities and legitimise their presence as camp followers, Harnett and his partner Ben Crouch would acquire licences as army suttlers – purveyors of drink and sundries to the troops. 'They generally obtained the teeth on the night succeeding the battle, only drawing them from those soldiers whose youth and health rendered them peculiarly fitted for the purposes to which they were to be employed.'[23]

It was an international trade. Riding past a burial pit in the process of being filled in the days after the battle of Waterloo, a gentleman noticed 'some Russian Jews . . . assisting in the spoliation of the dead, by chiselling out their teeth'. In keeping with the casual anti-Semitism of the time, this type of profiteering, conducted 'with the most brutal indifference',[24] was commonly ascribed to the Jews. Allegedly, it was 'the number of Jews . . . who gradually entered into this traffic' that explained the diminution of profits complained of by English 'tooth drawers' like Ben Crouch, who 'became very poor'[25] in consequence. 'Polish Jews were very active at this work', wrote a journalist of the 1840s, who remembered 'a British dentist nicknamed *Dr Pulltuski* from the notoriety of his dealings with them'.[26] A French dentist referred with nostalgia to 'the most precious harvest of all', provided by the battle of Leipzig in 1813: 'The German universities [in that year] turned out many youths in their very bloom; and our [French] conscripts were so young that few of their teeth had been injured by the stain of tobacco.'[27] As late as 1865, during the last year of the American Civil War, although the craft of dental prosthetics had advanced considerably, it was reported that 'dentists . . . do not trouble themselves to make artificial teeth. Taking advantage of the blessings which balance the horrors of war, they furnish [customers] with sets of real ones. Amongst the enterprising hordes which follow the armies of the North are certain practitioners, who, after a battle, may be seen stooping over the prostrate forms of the young soldiers. Veterans they leave to their repose, devoting their attention only to the raw levies . . . They are rifling their mouths [of teeth]. These, when collected, are packed in boxes and sent over to the London dentists.'[28] But in memory of the rich crop of June 1815, such dentures were still known as 'Waterloo teeth' and greatly preferred by the fashionable to those of doubtful and unwholesome provenance taken in peacetime from corpses of the old, the diseased or the hanged.

*

The local peasantry and 'the worst and most desperate characters from Brussels and other places'[29] were said to have taken 'the greatest share of the spoils of the field of battle [because the] soldiers were too much exhausted to anticipate them in this particular',[30] but dead and wounded alike were also extensively pillaged by the troops that survived them. An English officer, lying helpless in a heap of dead, witnessed the plunder and murder of a young crippled ensign by a Prussian rifleman. The officer was saved from a similar fate by the timely intervention of two English Grenadiers. After killing the Prussian, and adding his loot to their own, the elder of the pair cheerfully justified 'collecting lost property' from the field: 'Well, we fought hard enough yesterday to allow us a right to share what no one claims, before the Flemish clowns come here by cock-crow.'[31] Despite William Tomkinson's high-minded insistence that the British army 'did not allow such proceedings', he admitted that many of his own men were also 'looking after plunder'. He emphasised, however, that theirs was selective – taken from the enemy's dead, not their own – and that only 'excellent *French* watches' were being sold.[32] Ensign William Leeke of the 52nd Regiment bought a brace of French brass-barrelled pistols, with which he tried and failed to put a wounded horse out of its misery. The animal was finally shot by a passing Prussian sergeant, and Leeke, somewhat ashamed of his purchase, threw the pistols away.[33] A junior officer in the 1st Royal Scots appeared to condone but not benefit from the trade: 'Plunder was for sale in great quantities, chiefly gold and silver watches, rings, etc., etc. Of the former, I might have bought a dozen for a dollar piece but I do not think any officer bought . . . probably expecting (as I did) that in a few days our pockets would be rifled of them as quickly as those of the French had been.'[34] Many were unaware of how comprehensively the French had been defeated and naturally expected to be called upon soon to engage the enemy again.

Private George Farmer of the 11th Light Dragoons was a typical looter. When the fighting finished and his regiment received the order to dismount and rest, he and a few like-minded companions set out across the nocturnal battlefield in search of spoils. 'It is one of the worst results of a life of violence', Farmer confessed, 'that it renders such as follow it selfish and mercenary [and] when the bloody work of the day is over, the survivor's first wish is to secure, in the shape of plunder, some recompense for the risks which he has run and the exertions which he has made. Neither does it enter into [his] mind . . . to consider whether it is the dead body of a friend or of a foe from which he is seeking his booty.'[35] They rode over ground covered with the bodies of the wounded and slain, human and animal. In some places the corpses lay wedged so closely together that it was impossible to avoid trampling them under the horses' hooves. The little party of dragoons dismounted to search through knapsacks for valuables, rarely finding more than a spare shirt, a pair of shoes, some tobacco or perhaps a bag of salt. They had the additional aggravation of catching their spurs in the uniforms of tangled bodies, and of tripping and sprawling over those they plundered.

Private Farmer had a more lucrative prize in mind than the meagre spoils of a common soldier's knapsack. During the last stage of the battle, advancing in the failing light against the routed French, he had seen a young English officer shot from his saddle. As the body hit the ground, Farmer saw the gold seals hanging from his waistcoat glint in the twilight, promising a gold watch concealed in the fob. Having memorised the place, he returned to claim the possessions of this fallen hero. But others had been before him, and watch, seals, everything of value had been taken, including clothes. Farmer could see the hole made by the lead ball, exactly in the middle of the naked chest.

Some had even found opportunity for profit during the battle. No sooner had the top-hatted General Picton fallen from his horse, a musket ball through hat and temple, than one of his own infantry division, a Grenadier of the 28th, was 'endeavouring to take his spectacles and purse'[36] from his trouser pocket. Private William Wheeler and two companions of the 51st Regiment, having shot a French officer, divided between them the proceeds of forty double napoleons and the gold lace from his uniform.[37] Friedrich Lindau, a rifleman in the King's German Legion, shot a French cavalry officer from a loophole in the barn wall at La Haye Sainte, and during a brief sortie was able to snatch his watch and chain. The wounded man reached for his sabre to resist, but Lindau clubbed him in the head with his rifle butt. He took a purse of gold coins from the officer's saddlebag but was cheated of a gold ring on his finger by the approach of enemy cavalry. Later in the day, Lindau was taken prisoner only to be plundered in turn by his captors, and relieved not only of the coins but of three watches: two of silver and one of gold.[38] Thomas Howell, of the 71st Highland Light Infantry, described how, even under attack from French cavalry, the defenders of an infantry square could still find plunder in passing: 'A French General lay dead in the square; he had a number of ornaments upon his breast. Our men fell to plucking them off, pushing each other . . . and snatching at them.'[39] Lieutenant Colonel Frederick Cavendish Ponsonby of the 12th Light Dragoons – air whistling from a lance wound in the back – was plundered of money and cigars by a French skirmisher, then by a Prussian, but was finally protected from further depredation after the fighting by an English looter of the 40th Regiment on the promise of a reward.[40]

The Prussians, Georgy Capel wrote, 'are the greatest Plunderers that ever existed'. A month after the battle, she was shown two diamonds taken from a dead Prussian's pocket by a camp follower, the wife of an English soldier. The woman had offered them to a remarkably honest Brussels jeweller for forty francs and was told they were worth at least £6,000. 'It is wonderful,'

Georgy told her grandmother, the Dowager Countess of Uxbridge, 'the immense quantities of jewels which have been found amongst the dead on the field of Battle, particularly amongst the Prussians.'[41]

Looting of the five square miles continued. On 22 June, 'groups of peasants [were] parading all over the plain in search of plunder'.[42] Over a month later, the Irish politician and Admiralty Secretary John Wilson Croker saw 'people searching for some remains of plunder, but they had not got much, as the whole had been already carefully gleaned over'. Nevertheless, he noted, 'two boys had [found] two English Lifeguardsmen's swords'.[43] And much later, chance discoveries would generate great excitement in the locality, as when a boy picked up 'a double Napoleon wrapt in paper', causing all who heard of it, for days afterwards, to eye the ground and 'look among the stubble or grass in hope of the like good luck'. Local legend kept such dreams alive. It was said that 'an English General', lying wounded in the sandpit near La Haye Sainte, had buried 'a bag containing 200 Napoleons'.[44] The legend was believed even after persistent digging had failed to uncover the fabulous hoard. But the peasants would continue to pick up, and in succeeding years to plough up, 'things of no intrinsic value, but upon which curiosity sets a daily increasing estimate', as one writer observed, '[and] almost every hamlet opens a mart for them as soon as English visitors appear'.[45]

*

Riding across the battlefield on 20 June, Sir George Scovell's groom, young Edward Heeley, was tempted to pick up a souvenir from the debris lying on the ground, 'as a relic [of] this great action', but remembered his strict orders not to dismount lest he be conscripted into helping to dispose of the dead. This task fell – along with the more profitable opportunities offered by the clearance – to the peasants of the locality, and a hundred men had been employed for the purpose from the surrounding parishes.[46] Some were said to have been forced to the work at bayonet point by the Prussians, and 'many were put to death for refusing'.[47] Burial parties consisted of five or six men and an officer, who took account, where possible, of any property that might identify corpses, before stripping them – if not already stripped – and loading them on to wagons; then tumbling them, thirty or forty at a time, into large pits about six feet deep, fifteen or twenty feet square. 'It is quite astonishing', Heeley noted, 'what little effect such a scene has on a person, after seeing it for the first time. You feel quite indifferent about it, the faces of the dead were very much disfigured and ghastly, but the parties who were burying them seemed to be joking as if at any other ordinary employment.'[48]

The clinking of hammer on chisel beside the burial pits – as the 'Russian Jews' extracted their livelihood from the jaws of the dead – sometimes seemed to echo back across the field as pistol fire. 'Parties were out shooting such of the wounded horses as were yet alive, which at a distance sounded like skirmishing.'[49] Dead horses were rolled on to their backs, stiff legs pointing skyward like upturned tables, for the convenience of farriers prising iron shoes from hooves, 'so that nothing was lost of the least value'.[50] In this attitude the carcasses were left, some 'inflated to an enormous size',[51] until dragged to burial pit or bonfire.

By 22 June they were killing some of the human wounded as well. An eyewitness described patrols of Prussian soldiers shooting the most severely injured of their own army – and those of the French – who were beyond help. 'Although it seemed a piece of barbarity at the time . . . it was a great act of charity, as their sufferings must have been truly awful, with the heat and lack of anything to quench their thirst for three days under a scorching sun.'[52]

During the first few days, the dead horses were disposed of by burial, but even the biggest pits failed to accommodate large enough quantities of them, and thereafter, fire became the only practical expedient. Disposal of the human dead rapidly reached

a similar point of crisis, the sultry June weather lending urgency
to the clearance. Two days after the battle, the unburied dead,
'already offensive, were shocking to look at'. By noon on the
fourth day, the stripped corpses presented a truly fearsome sight.
'The weather was hot almost beyond endurance, and the smell
arising from the carcasses insufferable.'[53] While the bodies shaded
by trees, in the neighbourhood of Hougoumont, 'retained their
natural whiteness',[54] the skin of those exposed to the sun on open
ground had turned almost black, faces swollen, bellies grossly
distended as the gases of decay accumulated inside.

From hastily filled burial pits, here and there a human leg or
a decomposing arm appeared above the inadequate covering of
soil as though reaching up from the grave. And as the hot dry
weather baked the soil, more corpses were exposed: 'the ground
cracks or opens, and as the bodies . . . are not above a foot
below the surface, they may still be seen in many places'.[55] The
problem was exacerbated by over ten days of continuous wet
weather towards the end of July, 'more continued rain than I
ever saw', the former Irish barrister John Wilson Croker wrote,
'except at Cork when I used to go the *summer circuit*'.[56] By
August, 'numerous parties of the peasantry were employed in
raking more earth over the bodies, their first thin covering of
mould having been in many instances washed away by the
rains'.[57]

Less than a week after the battle, the logistics of disposal called
for drastic measures. 'The [attempt] to bury the vast number of
dead on the field has been given up,' Captain Courtenay Ilbert,
of the Reserve Artillery, wrote to his wife on 23 June, 'so now
they are burning them in heaps.'[58] In the courtyard at Hougoumont,
it was reported, 'they have been obliged to burn upwards of a
thousand carcasses, an awful holocaust to the War-Demon'.[59]
Another commentator reported 'huge piles of human ashes, dreadfully offensive in smell'.[60] Soon even the dignity of an exclusively
human funeral pyre was denied them: 'impossible to bury the
killed', wrote a hospital assistant, George Finlayson. 'They are
thrown with [the] horses on one heap and burnt.' But even

incineration was occasionally not wholly effective, and 'so great were the number of the slain' in the area around Hougoumont 'that it was impossible entirely to consume them. Pits had been dug, into which [the corpses] had been thrown, but they were obliged to be raised far above the surface of the ground. These dreadful heaps were covered with piles of wood, which were set on fire, so that underneath the ashes lay numbers of human bodies unconsumed.'[61] Writing on 26 June, Finlayson estimated that 'the field of battle will be clean of the dead by today'.[62] But the dead were burning a week later, and in mid-July, the huge piles of ash were still smoking. And as local farmers collected in what remained of their harvest following the battle, corpses were still being discovered. Georgy Capel wrote to her grandmother on 15 July: 'A great number of bodies have been found in the corn by the Reapers within the last day or two.'[63]

Many horse carcasses, unburned and unburied, were left on the ground to rot, preyed on by the 'incalculable swarms of carrion flies' that caused such annoyance to tourists that summer. Visitors to the field took with them 'large quantit[ies] of camphor . . . as a preventive against infection',[64] and Walter Scott thought it 'wonderful that a pestilential disease has not broken out, to sum up the horrors of the campaign'.[65]

Late summer in Belgium was unhealthy at the best of times. 'The lower, flat, wet, and marshy districts,' remarked Professor John Thomson of Edinburgh University:

are subject to fevers, which prevail epidemically towards the end of summer and the beginning and middle of autumn. It is well known that these fevers begin earlier or later, are of shorter or longer duration, and are attended with milder or more alarming symptoms, according to the various degrees of heat and moisture of the season, according to the greater or less stillness of the atmosphere, and also according to the degree and continuance of exposure to the air, which stagnates or moves slowly over the low, marshy, putredinous ditches, and over the oozy beds of the rivers, with which that country abounds.[66]

Even low-lying areas of the capital were annually at risk from contagion, but in the summer of 1815 – 'the streets crowded with wounded wretches and with waggons filled with dead and dying [and] the atmosphere so much affected' – the prospect of a particularly virulent fever season seemed greatly increased. In addition there were 'Hundreds of dead horses lying [in the Park] having been shot since they came into the Town, [and] upon the Ramparts . . . 3,000 dead bodies [were] exposed, there not being room to bury them.' It was small wonder that 'many English [residents were] thinking of quitting Bruxelles in fear of pestilence'.[67]

III

'OUR work behind the lines was grim in the extreme, and continued far into the night.' John Haddy James, assistant surgeon to the 1st Regiment of Life Guards, was reticent about his experiences during the battle, sparing future readers of his diary those scenes 'all too horrible to commit to paper'. Likewise, in the days that followed, assisting with wounded still on the ground and intermingled with the dead: 'Of these corpse-strewn fields I prefer to say little,' he wrote to a friend in England, 'the sights and sufferings were of such horror.' Written for posterity, his journal expressed a degree of empathy, unusual for a military surgeon, with the plight of the injured:

> The silent heroism of the greater part of the sufferers was a thing I shall not forget. When one considers the hasty surgery performed on such an occasion, the awful sights the men are witness to, knowing that their turn on that blood-soaked operating table is next, seeing the agony of an amputation, however swiftly performed . . . then one realises fully of what our soldiers are made.[1]

By contrast, the comment of hospital assistant Isaac James, after several days' duty, bore the terse stamp of fatigue: 'We have had lots of legs and arms to lop off.'[2] Another hospital assistant specified the ratio of surgical practice: 'There are perhaps 15 or 16 legs taken off for one arm.' It was best not to think too deeply of the human being beyond the stump.

The civilian Charles Bell had some experience of military surgery, having tended wounded from Corunna on their arrival at Portsmouth six years earlier. That experience had furnished material for a sixty-four-page *Dissertation on Gunshot Wounds*, and enough drawings for a further thirteen pages illustrating the most interesting injuries. When news of Waterloo reached London, he had recognised the opportunity for further research. 'Johnnie!' he shouted to his brother-in-law. 'How can we let this pass? Here is such an occasion of seeing gun-shot wounds come to our very door. Let us go!' Following the week he and John Shaw spent in Brussels, Bell wrote of the extreme clinical detachment and conscious suppression of feeling for the 'objects' under his knife and care: 'To give one of these objects access to your feelings was to allow yourself to be unmanned for the performance of a duty. It was less painful to look upon the whole than to contemplate one object.'[3]

In his *Report on Observations made in the British Military Hospitals in Belgium*, Professor Thomson recalled that something akin to Bell's emotional disengagement from his patients was commonly felt by experienced military surgeons as an even wider sense of alienation: 'Several [medical] officers confessed to me, that the sight of so much misery as presented itself after the battle of Waterloo, rendered them indifferent to life; and that, in the state of intense excitement in which they were for some days, they lost all recollection of, and regard for, themselves.'[4] This was confirmed by hospital assistant John Davy, and in nearly identical terms, writing home to his mother that 'most of those who attended [the wounded] became indifferent to life and in my own case at least, little regard for self remained'. He added, 'the horrors of the hospital continued to increase, the cries of the wounded were terrible, especially those of the Belgians'.[5]

*

Having arrived in Belgium on 8 July, accompanied by William Somerville, head of the Army Medical Department for Scotland, and having visited every hospital in Brussels, Antwerp and points between, John Thomson was able to document four distinct categories of injury: incised wounds inflicted by sabre, punctured wounds from lance or bayonet, contused and lacerated wounds from cannon round, case shot or shell fragment, and wounds by gunshot.

Lieutenant George Simmons of the 95th Regiment of Foot had been hit in the back by a musket ball which broke two ribs near the spine, and passed through liver and lung to lodge near his breast bone. Face down in mud he lay unnoticed and trampled for a time before being taken to the shot-riddled building that served as a field hospital at Mont-Saint-Jean farm, some 700 yards behind the Anglo-Allied front line. Here an incision was made 'under the right pap', the ball extracted, and a quart of blood taken from his arm. The battle was still undecided and the threat of capture by the advancing French, should the line not hold, made escape imperative. Patched up and barely conscious, Simmons was helped on to a horse and rode the twelve miles to Brussels in considerable agony, the animal's rhythmical movement pumping blood from his wounds and causing splintered bone to 'cut the flesh to a jelly'.[6] He was billeted with a Belgian family and a surgeon sent for. His wounds were poulticed and another quart of blood taken. Over the following four days, the surgeon relieved him of a further six quarts.*

Venesection, or bloodletting, was a trusted panacea – especially for wounds to the head and chest – and had been so for centuries. Taking away blood was thought to relieve the inflammation of an infected wound. It was deemed equally effective in reducing fever, preventing gangrene, even in restoring the senses following a concussion. Also, common sense suggested that lowering the blood pressure by copious bleeding could only be beneficial in slowing, or stopping, an internal haemorrhage. Venesection was,

---

* A total of sixteen pints in five days.

however, entirely futile and a patient often recovered in spite, rather than because, of such treatment.

The crisis in George Simmons' condition was reached a fortnight after his wounding. Convulsions and vomiting gave way to 'a violent inflammation'. He was bled three times and the inflammation appeared to recede, or perhaps it was that he merely looked paler and felt calmer for the loss of blood. The medical regimen went on for seven days: 'bled regularly two or three times a day'. The inflammation returned, 'with far more violence than ever'. His liver was swollen and painful, the area of his body around it 'a good deal enlarged'. Despite its failure to alleviate these alarming symptoms, Simmons had complete faith in the treatment he was being given: 'Bleeding was the only remedy.' After another week of 'intolerable burning pain in the liver'[7] and daily bleedings, his surgeon drained 'two large basins' of blood from his arm. 'The pain abated much' and Simmons lost consciousness. It was then decided that 'general bleeding' should be discontinued and 'local bloodletting'[8] tried instead. Thirty leeches were applied to his side on the area over his swollen liver. Another twenty-five were applied to the same spot the following day, and the day after, twenty-five more.* 'The last application of them was horrible,' he told his family:

My side was inflamed and nearly raw from the biting of the others. I got fresh leeches every time; they bit directly. I was in the greatest state of debility when the last were put on the raw part; all taking hold at once made me entirely mad with anguish. I kicked, roared, and swore, and tried to drag them off, but my hands were held. Such torture I never experienced.

No further blood was taken, and for three days he lay in a stupor, his life despaired of. Then on the third day he woke to feel his body 'very wet', and when the bedclothes were turned down, a

* One leech gorges between 20 and 30 ml of blood; thirty leeches around 750 ml.

considerable quantity of pus was found to have seeped through the dressings on his chest. 'The plaster was taken off the wound,' he recalled, 'when the matter flowed as from a fountain.' This discharge alleviated both fever and swelling. 'I was immediately rational and my body began to decrease, I knew . . . my life was saved.'[9]

The majority of incised wounds Thomson documented had been delivered by sabre stroke from horseback upon French infantrymen. They were consequently inflicted 'for the most part upon the upper region of the head, or upon the temples, face, back part of the neck, and shoulders'. The survival of some of these victims was little short of miraculous. One man had the back of his skull sheared off, exposing a considerable area of brain surface. During an attack of inflammation, 'a tendency to protrusion of the brain' was noticed, accompanied by 'a slight degree of stupor with loss of memory'. The inflammatory state was 'subdued' – no doubt by bleeding the patient – and 'the brain sunk to its former level, the stupor went off, and the memory returned'. Another Frenchman suffered 'a remarkable sabre-cut in the nape of the neck', exposing the cerebellum, or base of the brain, which 'was seen pulsating for a period of eight weeks'. According to Thomson, the patient suffered no serious ill effects, 'but, like several others who had received deep cuts on the back part of the neck . . . complained of great feebleness in the lower extremities'.[10]

The curved sabre was primarily a slashing weapon. Not so the straight weapon used by French heavy cavalry. Charles Bell saw one extraordinary stab wound to an English officer from a cuirassier's sword which 'pierced the back and upper part of the thigh, went through the wood-work and leather of the saddle, and entered the horse's body, pinning the man to the horse'. Bell could not help but be impressed: 'The force with which the cuirassiers came on is wonderful.'[11]

Punctured wounds were for the most part inflicted by lance, fewer by bayonet, the nature of each weapon carrying greater and lesser prospects for the victim's recovery. 'In piercing the body, the lance cuts more than the bayonet,' observed Thomson, 'and, by the greater haemorrhage which it occasions, it is probably more deadly in its effects.' However, 'lance-wounds in general healed very readily, much more so than those made by the bayonet'.[12] Frederick Cavendish Ponsonby sustained no fewer than seven injuries, the most serious of which was a lance-punctured lung. His surgeon believed he 'had some faint hopes of recovery', and warned him not to speak, 'for fear of causing the wounds in his lung to bleed afresh'.[13] It was presumably to counterbalance the internal haemorrhage that an aggressive course of venesection was prescribed along with the enforced silence. Over the following forty-eight hours the crisis passed and Ponsonby survived to tell the story of his night abandoned on the battlefield at the mercy of French and Prussian plunderers. His recovery was attributed to 'excessive bleeding'.[14]

Thomson subdivided the damage caused by cannon round, shell fragment or canister shot into two categories. Flesh might be contused or lacerated – bruised or ripped open – depending upon the speed and angle at which the man was struck.

The injury sustained by Sir William Howe De Lancey was a contused wound. The acting Quartermaster General had been hit in the back by a spent cannon ball as it ricocheted from the ground. Despite its reduced velocity and the glancing contact made, it was powerful enough to knock him over the head of his horse to a distance of several yards. Even so, it was not at first entirely clear that he had been physically wounded at all. His skin was not broken, nor was the fabric of his uniform torn, and it was thought that he had fallen victim to a spurious phenomenon known as the 'wind of a ball'. There was a belief in some medical circles that the pressure of displaced air as a missile passed within a fraction of an inch of the body could have nearly as destructive an effect on the internal organs as an actual blow, and yet leave little or no external trace. An outlandish theory had it that the damage might be caused by an electrical charge produced by the flight of the ball, akin to a lightning bolt.

The full extent of De Lancey's injury would only be revealed by autopsy. Nearly the entire left side of his ribcage had been detached from the spine, and the shattered fragments of one rib driven into the lung. Medical treatment was conventional and a surgeon paid regular visits 'to bleed him constantly'.

Magdalene De Lancey had been in Antwerp on the morning after the battle and was relieved that her husband's name was not on an early list of casualties. Hours later she was told that there had been an oversight but that he was 'only wounded', then that he was 'only desperately wounded' and finally that he was 'alive, but was not expected to live'. She made haste to join him. But on the road to Brussels a chance encounter with a friend – who could not meet her eyes – extinguished her last hope with the news that 'it was all over'. She returned to Antwerp, only to be told that 'Sir William was alive, and that there were even hopes of his recovery'.[15] She set out again, arriving at Mont-Saint-Jean in the afternoon of 20 June. During the six days her husband took to die, Lady De Lancey became adept at applying leeches.

In the report of his observations on military hospitals, John Thomson made no mention of lacerated wounds to the head, thorax or abdomen, because the effect of a direct impact of cannon round, shell fragment or canister shot, travelling at full speed, on any part of the body but an extremity, would have rendered a man beyond hospital treatment. Had the ball that wounded De Lancey not been spent and at a tangential angle, it would have torn him apart, denying his wife the scant consolation of nursing and bidding him goodbye. Presented with a lacerated wound to an arm or leg, however, especially one comprising extensive bone damage to the joint – or even a similarly destructive gunshot wound – the surgeon usually had but one course of action.

Among the most formidable procedures he would be called upon to perform, amputation was categorised as a 'capital operation', the term giving due recognition to the risk to a patient's life. Generally that risk was offset by necessity, and the danger, were it not taken, of death from gangrene. There was a maxim that it was better for a man 'to live with three limbs than to die with four'.[16]

For the capital operation, a capital knife; the surgeon would have the choice of at least two: short to take off an arm or the lower leg, longer to encompass the thickness of a thigh. The customary method of severing a leg above the knee required a supple wrist, practised speed and two continuous circular cuts. A minimum of two assistants was needed, one to control the bleeding and manage the tourniquet, the other to restrain the wounded man unfortunate enough not to lose consciousness during the process. Passing his operating hand under the patient's limb and reaching back over the top – with the knife pointing towards his own chest, and the heel of the blade as far round the circumference of the thigh as possible – the surgeon would begin his first incision. Drawing the knife away from himself in a single, steady, circular sweep, dividing skin and fat layers to muscle depth all the way around, and utilising the whole length of the blade from heel to tip, he would bring both knife and incision back to their starting place. This was known as the *coup de main*. A skilled practitioner could alter his grip on the knife as he approached completion of the circuit without interrupting its course. An assistant would then 'retract' the cut layer of skin and fat, pulling it back from the incision to expose a couple of inches of muscle. This ensured that a skirt or tube of skin would hang over the amputation to cover the stump. With a tourniquet applied, or the assistant pressing down on the main artery with his thumbs, the surgeon would make his second circular cut in the same way as the first but higher on the leg, at the level of retracted skin, and slicing down through the muscle all the way to the bone. That vigorous stroke was called the *coup de force*. The muscle was then retracted by throwing a split linen sheet round the raw, cut surface and hauling it back to expose two or three inches of bone to the surgeon's tenon saw. The higher the bone was sawn, the more muscle would cover it when the retraction was released, and the thicker and more comfortable the pad of flesh would be when the skin was closed over the stump. The operation took less time than the description. 'Removal of a limb should not occupy two minutes,' George James Guthrie would tell his students. Securing the ten or so severed blood vessels – especially the arteries – with silken ligatures takes longer, he added, 'and this should be done without reference to time'.[17] However, the luxury of time, as well as textbook precision, would have been sacrificed between lecture theatre and the shambles of a busy field hospital. Sergeant Johann Heinrich Doring of the Orange Nassau Regiment passed one on the outskirts of Waterloo village in the early morning of 19 June: 'a place in front of a barn was full of amputated legs and arms, some still with parts of uniforms, and the surgeons, with rolled up sleeves like butchers, [were] still busy at work. The scene looked like a slaughterhouse.'[18]

On the previous evening, the house of Monsieur Hyacinthe Joseph-Marie Paris, at the north end of the village on the Brussels road, was the setting for one of the most illustrious amputations of the entire Napoleonic War period. Removal of the Earl of Uxbridge's right leg, shattered at the knee joint by a piece of grapeshot, was a more considered and careful operation than most. The Duke of Wellington's friend and physician, John Robert Hume, consulted half a dozen other surgeons before going to work with a brand-new capital knife borrowed for the occasion, his own having 'been a good deal employed during the day'. With the tourniquet applied and the assistants standing ready, Uxbridge said to Hume:

'Tell me when you are going to begin.'

'Now, my lord.'

And putting a hand up to his eyes the patient replied: 'Whenever you please.'

As well as the undivided attention of an expert surgeon and the razor sharpness of a pristine blade, his lordship had the benefit of a more sophisticated surgical procedure than those being carried out in the barn down the road. Hume slid the knife point horizontally into the meat of the inner thigh, over the bone, until it emerged from the other side, then sliced outwards at an oblique angle in the direction of the smashed knee to form a curved flap of skin and muscle. He made another incision, his knife entering close to the starting point of the first, but transfixing the thigh this time below the bone and as nearly parallel to the initial passage of the blade as possible, before again slicing out to form a second flap . . .

There had been considerable dispute some decades earlier between 'Flappers and Anti-Flappers'[19] concerning this alternative to the standard circular incision. Its principal advantage, the Flappers argued, was that it gave greater coverage to the bone and allowed for a neater, tapering stump to be tailored, best suited to the fitting of a prosthetic limb.

. . . Having slit through the inch or so of tissue separating the ends of his two cuts on the outside of the thigh, and having retracted the skin, Hume divided the muscles down to the bone in the usual way with a single circular stroke. With the muscles retracted, he began to saw through the femur. At one point an assistant supporting the leg inadvertently raised it fractionally, bringing the ends of the bone together and trapping the blade in the cut. 'Damn the saw!' Hume muttered angrily. Uxbridge raised his head and smiled, 'What is the matter?'[20] Hume claimed this was the only sound he made throughout, but another remark was attributed to him by his aide-de-camp, Captain Wildman: 'that he thought the instrument was not very sharp'.[21] Uxbridge's sang froid was the stuff of legend: 'during the whole operation he neither uttered groan or complaint nor gave any sign of impatience or uneasiness'. When the ordeal was over, Hume observed: 'His skin was perfectly cool, his pulse which I was curious enough to count gave only 66 beats to the minute, and so far was he from exhibiting any symptoms of what he had undergone in his countenance that I am quite certain had anyone entered the room they would have enquired of him where the wounded man was.'[22]

The severed leg was to receive reverent interment by Monsieur

Paris in his garden, a willow tree planted on top of it and a grandiose epitaph inscribed on stone.

*

Every conscientious surgeon would admit that the removal of a man's arm or leg, no matter how skilfully executed, was a failure, and that 'to save one limb [was] infinitely more honourable ... than to have performed numerous amputations, however successful'.[23] Guthrie expressed it succinctly as being 'the last resource and the opprobrium of surgery'.[24] Ironically, caution seemed to carry a marginally greater risk to the patient's life than daring. Of a sample 371 capital procedures performed on the British wounded of Quatre Bras and Waterloo, 146 were 'primary amputations' – operations carried out within twenty-four hours of injury – and of these, thirty-two, one in almost five, perished under the knife or of post-operative infection. Of the other 225 'secondary amputations' – cases in which surgery was delayed for days or even weeks – eighty-three had fatal outcomes, a mortality rate close to one in three. John Davy's initiation to operative surgery in one of the smaller of the Brussels hospitals was even more disheartening: 'Most of the capital operations, such as amputations of the thigh, proved fatal.'[25]

The longer the interval between injury and amputation, the greater the danger. When Lieutenant William Hay of the 12th Light Dragoons visited his friend Captain Sandys at a house in Brussels on 20 June, Sandys complained bitterly at not receiving attention from any medical man since he was brought in. Hay hurried off in search of help to a nearby convent that was being used as a temporary hospital: 'The long passages, corridors, yards, and every space of ground in and about the place, was covered with wounded soldiers, lying, sitting, or reclining.' He entered 'a long, broad room with a table down the centre on which were lying some twenty or thirty fellows, under the operation of the doctors' knives'. He waited until one young surgeon finished amputating a leg and returned with him to Captain Sandys.

'Oh! I am so sorry I gave you the trouble,' the patient exclaimed when they entered. 'I feel much better, all the pain has left me, I suffer only from coldness in my feet.'

Hay stepped out of the room while the surgeon made his examination.

'I regret to say your friend cannot live many hours,' he whispered as he left a couple of minutes later. 'Mortification has set in, and his suffering will soon be at an end.'

Sandys died that night.

Mortification – as tissue perished, deprived of blood from blocked and damaged vessels – was one consequence of delay. Another was the creeping sepsis of blood poisoning. The two conditions were distinguished by the terms dry and wet gangrene. The French had a term – *purriture hôpital* – for the wet variety: hospital rot.

'Surgeons no longer hesitate,' reported John Hennen, director of one of the main Brussels hospitals, 'and even patients appreciate their motives justly, and attribute the loss of limbs to the fire of the enemy rather than to the incision knife of their friends.'[26]

Not all were so compliant. Charles O'Neil rejected a surgeon's advice that his arm be amputated, ignoring warnings that otherwise it would mortify and cause his death. He was mistakenly convinced that 'for every *joint* amputated the operating surgeon obtained an enormous price from the government'. And his suspicions seemed only bolstered when, at the end of that day, 'three carts, laden with legs and arms, were carried away, leaving many hundreds of poor fellows on the invalid list for the remainder of their lives'.[27] O'Neil kept his arm, and with no ill effect. Edward Heeley also expressed mistrust of the surgeon's trade after walking past one of the Brussels hospitals: 'The legs and arms lay in heaps in the yard, many a poor fellow had a limb cut off when it was not necessary, just that the young doctors might try their skill.' Heeley was also a witness to the grim routine of surgical failure:

It was full employment for several men to sew up the dead in their blanket as fast as they died. They then dragged them to the top of the stairs and gave them a push and others at the bottom of the stairs put them into a cart, and away they went in cart loads, and loads of deal coffins were taken to Waterloo by officers' servants and others to bury the officers in.[28]

*

The flow of casualties entering Brussels from Quatre Bras and Ligny had become a flood after Waterloo. Throughout the city and its suburbs the doors of houses containing wounded were marked in chalk '*Militaires blessés*'[29] for the convenience of visiting medical men. Sometimes the inscriptions specified '"1, 2, or 3 *blessés*" . . . Sometimes it was "2 *officiers blessés*" and on one door . . . "2 *Anglais, et* 2 *Ecossois blessés*".' The Scots were particular favourites. There was a saying among families that had soldiers of the Highland regiments billeted on them: '*Les Ecossois sont lions dans la bataille, et agneaux dans la maison.*' Lions in the field, lambs in the home. After the battle, there were families who went out 'some miles to meet "*Notre Ecossois*"'[30] on their limping return. While some commentators demonised the rural population near the battlefield as plunderers and even casual murderers of the wounded, the respectable citizens of Brussels were generally praised for their hospitality. 'To their everlasting credit,' William Hay wrote, 'I found not only the whole of the rooms in the houses of the best families occupied by the men of the British Army, but the ladies of the houses attending and dressing their wounds, and nursing them like their own children.'[31] As he and William Somerville made their survey, John Thomson reported:

In the course of our visits to wounded officers, in private quarters, we had frequently occasion to observe the sacrifices which the inhabitants cheerfully made of their accommodations and comforts to their wounded guests, the personal services which

they rendered, and the kindness they showed in presenting them
with wine, fruit, and other luxuries.[32]

Private hospitality was limited, however. The majority of the
10,000 Anglo-Allied wounded were distributed across the city
to more impersonal and crowded accommodation, or else taken
by canal boat to Antwerp. There were five main hospitals in
Brussels: Sainte-Elisabeth, Notre Dame, the Orpheline, the
Annonciade and a Jesuit institution. In addition, there were over
twenty establishments hastily commandeered to receive an influx
of war-torn wretchedness that seemed to have caught the medical
authority unawares. 'It was thought that we were prepared for
a great battle,' remarked Charles Bell on his arrival at the end
of June, 'yet here we are, eleven days after it, only [now] making
arrangements for the reception of the wounded. The expression
is continually heard, "We were not prepared for this."'[33] And the
makeshift provision was often of variable suitability. A building
known as the Petit Chateau, 'situated among the stagnant waters
and the filth of the town'[34] close to the canal, was rife with
malarial fever and typhoid, as well as the prevailing disease of
Brussels, pulmonary tuberculosis. Some medical opinion had it
that a wounded man stood a better chance of recovery the longer
he stayed *out* of hospital.

When the Whig politician Thomas Creevey visited the battlefield just two days after the fighting, he was shocked less by
the grisly spectacle of unburied corpses than by the untreated
wounded, and expressed 'regret at the wounded people being
still out'. However, the man who had recently relieved Lord
Uxbridge of his leg reassured him as they rode back to Brussels.
'The two nights they have been out is all in their favour,' Hume
said heartily, 'provided they are now got into hospitals. They
will have a better chance of escaping fever this hot weather
than our own people who have been carried into hospitals
first.'[35] But despite the requisition of every available vehicle to
transport the wounded – 'even elegant equipages, landaulets,
barouches and berlines' – ten days after the battle 'they [were]

yet far from being all brought in'.[36] Lord Arthur Hill, who had accompanied Creevey on his visit to the field and given brandy and water to a number of the wounded, apologised to a sergeant of Napoleon's Imperial Guard with a smashed thigh bone for his not being brought off sooner, 'on account of the numbers of our own men we had to take care of'.[37] The French wounded were indeed the last to be dealt with, some having lain untreated for more than a fortnight. It was reported that 'at the end of ten, twelve, and fifteen days there were found among the dead a great number of wounded, who, from hunger or madness, had torn with their teeth the carcasses of men and horses'.[38] Some had been 'collected [from] all over the country[side] by the peasantry, and dragged from barn to barn, often without food or dressings'.[39] Of those who were finally given medical aid, 'a great proportion . . . had compound fractures in a gangrenous state and filled with worms'.

The last building in Brussels made ready to receive the wounded – and as a consequence filled exclusively by the French – was the barracks of the Gens d'Armerie in the reputedly unhealthy lower part of town. Charles Bell watched its occupation on 1 July with mixed feelings, inspired by suffering patients who were at the same time enemies and prisoners of war. 'These fellows are brought from the field after many days on the ground, many dying, many in . . . agony, many miserably racked with pain and spasms,' he wrote to his brother. And yet, although laid out 'naked or almost so' in beds close to the ground, a hundred to a row, they still bore an air of menace:

Tho' wounded, low, exhausted, tho' *beaten*, you would still conclude . . . that those were fellows capable of marching, unopposed, from the west of Europe to the east of Asia. Strong, thick-set, hardy veterans . . . they cast their wild glance upon you, their black eyes and brown cheeks finely contrasted with their fresh sheets . . . From all I have seen and heard of their fierceness, their cruelty, and bloodthirstiness, I cannot convey to you my detestation of this race of trained banditti. Whether they are put to the sword, or kept in subjection until other habits come upon them, I am convinced that these men cannot be left to the bent of their propensities.[40]

Bell had spent the first few days after his arrival in Brussels visiting four of its main hospitals, making sketches of noteworthy injuries, and drinking coffee in the Park while he finished his drawings and wrote up his observations. However, finding 'that the best cases, that is the most horrid wounds, left totally without assistance' were to be found among the French, he pursued his researches surrounded by 'the most shocking sights of woe . . . accents of entreaty . . . and *noisome smells*' in the Gens d'Armerie. During his waking hours he was assailed from all sides by the cries of '*Pansez! Pansez!*' – to tend their wounds – or to operate: '*Coupez! Coupez!*' He was unable to sleep because 'what was heart-rending in the day was intolerable at night'. At half past four in the morning he wrote to Theodore Gordon, superintendent of the Gens d'Armerie, offering to perform all the necessary capital operations. It would be two days' work, he estimated. It took him three:

At six o'clock I took the knife in my hand, and continued incessantly at work till seven in the evening, and so the second and the third day. All the decencies of performing surgical operations were soon neglected. While I amputated one man's thigh, there lay at one time thirteen, all beseeching to be taken next; one full of entreaty, one calling upon me to remember my promise to take him, another execrating. It was a strange thing to feel my clothes stiff with blood, and my arms powerless with the exertion of using the knife![41]

It was generally believed that topography – or at least proximity to sea level – was a significant factor in the spread of gangrene and attendant fever among the wounded. Four of the main Brussels hospitals – the Jesuits, Notre Dame, Orpheline and Annonciade – were in the higher, healthier parts of town. While the danger might be circumvented in a clean and well-aired building like the Sainte-Elisabeth Hospital – despite its unhealthy location – it was nevertheless noted there that 'some cases of gangrene appeared, but originally and principally in the *lowest* wards'.[42] The connection between height and health, depth and disease seemed to be confirmed by the conditions and disastrous mortality rate of a temporary hospital established for the Brunswick troops north of Brussels, at Laeken. It lay 'on a swampy flat covered with trees, through which the great Antwerp canal was cut, and the Dyle and several tributary branches crept along'. The wounded lay on the floors 'and were much crowded'. Here post-operative gangrene flourished, frequently seizing a stump within three hours, with fever killing the patient a day or two later. 'Twenty-eight days after the battle, one solitary survivor alone marked the performance of a successful amputation.'[43] Understandably, Dr Pockel, medical director at Laeken, began to urge restraint on his surgeons – and with gratifying results:

> These fatal symptoms . . . induced us to leave many of the great wounds to nature, and the more as we observed that by thus leaving them, the traumatic fever was not excessive. This circum-stance enabled us to effect the cure of some of the most serious injuries, cases which, according to the rules of military surgery, would have demanded amputation.[44]

However, the French wounded were often so far gone from expo-sure and neglect as to render such a conservative approach out of the question. But, even if they had escaped contracting infec-tion during their days and nights among the dead in the humid conditions of the battlefield, infection awaited them more surely at the 'unfavourably placed'[45] Gens d'Armerie. Theodore Gordon described the deadly welter of complications following many an amputation:

> The patient becomes restless and uneasy; he has a sense of pricking, shooting, and lancelating pain in the stump, . . . he becomes hot

and thirsty; his pulse is jarring, and the whole arterial system [is] in a very tumultuary state; a rigor, and the paroxysm of intermittent [malarial fever] has . . . about this time intervened. A small dark-coloured spot is observable, not always confined to the edge of the sore; its circumference is very tender; the centre itself is by no means so; . . . it spreads, the whole face of the stump becomes gangrenous. The constitutional symptoms keep pace with the local ones. The tongue becomes furred; delirium, with the greatest prostration of strength, and a yellow suffusion of the skin, generally closes the scene.[46]

It did not occur to anyone that the spread of gangrene and septicaemia from stump to stump might have been accelerated less by the position of a hospital or its closeness to the canal than by infected tissue, pus and blood from one patient's wounds being passed to those of another on the blade and hands of the surgeon.* It was perhaps no reflection upon Charles Bell's surgical skill, but rather a result of the standards of hygiene prevailing at the time, that ninety per cent of the men on whom he operated during those three hectic days at the Gens d'Armerie died shortly after.

*

'The scene was now entirely divested of its more horrifying features.' Forty days after the battle, when the Edinburgh advocate James Simpson visited a military hospital in Antwerp, he found 'a general air of comfort and comparative ease'.[47] Ironically, the Caserne de Façon, 'one of the finest barracks in Europe', which now contained 800 of the British wounded, had been built by Napoleon to house troops intended for his projected invasion of

---

* The connection would not be made for another thirty years, until Ignaz Semmelweis first suggested in 1847 that the incidence of septicaemia in the Vienna General Hospital could be reduced if doctors washed their hands between performing autopsies in the mortuary and carrying out gynaecological examinations on the maternity ward.

England a decade earlier: 'the destined plunderers of London', as Simpson put it. He also pointed out that the conquering army 'were further indebted to [Napoleon] for the industry with which he had fitted up all the convents of Antwerp as barracks [and] nothing could be more convenient and satisfactory than their easy conversion into hospitals with the best possible accommodation . . . striking examples of the *reversal* of French *destinies*, which the times had produced'.

Bonaparte had also made indirect provision for the French wounded. La Corderie – a ropeworks attached to the naval arsenal, consisting of a single ground-floor chamber a quarter of a mile long, sufficient to lay out the cable for a first-rate ship of the line – contained about 1,500 men, with beds laid side by side in four rows from end to end of the immense space. Simpson made his first approach to the enemy with some trepidation: 'A little hesitation in mingling with these ferocious and exasperated men was not unnatural; but . . . unnecessary. Insult was certainly the utmost which a stranger apprehended; but even this had no place, where all were engrossed with their own sufferings: humbled in a consciousness of their irretrievable defeat.' They were, he added, 'under excellent *surveillance* and discipline', emphasising that although wounded and helpless, the inmates of La Corderie were nonetheless prisoners. Simpson was conducted around the Façon and Corderie by his Edinburgh friends William Somerville and John Thomson. They pointed out a man who had flourished his severed arm above his head with a shout of '*Vive l'Empereur!*' and another who had remarked as preparations were made to take off his arm that one thing would cure him, save his limb and spare the surgeon's trouble: 'a sight of the Emperor!' He died under the knife, staring at his own blood, declaring 'that he would cheerfully shed the last drop in his veins for the great Napoleon'. Yet another said to the surgeon probing for a musket ball close to his heart, 'An inch deeper, and you'll find the Emperor!'[48] There were many such stories of incorrigible loyalty. According to one, the restored French

King made a magnanimous gesture towards those of his unruly
subjects injured in the battle:

> Louis XVIII sent an officer . . . to inquire if they were in want of
> anything, and to afford assistance to those who required it. He
> visited every one of the hospitals [containing French wounded];
> but . . . could not prevail on one of them to accept of assistance
> from him, in the name of his sovereign. They had no king but
> one, '*Vive l'Empereur!*'

It was a constant cry, and one man, close to death, converted it to
a tuneless incantation that he chanted over and over until the breath
left him: '*Vive l'Empereur! Vive l'Empereur! Vive l'Empereur!*'[49]

IV

THE curious came from Brussels and beyond to view the field, the beginning of a stream of tourists that would continue for the next two centuries. The first party appeared on the morning of the 19th while the battle-soiled men of 'G' Troop were sitting on stacked piles of French cuirasses to feed. Hands, face and clothes 'begrimed and blackened with blood and smoke', Captain Mercer rose and spoke to a middle-aged gentleman who 'approached holding a delicately white perfumed handkerchief to his nose; stepping carefully [around] the bodies . . . to avoid polluting the glossy silken hose that clothed his nether limbs'.[1]

Charlotte Waldie thought this impulse to view the scene so soon after the battle despicable. 'There were those of my own country, and even of my own sex', she exclaimed:

whom I heard express a longing wish to visit . . . the fatal field of Waterloo! If, by visiting the dreadful scene of glory and of death, I could have saved the life, or assuaged the pangs, of one single individual who had fallen for his country, gladly would I have braved its horrors; but for the gratification of an idle, a barbarous curiosity, to gaze upon the mangled corpses of thousands; to hear the deep groans of agony, and witness the last struggles of the departing spirit – No![2]

Basil Jackson told of an excursion made from Brussels of a party of English ladies and gentlemen: 'Not aware of the shocking sights offered by a battle-field . . . a single glance so shocked our fair countrywomen, as to make them fly away like scared doves.'[3] By contrast, Mr Creevey, who visited on Tuesday 20 June, expressed 'great surprise . . . at not being more horrified at the sight of such a mass of dead bodies'.[4] The Scottish gentleman who had paid his respects to the field of Quatre Bras on 17 June had returned from Antwerp to Brussels with his ailing wife and lost no time in visiting the field of Waterloo on the Wednesday:

> The first thing that struck him at a distance was the quantity of caps and hats strewed on the ground. It appeared as if the field had been covered with crows. When he came to the spot, the sight was truly shocking. At first there was a prodigious preponderance of British slain, which looked very ill; but more in advance, the revenge made itself dreadfully marked, for ten French lay dead for one British. The field was so much covered with blood that it appeared as if it had been completely flooded with it; dead horses seemed innumerable.

Major W. E. Frye, on extended furlough from his regiment in Ceylon and staying in Brussels as a tourist, visited on the 22nd. 'The sight was too horrible to behold,' he wrote. 'I felt sick in the stomach and was obliged to return . . . For my part I shall not go a second time.' It was suggested 'that they who went to see the field of battle from motives of curiosity would do well to take with them bread, wine and other refreshments to distribute among the wounded, and most people did so'.[5] Some 'supplied them with spirits, or other strong fluids', remarked the abstemious editor of the *Champion*, John Scott. Drunkenness was thereby added to the horrors of the field, and produced 'exhibitions [compared] to which the mere heaps of the bodies . . . were pleasant sights . . . and what with pain, intoxication, and the recollections of the battle, these poor creatures displayed an extravagance in their wretchedness, which had a tremendous effect'.[6]

Tourists were sometimes exposed to more alarming encounters than with the drunken wounded. 'Prussian stragglers robbed many persons on the field,' reported James Simpson. On the Thursday after the battle, a party of four Belgian citizens was confronted by a mounted Prussian hussar with a drawn sabre. 'Your watches, your money,' he demanded, 'or I will cut you down!' Having surrendered their valuables, the quartet returned to Mont-Saint-Jean, where they met four Englishmen who reported 'that they too had allowed this fortunate hussar to serve them in the same manner'. When he heard the story, Simpson was ashamed of his countrymen and remarked, 'I do not think that *every four* Englishmen would have been robbed by one man, however completely armed or mounted.'[7] Three weeks later, the dauntless Miss Waldie deprecated stories of 'deserters' and 'armed desperadoes' who 'sometimes alone, and sometimes in a gang' robbed civilians and plundered the locality. She believed that 'most of the horrible stories . . . were entirely devoid of truth', and for her part had 'never heard of any well-authenticated murder that they committed'.[8]

*

The last of the wounded had been removed from the field by the time Lady Charlotte Uxbridge visited on 1 July. 'Oh! What a sight,' she wrote on her return, '& yet I would not have missed it for the world.'[9] Only four days earlier, she had declined to join an excursion, thinking that she lacked 'the courage to *look* if [she] went'.[10] And even having at last decided to go, in the company of Lady Fitzroy Somerset, she still had misgivings: 'We are both dying to see that fatal spot & yet we are both frightened to death at the thoughts of it.'[11] Travelling in a green barouche, drawn by four coach horses and driven by a postilion, the two ladies were accompanied by Lord and Lady Seymour and Captain Wildman – who had been 'slightly [wounded] in the foot'.[12] They visited the houses in the village of Waterloo, 'where [their husbands'] poor limbs were amputated', Somerset's arm and

Uxbridge's more celebrated leg. Charlotte was taken into the garden by Madame Paris, the farmer's wife. 'She . . . show[ed] me where his poor dear *dear* leg was buried, & she has promised me to plant a tree over the spot.' The road from Waterloo to the battlefield was 'dreadfully disgusting, the smell from the dead horses is so horrid', wrote Charlotte, 'but the field itself *is perfectly sweet*'. The sweetness of the field was perhaps only relative, because 'in one part there was still a pile burning of dead bodies which were consuming by fire. There was nothing *to be seen* but straw & smoke!' The heaps of earth, 'where the poor dead bodies have been buried', covered the area 'as thick as *mole hills*'. Captain Wildman was able to show her the exact spot where Uxbridge had been hit, but 'he could not satisfy [Lady Somerset's] curiosity so well'. The battlefield litter, so fascinating to other visitors, seemed to hold no interest for Charlotte. 'The whole ground . . . is *covered* with caps, helmets & different bits & scraps of all sorts but nothing worth picking up. It has been so completely searched that nothing remains.'[13] Both ladies, however, brought home grapeshot. Charlotte's was of the precise size that had wounded her husband and fitted exactly the hole made in his trousers. She kept the trousers as a relic, but yielded to the entreaties of Monsieur Paris, who had so reverently buried the leg, that he might be allowed to keep the boot. He offered her two guineas for it but she did not say whether she took his money.

Writing a fortnight later, on 15 July, Lady Charlotte's niece, Georgy Capel, reported that the 'pestilential air of Brussels [was] clarified', many of the wounded being encamped outside the city, while the dead horses and 3,000 human corpses previously exposed on the ramparts had finally been disposed of. Her aunt had told her that 'the Field of Battle is now quite sweetened', but Georgy thought the hot weather would not allow it to remain so. She was right. That same day, Charlotte Waldie overcame her earlier qualms at gratifying 'an idle, a barbarous curiosity', in the company of her brother, her sister and other ladies and gentlemen. 'The effluvia,' she wrote, 'even beneath the open canopy of heaven, was horrible; and the pure west wind of summer, as it passed us, seemed pestiferous, so deadly was the smell that in many places pervaded the field.'[14] And yet a week later, when Lord Grantham and Sir Lowry Cole rode across it, no mention was made of the smell. 'It was then so completely cleared of the dead, who had been buried or burnt, that nothing disgusting or unpleasant was to be seen.'[15]

Georgy Capel had been told about the battlefield, of the 'thousands of the most moving English and French Letters . . . and caps pierced with Balls and all the inside filled with congealed Blood'.[16] But it was not until the beginning of August, nearly seven weeks after the battle, that she saw the field for herself. She and her younger sister Muzzy were escorted by the Duke of Richmond, who was something of an authority: he had been a spectator at the battle until three o'clock in the afternoon of 18 June and had since made no fewer than three visits to the field – 'and knew all the particulars'.[17] Even so, Georgy would have preferred seeing it in the company of a military man like her uncle: 'someone who would . . . explain all I wish to know in their own language, not *womanised*, for tho' I do not pretend to understand their *military* terms it loses much of the effect when the same sense is conveyed in *civil* terms'. But Lord Uxbridge, newly created Marquis of Anglesey by the Prince Regent, had by then returned with his wife to England, inadvertently taking his niece's two-volume *Campaigns in Spain and Portugal* – with which, perhaps, she had been trying to master military terms – in his baggage.

Georgy described the road through the forest of Soignes, the 'mounds of earth covering dead horses . . . caps, broken swords and knapsacks stript of their contents'. She noticed incidental details, such as 'damaged biscuit' by the wayside and corn spilt from the commissary wagons, which had now begun to sprout in the wheel ruts.

In the village of Waterloo, where the Anglo-Allied army's headquarters had been established on 17 June, the illustrious names were still to be seen chalked on the doors. Charlotte Waldie noticed those of 'His Grace the Duke of Wellington', 'His Royal

Highness the Prince of Orange', and 'other pompous titles', contrasting strangely with the lowly habitations on which they were inscribed. She noted also:

> the lamented names of Sir Thomas Picton, Sir Alexander Gordon, Sir William De Lancey, Sir William Ponsonby, and many others who now sleep in the bed of honour. Volumes of sermons and homilies upon the instability of human life could not have spoke such affecting and convincing eloquence . . . as the sight of these names, thus traced in chalk, which had been more durable than the lives of these gallant men.[18]

In fact the names had been rendered more durable still by the inhabitants, who had 'been at pains to preserve the chalking on the doors',[19] probably re-chalking them following heavy rainfall. The names attracted tourists, eager to see the rooms where the great men had passed the night before the battle: the chairs they had sat on, the tables they had dined at, the beds they had slept in. Georgy and Muzzy were shown the room in which their uncle's leg had been amputated, and the chair in which he had sat during the operation, '*with blood* upon it'. Madame Paris showed them the other prized relics of the house, 'his boot which had been cut off, and the bedding, also covered with *his* blood'. They were taken to see the place where the leg was buried – 'overgrown *with weeds, which we cleared away*' – and told that a stone with an inscription had been ordered from Brussels to be laid above it. They visited the Duke of Wellington's quarters and were shown the wounded Prince of Orange's bed, 'covered with blood', and the door upon which he had been carried there.

'I supposed Waterloo was close to the field,' John Scott wrote, 'but it was not.' It was nevertheless doing a roaring trade as a stopping-off place for refreshment: 'Every inn had chaises, gigs, fiacres, cabriolets and carriages crowded round its door, just as you see in the neighbourhood of a horse-race or boxing match. Luncheons, dinner, drinking, at every public-house.'[20]

A mile beyond Waterloo, most tourists would leave their

carriage at the village of Mont-Saint-Jean and perhaps engage a battlefield guide. A local man, whose house had been filled with wounded after the battle, found regular employment as such and professed a deep hatred of Napoleon. 'And all for one man!' he would say. '*Ce coquin!*' He would tell his English clients of the sufferings he had witnessed, 'nothing but sawing off legs, and sawing off arms'. Then he would repeat his refrain: '*Oh mon Dieu!* And all for one man!' And, following Bonaparte's capture and exile, he would add: 'Why did you not put him to death?'[21]

From Mont-Saint-Jean, tourists would continue the short way to the battlefield on foot. The road climbed gradually until it passed through a cutting at the centre of the ridge along which the Anglo-Allied lines had deployed. In sight of the field for the first time, tourists became aware of 'a long line of immense fresh-made graves' in front of the hedge that was fancifully supposed to have given the farm of La Haye Sainte – 'The Sacred Hedge' – its name. Along the top of the ridge, to the left of the road, extended another long line of 'tremendous graves'.[22] Scrambling up the steep side of the cutting to the right of the road, tourists would reach the so-called 'Wellington tree', a solitary elm on the ridge overlooking La Haye Sainte, from the vicinity of which the Duke had watched the battle's progress. Riddled though it was with lead musket balls and iron shot, 'its branches and trunk . . . terribly splintered', the tree lived, a symbol of nature's endurance through adversity. Those wanting a memento cut out a musket ball or tore off a strip of bark. What the battle had failed to kill, the tourists' penknives achieved, and the tree perished.* In front of Hougoumont, two centuries later, less iconic trees still stand, pitted with holes from the combat, although the musket balls themselves have long since been prised out by souvenir hunters.

The two Capel girls walked, with the Duke of Richmond,

---

* Chopped down in 1818, it was sold to Mr John George Children of the British Museum, who had mementoes carved from its wood, including three chairs. In the coronation year of 1838, one was presented to the Duke of Wellington, another to Queen Victoria and the third to the Duke of Rutland. Mr Children also had a cabinet made of the wood to contain his collection of minerals, and several smaller items that he gave to friends (see *Illustrated London News*, 27 November 1852).

along the ridge, tracing the right wing of Wellington's front line, towards the ruins of Hougoumont, disturbing 'thousands of crows and ravens from their ungrateful office' among the shallow graves. Like many a young person of the time with romantic sensibilities, Georgy was thinking of Ossian: 'the leaves whirl round the wind and strew the graves of the dead – at times are seen the Ghosts of the departed when the musing hunter alone slowly stalks over the field'.[23]

The chateau of Hougoumont was a major battlefield attraction. Visitors would be taken to see the chapel miraculously spared by the fire that swept through other parts of the building, leaving only the feet of the wooden crucifix scorched. Outside, the man-high splash of blood on a wall would be pointed out, where 'some poor fellow must have been knocked to pieces against it by a cannon ball'.[24] At Hougoumont, the fighting had been particularly savage, the slaughter immense, the bonfires higher than elsewhere. The Reverend Rudge described an outbuilding in which many bodies had been burnt and where the ashes lay three feet deep. He took home 'a small piece of a skull . . . found there, and upon which the suture of the skull was very perceptible'.[25] Tourists would be shown 'a mound where the bodies of 600 Frenchmen had been burnt'. The guide would demonstrate the assertion by poking a stick into the base and scraping out ash and, perhaps, 'the calcined bone of a finger', while 'a perceptible smell of ammonia'[26] escaped from inside. Charlotte Waldie was shown another pile where, the guide told her, the bodies of British Guardsmen had been consumed. She collected a handful of these ashes and folded them into one of the pieces of paper she found scattered about. Later she would write: 'Perhaps those heaps that then blackened the surface of this scene of desolation are already scattered by the winds of winter, and mingled unnoticed with the dust of the field; perhaps the few sacred ashes which I then gathered . . . are all that is now to be found upon earth of the thousands who fell upon this fatal field!'[27] She refused, on principle, to look at the skeleton of a calf that had perished when one of the outhouses caught fire. Another lady of the party went into transports of sentimental grief: 'it seemed to fill her mind with more concern than anything else'. But Charlotte, who had seen the ash remains of countless dead, and been told of the wounded men burned alive in the chateau, remained unmoved by the creature's fate. The other lady – finding no melting fellow feeling from Charlotte – tried to engage Charlotte's sister instead, 'and began to bewail the calf anew'. Finally, Jane Waldie lost patience: 'I don't care if all the calves in the world have been burnt,' she snapped, and they heard no more from the animal lover.[28]

*

For the first month or so, mementoes could still be picked up off the battlefield by tourists. John Scott found a twelve-pound cannon ball and carried it 'for five or six miles in a blazing day', determined to take it home as a trophy 'with the cuirass and other spoils of battle'[29] he had secured. Meanwhile, the commercial trade in 'cap plates, cuirasses, &c.' boomed. 'At first these things were bought by the curious cheap enough,' wrote John Wilson Croker in late July. 'Now the purchasers are more numerous and the commodity rarer, and therefore their prices are much enhanced.'[30] The local peasants had collected 'a vast booty' from the field and 'many of them [were said to have] made some hundred pounds'[31] from it. James Simpson was one of a party of tourists who visited six weeks after the battle. In the village of Waterloo his friend bought a cuirass, and a brace of pistols purportedly 'found in the cloak case of a French general', from an old woman who was suspicious of the three guineas offered in payment. Despite assurances 'that in Brussels she could . . . exchange them for twenty-six francs each', she hesitated, pleading her poverty, afraid that she was being swindled. At last she took the money. '*Vous êtes Anglais,*' she said, '*et les Anglais ne trompent jamais.*' The English never deceive.[32]

Visiting the field in the company of Sir Robert Peel and the Duke of Richmond, Croker paid one napoleon for a cross of the Legion of Honour, 'taken from a dead French officer', as a present for his wife, and bought half a dozen broken eagle cap badges for one franc apiece. Peel paid two napoleons for 'a very handsome cuirasse'.[33] The Duke of Richmond, as a frequent visitor, had already bought a dozen of them. In August, Walter Scott bought the back plate of a cuirass perforated by a musket ball. 'From the edges of the hole being turned outwards, it appeared that the shot must have [passed through the breast plate and] the body of the unfortunate wearer.'[34] It cost Scott five francs, but he paid twenty for a more ornate inlaid specimen purchased later in Brussels.[35]

La Belle Alliance – the inn at the centre of the French front line – was full of such merchandise, and 'Cuirasses, helmets, swords, bayonets, feathers, brass eagles, and crosses of the Legion of Honour, were to be purchased here.'[36] Not content with the peasants' battlefield gleanings, some people were attracted by the fabric of the iconic building itself, outside which Wellington and Blücher were supposed to have met after their victory on the night of 18 June. One tourist carried away a brick, while 'a more wholesale amateur'[37] bought the door for two gold napoleons.

English visitors would be shown a straw-bottomed chair upon which the Duke of Wellington reportedly sat momentarily after the battle. The building was 'of the poorest; consisting of two rooms, with two smaller back rooms, a passage, and some miserable holes up stairs'. The proprietor had painted above the door, 'in very large and rude letters in black, on a white-wash ground, *"Hotel de la Belle Alliance"*'.[38] Soon it would be repainted 'A la Belle Alliance & Wellington Hotel', and the walls of its two main rooms covered with tourist graffiti. 'John Todd', one of them read, 'came to the field of battle at Waterloo, the 10th of July, 1815.' Another visitor had signed his name, 'Thomas Jackson', only to have it libelled by another hand: 'he was hanged at the last assizes, for sheep-stealing!' A portrait drawing had been attempted of 'Thomas Sutcliffe, of the second Life Guards', against which some wit had written 'ugly *theef*'.[39]

Typical of a class of English tourist, combining a foreign jaunt

with patriotic fervour and flocking to Waterloo just as soon as
their clerkships in London offices allowed, were the 'Brentford
lads' who arrived in August. They hired a peasant guide in Mont-
Saint-Jean, bought three pints of brandy to get them round the
battlefield, and a plentiful supply of snuff to neutralise the 'stench'
they had been warned of. They flirted with some girls bringing
in the harvest near La Belle Alliance and were excited to see a
man's leg lying in the stubble, looking 'very fresh'. They hated
the food served at the inn – fatty yellow bacon and meat that
was almost raw – and suspected it had been carved from dead
men. Two of the 'lads' pulled off a finger each from a decomposing hand they saw sticking out of the ground. They assumed
it to be a Frenchman's hand and took the fingers back with them
to England pickled in spirits.[40]

*

Other tourists arrived – seeking sublimity rather than vulgar
sensation. Walter Scott was the earliest of the poets. On 31 July,
before he had even boarded the ferry at Harwich and not a
word of it written, *The Field of Waterloo, a poem*, was reported
as 'In the Press, and speedily will be published'. He reached the
battlefield on the ninth day of that hot month, when the still
prevailing smell of putrefaction gave one verse of his epic the
immediacy of heightened journalism:

> And feel'st thou not the tainted steam,
> That reeks against the sultry beam,
>   From yonder trenched mound?
> The pestilential fumes declare
> That Carnage has replenish'd there
>   Her garner-house profound.[41]

Published in late October, the poem carried a disclaimer: any
imperfections resulted from it having been 'composed hastily,
during a short tour of the continent, when the Author's labours

were liable to frequent interruption'. Scott mentioned, in the poem's defence, 'that it was written for the purpose of assisting the Waterloo Subscription' to relieve the suffering of the wounded and their families. This may have blunted the harsh critical reception, and the opinion that it fell far short of the battle of Flodden in the author's earlier *Marmion*. His laudable motives, however, did not spare him from occasional anonymous squibs in the press:

> How prostrate lie the heaps of slain
> On Waterloo's immortal plain!
> But none by sabre or by shot,
> Fell half so flat as WALTER SCOTT . . .[42]

After Scott came Robert Southey, the Poet Laureate, visiting the field on 3 October for a more considered, ambitious and pedestrian work befitting his office: *The Poet's Pilgrimage to Waterloo*. The air was still foul, and, like Scott, Southey met the challenge of making poetry from stench:

> And sometimes did the wind upon its breath
> Bear from ill-covered graves a taint of death.[43]

Each site and gruesome detail provided the content of a sonorous stanza – from La Haye Sainte . . .

> Set where thou wilt thy foot, thou scarce canst tread
> Here on a spot unhallowed by the dead.[44]

. . . to the smeared wall at Hougoumont:

> Of all the blood which on that day was shed
> This mortal stain alone remained impressed,
> The all-devouring earth had drunk the rest.[45]

Even the local guide's uncharitable views on the treatment of Napoleon were incorporated:

For him alone had all this blood been shed,
Why had not vengeance struck the guilty head?
. . . One man was cause of all this world of woe,
Ye had him, and ye did not strike the blow!⁴⁶

Lord Byron arrived in the spring of 1816, and if the place still smelt, he made no mention of it. He galloped across the field on a Cossack horse hired in Brussels, made 'a tolerably minute investigation' of the area, and 'purchased a quantity of helmets [and] sabres', but thought it 'not much after Marathon & Troy – Chaeronea & Platea', the classical battle grounds he had already visited. An admirer of Bonaparte, he conceded that he was prejudiced, despising, as he did, both 'the cause & the victors' – any victory, indeed, which included 'Blucher & the Bourbons'.⁴⁷ And yet Canto III of *Childe Harold's Pilgrimage* contains some of the most resonant, and arresting, lines ever written on Waterloo:

Stop! – for thy tread is on an Empire's dust!
An earthquake's spoil is sepulchred below!

In the summer of 1817, J. M. W. Turner stopped to make studies for a large painting intended for the following year's Royal Academy exhibition. In a little sketchbook he jotted down pencil drawings of La Haye Sainte and the ruins of Hougoumont, scribbling notes of what his guide told him: '4,000 killed here' on one page; 'Hollow where the great carnage took place of the Cuirassiers by the Guards' on another. Back in London, he produced two watercolours, looking south from the British position on the ridge to the left of the road, close to the place where General Picton was killed. One shows the field much as he had seen it – albeit with the picturesque additions of a spurious flock of sheep and a horse skeleton in the foreground, while jagged lightning provided drama in the middle distance.⁴⁸ The other is closer – in subject matter at least – to the final oil painting. The bottom third of the composition is occupied by a dozen or so dead bodies: French infantrymen, Cuirassiers, Gordon Highlanders, horses. The limber box of a dismantled English cannon bears the initials 'GR III'; a French saddle cloth the letter 'N'. A litter of bodies cresting the ridge diminishes with distance, fading off the paper to the right. And yet, despite the dark, storm-laden clouds on the horizon and the customary lightning bolt, the scene is diminished in sunlight – the inexpressible scale of carnage rendered finite and inconsequential by its visibility.[49]

Not so the brooding canvas exhibited in the Royal Academy's Great Room at Somerset House during the spring of 1818. Despite three disparate light sources, little can be seen clearly. Off to the right, Hougoumont is on fire, shrouded in smoke, the flames only serving to throw the building into silhouette, any details noted in the pencil sketches the previous summer lost in darkness. The starkest illumination – shed by a flare or rocket supposedly fired to discourage looters – casts a silvery glow akin to moonlight across the distant rolling landscape, glimpsed between black banks of cloud. Finally, the light of a single flame – carried by a figure in the foreground – shows a densely packed mass of bodies. But in the profound shadow extending to either side of this sulphurous yellow oval, and in the intervening blackness of the middle ground separating it from the harsher light of the flare, countless more corpses are to be imagined than painted. There, unseen, are the sublime horrors that Edmund Burke ascribed to the domain of obscurity.[50] Attached to the painting's catalogue entry was a verse from *Childe Harold's Pilgrimage* recalling the Duchess of Richmond's ball and the brief chronology of slaughter:

Last noon beheld them full of lusty life,
Last eve in Beauty's circle proudly gay,
The midnight brought the signal-sound of strife,
The morn the marshalling in arms, – the day
Battle's magnificently-stern array!
The thunder-clouds close o'er it, which when rent
The earth is covered thick with other clay,
Which her own clay shall cover, heaped and pent,
Rider and horse, – friend, foe, – in one red burial blent![51]

On 17 July 1820, the Wordsworths came: William, his wife Mary and sister Dorothy. By then, the ruined parts of Hougoumont had been 'ridded away', the damage done to La Haye Sainte repaired, 'thus hastily removing from the spot all vestiges of so momentous an event', which, Dorothy felt, lacked gratitude. She thought – as Byron, Southey and Scott had thought before her – of the bodies buried underfoot, and although the smell of decay no longer hung on the air, a miasma might still be fancied, providing the sublime frisson to those possessing the necessary poetic sensibility. William sensed it and sometime later – as was his custom – crafted part of his sister's journal into a poem: 'After Visiting the Field of Waterloo'. But Dorothy's more immediate, plainer prose makes, perhaps, the greater impact across the centuries. 'There was little to be seen,' she wrote, 'but much to be felt; – sorrow and sadness, and even something like horror breathed out of the ground as we stood upon it!'[52]

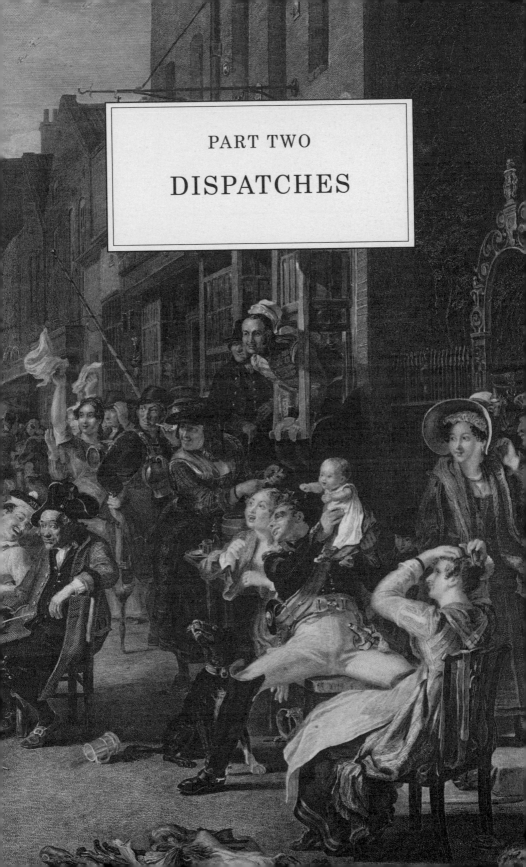

PART TWO

DISPATCHES

I

MIDNIGHT aboard the Channel packet *Maria* – Sunday passing into Monday 19 June – and Mr Sutton was bringing the first news of victory. Variously referred to in English newspapers over the following days as 'Captain', 'Packet Agent', or 'a most active officer',[1] Sutton was, according to *The Times*, 'proprietor of the passage vessels sailing between [Colchester] and Ostend'. Visiting the Belgian port on business, he had heard reports of the outbreak of hostilities and 'with great zeal and alacrity ordered [the *Maria*] to sea without waiting for passengers'. Setting sail between eleven and twelve on the Sunday night, she docked at Colchester next morning and Mr Sutton 'made the best of his way to town to relieve the anxiety of government and the public by the earliest information'.[2] In London, the War Office issued a short bulletin the following day, Tuesday the 20th:

A Captain of one of the Ostend packets brings an account of much severe fighting between the British and Prussians, and the French commanded by BUONAPARTE in person. The Duke of WELLINGTON having reached Nivelles on the 16th, attacked BUONAPARTE on the 17th, and, after a most obstinate struggle, drove him back in the first instance to Fleurus, and subsequently across the Sambre to Charleroi, which was burnt by the French. It was supposed that the British and Prussians were following up their success, as cannonading was heard on the 18th.

The information Sutton had acquired in Ostend was garbled in that it conflated the actions of 16 and 18 June into one battle on the 17th. But such as it was, it gave the *Morning Post*'s second edition on the 20th 'the supreme happiness' of an exclusive: 'the important and glorious intelligence of the defeat of BONAPARTE, in his first desperate efforts by the great and illustrious WELLINGTON, his country's pride and boast and the destined saviour of Europe and the whole civilized world'.

Other London papers printed the *Post*'s information on the following day, headlined: MOST DREADFUL BATTLE, AUSPICIOUS OPENING OF THE CAMPAIGN, COMPLETE REPULSE OF BUONAPARTE, and waited impatiently for the confidently anticipated arrival of official dispatches from Belgium. *The Times* asserted that Mr Sutton's initiative had provided a creditable lesson in the rapid dissemination of information: 'We cannot quit the subject without expressing some surprise that, in the present critical conjuncture of affairs, some arrangement has not been adopted by Government for securing the regular transmission of dispatches by the route through which the present intelligence was so laudably transmitted.' And the *Morning Post* showed gratitude for its exclusive by giving Mr Sutton's business a valuable endorsement: 'We were not aware of the facility . . . of the short passages which the packets, lately established at Colchester, usually make to and from Ostend. Government will probably feel it advisable to take more notice of this port.'[3]

Yet only a matter of days previously, before even the vaguest rumour of opening hostilities had crossed the Channel, members of the public craving up-to-date information might have been reassured by the following report:

Government has employed the means for the most rapid convey-ance of news which the ingenuity of modern discovery will allow. A succession of vessels stationed between Ostend and Deal, provided with all the expedients of telegraphic communication both for the day and night; and from Deal the land telegraphs, it is well known, confer with the Admiralty. By the application of these contrivances to maritime intercourse the event of a battle will be transmitted from Ostend in a few minutes.[4]

But this was wildly optimistic. Telegraphy by semaphore across the Channel was in theory possible but it would not be employed in June 1815. Instead the time taken for news of the battle of Waterloo to be transmitted from Ostend to London was very much dependent upon the vagaries of weather and wind.

*

The Right Honourable Maurice FitzGerald, 18th Knight of Kerry, stepped ashore from the *Leveret* sloop of war at Deal on the morning of Monday 20 June carrying an urgent dispatch to the First Lord of the Admiralty, Lord Melville, from Sir Pulteney Malcolm. Rear Admiral Malcolm was in command of the North Sea squadron stationed on the Scheldt river, providing support for the Anglo-Allied army and maintaining a line of communication to the government in London. Service etiquette forbade even a senior naval officer from entering into details on military matters before the commander-in-chief of land forces had made his report, and the Duke of Wellington had declared on the Sunday morning at Waterloo 'that he would not write a line until he had fought a battle'. As a result, only the vaguest accounts – from smugglers operating in and out of the French ports, and from Mr Sutton out of Ostend – had so far reached Whitehall, and London was 'inundated with the most alarming and dangerous rumours'. Speculation was rife in the partisan clubs of St James's: the Tory White's and the Whig Brooks's. Also, 'from the length of time since [the Cabinet] had received any positive communication from the Duke . . . considerable anxiety undoubtedly existed'. To allay that anxiety without offending protocol, Malcolm had asked the civilian Maurice FitzGerald to deliver a letter to Lord Melville – ostensibly a letter from one navy man to another, but a letter intended to be shared with the Prime Minister, Lord Liverpool, the Foreign Secretary, Lord Castlereagh, and Cabinet ministers of both the Lords and Commons. It was important that 'alarming and dangerous' rumours be superseded by accurate and balanced intelligence, that 'the bane of a serious disaster to the Prussian arms [at Ligny] was qualified . . . by the antidote of the Duke's success at Quatre Bras'.

FitzGerald left Ghent for Ostend after seven in the evening of 18 June, boarded HMS *Leveret*, the vessel provided by Malcolm, and after 'rather a slow passage' to Deal reached the Admiralty in London at 4.30 in the afternoon of the 20th, to be told that Lord Melville had just departed for the House of Lords. FitzGerald followed and delivered Malcolm's dispatch, comprising just a few lines: that Bonaparte had defeated the Prussians 'with great loss'; that when last seen, at half past ten on Sunday morning, the Duke of Wellington was 'with the army in position on ground which he had already examined, determined to give battle, and confident of success, and that he was in military communication with Marshal Blücher'; finally, that the Knight of Kerry, bearer of the letter, 'could furnish all particulars which were as yet known, for the information of the Government'. Lord Melville summoned the Cabinets of both Houses to the Chancellor's room and FitzGerald 'was requested to communicate the particulars referred to'.

FitzGerald began by asking how far the government was informed of what had already occurred in the campaign.

They knew nothing, said Lord Liverpool.

Had they not heard of the battle with the Prussians?

'No,' said Lord Liverpool.

Had they not even heard that Napoleon had moved his army?

'Reports by smugglers to that effect have come across,' Lord Liverpool replied, 'but nothing certain.'

FitzGerald then recounted what he knew of the opening skirmishes, and 'the driving in of the Prussians' on the 15th. He gave a detailed account of 'the glorious battle of Quatre Bras', as he had heard it from 'a gallant officer of the Rifle Brigade . . . who was wounded there'. He spoke of 'the Duke's thorough knowledge of the ground which he had occupied on the morning of Sunday (the 18th)'. Finally, he 'endeavoured to impress on them the utmost confidence in the success of the Duke of Wellington in any battle that should take place'. His Majesty's ministers 'expressed their great relief and gratification at the intelligence'. FitzGerald might also have communicated the additional, unconfirmed information shouted to him from a mail boat that overtook his own slower vessel in mid-Channel on 19 June: 'reports had just arrived that the Duke . . . was driving the French at all points'.[5]

*

As the *Maria* sailed out of Ostend late on Sunday night – Mr Sutton its proprietor and sole passenger – the Duke of Wellington was at his headquarters in Waterloo. Returning from the battlefield at about nine or ten, he had visited Sir Alexander Gordon, his friend and favourite aide-de-camp, whose leg had been amputated close to the groin some hours before. He had delegated General Pozzo di Borgo – Corsican-born Russian commissioner and Tsar Alexander's agent in the Anglo-Allied army – to write to Louis XVIII in Ghent: 'Tell him only that Napoleon is utterly defeated: that in less than a fortnight I shall be in possession of Paris, and hope very soon after to see him reinstated: say that excessive fatigue prevents me from writing.'[6] The mood at supper was subdued. Wellington ate with another aide-de-camp, Lieutenant Colonel Fremantle, and his old comrade-in-arms, the Spanish General Alava, at a table set for several more. 'The Duke said very little, ate hastily and heartily, but every time the door opened he gave a searching look, evidently in the hope of some of his valuable Staff approaching.' Some were dead or dying, others maimed. 'When he had finished eating, [Wellington] held up both hands in an imploring attitude and said, "The hand of Almighty God has been upon me this day."'[7] His only other recorded remark at table was a toast drunk with Alava: 'to the memory of the Peninsular war'.[8] Then he retired to his bed.

*

By two o'clock that morning, the twenty-three-year-old Major General William Frederik, Prince of Orange, was in Brussels and writing to his parents: 'Victory! Victory! . . . We have had a magnificent affair against Napoleon today [sic] . . . I am wounded by a ball in the left shoulder but only slightly.'[9] Five years later, King William I of Holland would raise a 140-foot mound of earth, topped by a thirty-one-ton iron statue of a lion, to commemorate his son's wound, on the spot at which it was inflicted. A number of historians have maintained that the lives of a great many of the men under the Prince's command might have been spared had he been wounded and carried from the field at the start of the campaign. Recent studies, however, suggest that his murderous incompetence has been exaggerated.

At three o'clock in the morning, the governor general of the Belgian provinces, Baron de Capellen, issued his fifth bulletin to reassure the citizenry of Brussels as to their Dutch saviour's welfare: 'The valuable life of that hero, who so greatly contributed to the victory of yesterday, and who has just acquired so many new claims to our gratitude, has been preserved.' The bulletin continued:

> The battle of yesterday was sanguinary, and the result brilliant. The army of Field-Marshal the Duke of Wellington covered itself with glory. The victory was complete. The enemy was totally defeated and put to the rout. He lost more than 100 cannon. Prince Blücher having joined the Duke of Wellington, their armies are pursuing the enemy beyond Genappe.[10]

It was some time after half past three, with dawn approaching, when Dr Hume tapped on Wellington's door. Sitting up in bed, his face still grimed by the previous day's dust and sweat, the Duke reached out a hand and Hume held it while reporting that Gordon had just died in a neighbouring room. As he recounted the lengthening roll of other casualties, Hume recalled, 'I felt his tears dropping fast upon my hands, and looking towards him, saw them chasing one another in furrows over his dusty cheeks.'

Then, brushing his eyes dry with his left hand, 'Thank God,' he said, 'I don't know what it is to lose a battle; but certainly nothing can be more painful than to gain one with the loss of so many of one's friends.'[11] The sentiments would find re-expression, refined to a laconic aphorism and its numerous variants: 'Nothing except a battle lost can be half so melancholy as a battle won.'

Left alone, Wellington washed and dressed, then sat down to write his report of the previous four days, addressing it to Lord Bathurst, Secretary of State for War and the Colonies. It was begun in the village of Waterloo, completed, fair-copied and signed in Brussels later that morning; published in the *London Gazette* and reprinted in whole or in part by every British newspaper; read, reread and argued over during the days, weeks, months and years to come. The Waterloo dispatch was composed in such a brusque, unadorned style, it is said to have given the impression – at a first reading – that Wellington had lost the battle. Nearly half the document was devoted to the early movement of the campaign, the inconclusive but costly action at Quatre Bras and the retreat to Mont-Saint-Jean. The Duke's account of the battle on 18 June reflected the dogged attrition of an 'arduous day', of positions 'maintained', of attack and counterattack, of the defence, loss and recapture of La Haye Sainte. Only towards the end – as towards the end of the day itself – was there reference to what might be called a victory, although that word did not appear in the dispatch itself:

> I determined to attack the enemy, and immediately advanced the whole line of infantry, supported by the cavalry and artillery. The attack succeeded in every point; the enemy was forced from his position on the heights, and fled in the utmost confusion, leaving behind him, as far as I could judge, one hundred and fifty pieces of cannon, with their ammunition, which fell into our hands.

A careless reader overlooking those few lines might well have assumed a different outcome, given the reckoning that followed: 'Your Lordship will observe that such a desperate action could not be fought, and such advantages could not be gained, without great loss; and I am sorry to add that ours has been immense.'

The catalogue of dead and wounded was inevitably repetitious. By the death of General Picton 'His Majesty has sustained the loss of an Officer who has frequently distinguished himself in his service.' Sir Alexander Gordon was 'a most promising officer, and . . . a serious loss to His Majesty's service'. The Duke's announcement of De Lancey's death – 'a serious loss to His Majesty's service and to me at this moment' – was seven days premature, however. When rectifying the error in a postscript, he was 'very happy to add, that Colonel De Lancey is not dead, and that strong hopes of his recovery are entertained'.

His Royal Highness the Prince of Orange was complimented for the 'gallantry and conduct' shown prior to receiving the musket-ball wound 'which obliged him to quit the field'. More controversially, Lord Uxbridge appeared to be credited with no other contribution to the battle than getting wounded: 'after having successfully got through this arduous day, [he] received a wound by almost the last shot fired which will, I am afraid, deprive His Majesty for some time of his services'. Caroline Capel would take particular exception to the slighting notice of her brother, when this 'odious Dispatch in which no one is done justice to'[12] was published. Lady Uxbridge felt the same as her sister-in-law, despite her easy-going husband's readiness to give Wellington the benefit of the doubt: '[Paget] is so generous about the expressions or rather *no expression* in the [dispatch], he says he is sure the Duke means kindly & appreciates him which is enough for *him*, but *not* so for us . . . He says that the Duke has a cold dry manner about everything.'[13] Family feelings would be somewhat soothed by the Prince Regent's elevation of Paget to 'the name, stile, and title of Marquess of Anglesey'.[14]

If the Duke's 'cold dry manner' restricted the tone of his comments to the neutral and the moderate, his muted expressions of approval glowed all the warmer by contrast: 'It gives me the greatest satisfaction to assure your Lordship that the army never, upon any occasion, conducted itself better . . . and there is no Officer, nor description of troops, that did not behave well.'

He did not mention the flight of the Cumberland Hussars, nor their commanding officer Lieutenant Colonel Hake, who would later be court-martialled and dismissed from the service.

Wellington was scrupulous in acknowledging the Prussians' contribution to the day: 'I should not do justice to my feelings or to Marshal Blucher and the Prussian army, if I did not attribute the successful result of this arduous day to the cordial and timely assistance I received from them.' At the same time he was careful not to surrender too much of the credit for defeating Bonaparte. This resulted in a complex, almost unintelligible exercise in conditionality:

> The operation of General Bülow, upon the enemy's flank, was a most decisive one; and even if I had not found myself in a situation to make the attack, which produced the final result, it would have forced the enemy to retire, if his attacks should have failed, and would have prevented him from taking advantage of them, if they should unfortunately have succeeded.[15]

Semantic contortions aside, the broad intelligence Wellington's dispatch would convey to Lord Bathurst, and beyond him to the Prime Minister, to the Foreign Secretary, to the Houses of Commons and Lords, to the citizenry of London and in time to the population of England, Wales, Scotland and Ireland, was essentially the same as the percussive phrase chanted jubilantly by survivors of the Highland regiments in the streets of Brussels that morning of 19 June: 'Boney's beat! Boney's beat! Boney's beat!'

*

According to François de Chateaubriand, the dispatch informing Louis XVIII 'that Napoleon [was] utterly defeated' was brought to Ghent by a Russian officer on the staff of Pozzo di Borgo at one o'clock in the morning of 19 June.[16] Another account has it delivered twelve hours later at one in the afternoon: a gentleman was standing opposite the Hotel d'Hane Steenhyse – the French King's residence in exile – when he saw the officer, 'covered with dust', dismount from his horse and run into the building. The gentleman followed him inside and witnessed his meeting with the King. 'We have taken all the heavy artillery,' he heard the officer say. 'Victory is ours!' The gentleman heard more: 'that the battle of Sunday had been general along the whole line, and had continued nine hours, – that a great number of prisoners had been taken – the French retreating in the greatest confusion . . .' He watched as the King, in tears, embraced the messenger and kissed him on both cheeks. Having seen and heard enough, the gentleman immediately left Ghent for Ostend, where he boarded a packet called the *Nymph*, which sailed at eight o'clock that evening. He arrived in Deal during the early hours of Tuesday 20 June, making his way from there by the fastest means possible to London.

In yet another version of the story, the dust-covered officer arrived at the Hotel d'Hane Steenhyse in the morning, the royal family being at breakfast and the King in his dressing gown. The gentleman observed everything from the street, through an open window, heard nothing distinctly but judged the tenor of the news from the smiles, the laughter and the dumb show of embrace and kisses. It was also said that at Ostend, before boarding the *Nymph* on the evening of the 19th, the gentleman met Admiral Malcolm 'but told him nothing [and] declared that he knew no news'.[17] Malcolm had earlier sent Maurice FitzGerald on board HMS *Leveret* with information that was over twenty-four hours old. As the *Nymph* sailed out of port, passengers 'saw a dragoon run down to the beach, take off his cap and wave it in the air. They wondered what it could mean, but none guessed.'[18] Still the gentleman said nothing.

The 'Gentleman who was at Ghent',[19] as the *Morning Post* referred to him, was not identified in the newspapers, although one source supplied an initial, a home town and an air of wilful mystery to the gentleman's anonymity, calling him 'Mr C. of Dover'.[20] Later it was alleged that this individual, so fortuitously

stationed in front of the Hotel d'Hane Steenhyse, had a devious,
even sinister, motive in getting reliable news of the battle's outcome
to London. The Duke of Wellington was not alone in his conviction that the gentleman was 'a Jew in the service of [Nathan
Mayer] Rothschild',[21] and it was to become generally accepted
that the financier used the information his spy brought back to
make a killing on the stock market, enriching himself by several
million pounds and ruining a number of his competitors. Fuelling
two centuries of anti-Semitic conspiracy theory, the story evolved
into a number of variant legends. In one version, Rothschild's spy
– a Mr Roworth – instead of loitering in Ghent stayed at Ostend
and brought his paymaster 'a Dutch paper giving the news of a
great English victory, but with confusing details'.[22] In another,
Roworth actually 'slept the night before it on the battle-field,
under some slight shelter [and] as soon as the total defeat of
Napoleon was assured, he made a rapid journey to the coast, and
crossed the channel in an open boat'.[23] In yet another, dispensing
altogether with his intermediary, Rothschild himself observed the
battle from horseback on high ground above Hougoumont,
galloped to the coast and crossed the Channel in a raging storm.[24]
Yet another version involved carrier pigeons.

There is a similar disparity in the accounts of what happened
when the messenger reached London. In one version the gentleman
delivered his information to Rothschild and was then sent on to
inform the Prime Minister.

> Lord Liverpool could make nothing out of the man, and after
> examining and cross-examining him for some time, he felt increas-
> ingly sceptical as to the authenticity of the news which he brought.
> He then sent for the Admiralty Secretary, John Wilson Croker and
> told him that the messenger had come from Belgium with the
> tidings of victory, but that his story was confused and it was
> therefore difficult to accept it as genuine.

Croker questioned the man at length and succeeded in extracting
from him three salient facts: that the French King had been in

his dressing gown when he received the messenger; that he had embraced and kissed him; and finally that he had kissed him on both cheeks. At which point Croker turned in triumph to the Prime Minister: 'My Lord, it is true; his news is genuine.'[25]

Another version had Rothschild and his brother-in-law Benjamin Cohen trying in vain to gain admittance to the Foreign Secretary, Lord Castlereagh, but being turned away by the butler: 'His Lordship is sleeping and is not to be disturbed.'[26]

Common to all versions of the story was the use Rothschild made of the information after – or even before – passing it to the government. The financier is said to have taken up his customary position in the Exchange, leaning against the so-called 'Rothschild Pillar' – the first one on the right inside the Cornhill entrance of the building – and, with a depressed expression, made surreptitious signals to his agents around the trading floor to sell 'consols' – fixed-interest government bonds. By selling consols at such a rate he is said to have given a clear impression that the war was not going well, even that Wellington's army had suffered a disastrous defeat. In the absence of official information – and despite the 'auspicious' news from Mr Sutton that had been published the day before – rumour spread that 'Rothschild knows something'. Other investors followed his lead and began to sell their consols in panic. Prices fell. Then, when the market had slumped and the value of consols had reached its nadir, there were more surreptitious signals from the 'Rothschild Pillar' and his agents started to buy cheaply everything that had previously been sold, in time to take advantage of the inevitable surge in confidence and prices when trading opened on the morning of Thursday 22 June, following official confirmation of the battle's true outcome.

That Rothschild made 'millions' from this cynical manipulation of intelligence, even that the house of Rothschild owed the very basis of its vast fortune to the slaughter of the battle, is, however, a considerable exaggeration. It has been calculated, according to the Stock Exchange rates of the period in question, that in order to make a million pounds' profit from buying consols, the sum of £14.125 million would need to have been speculated, and such a purchase, under the rules governing the Stock Exchange at that time, would not have been permitted. The maximum expenditure allowed was £100,000, and this would have brought a profit of £7,080 – hardly the foundation of a financial empire. Rothschild would have faced fewer investment restrictions if he had speculated in 'omniums' – a particularly volatile kind of government stock, vulnerable to fraudulent manipulation because it was a sure gauge of market confidence. Only a year before, in June 1814, the naval officer Thomas Cochrane had been tried in the Court of King's Bench, accused, with two accomplices, of boosting the value of omnium stock with spurious intelligence that Napoleon had been captured and cut to pieces by Cossacks. But, according to the present Baron Rothschild, 'there would have been no possibility of . . . buying enough . . . Omnium stock [in June 1815] to make a profit of £1 million. The market was not big enough.'[27]

Discrediting the myth of 'millions' does not preclude some profit having been turned on the Exchange in those uncertain days. On Wednesday 21 June, as rumour of defeat was overtaken by rumour of victory, the *Sun* noted:

> The state of the Money Market affords strong presumption that . . . intelligence has been received . . . Though nothing Official was known upon 'Change . . . no doubt seems to be entertained of the success of the Allies. The Jews, who seem to be in the secret, are buying largely, and Omnium, which opened at 4 per cent was, at one o'clock, 5¾ per cent Premium.[28]

The Times observed: 'some houses generally supposed to possess the best information were among the purchasers'.[29]

But even as prices rose, rumours that Wellington had been beaten continued to circulate. Major Sir Robert Wilson, a Whig with strong republican sympathies, who had been unable to disguise his satisfaction when Napoleon escaped from Elba, 'was the bird of ill-omen at Brookes's [*sic*], the constant harbinger of bad news, which he propagated as coming from the most undeniable authority of his private correspondents abroad'.[30]

*

At six o'clock in the morning of Sunday 18 June, the citizens of Paris had been roused by a hundred-gun cannonade of celebration. In various parts of the city placards were posted, giving news of Ligny and Quatre Bras that was equally rousing:

> The Emperor has just obtained a complete victory over the united Prussian and English armies, under the command of Lord Wellington and Marshal Blücher. The enemy experienced a dreadful overthrow. Wellington and Blücher saved themselves with difficulty. They were routed in all directions. We have already several thousand prisoners, and forty pieces of cannon. – Prisoners every instant are announced.

The statement was signed by Marshal Davout, Prince Eckmühl, Minister of War.[31]

That Sunday morning the *Moniteur Universel*, the French government's official journal of report, provided the text of a telegraphic dispatch sent from Lyons the previous morning but dated 15 June. With the necessary brevity of semaphore it reported the opening clashes of the campaign in the Charleroi region: 'The enemy was attacked this morning. We have taken six hundred prisoners, a colonel and a major among them; we have killed two or three hundred men.' The *Moniteur* also printed in full the Emperor's most recent proclamation to his troops. Delivered at Avesnes, on the 14th, it was intended to urge the army and French nation to a defensive war by reference to victories achieved that day in 1800 and 1807, over Austria and Russia respectively. 'SOLDIERS', it began:

> This day is the anniversary of Marengo and of Friedland, which twice decided the destiny of Europe. Then, as after Austerlitz, as after Wagram, we were too generous! We believed in the

protestations and in the oaths of princes whom we left on the throne! Now, however, coalesced among themselves, they would destroy the independence and the most sacred rights of France. They have commenced the most unjust of aggressions. Let us march then to meet them. Are they and we no longer the same men? SOLDIERS! At Iena, against these same Prussians, now so arrogant, you were one against three, and at Montmirail one against six!

Unable to claim like victories over the British, he had only to remind his troops of the privations endured by French captives of the Peninsular campaign aboard the infernal prison ships anchored in the Medway to inspire them with a persuasive combination of fear and hatred: 'Let those among you who have been prisoners of the English, detail to you the hulks, and the frightful miseries which they suffered!' He reminded them also that many of the soldiers they would be facing – among the alliance fighting alongside the British – were themselves representatives of oppressed nations and that the yoke of the decadent, despotic hereditary powers they were being forced to defend was as irksome to them as it would be to the French nation in the unthinkable event that the campaign should fail:

The Saxons, the Belgians, the Hanoverians, the soldiers of the confederation of the Rhine, lament that they are compelled to lend their arms to the cause of princes, the enemies of justice and the rights of all nations; they know that this coalition is insatiable. After having devoured twelve millions of Poles, twelve millions of Italians, one million of Saxons, six millions of Belgians, it must devour the states of the second rank of Germany. The madmen! A moment of prosperity blinds them. The oppression and humiliation of the French people are beyond their power. If they enter France, they will there find their tomb.

Finally he rallied his forces with a call to arms intended to echo back across France and forward to the Belgian province they were about to invade:

SOLDIERS! We have forced marches to make, battles to fight, dangers to encounter; but, with steadiness, victory will be ours; – the rights, the honour, the happiness of the country will be re-conquered! To every Frenchman who has a heart, the moment is arrived to conquer or perish.[32]

On Monday morning, 19 June, the day after these exhilarating pronouncements were published, the *Journal de Paris* contained a report, dated the 16th, 'from behind Ligny at half past eight in the evening'. The army was advancing from Fleurus in pursuit of the enemy. At noon a message reached Paris by telegraph bearing the 'satisfactory' intelligence that La Haye Sainte and Mont-Saint-Jean 'had been carried by our troops'. Then, towards midnight, the Marquis de Caulaincourt, Minister for Foreign Affairs, was sitting alone in his office when a servant brought him a note, just delivered by 'a gentlemanly-looking man' who 'appeared rather agitated'. It was in Latin and unsigned: 'The army has been destroyed.'

Caulaincourt ordered a carriage and had himself driven to the house of the Comte de Carnot, Minister of the Interior. Carnot had received an identical message. Together they visited the man they suspected of being the instigator, if not author, of the intelligence: Joseph Fouché, Duc d'Otronte, Minister of Police . . .

The opportunist survivor of a quarter-century's political turmoil – outlasting Revolution, Terror, Directory, Consulate and Empire – Fouché was a master of intrigue. He had plotted against Napoleon before, had been instrumental in returning the Bourbons to the throne in 1814, only to be reinstated by his former master as Minister of Police during the Hundred Days. 'I did not want Napoleon any more,' he later admitted, 'and knew that if he were victorious in [the Belgian] campaign, I would continue to suffer his yoke along with the rest of France, as a victory would prolong his disastrous rule.'[33] To prevent such a victory he had been in regular covert communication with the Duke of Wellington, in all probability supplying him with the highly detailed account of 'the strength and disposition of the French army'[34] that the Duke circulated to his allies on 16 May 1815.

... It was two o'clock in the morning when Carnot and Caulaincourt confronted Fouché in his bedchamber, showed him the notes they had received and demanded an explanation. His face as blank and composed as that of a corpse, Fouché assured them that he knew nothing about the matter. The two men left more than ever convinced 'that he knew everything'.[35] The controlling centre of an extensive web of agents, spies and informers, the Minister of Police was most likely to have received news of the Belgian catastrophe before anyone else and to have kept it secret before divulging it in the most insidious manner – at dead of night, by mysterious messenger and anonymous note – so as to create the maximum instability and anxiety in government circles. During the days following the Emperor's hoped-for defeat and second abdication, Fouché would set about orchestrating overtures of peace and a smooth transition from imperial rule, always ensuring that he retained his sinister power under a weakened constitutional Bourbon monarchy.

At six o'clock in the morning, Tuesday 20 June, a telegraph arrived in Paris with news of the defeat, but the information was withheld from the public. Instead, further four-day-old intelligence appeared in the press. That night Caulaincourt received word that he was to expect the Emperor at the Elysée Palace early the following morning. His arrival was also kept secret, but a dispatch was published the same day from a member of the General Staff which began: 'The armies of France have continued to immortalise themselves on the plain of Fleurus.'[36] It was dated 17 June. Readers of the *Journal de Paris* and the *Moniteur Universel* may well have wondered what they were not being told. Rumours had already begun to spread.

A French correspondent of John Scott wrote of 'a rushing whisper over Paris, increasing to a buzz in the Cafés, &c. that the army had suffered a great defeat'. It was claimed that Lucien Bonaparte, the Emperor's brother, had sold twelve million francs' worth of government stock and that as a result the value of stock had fallen, causing 'the greatest agitation on 'Change'. At nine o'clock in the evening, 20 June, the Parisian gentleman recorded:

> The news keeps us all on our feet, streaming to the places where our anxiety is most likely to be relieved. Questions are put by every one to his neighbour, who again looks to him for satisfaction. People throng towards the Tuileries, the barriers, &c. The report of a lost battle gains ground – Buonaparte has been killed – Jerome [his youngest brother] is arrived wounded from headquarters. The officers and Buonapartists evince consternation.

That night there were disturbances in the theatres, and audiences called on orchestras to play *La Marseillaise*.[37]

The following morning, although still no official intelligence had been published, everyone was convinced: 'The army is lost – annihilated! . . . Buonaparte is in Paris – wounded – killed! Not two hundred of the Imperial Guards remain. Whole corps have passed over to the king – the Allies are rapidly marching on Paris!'

Two hours later, the Chambers of Peers and Representatives – the upper and lower houses of parliament – were said to be in emergency session and rumour continued to flood the streets:

> Great crowds on the boulevards. Every one asking – no one able to answer, except with fancies. The news of the defeat, however, with every possible aggravation, is loudly talked of. The officers and agents of the Police interfere harshly with the assemblages in the streets to stop the circulation of the dreadful stories. – At one or two points smart conflicts took place in consequence.

By two o'clock in the afternoon, the news was 'fully confirmed'.[38] A second edition of the *Moniteur* printed the Emperor's own account of the campaign. It ended with the words: 'Such has been the issue of the battle of Mont St Jean, glorious for the French armies, and yet so fatal.'[39]

That same morning, a small item in the *Journal de Paris* suggested that society might continue to find amusement in the dark days to come. The previous evening, at the Gaiety Theatre, a musical entertainment in one act received its first performance and ecstatic applause. Set in a village 'some leagues from Paris', *The Montargis Dog and the Magpie of Palaiseau; or Crime struggling with Virtue* featured a pair of young lovers, a comic bailiff, a chorus of market traders and carnival folk, a ballet of dogs and magpies, and a song every few minutes. 'This is the most hilarious comedy imaginable,' the critic raved. 'It was a festival of animals. The theatre was like a menagerie, the audience laughed like beasts, and the orchestra played. Where better to take the family?'

*

In London on Wednesday evening, 21 June, society also went about its pleasures. Mr Vezey-Fitzgerald gave a grand entertainment at his home in Great George Street to assorted lords and ladies, earls and countesses, marquesses and marchionesses, viscounts and knights of the realm. In Portman Square, the Dowager Countess of Clonmell held a 'grand rout', boasting a similarly exalted company, which included the retired tragedienne Mrs Siddons, and Mrs Fitzherbert, illegitimate wife of the Prince Regent. Her ladyship's son, the Earl of Clonmell, made an appearance at both gatherings. There was a ball at the home of Sir George Talbot and his daughters in New Burlington Street, while south of Piccadilly, at 1 St James's Square, Lord and Lady Grantham were giving 'a grand turtle dinner'; among the 'large party of fashionables' attending were the Russian ambassador and his lady, the Duke of Devonshire, the Earl and Countess of Jersey, Lord and Lady Morpeth, and Lord and Lady Boringdon. On the opposite side of the square, at number 16, the West Indies merchant Mr Edmund Boehm and his ambitious wife were entertaining His Royal Highness the Prince Regent with 'a grand dinner' and a ball to follow. Those invited to meet the esteemed guest included the Prince's brother, His Royal Highness the Duke of York, the Earl of Cholmondely, General Bloomfield, the Hon. Mr and Mrs Edward Bouverie, and Lord and Lady Castlereagh. The Foreign Secretary and his wife would have had the shortest of strolls from their house at 18 St James's Square, on the corner of King Street.

Thomas Raikes was dining with a large party that evening at the home of the Drummond-Burrells – the future Lord and Lady Willoughby de Eresby – in Piccadilly. Sir Henry 'Kangaroo' Cooke was there, as was his crony, 'the bird of ill-omen', Sir Robert Wilson. 'Have you heard any news?' Margaret Elphinstone, daughter of Admiral Lord Keith, whispered to Raikes. She added that she feared from Wilson's 'grave portentous countenance' that some disaster had happened. For his part Raikes had little confidence in the rumours of an allied defeat because he 'had heard that Rothschild was purchasing stock largely, and that the funds had risen two per cent'. After the ladies had retired, Wilson imparted his news to the gentlemen over port and cigars: 'he had received a private dispatch from Brussels, announcing the total defeat of the Anglo-Prussian army by the French, with the additional circumstance that Napoleon, after his decided victory, had supped with the Prince d'Aremberg at his palace in that city'. When Raikes and other gentlemen expressed doubts about the information, Wilson 'offered readily to bet any sum on the strength of his dispatches'.[40] Raikes bet four or five hundred pounds against and others followed, some raising the stakes to more than £1,000.

Another exclusively masculine company was assembled at 44 Grosvenor Square, where Lord Harrowby was hosting one of his regular Wednesday Cabinet dinners. The Prime Minister, Lord Liverpool, was there, as was the Chancellor of the Exchequer, Nicholas Vansittart, and the Secretary of State for War and Colonies, Lord Bathurst. The attendance of Bathurst at this particular dinner may have attracted a number of other Cabinet members who would otherwise – like Lord Castlereagh – have taken advantage of alternative social engagements that evening.

'It was well understood . . . that the Despatch, whenever it arrived, would be taken in the first instance to the War Secretary . . . and therefore several members of the Cabinet felt great pleasure on the 21st, in accepting [Harrowby]'s invitation to dinner, in order that they might be on the spot when the Despatch arrived.' But their dinner was not interrupted. 'They dined, they sat. No Despatch came.'[41]

*

In Brussels two days earlier, Wellington's report, so eagerly awaited by the gentlemen in Grosvenor Square, had concluded: 'I send, with this dispatch, two eagles, taken by the troops in this action, which Major Percy will have the honour of laying at the feet of his Royal Highness. I beg leave to recommend him to your Lordship's protection.'

It is said that Percy was the only one of the Duke's aides-de-camp left alive or uninjured after the battle. This was not so. However, following the death of Colonels Canning and Gordon, the highest-ranking officer of the remaining six aides-de-camp was Colonel Fremantle, and he had already been given the honour of bringing home the dispatch after Wellington's last comparable triumph, the battle of Vitoria in June 1813. If such a pecking order entered into consideration at all, then Major Henry Percy would have been given the commission as the next highest in rank.

Entrusted with the Duke's letter, Percy folded and placed it for protection inside a small memento of the Duchess of Richmond's ball. It is not known who his dancing partner was on the evening of 15 June, but as the handsome young major hurried away about the business of war, she had pressed upon him her purple velvet handkerchief sachet. Put to no use at Quatre Bras and Mont-Saint-Jean, the perfumed keepsake had lain forgotten in his pocket over the following three days. On 19 June it provided a perfect fit for his momentous charge.

Still dressed in the clothes he had worn in the battle of the previous day, the coat heavily stained with the blood of an officer killed close by him, he left Brussels by coach about noon, the captured eagle standard of the 105th Regiment sticking out of one window, that of Napoleon's 'Invincibles', the 45th – inscribed with *Iena, Austerlitz, Wagram, Rylau* and *Friedland* – out of the other. The pace was slow over rutted roads made near impassable in places by the heavy rains, and progress continued sluggish the whole seventy miles by way of Ghent to Ostend. So it was not until one o'clock in the afternoon of the following day that Percy carried his prizes aboard the sixteen-gun brig-sloop HMS *Peruvian*, commanded by Captain James Kearney White. The captain's log records that at four o'clock they 'Tacked – at Ostend' and at half past six 'Set sail'.

Given favourable winds, the sixty-odd-mile crossing from Ostend could have been accomplished in eight to nine hours or even less, although the average was between ten and twelve.[42] The *Peruvian*'s log for that night recorded 'Winds East, light breezes – clear.' At three in the morning, with what little wind there was dropping, Captain White ordered more canvas spread: 'Made sail, light breezes – clear.' Five hours later, at eight o'clock, the vessel was barely moving: 'Nearly calm.' By half past eleven, almost twenty hours after leaving port and with no imminent prospect of making further headway, Percy voiced his impatience to the *Peruvian*'s commander, who ordered every inch of canvas spread: 'Light airs, made all possible sail.' When this too proved futile, Captain White told Percy that if he agreed to entrust himself, the dispatch and the eagles to his care, they could reach Broadstairs in five hours. Percy agreed, and the log recorded: 'Out gig.' Enthused by his incidental part in this glorious moment of history, Captain White had made the extraordinary decision to abandon his becalmed ship. The gig was lowered and crewed by four strong oarsmen. White himself took an oar, Percy, who had rowed at Eton, took another. With the eagles safely stowed, they pulled towards the English coast. According to the *Kentish Gazette*, 'four hours after, [they] landed in safety at Broadstairs; these gallant fellows having rowed 38 miles in that time'.[43] A building in the vicinity where Percy and White are said to have rested with the trophies is still called 'Eagle House'.

Where and from whom they hired the chaise and four that took them to London is not known, neither is the name of the driver, the fare agreed on, nor any of the other practical considerations so readily forgotten in the telling and retelling of such a legendary dash to glory. The horses would have been changed every twelve to fourteen miles, at staging posts in Canterbury, Sittingbourne and Rochester. Each stop would have attracted wondering locals to stare at the two men, in navy blue and battle-soiled army scarlet; at the heavy, gold-embroidered standards, and at the eagles, one of which was said to have been still smeared with blood and mud, the other much hacked about by sabre blows and barely attached to its pole.

They entered London at dusk, clattering along the Old Kent Road, crossing Bermondsey New Road into Kent Street and on to the junction with White Street. Alongside the church of St George the Martyr they turned left down Blackman Street for some 400 yards, bearing right into Borough Road and skirting the high wall of the King's Bench prison, topped with *chevaux de frise*. The length of Borough Road brought them to the Obelisk, marking a mile to Palace Yard and Parliament. Westminster Bridge Road took them curving towards the river and across the bridge. Passing the old Palace of Westminster on the left, they turned right along Parliament Street and on to Whitehall, before turning left into Downing Street. At the far end of that short cul-de-sac they pulled up in front of number 14. Two doors down, at number 12, Secretary to the Treasury Charles Arbuthnot had just returned from the House of Commons, and was sitting quietly in his study when he heard an uproar in the street. He thought at first it was a mob demonstrating its anger at the Corn Laws – not an uncommon feature of London life at the time – but stepping outside, he found instead a jubilant crowd gathered around the chaise and the eagles, and Major Percy enquiring at the door of the Colonial Office for Lord Bathurst. Arbuthnot knew exactly where his lordship and other members of the Cabinet were to be found that night. Getting into the carriage with Percy and White, he instructed the driver and they set off again, followed by the London mob – attuned as readily to celebration as to resentment and violence. Turning back into Whitehall, they forked left at the statue of Charles I and into Cockspur Street, then Haymarket, then left along Piccadilly, turning right up Bond Street before going left into Grosvenor Street and on to Grosvenor Square.

Having waited all evening for the expected dispatch, the party of ministers attending Lord Harrowby's Cabinet dinner had begun to disperse, disappointed, but a number were still in conversation on the pavement outside, as though reluctant to abandon hope of the messenger's arrival. Suddenly there was a gathering roar of shouts and cheering in the distance, but getting closer. Then, into the square came the carriage – seemingly transfixed by the two eagle standards – and 'escorted by a running and vociferous multi-tude'.[44] Out jumped Major Percy followed by Mr Arbuthnot. They ran into Lord Harrowby's house, along with his lordship's returning dinner guests. The excited crowd waited. After a time Arbuthnot was sent out on to the top of the steps to announce the news. He ended by saying: 'In short, the French army is entirely destroyed!' As the people bellowed their approval, Lord Harrowby might have been heard calling from inside: 'I beg your pardon, Mr Arbuthnot – but not exactly – I think you are going a little too far.'[45] It was not after all clear, from a first hasty perusal of the dispatch, how great a victory had been achieved. As they read through it again, ministers asked Percy for more details:

'What number of prisoners have been taken?'

'I saw a column of 10,000,' he replied.

'How many of the enemy's cannon?'

'All.'[46]

They read on. Someone asked the major another question, but there was no answer. Having had little or no rest for the previous four days, he had fallen asleep in a chair.

But before he could sleep properly that night, Percy had one more commission to fulfil. Lord Liverpool, having read the final lines of Wellington's dispatch, said: 'You must come immediately with me to the Regent.' The major got back into his chaise, this time with Liverpool at his side, Captain White and Arbuthnot having by this time melted from the company, as from the story.

The Prime Minister at first proposed using his own carriage.

'But what is to be done with the Eagles?' said the major.

'Let the footman carry them,' his lordship replied.

In later years Percy would recall the suggestion with disgust, but at the time he politely insisted that they and the eagles travel in the chaise.

Back along Grosvenor Street they went, then right, down the length of New and Old Bond Street, sharp right into Piccadilly and immediately left down St James's Street. The attendant crowds had grown, newcomers being told by those a little better informed: 'Wellington is safe!' This was not a victory like that of Trafalgar ten years earlier – a victory tempered by the death of a national hero. 'We don't know what the news is,' those nearest the carriage shouted back into the crowd, 'but Wellington is safe!'[47]

Sir Robert Wilson had arrived at Brooks's following dinner at the Drummond-Burrells. In an upper room facing on to St James's Street, he and another pro-Bonapartist Whig, Charles Grey, were holding the floor with news of Wellington's defeat. They 'demonstrated satisfactorily to the crowded audience that Boney had 200,000 men across [the] Sambre, and that he must then be at Brussels'. The club's betting book recorded no wagers laid that night, either for or against the truth of Wilson's assertions, but as he was reading out a letter 'announcing that the English were defiling out of the town by the Antwerp gate', shouts were heard in the street and everyone went to the windows. They saw the crowds below, the chaise and four, the eagles. Sir Robert no doubt calculated how much his wagers earlier in the evening had cost him. 'We are good people,' another Brooks's member reflected later, 'but sorry prophets!'[48]

It was gone midnight at 16 St James's Square. Remnants of a lavish dinner were being cleared away and replaced by an equally lavish supper for the ball guests arriving with unusual punctuality in deference to His Royal Highness the Prince Regent. Everything was going so well. 'Mr Boehm had spared no cost to render it the most brilliant party of the season.' Upstairs in the ballroom the tall windows had been left wide open because of the sultry weather. The Prince was just approaching the dais on which his chair had been placed as the band struck up and the first quadrille began to form. Suddenly, from outside, came 'vociferous shouts' rising and combining to a thunderous roar. The band fell silent, the forming quadrille broke up and everyone – dancers, dowagers, dukes and duchesses alike – rushed to the windows 'without the slightest sense of decorum'. Mrs Boehm watched, appalled, as down in the square

> an enormous mob [came] running by the side of a post-chaise and four, out of whose windows were hanging . . . nasty French eagles. In a second the door of the carriage was flung open, and without waiting for the steps to be let down, out sprang Henry Percy – such a dusty figure! – with a flag in each hand, pushing aside everyone who happened to be in his way, darting up stairs, into the ball-room, stepping hastily up to the Regent, dropping on one knee, laying the flags at his feet, and pronouncing the words 'Victory, Sir! Victory!'[49]

The Prince adjourned, with the rest of the gentlemen, into a neighbouring room to read the dispatch, and left the ladies fluttering their fans nervously in the warm night air from the open windows.

Left alone for the evening at 18 St James's Square, Lady Emma Sophia Edgcombe, twenty-four-year-old niece of Lord and Lady Castlereagh, had heard the commotion of Percy's arrival. Soon afterwards she received a note from her aunt, instructing her to dress and join her directly. She arrived at number 16 and found the gentlemen still in conference and the ladies 'silent, too anxious to talk, and longing to hear more'. The portly dandy Lord Alvanley was the first gentleman to emerge, horrifying them with names of the dead and injured. The Guards, he declared, with his characteristic lisp, 'have thuffered theverely!' Then he slipped away to carry the news among the rest of society, leaving Lady Edgcombe concerned for the safety of her brother Ernest, an ensign in the 1st Regiment of Foot Guards, although aware that 'the fate of a subaltern could not be known'. The Prince Regent emerged from his conference in tears. 'It is a glorious victory and we must rejoice at it,' he told the ladies, 'but the loss of life has been fearful, and I have lost many friends.'[50] Then he called for his carriage and left. His brother, the Duke of York, followed, then everybody else. Mrs Boehm's glittering assembly dispersed into the darkness:

> Ladies of the highest rank, who had not ordered their carriages till four o'clock a.m., rushed away, like maniacs, in their muslins and satin shoes, across the Square; some accompanied by gentlemen, others without escort of any kind; all impatient to learn the fate of those dear to them; many jumping into the first stray hackney-coach they fell in with, and hurrying on to the Foreign Office or Horse Guards, eager to get a sight of the List of Killed and Wounded.

Within twenty minutes, only the host and hostess remained in their desolate ballroom. 'Even the band had gone', and the splendid supper provided for their guests lay spread in the dining room untouched. Sixteen years later, the widowed Mrs Boehm still harboured the vivid and bitter memory:

> All our trouble, anxiety, and the expense were utterly thrown away in consequence of – what shall I say? Well, I must say it – the unseasonable declaration of the Waterloo victory! Of course, one was very glad to think one had beaten those horrid French and

all that sort of thing; but still, I always shall think it would have
been far better if Henry Percy had waited quietly till the morning,
instead of bursting in upon us, as he did, in such indecent haste:
and even if he had told the Prince alone, it would have been better;
for I have no doubt his Royal highness would have shown consideration enough for my feelings not to publish the news till the
next morning.[51]

But such intelligence, so long arriving, was spreading fast through
the town, 'and all the world was out of doors during the best
part of the night, asking news of their neighbours'.[52]

Sometime after Sir Robert Wilson left the Drummond-Burrells'
dinner, taking information of Wellington's defeat to Brooks's,
Thomas Raikes went to show his face at the Talbots' party in
New Burlington Street. He arrived to find 'the whole house
in confusion and dismay; ladies calling for their carriages, and
others fainting in the anteroom'. He claimed that it was Lady
Castlereagh who had caused this panic, having come directly
from the Boehms' ruined soirée, bearing joyous news of victory
and a partial list of killed and wounded. Raikes noticed 'particularly the Ladies Paget', wife and daughters of Lord Uxbridge.
They had just been informed of the amputation of his right leg
and 'seemed in the utmost distress'. In a memoir written half a
century later, Lady Edgcombe – by then the septuagenarian
Countess Brownlow – was careful to exonerate her aunt of a
callous lack of feeling: 'Immediately on hearing the details from
Lord Alvanley, [Lady Castlereagh] made me write a note of excuse
to Sir George Talbot both for herself and me, as she properly felt
that going to a ball under such circumstances was quite out of
the question.' Instead, it was Lord Alvanley himself to whom she
gave 'the credit of having sent half the ladies into fainting fits
and hysterics'.[53]

Major Percy was promoted lieutenant colonel by the Prince
Regent – just as Major Fremantle had been after delivering the
Vitoria dispatch two years earlier – this being a perquisite of
bearing such news. Exhausted by a day of battle and three days'

travel, in the early hours of Thursday 22 June Percy had himself
driven to his father's home in Portman Square. Here at last he
was able to sleep. Undressing for bed, he laid aside the uniform
coat stained with a brother officer's blood. As he unwound the
scarlet sash at his waist, fragments of the officer's brain dropped
from its folds on to the floor.[54]

II

ORDINARILY the *London Gazette* – 'Published by Authority' of His Majesty's Britannic Government – appeared twice weekly, on Tuesdays and Saturdays, variably priced between sixpence and four shillings. It would contain royal proclamations, government announcements, notices of parliamentary Acts, naval and military promotions, and the names of all gentlemen recently declared bankrupt together with proceedings against them in the Court of Insolvency. Occasionally a 'Supplement' to the Saturday issue might be published on Monday or to that of Tuesday on Thursday. Extraordinary events, however, called for an issue of the *Gazette* that was not merely supplementary to a preceding one. So on the morning of Thursday 22 June, as placards were hung on the gates of the Mansion House and cannon fired in jubilation from the Tower and in the Regent's Park, a *London Gazette EXTRAORDINARY* brought the full text of the Waterloo dispatch to public attention.

The history painter Benjamin Robert Haydon secured his copy and read it through four times at a single sitting. He was unable to paint for excitement and because his servant and model, Corporal John Sammons, late of the Horse Guards – who 'seemed astounded that the Battle of Waterloo had been won and he not present'[1] – had taken himself off to get drunk with his former comrades in arms. Haydon read the *Gazette* again before going to bed and 'dreamt of it & was fighting & waking all night', getting up the next morning 'in a steam of intense feeling'. He read it yet again and ordered the *Courier* for a month. Then he went to a confectioner's shop and read all the London papers till his stomach ached. By the following day he had read the *Gazette* so many times he knew it by heart.

He dined with Leigh Hunt on Sunday 25 June, the battle monopolising conversation and fuelling argument.

'Terrible Battle this, Haydon.'

'A glorious one, Hunt.'

'Oh, certainly.'

But Hunt had more sympathy for Bonaparte than for the alliance of despotic princes that had defeated him. After all, he and his brother had just completed a two-year term of imprisonment for libelling the Prince Regent. He argued that, even vanquished, 'Buonaparte may be the means of producing something better because he is not so powerful as he was formerly, to push his victories to the extent he did, so that he may work an improvement in others, and be even under its influence himself.'[2] Hunt had concluded his *Examiner* editorial published that morning with the fervent hope that some benefit might issue from the carnage:

In one point of view, nothing but affliction and disgust present themselves to the mind at the sight of so many lives destroyed, so many public burdens increased, and so much misery of all sorts occasioned to families; but in another point, the very excess of the thing produces a hope of better days; for if both parties should be speedily exhausted, there will be good ground for their coming to a reasonable accommodation; and if the war should last long, and they should go on so as to make any material and final exhaustion of their respective military strengths, there is hope that the mere brute force of governments may be obliged to lie quiet a little, and the civil power, intellect, and rights of the community at large, be heard and be felt in their own cause.[3]

But Haydon had no patience with such nuances. For him the matter was simple: the Duke of Wellington had 'saved for this age the intellect of the world', while, 'had Napoleon triumphed we would have been brought back to barbarism'. Having visited Paris the previous year, he had little faith that any 'reasonable accommodation' was to be expected from the French:

> Vain, insolent, thoughtless, bloodthirsty, and impetuous by nature, – so susceptible to glory as to have their little sense blinded by that bubble, a people who are brilliant without intensity, have courage without firmness, are polite without benevolence, tender without heart, – pale, fierce, and elegant in their looks, depraved, lecherous, and blasphemous in their natures! Good God![4]

When the first British troops began to arrive back in London, Corporal Sammons brought several wounded men of his acquaintance to Haydon's painting room, where his master and the Scottish artist David Wilkie listened with relish to gruesome tales of close combat. One man described Corporal John Shaw cutting a Frenchman 'right through his brass helmet to the chin' so that 'his face fell off him like a bit of apple'. Another had watched Shaw die, his 'side torn off by a shell'. Private Hodgson of the 2nd Life Guards regaled the two painters with a first-hand account of fighting a Cuirassier: 'The first cut he gave was on the cuirass [and] the shock nearly broke his arm . . . [then] dropping the reins, and guiding his horse with his knees, as the Cuirassier at last gave point, [Hodgson] cut his sword hand off, and then dashing the point of his sword into the man's throat turned it round and round.'

Wilkie would later paint his masterpiece for the Duke of Wellington – *The Chelsea Pensioners Reading the Waterloo Dispatch* – asking and receiving from His Grace the astonishing sum of 1,200 guineas for it. One particularly telling detail of the crowded composition moved the French painter Théodore Géricault to tears: a young woman – mouth and nose obscured by a corner of the *Gazette Extraordinary* – all eyes as she anxiously scans the casualty list. The painting would be the sensation of the 1822 Royal Academy exhibition. For his part Haydon would receive a commission from a consortium of Liverpool gentlemen for a life-size picture of the Duke and his horse imagined surveying the field of Waterloo twenty years after. He would also paint twenty-six versions of another imaginary scene: *Napoleon Musing on St Helena*. But for the time being, both painters were content to listen, agog, to the soldiers' tales, and they 'kept the poor fellows long and late, and rewarded them well'.[5]

However, there were other civilians who were unwilling to hear or speak of the battle. On 28 June at Trostan Hall, Suffolk, none of the dinner-party guests 'durst even mention the subject'[6] in the presence of their host, the radical lawyer Capel Lofft, so distressed was he by Bonaparte's downfall. The embargo was 'concerted separately with each of the guests as he arrived; it was understood that this precaution was requisite to ensure [Lofft's] attendance at dinner'.[7]

Nobody took the news of Waterloo so badly, according to Haydon, as did William Hazlitt: 'It is not to be believed how the destruction of Napoleon affected him; he seemed prostrated in mind and body: he walked about unwashed, unshaved, hardly sober by day, and always intoxicated by night, literally, without exaggeration, for weeks . . .' And around this shambling malcontent a drunken multitude rejoiced.

The guns that thundered across London at ten o'clock on the morning after Percy's arrival with the Waterloo dispatch marked the official start of national celebrations. When darkness fell, celebration required illumination: the most rudimentary means was a lamp or candle placed in the window, more sophisticated displays being made with coloured designs painted on parchment and lit from behind, while the most elaborate were those in which entire buildings flamed with multicoloured configurations of oil lamps. Business thrived on fulfilling the demand for patriotic show.

'IN Honour of the GLORIOUS VICTORY', Fawley's Manufactory in Blackfriars Road offered 'A large ASSORTMENT of

ILLUMINATION TRANSPARENCIES, designed by the first Artists, and painted in a very superior style, for the present glorious occasion, to be LENT or SOLD.'⁸ The New Metallic Colour Works in Brydges Street, Covent Garden, respectfully informed the public 'that ILLUMINATION LAMPS, of all colours, ready attired for lighting, with Devices, Transparencies, &c. may be had on the lowest terms' from their warehouse in Old Street, opposite Vinegar Yard, and that 'Public Buildings and Gentlemen's Houses [were to be] illuminated on very low terms, at the shortest notice'.⁹ The last time illuminations had been required on so large a scale by the 'Nobility, Gentry and others' was just a year before, to celebrate the 'Proclamation of Peace'. On that occasion a Lambeth iron-monger by the name of Turk boasted a stock of 'thirty thousand and upwards' of such lamps at '7/6 per dozen and devices appropriate'.¹⁰

By Friday night London's West End was 'in a blaze', drawing crowds into the streets 'greater, if possible than on the first night of lighting up in honour of the Victory of Vitoria'. The most common illuminations comprised initials: 'GR' or 'GRIII' for King George, 'GPR' for the Prince Regent, one surmounted by a crown, the other by the Prince of Wales feathers. The Duke of Wellington was sometimes represented by 'DW', or a 'W' stood for both the hero and his battle. Elsewhere his name appeared in full, sometimes alongside that of his Prussian ally. 'WELLINGTON and BLÜCHER' adorned the Horse Guards in Whitehall with laurel branches picked out in green lamps. The House of Commons display had 'WELLINGTON, BLÜCHER, and VICTORY' in gold, branches of laurel, 'pyram-idal rows of lamps; a triumphal arch in the centre [with] parallel rows of lamps, red and yellow'. Along the facade of the Admiralty was emblazoned 'WELLINGTON UNCONQUERED'. Lord Castlereagh's office had the letters of WELLINGTON arranged in a semicircle over the portico, three rows of laurels underneath, crossed swords at the base and the British Star, surmounted by an imperial crown, flanked by English and Prussian standards unfurled. And on the parapet of the building cannon and cannon balls were composed in yellow lamps, laurels in green, with the Prince Regent's initials, 'GPR', and the names of the allies, 'BLÜCHER' and 'ORANGE', all 'wreathed with lamps'. The house of Charles Arbuthnot, who had travelled with Major Percy on the final leg of his journey only forty-eight hours earlier, was decorated with the captured eagle standards portrayed in lamps. The eccentric radical, and epic pedestrian, John 'Walking' Stewart illuminated his house in Cockspur Street with a transparency reading: 'The Secret of British Victory is in the Bayonet.' The Ordnance Office, predictably, had a design of 'cannon placed in every appropriate situation, with castellated ornaments and emblems of military tactics'. The Opera House in Covent Garden particularly excelled in allegorical artistry: 'A grand Transparency, representing Britannia succouring France, personified by an interesting Female figure in a suppliant posture, attired in a robe covered with *fleur de lis*; on her side stands the British Lion. A group of attributes, and above, with expanded wings, appears a figure of Fame sounding the trumpet.'[11]

The most entertaining illuminations were those put up in front of commercial premises with perhaps as much an eye to the attraction of custom as inspiring patriotic sentiments. The publican of a tavern under the sign of the cockerel devised a large transparency of a game bird strutting over his fallen adversary above the legend 'ENGLAND THE COCK OF THE WALK!' The publisher and print seller Rudolph Ackermann advertised his 'Repository of Arts' in the Strand with 'a most humorous Transparency, about fifteen foot long' designed by Thomas Rowlandson:

> The Duke of Wellington, Bonaparte, and Prince Blücher, all on horseback: Bonaparte flying frightened, and pursued by Wellington, is running direct into the arms of Blücher, who is prepared to meet him with an engine of destruction (an English blunderbuss). The desperate situation of Bonaparte is finely depicted, not only in his countenance but even in his frightened horse. His eagles are seen to fly from him in swarms.'[12]

Further along the Strand from Ackermann's, outside Somerset House
– its entire front shining with 'WELLINGTON TRIUMPHANT',
a 'W' enclosed within two branches of laurel, and 'a star of great
magnitude atop the pillars and cornices' – crowds blocked the street
and refused to let carriages pass until the coachmen 'took off their
hats as an acknowledgment of the favour'. The tossing of squibs
and firecrackers into gentlefolk's coaches was a popular jape, 'and
the alarm which the ladies were consequently thrown into appeared
to delight John Bull exceedingly'. Jokes were invented and told,
circulated and printed in the press: that Napoleon had wanted to
reach Brussels but he couldn't get past *Uxbridge*; that Napoleon's
marshals did not have any Orders of the Bar but now they had a
lot of *Crosses*; that Wellington had never seen Bonaparte before
but now he had seen him both *before* and *behind*.

*

As celebrations continued, those that mourned were not forgotten.
Joseph Ballard, 'a young Boston merchant' visiting London, was
appalled at the degree to which the English were 'forever upon
the alert to make money out of everything'.[13] He noticed particularly an enterprising undertaker whose advertisement appeared
in the *Morning Chronicle* offering repatriation of the dead:

> To the Relations and Friends of those who have FALLEN in the
> late Glorious VICTORY. – The anxious desire naturally prevalent
> for the possession of the remains of a beloved Relation being
> seldom capable of gratification, from the great difficulty of the
> removal . . . a Gentleman who has peculiar advantages by an
> establishment at Ostend, as well as at Bruxelles, and proposes
> to facilitate that difficult task, and to undertake their speedy
> removal to London or elsewhere, by a mode of envelopement
> superior to leaden enclosures in many respects.[14]

For every man killed there was a circle of relatives requiring
black. Layton and Shears, of Henrietta Street, Covent Garden,

announced a 'NEW ARTICLE for FAMILY MOURNING . . . just invented . . . which never creases or tumbles, possessing a degree of softness peculiar to itself, the colour of which is a beautiful jet black, warranted never to turn brown'. The same firm also offered: 'of their own manufacture Bombazeens of matchless colour and quality, from 2s. 6d to 5s. 6d per yard; Italian Gauzes, Crapes, Lustres, Poplins, Satins, striped Gauzes, and every article of fashionable Mourning'.[15] Thomas & Co. of Fleet Street informed customers they had 'recently laid in a very extensive Stock of everything suitable for Fashionable Mourning' and tried to undercut competition by offering it 'at least 20 per cent below the usual prices'.[16]

Royal protocol necessitated the court going into two months of suitably ostentatious mourning for 'his late Serene Highness The Duke of Brunswick Oels'. The hero of Quatre Bras and noblest-ranking fatality of the Waterloo campaign was nephew to George III and brother-in-law to the Prince Regent through his despised and estranged wife Princess Caroline. The requirements of court mourning were stipulated by the Lord Chamberlain's office and published in the *Gazette*:

The Ladies to wear black silk, plain muslin, or long-lawn crape, or love hoods, black silk shoes, black glazed gloves, and black paper fans. Undress – Black or dark grey unwatered tabbies. The Gentlemen to wear black cloth, without buttons on the sleeves or pockets, plain muslin or long-lawn cravats, and weepers, black swords and buckles. Undress – Dark grey frocks.[17]

The period of 'deep mourning' was to last a month, 'the first fortnight in the second month to be half mourning, and the last fortnight of the two months to be slight'.[18]

*

In marked contrast to the Prince Regent's enforced, uncharacteristic and doubtless reluctant sobriety of dress and demeanour, the flamboyant Grand Gala Nights at Vauxhall Gardens, advertised as 'Under the Patronage of His Royal Highness', continued. On the night Percy arrived with the Waterloo dispatch, Sir Edwin Sandys, director of music at Vauxhall, raised his baton and the band struck up with a Handel aria from *Judas Maccabaeus*, dedicated in 1747 to George II's son William Augustus, Duke of Cumberland, known as 'Butcher' Cumberland after his brutal suppression of the Jacobite rising the previous year. Subsequently used as an anthem to any victorious commander, after 18 June 1815 it would be inextricably identified with the Duke of Wellington:

> See, the-e conqu'ring he-he-he-he-hero comes!
> Sa-a-a-a-ound the trum-pets, bea-ea-eat the drums.[19]

Two nights later the hero's name was honoured in fire at Vauxhall by the most dazzling display of illuminations London had to offer:

> Pre-eminently distinguished, the name of the immortal WELLINGTON and his brave army, [were] inscribed in prodigious large Roman characters, in gold coloured lamps, thickly surrounded and interspersed with diamond and laurel leaves, the fresh green of which, contrasted with the broad glare of the lamps, which had the most happy effect, and softened that light which would other-wise have been almost insupportable . . . The amusements concluded with a grand display of Pyrotechnic invention . . . The last subject exhibited was the front of a Grecian temple, in the centre of which appeared the word WELLINGTON in characters of living flame.[20]

*

Just a week after the dispatch arrived, at one o'clock on 28 June, a large gathering of 'MERCHANTS, BANKERS,

TRADERS, and others'[21] assembled at the City of London Tavern in Bishopsgate Street, 'to consider of the propriety of a PUBLIC SUBSCRIPTION for the RELIEF of the SUFFERERS in the late GLORIOUS BATTLES'.[22] The first to donate was a Mr John Fuller, who promised 200 guineas and made a speech hoping that other gentlemen would follow his example 'and leave off buying baubles and nonsense, and a pack of fooleries, at the sales and exhibitions of Bond Street'. The hundred or so individuals and businesses represented at the meeting subscribed immediately the further sum of £9,488. On 30 June, the fund had increased to £21,216, a week later to £38,171, and by 13 July it stood at £74,540. 11s. 8d. The *Morning Post* of 9 August published some lines of verse ON THE WATERLOO SUBSCRIPTION REACHING THE SUM OF ONE HUNDRED THOUSAND POUNDS:

> Hail, Britain! Thy bounty, beyond all dispute,
> Must with wonder strike other lands dumb;
> When they see that thy heroes, as victory's *fruit*,
> Receive from thy kindness *a plumb.**
> A *plumb* for those who fought and bled,
> Already they declare;
> But some have confidently said,
> We'll make that *plumb* a *pair*.

The City of London's lead was quickly followed by the City of Westminster, and during 'a most respectable meeting of . . . Noblemen and Gentlemen'[23] at the Thatched House Tavern in St James's, with HRH the Duke of York in the chair, it was agreed 'That a general Subscription be entered into for the special relief of the relations of the Soldiers of the British Army . . . who fell in the Battle of Waterloo . . . and that the subscriptions so raised

---

* PLUMB. An hundred thousand pounds (*A Classical Dictionary of the Vulgar Tongue*, 2nd edition, corrected and enlarged, 1788).

should be consolidated into one Fund with those obtained in the City of London.' By the middle of August, subscriptions from Westminster amounted to £23,774.17s.11d, while those to the City of London had reached £110,420.8s. It was reported that 'Similar Subscriptions are making in Southwark, Dublin, Edinburgh, Glasgow, Liverpool, Manchester, Birmingham, Bristol, Northampton, Leeds, York, Exeter, and other Cities and Towns of the Empire, and are [expected] in the Eastern and Western Colonies and Dependencies.'[24]

On 27 June, the same day as the inaugural meeting at the City of London Tavern was advertised in the *Morning Post*, management of the King's Theatre announced its own charitable plans:

IN HONOUR of the ever MEMORABLE BATTLE GAINED OVER the FRENCH . . . at WATERLOO, and for the BENEFIT of the DISTRESSED WIDOWS and CHILDREN of those SOLDIERS who have so BRAVELY and GLORIOUSLY FALLEN on the occasion. The Nobility, Subscribers to the Opera, and the Public are respectfully informed that on Thursday, the 6th of July, a GRAND PERFORMANCE will take place at this Theatre, arranged and composed for the exclusive purpose above mentioned. Full particulars of which will be announced in a few days.[25]

Within three days the programme was taking shape. One act of an as yet unspecified GRAND SERIOUS OPERA was to be performed, followed by 'an appropriate Address, written by a distinguished literary character'. Beethoven's 'celebrated Battle Piece' – composed in commemoration of Wellington's triumph over the French at Vitoria – was to be given, by permission of the Prince Regent, to whom it had been dedicated in 1813. The evening would conclude with 'a splendid Ballet Cantata, composed and arranged for the occasion . . . music by Laverati; the Dances by Mr A. Vestris, in which all the Opera Performers, and the whole of the Corps de Ballet will be brought forward. The stage will be greatly extended;

and the triumph of a most magnificent and classical order.'
The classical dress would do little to disguise the topicality
of the entertainment: CAESAR'S TRIUMPH OVER THE
GAULS. There would be military bands playing at the entrances
to the theatre and the whole building was to be 'superbly
illuminated, and decorated with laurel'.[26]

III

NEWS of Waterloo radiated from London by mail coach – 300 miles to the west, 600 to the north – just as news had travelled of earlier victories at Trafalgar, Coruña, Badajos, Salamanca, Vitoria and Toulouse. The young Thomas De Quincey knew the mail coaches well, going frequently to and from his Oxford college as an outside passenger between 1803 and 1808. He claimed to have travelled on the coach that took news westward of the battle of Talavera in the summer of 1809. 'The national organ for publishing these mighty events', the great chocolate-brown carriage was decorated on such occasions with flags and branches of laurel and oak, the horses' harness with ribbons. The driver up front on his box and the guard at the rear with horn and blunderbuss, each dressed in the scarlet livery of the Royal Mail, wore sprigs of oak and laurel leaves in their gold-braided hats.

Scores of such coaches, each carrying mail, 'express letters' and the latest editions of the London papers, would be drawn up in double file in front of the General Post Office in Lombard Street, stretching in both directions from the Mansion House to All Hallows Grass. Then, one by one, as lids were slammed and locked on mail sacks, and destinations bawled out by Post Office officials, they set off, 'Going down with Victory', towards Lincoln, Winchester, Portsmouth, Gloucester, Oxford, Bristol, Plymouth and Truro; to Manchester and York, to Newcastle, Edinburgh, Glasgow, Perth, Stirling and Aberdeen.

In Liverpool, at nine o'clock on Friday morning, 23 June, a second edition of the weekly *Mercury* was printed carrying an alarming report that, following the Duke of Wellington's withdrawal to Waterloo, 'it is positively asserted that Brussels will be given up should it be found necessary for the allied armies to continue to retreat'. Then at ten o'clock the 'Alexander' mail coach arrived, having made the journey from London in just twenty-seven hours. A third edition of the *Mercury* immediately went to press, followed by a fourth at eleven o'clock, announcing 'the most brilliant and complete Victory ever obtained by the Duke of Wellington, and which will for ever exalt the Glory of the British Name'. The sight of that decorated mail coach bringing the news to Liverpool was the first that an American, lately disembarked from New York, knew of 'the wonderful events . . . taking place in the political world'.[1] The future author of 'Rip Van Winkle' and 'The Legend of Sleepy Hollow' had arrived to take control of his family's foundering trading company. An admirer of Bonaparte, the son of a rebel against the English crown, and named after the American commander in the War of Independence, Washington Irving had no taste for the subsequent rejoicing.

Another mail coach brought the news to Yorkshire and the *Leeds Mercury* reprinted the *Gazette,* 'this moment received', in full. It was a document, the editorial declared, 'eradiated with the most brilliant rays of glory; but the characters . . . written in copious streams of the best blood of our country – shed, we hope, to secure the happiness and permanent tranquillity of Europe'.[2]

In Cumbria, Dorothy Wordsworth found the particulars of the battle 'dreadful', thought the joy of victory 'an awful thing' and had 'no patience for the tinkling of our Ambleside bells on the occasion'. Nonetheless, she admitted, 'saving grief for the lamentable loss of so many brave men', she read the newspapers 'with unmingled triumph'.[3]

The mail coach arrived in Edinburgh on the morning of the 24th, bringing a letter from the Lord Provost, Sir John Marjoribanks, Member of Parliament for Bute, sent from London in the early hours of Thursday: 'As the feelings of those who have near relatives in the army must be on the stretch, I cannot help gratifying the inhabitants of the good town [of Edinburgh] with the communication by express of the greatest intelligence that ever came to Britain.' The *Caledonian Mercury* reported that this letter, brought to its desk by Mr Kerr of the Post Office, 'has thrown the city into a greater state of extacy than we ever remember to have witnessed'.[4] Every church bell in the city rang for most of the day by order of the magistrates, and at six o'clock on the Sunday morning 'a round of the guns from the Castle announced the glorious news'[5] to anyone still not aware of it.

The Glasgow mail, in addition to the customary oak, laurel and ribbons, flew a red flag from its roof. The guard blew his horn repeatedly as the carriage thundered along Gallowgate, and coming to a halt at the foot of Nelson Street, he fired his blunderbuss into the air. All who heard the signal made a rush for the Tontine Coffee Room to read the papers. But before a broadsheet had been opened, most of the crowd would have been in possession of the general particulars from the mouth of the guard himself.[6]

And so the news crossed the country. Until the end of the century old men and women would tell of the day when history rattled into town, village and hamlet, decked in laurel. The advocate of proportional representation, Thomas Hare, would tell his grandson how, at the age of nine, he ran barefoot alongside the mail coach as it entered Dorchester. Ann Cox was forty-five years old when she saw it arrive in the nearby Dorset village of Beaminster. She would tell her granddaughter of the breathless driver announcing 'Bloody News' to the excited residents, and the granddaughter, Annie Trotman, would in time tell the same story to her own grandchildren, who would pester her to repeat it, thrilled each time at hearing the old lady utter such a coarse phrase as 'Bloody News'.[7]

Intrinsic as it was to the dissemination of intelligence, the mail coach was an engine of national coherence, bringing to all parts of the country a sense of participation in the victory of Waterloo. Small wonder it was not so much that event itself as the epic broadcast of the news that roused the imagination and haunted the opium dreams of Thomas De Quincey for the rest of his life:

> Tidings had arrived . . . of a grandeur that measured itself against centuries; too full of pathos they were, too full of joy . . . to utter themselves by other language than by tears, by restless anthems, by reverberations rising from every choir of the *Gloria in excelsis*. These tidings we that sate upon the laurelled car had it for our privilege to publish among all nations . . . We waited for a secret word . . . At midnight the secret word arrived; which word was – Waterloo and Recovered Christendom! The dreadful word shone by its own light; before us it went; high above our leaders' heads it rode, and spread a golden light over the paths which we traversed. Every city, at the presence of the secret word, threw open its gates to receive us. The rivers were silent as we crossed. All the infinite forests, as we ran along their margins, shivered in homage to the secret word. And the darkness comprehended it.[8]

*

News continued to reach London from France, keeping the daily papers at a high pitch of excitement. On Monday 26 June, the *Morning Chronicle* stopped its presses to announce 'extraordinary and unlooked-for consequences that resulted from the brilliant victory'. Two days later, on the Wednesday morning, the information had travelled 275 miles north and Dorothy Wordsworth saw the mail coach roll into Ambleside, a paper affixed to its side: 'Great News. Abdication of Buonaparte.' She regarded this as a piece of impertinence: 'What right has he to abdicate, or to have a word to say in the business!' She hoped only that the allied armies had finished the job and not stopped too soon, 'as they did before', only the previous year.

Soon after news of Bonaparte's abdication came news of his arrest, then of his assassination. Sir John Marjoribanks wrote to Edinburgh from the House of Commons at six o'clock in the evening of 27 June that an account had 'come from the City, within this half hour, that BONAPARTE is Murdered; I fully believe it'. Mr Robert Ward, member for Haslemere, appeared to be the most vocal in the corridors at Westminster, asserting 'that on Sunday last the disappointment and fury of the people of *Paris* were at their height, and that during a violent commotion BONAPARTE was assassinated. This information was received by Ministers through a private channel this afternoon. It is fully credited in the Ministerial Circles.'[9] Another Member of Parliament revealed the source of the private channel: 'as Mr R[othschild], who has the best intelligence, and has never deceived the Government, reports it, I believe it'. The story was believed because anything in those heady days was believed: all things seemed possible. 'Under all the circumstances of the present moment [it] is not improbable', ran one newspaper report. 'Fear, revenge, disappointment, shame, all the angry and furious passions and feelings are strongly excited by the scene now acting in Paris.'[10] But it was no sooner credited than discredited. Although the account was said to have been brought by 'a smuggler of some note'[11] to Mr Rothschild, when that gentleman was approached for confirmation 'he said that he had not received it through any of his own channels of information, and it was not believed'.[12] But within days it had been printed in newspapers throughout the country, along with equally far-fetched, as well as more accurate, intelligence. Because the majority of provincial newspapers were published weekly, most news would be out of date or suspect by the time it was read. A bank of capitals and exclamation marks confronting the citizens of Truro on Saturday morning, 1 July, conveyed the information overload amassed in just six days since they had opened the previous *Royal Cornwall Gazette*:

FURTHER IMPORTANT NEWS. GREAT VICTORY! – DESTRUCTION OF THE FRENCH ARMY! ABDICATION AND ARREST OF BUONAPARTE! TUMULTUOUS PROCEEDINGS OF THE FRENCH CHAMBERS! – REPORTED ASSASSINATION OF THE EX-EMPEROR! – RAPID ADVANCE OF THE DUKE OF WELLINGTON![13]

*

At the bottom of Haymarket, the King's Theatre was almost full on Thursday evening, 6 July, 'for the benefit of the Widows and Orphans of those brave men who so gallantly fell . . . on the plains of Waterloo'. *The Times* noted that although some boxes were left empty on account of bereavement in the higher circles of society, they still contributed to the relief of those in the lower. 'Nearly the whole had been actually hired and paid for, though the owners, from the recency of their own domestic afflictions, arising from the same cause as that which gave rise to the evening's assembly, could not appear in public.'[14] The programme opened with a performance of the last act of the 'grand serious opera' by Giovanni Liverati, *I Selvaggi* – The Savages. Then the actor Robert William Elliston strode on to the stage and delivered a patriotic address 'written . . . on the spur of the occasion',[15] intended to remind patrons why they were there:

> While acclamation sounds throughout the land,
> And Britons' hearts with extacy expand,
> Here shall the Cherub Charity repair,
> To save the mourning mother from despair;
> To soothe, by sympathy, acute distress,
> The soldier's widow, and the fatherless . . .

Twenty-odd lines in praise of the dead later, the anonymous author returned to this theme, assuring the audience that new-made orphans of 1815 – supported by their charity – might thereby live to defend the country in future wars:

> Some soldier's offspring, fostered by your aid,
> May rise, in time, your ornament and shade;
> The Warrior's Orphans, whom your bounties save,
> In freedom's cause shall every danger brave;
> Perhaps your sons may view with glad surprise,
> From some of these, a WELLINGTON arise!!!

The final two couplets, honouring 'Britain's Hero', roused the house to euphoric joy:

> 'Twas he who broke the thirsty lance of War;
> 'Tis he shall fix fair Peace in Triumph's car;
> To him a pyramid of Fame we'll raise,
> Long may he live to hear a grat'ful nation's praise!!![16]

As the clamour subsided, the actor came to the front of the stage and made an announcement: 'Ladies and Gentlemen, I am desired by the Manager to inform you, and I feel very proud in being the bearer of such glorious tidings, that his Grace the Duke of WELLINGTON is now in [possession of] Paris . . .'[17] Loud huzzas erupted from all parts of the pit, the five tiers of boxes and the gallery. A sceptic close to the stage demanded to know 'on what authority' the information came and 'the acclamation was redoubled' as Mr Elliston replied that it came on the highest authority – that of the Prince Regent himself. The news had been issued that very evening from the Prince's residence, Carlton House, less than fifty yards from the theatre.

The next item on the programme was Beethoven's *Battle Symphony*, producing 'the same rapturous applause which has always followed its performance elsewhere'. This was followed by the National Anthem sung by the opera soloists Madame

Sessi and Miss Griglietti, by Mr Elliston, and 'loudly chorused by the whole house'. The climax of the evening and 'allusive to the occasion' was *The Triumph of Caesar over the Gauls*, the ballet cantata 'got up in a hurry' but no less appreciated for that. It featured a grand procession, dancers, singers, a triumphal car drawn by horses from the Royal Circus and a striking transparency of the modern Julius Caesar, the hero of Waterloo himself.

*

Towards the end of June, Dorothy Wordsworth had written to her friend Mrs Clarkson, expressing a premature hope that Napoleon was 'now a safe prisoner, somewhere'. Following the announcement of his abdication and the false reports of arrest and assassination, the nation craved news of his capture and speculated how he would be dealt with when that desirable outcome was achieved. On Friday 21 July, Washington Irving wrote home to his brother Ebenezer in New York: 'As to Bonaparte, they have disposed of him in a thousand ways; every fat-sided John Bull has him dished up in a way to please his own palate, excepting that as yet they have not observed the first direction in the famous [recipe] to cook a Turbot – "first catch your Turbot".' On the same day, another *London Gazette Extraordinary* was published. Printed on one half-side of a single sheet, it comprised a dispatch from Lord Castlereagh in Paris little more than sixty words in length. The cover price of sixpence would have seemed an extravagant sum were it not for the importance of the intelligence it contained: 'that Napoleon Buonaparte, not being able to escape from the English cruisers, or from the guards kept upon the coasts, has taken the resolution of going on board the English ship Bellerophon . . .' Irving added a postscript to his letter: 'The bells are ringing, and this moment news is brought that poor Boney is prisoner . . . *John has caught the Turbot!*'[18]

A rumour spread that apartments in the Tower were being

prepared to accommodate the ex-emperor and 'some thousands of the populace waited a long time upon London Bridge in order to see him pass'.[19] The *Morning Post* of 26 July reported that he had been sent to Fort George on the Moray Firth in Inverness. The *Courier Extraordinary* reported that 'Bonaparte will be provisionally confined in the castle of Edinburgh'.[20]

It was claimed, in Brussels, that 'several miscreants had doubted . . . the entrance of the Allies into Paris . . . because this news had not been announced . . . by the ringing of bells. To give . . . more certainty of the capture of BONAPARTE, the bells of all the churches have been ringing the whole day, interrupted only by the sound of cannon and musketry.'[21] Writing to her grandmother, Georgy Capel reported 'Much and universal rejoicing . . . Squibs and Crackers, the whole town brilliantly illuminated . . . The streets filled with People the whole night and a general confusion . . . all over the Town. And . . . the few soldiers that are remaining, testified their noisy joy by loud cheers and songs.' Her younger sister Louisa described 'the Cannons firing from the Ramparts and guns in every corner of the Streets'. She could not help thinking 'how wonderful it is the *number* of *different* things that have occurred during the last *five weeks*, the *very different* sensation this firing gave us, from that on the 16th of June'.[22] Brussels itself seemed a different place when the more unsightly wounded were no longer seen. Instead there were 'fine young men, using crutches, or with arms in slings, strutting nevertheless with a gallant, coxcombical air . . . eyeing the pretty girls, and casting complacent looks at the symmetry of their legs'. John Scott, editor of the *Champion*, detected a definite erotic charge in the tenor of life, common perhaps after any armistice: 'A constant amatory parade up and down goes on in the streets and parks. The convalescent officers have but one pursuit; and the women of Brussels, high and low, married and single, are abundantly susceptible.'[23]

*

Back in England, the celebrations spread with the news. Under the heading 'TYRANT CONQUERED on the PLAINS of WATERLOO', the Globe Hotel in Exmouth placed an advertisement in the press announcing 'A BALL . . . to celebrate this glorious VICTORY'.[24] In the Suffolk village of East Bergholt, the painter John Constable attended a summer fair at the end of July and made an oil sketch of jubilant crowds, flags and an effigy of Bonaparte suspended from a gibbet.[25] At the Bull's Head, in Eyam, Derbyshire, 'the late glorious VICTORY' was celebrated by a 'PUBLICK DINNER', tickets at six shillings each, 'Malt Liquor included'.[26] One of the earliest formal celebrations was held much further north, in the Scottish Borders. Just eight days after news of the victory reached London, on Friday 30 June, a ceremony was held on the top of Peniel Heugh Hill in the county of Roxburghshire. 'The Marquis of Lothian's tenants', reported the *Kelso Mail*, 'have entered into a subscription to drive materials . . . for a monument to be erected . . . to commemorate the signal victory obtained . . . by the Duke of Wellington and the British troops over Bonaparte and his perjured forces.' Lord Lothian laid the foundation stone of a pillar, planned to be ninety feet high, and a toast to the health of the Duke of Wellington was proposed and drunk 'with the greatest enthusiasm, followed by three times three cheers'. Other toasts followed. So early was this celebration that the name of 'Waterloo' did not figure in the speeches. Instead, the battle was referred to by the title favoured by Marshal Blücher and reported as such in many of the first newspaper accounts. So when the hope was expressed that 'the armies of Great Britain ever acquit themselves, when called into action, in the same glorious manner', it was to the 'ever-memorable battle of La Belle Alliance'[27] that glasses were raised and emptied.

The most spectacular demonstration of patriotic fervour was staged some months later in Cumbria and organised by Robert Southey. 'I have set on foot a grand project', he wrote on 8 August: 'nothing less than that of rejoicing for the Battle of Waterloo and the capture of Bonaparte, by a bonfire on the top of Skiddaw, upon the Prince [Regent]'s birthday. It will be seen far into Scotland, and by all the country round.'

The most rounded and accessible of the higher Lake District peaks, at 3,054 feet, Skiddaw is the easiest mountain of its size to ascend in England. Nevertheless, the horse-drawn carts that carried a cannon and several tons of combustibles to the top with 'some *expence* as well as *labour*'[28] in the first weeks of August were said to be the first ever to have made the climb. The mound of tar barrels, oil casks, bundles of heather, peat and turpentine-soaked bales of hemp was erected in good time for the Regent's fifty-third birthday, Saturday 12 August, but 'the weather proving very unfavourable',[29] the celebration was postponed until the next clear evening. Unfortunately, no guard was mounted over the inflammable material, and between three and four on the Sunday morning, 'at a time when the sober part of mankind were at rest',[30] Southey's patriotic enterprise was subverted. Possessed by 'some malevolent spirit . . . gratify[ing] itself by the disappointment of others',[31] a 'set of miscreants'[32] climbed the mountain and lit the bonfire prematurely. So dense was the cloud cover that the futile blaze could barely be seen, even by the closest inhabitants of the area. Southey blamed 'the rabble here [in Keswick]' for the outrage, bemoaned the waste of the seven pounds it had cost to transport everything to the top and described the vandalism as a 'specimen of Keswick feeling'. They had even thrown the cannon on to the fire. 'I confess', he wrote, 'it would gratify me much to punish these fellows if we could fix upon them.'[33]

But the perpetrators were never identified and the motive for their action – whether a mischievous prank or a more considered work of sabotage – is not known. Ascending a mountain in darkness and thick fog – no matter how straight-forward the climb – would have entailed a considerable degree of effort and some danger for the sake of a mere prank. It is possible, however, that there was a more ideological purpose. Throughout England there were individuals who did not share in the national mood of jubilation at the downfall and capture of Napoleon; individuals who would have regarded a prominent display of triumphalism, such as that planned on Skiddaw, as distasteful, even abhorrent. It is possible that there were some in Keswick, also, determined to prevent the Poet Laureate's 'loyal effusion'.[34]

Whoever had set light to the pyre in the early morning of 13 August – and whatever their reason – that 'brutal act of malevolence' was but a temporary setback to Southey's plans. Over the following week carts carried more tar barrels and oil casks and hemp up the mountain, and by Monday 21 August another pyre had been raised, as high as, if not higher than, the first. The weather promised 'dusky but free from mists'[35] and the revellers began their ascent from Keswick in the late afternoon. The seventy-seven-year-old Lord Sunderlin rode up on horseback while his wife and their house guest James Boswell, son of Dr Johnson's biographer, joined one of the walking parties. William Wordsworth, his sister Dorothy, his wife and eldest son, John, had come over from Grasmere for the occasion. Robert and Edith Southey made the climb with their friend Mary Barker, two of their children, three maidservants, various neighbours and 'some adventurous Lakers'. Southey referred to the rest of the assembly as 'Messrs. Rag, Tag, and Bobtail'.[36] Sir George Beaumont, having 'imprudently walked to the summit in the morning',[37] had exhausted himself for a repeat of the exercise in the evening and had to be content with watching the distant conflagration from a window of Greta Hall, the Southeys' home. With him was Mrs Coleridge – at the best of times 'not equal to a walk of ten miles mountain road' – and her daughter, who was 'much too delicate to be permitted such a thing'. Young Sara had cried as she watched her cousins, the Southey children, setting out, 'protesting she could perform the thing with the greatest ease'. But it was to no avail and 'all set face against her attempting it'.

Hardier souls on the mountaintop sang 'God Save the King' and 'Rule Britannia' to the accompaniment of 'various wind instruments'.[38] They roasted beef, boiled plum puddings and drank 'a huge wooden bowl of punch'. Unlike the toasts drunk on Peniel Heugh Hill seven weeks earlier, those on Skiddaw pronounced the battle's now familiar name. Southey even used it in the invention of a joke: that the battle had been fought 'at a Waterloo . . . – or a place of water, & in honour of it Skiddaw should be converted to a Punchloo – that is to say a place of Punch'.[39] They drank to the health of the Prince Regent, the Duke of Wellington and Marshal Blücher, and at every toast and 'three times three' they fired cannon that had again been dragged to the summit for that purpose.* They rolled 'blazing balls of tow and turpentine' down the steep slopes and this, combined with the raging inferno produced by the mound of tar barrels, made it appear as though Skiddaw had become a volcano. It could be seen from well into Scotland and from more than sixty miles away to the south in Broughton, Lancashire. The spectacle exceeded all Southey's expectations of the sublime: 'The effect was grand beyond imagination. We formed a huge circle round the most intense light, and behind us was an immeasurable arch of the most intense darkness, for our bonfire fairly put out the moon.'

The only mishap occurred when someone, stumbling about in the dense shadows cast beyond the firelight by the ring of spectators, knocked over a large kettle of hot water intended for replenishing the punch. Enquiries were made as to who was responsible. 'It was one of the gentlemen,' said some who had seen it happen. They did not know his name 'but he had a red cloak on', and they pointed to a tall figure 'equipped like a Spanish Don'.[40] It was, in fact, a maroon cloak that Wordsworth had borrowed from the Laureate's wife, and it marked him out as the culprit. Led by Southey, the company took its good-natured revenge, surrounding the other poet, jabbing their

---

* Southey's joint toast to Wellington and Blücher was the occasion for another joke, based on the biblical verse about David and Jonathan: 'lovely and pleasant in their lives, and in their death they were not divided'. Southey justified toasting the commanders jointly, remarking: 'they were lovely at Waterloo and on Skiddaw they shall not be divided' (to Grosvenor Charles Bedford, 22 August, Bodleian Library, MS Eng. Lett. C. 25).

fingers at him and chanting a parody of the popular 'Catch for
Three Voices':

> 'Twas you, sir; 'twas you, sir,
> I tell you nothing new, sir,
> 'Twas you kicked the kettle down,
> 'Twas you, sir, you.*

As a result of Wordsworth's clumsiness, the last of the cold
water had to be heated for the punch, leaving none for the grog.
This meant that a number of gentlemen had no alternative but
to drink their rum neat, and by ten o'clock, when the time came
to return to Keswick, many were extremely intoxicated. 'One
fellow was so drunk', Southey recalled, 'that his companions
placed him upon a horse, with his face to the tail, to bring him
down, themselves being just sober enough to guide and hold
him on.' The descent became 'a track of fire',[41] from the torches
the company carried and the gobbets of pitch and tarred rope
that dropped and were left burning on the path behind. They
reached Keswick after midnight and 'the festivities were
concluded by a display of fire-works, and the ascent of a fire-
balloon, on which was inscribed the words "Wellington and
Waterloo"'.[42]

On the following Friday there was further celebration, this
time hosted by Lord and Lady Sunderlin at their residence on
the opposite side of Derwent Water. Several hundred people
came from the surrounding districts to see the fireworks: 'a
grand display of rockets, wheels, Roman candlesticks, &c. &c.'
as well as some launched from a raft in the lake. In front of
the house were three big transparencies. The first – painted by
'an eminent female artist' – represented the previous Monday's
great bonfire. The second had 'John Bull seated on a cask, with
a can of ale in his hand, viewing the Devil with Bonaparte on

---

* Garret Colley Wellesley, Earl of Mornington's original has the accusation: ''Twas
you that kissed that pretty girl'.

his shoulders'. The third was said to have been designed by 'one of the first artists in the kingdom' and showed the Devil throwing Bonaparte into a lake of fire. Another fire-balloon, ten feet high, eighteen feet in circumference, rose to the joyous huzzas of the crowd and floated, a diminishing flame, northwards across the lake into dark and distance. For some time it looked as though it was going to come down on Skiddaw, but no remains were found there the following day, 'although diligent search was made for them'.[43] Instead, a large iron ring and other fragments were reported to have fallen some twelve miles beyond the mountain, close to the little town of Wigton.

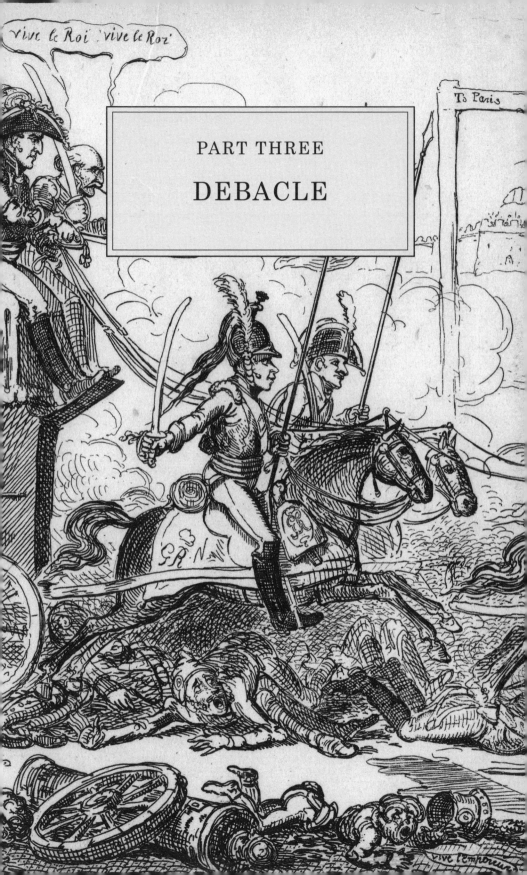

PART THREE

DEBACLE

I

TWELVE o'clock at La Bourse farm on the heights above Limale – night passing into the morning of Monday 19 June – and Marshal Grouchy was making his preparations for attacking the Prussian enemy. Half an hour earlier he had signed a dispatch to General Vandamme, whose III Corps was facing Wavre, Basse Wavre and Bierges from the opposite side of the river Dyle two miles away to the north-east. 'Since you have not yet been able to cross the Dyle,' he told Vandamme, 'kindly come immediately to Limale with your Corps, leaving only sufficient troops before Wavre to maintain our positions there.'

In front of the farm buildings commandeered by Grouchy for his headquarters were two IV Corps infantry divisions that he had led there the previous evening, together with the 21st Infantry Division that had taken part in the capture of Limale. Each infantry division comprised two brigades; a brigade two regiments; a regiment two or three battalions. A French battalion at full strength was supposed to number 840 men but in practice usually consisted of between 400 and 600. At that moment Grouchy had at his disposal nineteen infantry battalions supported by a combined complement of thirty-two pieces of ordnance. When Vandamme arrived with his III Corps, comprising a further thirty battalions, he was to assume overall command of the infantry. Off to the left of Grouchy's headquarters were four regiments of hussars and one of *chasseurs à cheval* under the command of General Pajol and supported by a single troop of horse artillery.

To carry out the last instructions received from the Emperor late the previous afternoon – 'keep manoeuvring in our direction, and . . . join us before any [enemy] corps places itself between' – Grouchy had first to dispose of the Prussian force ranged 'beak to beak' with his own troops across the intervening 500 yards of corn. His dispatch to Vandamme at 11.30 that night had read: 'We will then succeed, I hope, in joining the Emperor as he ordered. It is said that he has beaten the English but I have no more news of him and am having great difficulty giving him ours.'[1]

Vandamme did not comply with Grouchy's orders: instead of bringing his III Corps to Limale, leaving a token force opposite Wavre, he sent only a single infantry division, commanded by General Hulot, and four dragoon regiments under General Strolz, none of which would take any active part in the battle to come.

As he waited for dawn, Grouchy still had no reason to doubt the French victory at Mont-Saint-Jean, or to revise his belief that the Emperor had 'beaten the English'.

Meanwhile, on the opposite side of the plateau, along the edge of the Bois de Rixensart, rumour of Napoleon's defeat was spreading through the Prussian lines. Generallieutenant von Thielemann, assuming that Grouchy must also have heard about the French rout, fully expected him to retreat from the confrontation before dawn. Even some of Thielemann's own officers seemed to have abandoned the idea of the morning's fight, assuming the battle to be over. Oberstlieutenant von Ledebur, with five squadrons of hussars and two pieces of horse artillery, had marched off in the direction of Saint-Lambert to join the main Prussian army, while Major von Stengel, with three infantry battalions and three squadrons of lancers, would follow shortly after dawn. Only the French seemed to regard the battle as worth continuing. And as daybreak approached, to Thielemann's surprise, Grouchy's forces were still there.

Outnumbered by nineteen battalions to ten, Thielemann reinforced the centre of his line at a place called Point du Jour – Daybreak – with troops from Wavre, leaving only four battalions to hold the town in the stalemated contest with Vandamme's III Corps across the river. But that morning, above Limale, the Prussian guns were the first to fire.

With orders to prepare for a dawn attack, the French troops were taking advantage of the remaining hours of darkness to sleep. Infantry lay on the open ground in square battle formations, many with muskets clasped between their legs in readiness. At three o'clock, some forty-five minutes before sunrise, a Prussian round shot ripped a sentry in half outside Grouchy's headquarters and the ranks of sleeping troops started awake as shells and shot fell among them. Supported by the artillery fire, a Prussian cavalry brigade advanced on to the field. On the French left wing, General Pécheux's 12th Infantry Division had recovered quickly from the bombardment, and was ordered to march forward. Captain Charles François of the 30th Infantry Regiment described his men surprising an outpost of about 300 Prussians, bayoneting some, taking others prisoner.[2] The superior firepower of the French artillery raked the Prussian lines and succeeded in wrecking five of their cannon. The three French infantry divisions pressed steadily forward, a strong line of skirmishing troops ahead and unseen in the high corn. On the left, Pécheux's division, supported by Pajol's cavalry, and General Vichery's 13th Infantry Division in the centre advanced towards Thielemann's main force at Point du Jour between the Rixensart woods and Wavre. On the right, General Teste's 21st Infantry Division attacked Bierges. This village, with its fortified mill and bridge, was the key to Thielemann's defensive line, securing not only the Dyle crossing but also the southern approach to Wavre.

After some resistance, the outnumbered Prussians in front of Pécheux's division began to withdraw into the Rixensart woods.

As they fell back, some called on the French to desert, repeating the rumours that had filtered through their ranks during the night: that Bonaparte had been killed and his army destroyed. *'Kommen Sie mit uns, gut Franzosen,'* they shouted. *'Sie haben nicht mehr eine Armee. Napoleon ist tot!'*[3] Captain François and a number of his comrades who understood German were unsettled by what they heard.

At eight o'clock Thielemann received a dispatch from Generalmajor von Pirch,[4] containing positive confirmation of the allied victory at Waterloo. Rumour gave place to certainty and he rallied the 31st Infantry Regiment, driven from the Rixensart woods by Pécheux's troops. 'Children!' he shouted to them. 'Yesterday a great battle between Napoleon and Prince Blücher and Wellington took place. Napoleon has been totally defeated and is retreating. I have only just received this news, on my word . . . Take this wood now. Long live the King! Long live the Fatherland!'[5] He urged the men to cheer loudly and jump up and down between the bursts of cannon fire in an effort to demoralise the enemy and persuade them to retreat. Still cheering, the 31st Regiment charged into the wood, driving the French back to its southern edge. But the French, still oblivious to the outcome of yesterday's battle, had no reason to feel demoralised. Instead they retaliated. Reinforcements were brought up and, artillery firing directly into the trees, again drove the Prussians back in a wreck of splintered timber. The Prussians fought on until their ammunition was almost exhausted.

Towards nine o'clock, a combined French assault – Teste's division from the west and General Berthezène's 11th Division across the Dyle from the east – succeeded in gaining possession of Bierges. With the loss of this key position on his left flank, his right failing in the Rixensart woods and Pajol's cavalry manoeuvring north towards the village of Rosieren in the Prussian rear, Thielemann was in danger of being encircled. If he was to have any chance of continuing to fight after the news of yesterday's battle turned Grouchy's advance to inevitable retreat, Thielemann needed to preserve the troops that remained to him. He therefore ordered a withdrawal five miles north-east to Sint-Agatha-Rode in the direction of Louvain. The four Prussian battalions defending Wavre pulled out of the town, abandoning the smoking ruins to Vandamme's III Corps, who were at last able to cross the Dyle bridges so fiercely contested the previous day.

Grouchy had won. The precise number of French casualties is not known, but they were light at about two and a half thousand. Prussian casualties had been roughly the same, if anything slightly fewer, at 2,400 men and seventy-six officers – albeit from a strength outnumbered nearly three to one. The Prussians had fled the field, leaving behind five disabled cannon and a number of wounded. Grouchy's victorious army now occupied a two-mile line west to east, linking the villages of Rosieren, Chambre and La Bavette. The road to Brussels lay ahead and clear.

At half past ten, as the marshal was preparing to march on the Belgian capital, an aide-de-camp arrived from General Gressot, deputy chief of the Imperial General Staff. Haggard, wild-eyed, and as bone weary as his exhausted horse, he seemed 'the embodied image of defeat and ruin'.[6] So incoherent was Captain Dumonceau bringing news of the 'disaster of Waterloo'[7] that Grouchy thought him drunk or insane. In response to questions, he could only babble an involved and confused account of the battle, 'scarcely able to collect his ideas or to find his words'.[8] But at last the details he blurted out of disorganised troops, and losses of men, horses and equipment, convinced Grouchy of the true, terrible state of things.

Pajol recalled that the marshal cried as he broke the news to his officers. Vandamme's harsher comment was that he 'could do nothing but weep like an old woman'.[9] Aware of murmurs among his staff regarding his conduct of the campaign, and in particular his refusal to countenance General Gérard's suggestion, just twenty-four hours earlier, that they should 'march to the sound of the guns' instead of moving on Wavre, Grouchy made

the first of many reiterated statements in defence of his actions –
statements that would occupy him for the rest of his life. 'My
honour makes it a matter of duty to explain myself, in regard to
my dispositions of yesterday,' he began:

> The instructions which I had received from the Emperor, left me
> free to manoeuvre in no other direction than Wavre. I was obliged,
> therefore, to refuse the advice which General Gérard thought he
> had the right to offer me. I do ample justice to Gérard's talents
> and bravery; but you were doubtless as surprised as I was, that a
> general officer, ignorant of the Emperor's orders, and the informa-
> tion motivating a Marshal of France, under whose orders he was
> placed, should have presumed publicly to dictate to me, my line
> of conduct. The lateness of the day, the distance from the point
> where the firing was heard, the condition of the roads, made it
> impossible to arrive in time to share in the action which was taking
> place. At any rate, whatever the subsequent events may have been,
> the Emperor's orders . . . did not permit of my acting otherwise
> than I have done.[10]

Grouchy at first considered marching south-west to attack
the rear of Blücher's main force, which was pursuing the
remnants of the imperial army into France. No sooner considered than abandoned, this strategy would have involved pitting
his 30,000 men against an enemy more than 60,000 strong,
and with Thielemann's 12,000 harrying from behind. Vandamme's
bold plan of advancing on Brussels and freeing the French
prisoners there was likewise rejected as futile and equally
suicidal. Instead, Grouchy ordered a march south-east to Namur.
It began between eleven o'clock and noon. Led by Grouchy
himself, the IV Corps and ambulance convoy re-crossed the
Dyle at Limale, while Vandamme's III Corps went back through
Wavre and across its three bridges. Shadowing the Prussians as
far as Sint-Agatha-Rode, a rearguard action mounted by Pajol's
three regiments of hussars and Teste's infantry was so adept at
screening the retreat that it was not until six o'clock in the

afternoon that Thielemann became aware that Grouchy's main force had gone.

*

The day before Grouchy's forces made their disciplined with-drawal across the Dyle, the main French army's retreat from the field of Mont-Saint-Jean had been a stampede. On the road south, between La Belle Alliance and Genappe, Lieutenant Martin of the 45th Infantry Regiment struggled forward in the press and darkness. 'Vehicles of all types, guns and artillery caissons, still mounted cavalry, all attempting to force a passage through the middle of a dense crowd of fugitives and wounded who were thrown down and crushed in the mud . . . The confusion was constantly compounded by the arrival of more fleeing troops . . .' Fights broke out. Impatient horsemen slashed with their sabres at infantrymen, who retaliated with bayonet thrusts. Here and there a musket was fired. It was 'as if a new battle was being fought amongst the unhappy debris of [the] army'.[11]

Wellington's Anglo-Allied pursuit had halted at La Belle Alliance while that of the Prussians continued. Assembling his senior officers at half past nine that evening, Marshal Blücher had given orders that 'the last horse and the last man' were to be sent after the enemy. Generalmajor von Pirch's II Korps was to move east against Grouchy's forces, while three brigades of Generallieutenant Graf Bülow von Denewitz's IV Korps, supported in the rear by Generallieutenant von Zeiten's I Korps, marched south, towards Genappe, in pursuit of the main army.

Several sources refer to the Prussians taking prisoners; others suggest that little quarter was given. 'The slaughter of the fugitive French by the Prussian cavalry was very great,' recorded Captain Harry Ross-Lewin of the 32nd Regiment of Foot, albeit by hearsay. 'Nothing could exceed the animosity that existed between the troops of these two nations; and the victors unmercifully retaliated on the vanquished for former insults and injuries.'[12] According to Fleury de Chaboulon, an officer on Napoleon's staff, 'The

Prussians . . . treated with unparalleled barbarity those unfortun-
ates they were able to overtake. Apart from a few steady old
soldiers, most had thrown away their weapons, and were defence-
less; but they were nonetheless massacred without pity.'[13] South
of Plancenoit, at Le Caillou – Bonaparte's former headquarters
– the Prussians found French wounded in barns and outhouses
abandoned by the retreat. It is said that they bayoneted or clubbed
many to death before setting the buildings on fire and leaving
the rest to burn alive.

While the prospect of capture and summary execution by the
Prussians was a powerful spur, many French soldiers feared the
grim alternative of being handed over to the English, to be
confined in a floating hell on the Medway estuary. The words
of the Emperor himself would have been fresh in their minds
from the General Order issued four days earlier at Avesnes and
read aloud at the head of every regiment, urging them to 'conquer
or perish', recalling the consequences of defeat and imprisonment. Sergeant Mauduit, a grenadier of the Imperial Guard,
described the flight from these remembered horrors:

> A multitude of wounded, not wanting to return to the hulks, nor
> to fall into the hands of the Prussians . . . re-doubled their efforts
> to drag themselves along the road behind the able-bodied
> remnants of the army, but soon overwhelmed by fatigue and the
> need for medical attention . . . they fell to be dispatched by
> Bülow's uhlans and hussars. Some of our wounded blew their
> brains out rather than survive such a disaster or return to the
> English hulks.[14]

There were accounts of other suicides. 'A colonel, to avoid falling
into [Prussian] hands, blew out his brains. Twenty other officers,
of various ranks, imitated the example. An officer of cuirassiers,
seeing the [Prussians] approach, said: "They shall have neither
me nor my horse." With one pistol he shot his horse dead; with
the other himself.'[15]

Three miles south of La Belle Alliance the road passed through a defile as it approached the town of Genappe. The pressure of the dense flow of fugitives was concentrated, channelling the herd – 'confused, jostling, crushed'[16] – downhill through a winding main street towards the single crossing of the river Dyle, a stone bridge just over seven feet wide. With its narrow entry points a disciplined force might have held this town against the Prussians for hours. The Anglo-Allied army had managed it during their retreat from the French the day before. But all discipline had now gone. The provost marshal of the army, Baron Étienne Radet, tried to restore order but was beaten to the ground with musket butts. The chaos was exacerbated by all the slow-moving carriages, baggage carts, ammunition caissons, limbers and cannon. Some had been overturned, either by accident or deliberately to impede the Prussians. Elsewhere drivers had cut the traces and ridden their horses off, leaving the wagons behind. In places the main street was so densely packed with obstacles that troops were forced to crawl under the stationary vehicles to proceed.

Sergeant Mauduit of the 1st Grenadiers reached the outskirts of the town at about eleven o'clock. His regiment – the last of Napoleon's precious reserves – had until that time formed a rearguard to the retreat, marching in square, sometimes halting to face and drive back their pursuers. The moon had not yet risen fully, and as they approached Genappe through the darkness they came under fire, not only from the Prussian artillery on the heights behind them but from the panicking mob in front. Further progress into the town was impossible: 'All the baggage of the army; the wounded, the ambulances, the vehicles and the artillery . . . were all mixed up so that once you had got into the press, it would have been impossible to get out and you would have been dragged along despite your efforts.' In danger of being trapped between that seething mass and the pursuing Prussians, this last cohesive regiment of the Old Guard manoeuvred to the left, skirting Genappe and fording the Dyle further downstream. Crossing open country, 'all order was lost without it being possible to reimpose it'. A mile beyond the town they heard midnight sound from a distant church. 'Everyone marched in groups of several hundred, randomly following the tracks that . . . ran parallel to the main road heading for Charleroi.'[17]

The dispersal of the rearguard left Genappe defended only by a makeshift barricade of wagons thrown across the end of the main street. Blowing apart the obstruction with howitzer shells, the Prussians took possession of the town. There are no eyewitness accounts of what took place, only lurid hearsay: 'Eight hundred lay dead, who had suffered themselves to be cut down like cattle . . . The Prussians . . . galloped through the streets, and massacred, without remorse, every Frenchman who fell in their way. No resistance was offered . . . yet the slaughter continued with unabated fury.'[18] One particular atrocity was certainly apocryphal. General Duhesme, commander of the Young Guard, had been severely wounded at Plancenoit. Taken to Genappe, he was lodged at an auberge – the Roi d'Espagne – where he was in fact to be treated by Blücher's personal surgeon before dying of his injuries a couple of days later. Nevertheless, the legend persisted that he had been cut down at the door of the inn, while attempting to surrender, by one of the Black Brunswick regiment, whose commanding officer had been killed at Quatre Bras. The hussar was said to have brought down his sabre with the words: 'The Duke fell yesterday, and you shall also bite the dust.' The story was given such credence that three months later Robert Southey was shown blade marks in the door frame, and 'the blood-stains . . . not yet effaced'.[19] Another version of the story supplied further elaboration: Duhesme was not killed outright but later hacked to death in his bed by Prussian sabres while his helpless servant looked on.[20]

Another source claimed that as the Prussians went from house to house, all those French found still in possession of their weapons were bayoneted while the rest were made prisoner.[21] It was said that 2,000 were captured at Genappe alone.

Although Bonaparte himself had made his escape from the

chaos at Genappe around midnight, his campaign coach became the pursuers' greatest trophy of the night. According to one account, a postilion and two leaders fell to the fusiliers' bayonets while the driver was cut down with a sabre blow from Major von Keller, commander of the 15th Infantry Regiment. In a less dramatic version, the coach was found in a line of half a dozen carriages, each harnessed with six or eight horses, 'but there was nobody in sight'.[22] When the doors were forced open, it was found to contain everything the Emperor might have needed for a long campaign: 'a gold and silver *nécessaire*, including above seventy pieces; a large silver chronometer; a steel bedstead with merino mattresses; a pair of pistols; a green velvet cap; a pair of spurs; linen, and many other things for the convenience of travelling', including a library 'of near 800 volumes'. There was a richly embroidered scarlet burnous, a hat, a sword, a spare uniform and – presumably anticipating his ceremonial investiture in Brussels – 'a diamond head-dress . . . and an imperial mantle'.[23] Several bales of a proclamation were found, addressed 'to the Belgians and Inhabitants of the left Bank of the Rhine', printed in Paris before his departure:

> The ephemeral success of my Enemies detached you for a moment from my Empire; in my exile, upon a rock in the sea, I heard your complaint; the God of Battles has decided the fate of your beautiful provinces; Napoleon is among you; you are worthy to be Frenchmen; rise in a mass, join my invincible phalanxes to exterminate the remainder of these barbarians, who are your enemies and mine; they fly, with rage and despair in their hearts.[24]

It had been signed, presumptuously, 'At the Imperial Palace of Lacken'[25] – former summer residence of the governors of the Habsburg Netherlands, just north of Brussels – and post-dated 17 June 1815. Among other papers was a list of Bonapartist sympathisers in Brussels: 'twenty individuals whose persons and property were to be excepted from the general pillage [of the city], and whose names were communicated to the French soldiers'.[26] There were also 'lists of all [Bonaparte's] spies and emissaries in every country of Europe'. Blücher's chief of staff, General Gneisenau, observed that there were many Berliners implicated.[27]

To the men of the Prussian 15th Regiment, the coach contained plunder beyond a looter's wildest dreams: 'several boxes of mounted and unmounted diamonds, large silver services, with the arms of Napoleon, and gold pieces, with his name and portrait'. All ranks benefited. Within a week, Napoleon's seal ring 'blaze[d] on the hand of the hero Gneisenau', while 'subaltern officers . . . dine[d] off silver', and fusiliers were selling 'four or five diamonds, as large as a pea, or even larger, for a few francs'. In addition, 'a large quantity of diamonds of a middle size' had been seized, 'and one the size of a pigeon's egg'. The regiment resolved to give the finest as a present to the King of Prussia.[28] To His Majesty's kinsman George, the English Prince Regent, they gave a pair of Napoleon's spurs, 'having heard that [His] Royal Highness had a collection of arms and military accoutrements, to which these spurs might be deemed a curious addition'.[29]

*

The main Prussian pursuit halted at Genappe, men and horses exhausted. Blücher spent the night at the Roi d'Espagne. It seemed only apposite, the Duke of Wellington having slept there on the night of 16 June during the retreat from Quatre Bras to Waterloo. But the fleeing French would get no rest. A small force – comprising three squadrons of lancers and the fusiliers of the 15th Infantry – pressed on, personally led by Gneisenau. 'The French [army] being pursued without intermission, was absolutely disorganised,' he reported:

[They] had not expected to be so quickly pursued, [and] were driven from more than nine bivouacs. In some villages they attempted to maintain themselves; but as soon as they heard the beating of our drums, or the sound of the trumpet, they either fled or threw themselves into the houses, where they were cut down or made prisoners.[30]

A drummer boy was placed on one of the horses from Bonaparte's coach, with orders to beat out a steady, menacing rhythm to the pursuit. The trumpets sounded as they advanced through the night and the troops were encouraged to roar the great Lutheran hymn *Herr Gott dich loben wir* – Lord God, thy praise we sing. By such means did the relatively small force strike terror into their demoralised quarry. 'The consternation . . . was so great', a French source recorded, 'that large bodies of well-armed cavalry and infantry suffered themselves to be made prisoners, without attempting to defend themselves, by a few miserable lancers, whom they might have driven back by merely turning to face them.'[31]

An English officer, following in the wake of the Prussians, testified to the efficiency of this unequal hunt: among the 'abandoned guns, carriages, knapsacks, and muskets, [that] choaked [sic] up the ground', he noticed 'the bodies of Frenchmen only'[32] across the five miles between La Belle Alliance and Quatre Bras. It was said that 'Prussians killed many [allied] men whom the French had made prisoners, mistaking them for French'.[33] Such oversights were inevitable in the murderous euphoria, despite the clarity of the night. 'It was moonlight,' observed Gneisenau, 'which greatly favoured the pursuit, for the whole march was but a continued chase, either in the corn-fields or the houses.'[34] And the exhilaration of the chase was shared by an unnamed Prussian officer: 'We did not halt 'til day-break. It was the finest night of my life: the moon beautifully illuminated the scene, and the weather was mild.'[35]

*

Between one and two o'clock in the morning, Sergeant Mauduit and his companions from the scattered 1st Grenadiers regained the Charleroi road at Quatre Bras. A vast moonlit morgue stretched before them, strewn with over three thousand naked corpses left uncleared from Friday's battle. For more than half a mile they lay, many caked black with mud following Saturday's storm. They appeared to Mauduit 'like veritable spectres demanding of us . . . why they were not to be honoured with burial'. The road through the battleground crossed a small brook, turned into a torrent by the heavy rains. Here the parched fugitives quenched their thirst regardless of the two-day-old bodies drifting past or clogging the stream.

Further to the east, another landscape of human devastation opened for the Englishman Edmund Wheatley. A lieutenant in the King's German Legion, Wheatley had been taken prisoner at about six o'clock during the fighting around La Haye Sainte and was subsequently swept along in the French retreat. Robbed of possessions by his captors, he had been made to surrender his boots and force-marched barefoot. 'Every stone I trod on lacerated the bottom of my feet and the torture was acute,' he recalled. Then, on the plain bounded by the villages of Saint-Armand, Ligny, Sombreffe and Fleurus, the ground became more yielding. 'The multitude [of naked bodies] was so thronged I felt a temporary relief to my feet in treading on through soft jellied lumps of inanimate flesh. The French assured me they were all Prussians.'[36]

*

According to a correspondent in the town, the first French wounded and deserters had reached Charleroi at around seven o'clock on the Sunday evening, having left the battle long before it was decided. They were in 'the most terrible disorder', while their officers were heard voicing 'a thousand imprecations against this man [Bonaparte], who cannot satiate himself with blood'. Throughout the night the numbers of fugitives increased, although it was estimated that of 40,000 cavalrymen who had passed through the town on 15 June riding north, 'not 10,000 capable of service [had] returned'.[37]

Many avenues and squares of the town had been blocked with ammunition caissons, provision wagons and baggage carts ever since the beginning of the French invasion. All the wounded from Quatre Bras and Ligny, and the twenty-seven guns and other equipment captured from the Prussians on the 16th had added to the congestion – so that towards daybreak on the 19th, Charleroi had become so crowded that 'the horrible scenes of Genappe were renewed'. In the centre of the town was a bridge over the Sambre. It now represented to the exhausted and desperate men their only way home to France. The steeply descending road – the rue du Montagne – narrowed as it approached the bridge:

> Completely filled with the . . . mingled column of the retreating army . . . the space . . . contracting, all passage was obstructed. Horsemen, infantry, and carriages rushed on, contending who should cross first. The stronger unfeelingly thrust aside or trampled upon the weaker, and too often drew their sabres, or their bayonets, on those who offered any resistance.[38]

A troop of cuirassiers thundering across the bridge struck the wooden parapet on one side with such force that it gave way, plunging horses and riders into the river. Several drowned. Then a provision wagon overturned in front of the bridge. Other vehicles coming down the hill were unable to stop, crashed and added to the blockage, crushing men and horses to death and scattering sacks of rice and flour, loaves of bread and casks of wine and brandy into the road. As the famished troops struggled through the wreckage, many speared loaves on the points of their bayonets. Others attacked the barrels, staving them in with musket butts and gulping down the liquor as it poured from the splintered wood.

A hundred yards back from the bridge, a wagon containing the Emperor's private treasury – one million francs in gold and 200,000 in silver – was stalled in the crowd. Realising that he would not be able to get his wagon and six horses across the

Sambre, the hapless *commissaire* responsible for the consignment took the decision to open it and entrust the treasure – in 20,000-franc bags – to his men and to those of the escort. A careful record was taken of the number of bags given to each man and arrangements were made to meet on the opposite bank of the river with the money. Before the distribution could be completed, however, several shots sounded from the direction of the bridge. Someone shouted: *'Les prussiens! Sauve qui peut!'* The cry was taken up by others. Panic ensued. In the confusion around the treasury wagon, 'swords were drawn, bayonet thrusts exchanged, blood shed'[39] and all the cash bags were rapidly plundered and disappeared into the crowd.

It had been a false alarm: the shots had come from thirsty soldiers firing their muskets into unbroached barrels of wine and spirits. The Prussians were in fact some way behind, and would not reach Charleroi until midday. When they arrived, they found nine cannon and a hundred ammunition caissons abandoned in the streets. Everything else – provisions, money and baggage – had been 'pillaged by the populace' within three hours.[40]

An exaggerated report was printed in the London press that 'BUONAPARTE in his retreat set fire to Charleroi, and burnt it to ashes.' It was, the *Sun* informed its readership, 'an example which, we hope, will not be forgotten by the Allies in their progress towards Paris'.[41]

II

On Tuesday 20 June, Marshal Grouchy's orderly retreat reached Namur, twenty miles upriver of Charleroi, at the confluence of the Sambre and the Meuse. His army had marched in two parallel columns three miles apart. The IV Corps, and the wounded, formed the western column, marching from Limale and led by Grouchy himself, while to the east, from Wavre, General Vandamme led the III Corps and a regiment of dragoons. An advance guard of General Exelmans' remaining seven dragoon regiments had been sent ahead to secure the Sambre bridge at Namur, Grouchy's vital passage to the French border. The rearguard, comprising General Teste's four infantry regiments and three regiments of hussars led by General Pajol, continued to shield the retreat against pursuit from Generallieutenant von Thielemann's Prussians. Thielemann, however, duped and outmanoeuvred at Sint-Agatha-Rode on Monday, had been slow to give chase. It was not until Vandamme's eastern column was within five miles of Namur, on the Tuesday morning, that it was attacked from the north by twenty-odd squadrons of cavalry from Thielemann's III Korps, commanded by Generalmajor von Hobe, who succeeded in capturing three artillery pieces and fifty horses before turning their attention on Grouchy's column. At the same time, Grouchy was attacked from the west by a cavalry brigade and horse artillery, the advance guard of Generalmajor von Pirch's II Korps. Sent by Blücher to locate and intercept Grouchy's forces, Pirch had been on the march since eleven o'clock on Sunday night.

Marshal Grouchy – reviled by history for his failure to 'march toward the guns' and save the day for his Emperor at Mont-Saint-Jean – was masterly in retreat. He was able to push back Hobe's cavalry and move to support Vandamme's column – even to recapture the three French cannon and take another from the Prussians – while a rearguard kept Pirch's troops in check until the convoy of French wounded had reached the shelter of Namur's walls. Covering fire from Vandamme then enabled the rest of Grouchy's column to reach the principal gate into the town, the Porte de Bruxelles. Colonel Hubert-Francois Biot, aide-de-camp to General Pajol, was sent to enquire how long Vandamme thought he could hold his position. 'I will remain for as short a time as is necessary,' Vandamme replied. 'The position is terribly hot here.'[1] It was indeed hot. During the few moments their conversation lasted, Biot's horse suffered two musket-ball wounds. By three o'clock in the afternoon, Vandamme had successfully withdrawn and Grouchy's largely intact army was inside the town. The fighting retreat through the suburbs and down the long avenue approaching the Brussels Gate had been so effective, and the French musket fire so intense, that all the trees were stripped of their bark to the height of a man, and 'the blood of the fallen ran in the gutters'.[2]

Walloon and fiercely Francophile, the municipal authorities of Namur had received news of the catastrophe at Mont-Saint-Jean with dismay and made available 100,000 rations of bread and 100,000 of brandy to sustain the remaining third of the Emperor's army still capable of continuing the war. Citizens also lined the streets distributing bread, beer, wine and meat from tables laden with produce. 'They vied with one another to give us comforts,' recalled Biot. 'I saw women take wounded

men from the hands of able-bodied soldiers, urging the latter
to return and fight.'[3] And if there was an edge of reproof to
what was said, Biot did not acknowledge it. 'The people of
Namur ... showed us every imaginable kindness,' wrote
Colonel Fantin des Odoards. 'Every house received our wounded,
providing supplies in profusion to officers and men alike. Not
a wine cellar remained closed ... Elegant ladies ... showed
themselves to be just as attentive as the common women. On
all sides we heard words of concern for us, curses against the
Prussians.'[4]

While first Grouchy's corps, then Vandamme's formed up
and marched through the town and out by way of the Porte
de France on the south side, the northern gates were barricaded
and defended by Teste's 2,000 infantry rearguard, distributed
along the walls and behind the chest-high earth glacis, Namur's
only outer fortification. They faced a Prussian force of between
twelve and fourteen thousand. The heaviest fighting took place
east of the Porte de Bruxelles, at the so-called Iron Gate,
commanding the road to Louvain. The Porte de Fer was
defended by two companies of grenadiers and a brace of cannon
camouflaged with brushwood and loaded with canister shot.
Orders had been given to allow the enemy within point-blank
range before opening fire. When the Prussian 6th Infantry
Brigade, led by its second-in-command Colonel von Zastrow,
reached the gate's metal grilles, a devastating volley of grape
and musketry raked through the close-packed formations of
men. Volley followed volley until the survivors succeeded in
escaping the line of fire. Despite this carnage, two more equally
vain attempts were made on the same position. '[The Prussians]
seemed drunk,' Teste reported, 'their officers also, as they came
to the barricades to be killed on our bayonets.' His own officers
had no need to give orders to their men, but fired alongside
them with muskets dropped by the wounded. As supplies of
cartridges ran low, each man took particular care to mark
his enemy and bring him down. Of the 1,700 Prussians killed

or wounded in the action at Namur, the 6th Brigade alone lost forty-four officers and 1,272 men in front of the Porte de Fer. Pirch's report made clear who he held responsible, but the gallant Colonel Zastrow had not survived to be reprimanded:

> Carried away by his ardour and having imprudently advanced, paying no attention to the repeated recalls addressed to him, [he] was struck by a shot in the chest, on the line of skirmishers amidst whom he was standing . . . The 6th brigade distinguished itself in this fight but its over-hasty action caused the death of many of our men.[5]

Among other officers killed was Colonel von Bismarck, uncle to the future 'Iron Chancellor' of a united Germany.

It was eight o'clock in the evening when Teste's rearguard, ammunition spent, began to withdraw from their positions, after first destroying the Porte de Bruxelles with explosives. At about the same time, Prussian troops gained entry to the town through the windows and door of a custom house built into the wall and advanced, street by street, in pursuit. As Teste's men passed through the Porte de France, they found that the bridge over the Sambre had been so effectively barricaded that the only way across it was by walking single file along the stone parapets. Their cannon had to be abandoned to the Prussians. Meanwhile, behind them, a detachment of sappers halted the pursuers for a considerable time with a fusillade of musket fire from loopholes cut into houses on either side of the gate. They then set fire to heaps of tar-soaked straw and faggots, leaving the entire street and the Porte de France ablaze in the face of the Prussians, before making their own way across the Sambre along the parapets of the bridge. Generalmajor von Pirch was left in possession of Namur, but the army he had been sent to intercept was beyond his reach.

Marching south through the night along the right bank of the Meuse, towards the Belgian town of Dinant ten miles from the French frontier, Colonel des Odoards reflected on the warmth and loyalty of the people of Namur. Despite the destruction wrought in their town, they had cheered the defeated army on its way with prayers for an early return. 'Oh! Let us remember, if, in a happier day, we carry our weapons back into Belgium. We found there a friendship to shame France.'[6]

There would be a far colder reception from many of their own countrymen.

*

On Friday 23 June, 500 cartloads of wounded soldiers rumbled into Paris. 'The Parisians seem very little touched by the sight,' remarked John Scott's French correspondent. The following Sunday was 'one of the most careless and pleasant days . . . that I have known in Paris', he noted. 'The promenades were all crowded excessively. The ladies gay and gracious, the gentlemen alert and gallant. Plays, quacks, and sports, all took their usual stations, to attract the attention of the volatile Parisians, as in the most halcyon times.'

Only the walking wounded, 'the cadaverous frowning counte-nances of soldiers and officers', blighted the scene. It was just seven days, the correspondent observed, since the battle 'that laid France at the feet of Europe'. He was particularly intrigued to see whether these survivors 'excited much interest or pity'. He found they did not.

'Alas! Madame,' one veteran was heard to address a person of fashion, 'we have suffered a dreadful defeat.'

'What is that to me, Sir? The army got into the scrape, let the army get itself out.'

Scott's correspondent thought 'most people seem to agree with the lady's reply', and noticed that her indifference, even animosity, was shared by the lower classes: 'The long faces of the ferocious officers and soldiers attract the insults of the market-women, who during late years have lost all their Jacobin propensities and are now conspicuous for loyalty [to the King].'[7] It was less than a week after the Emperor's abdication, and caricatures of 'Monsieur

Bonaparte' had replaced the bloated images of Louis XVIII in all the print shop windows.

*

In the Roi d'Espagne at Genappe, during the early hours of 19 June, Marshal Blücher had dreamed of Paris. 'In his fantasies he painted the brightest pictures,' aide-de-camp Graf von Nostitz recalled, 'expressing the hope that he would rush ahead of the English army, reach Paris two days before it and enter the great city without any outside help. He even suggested that if he were able to sign the capitulation of Paris alone, he could demand reparations in which all the sums of money Prussia had earlier to pay to France would be refunded to the Fatherland.'[8] The old man was 'trembling in every limb'[9] from the strain of four days' combat, retreat and retaliation. But he was convinced that 'to take full advantage of the terror of the lost battle',[10] his army's onslaught into French territory could not be slowed. 'The orders for the [Prussian] advance', Nostitz commented, 'were thus expressed in such a way that one could almost say that they overestimated the strength of man and beast . . . Uninterrupted marching would . . . increase the strain particularly as not a single day of rest was planned.'[11] One consequence of this urgency was that for a time the army outpaced its supplies and the Prussian troops, already disposed to plunder, were unleashed on to France hungry as well.

Wellington's forward march would seem leisurely by comparison, and when Generalmajor Karl von Müffling, the Duke's Prussian liaison officer, ventured to suggest a more rapid advance, he testily explained that a speedier pace would divide the army from its supply train:

Do not press me on this point, for I tell you, it won't do. If you were better acquainted with the English army, its composition and habits you would say the same. I cannot separate from my tents and my supplies. My troops must be well kept and well supplied in camp, if order and discipline are to be maintained. It is better that I should arrive two days later in Paris, than that discipline should be relaxed.[12]

The Duke knew from experience in the Peninsular War that an efficient commissariat was essential, not only to discipline but to the winning of hearts and minds of a subject people. A well-supplied army had no need to plunder the country through which it marched. The provision of tents was equally important. The alternative of bivouacking 'was not suitable to the English character', as he was fond of asserting: '[The English soldier] got drunk & lay down under a hedge. Discipline was destroyed. But when [we] introduced tents, every Soldier belonged to his tent, & drunk or sober, he got to it before he went to sleep.' And when it was pointed out that the French army customarily bivouacked, he would reply: 'Yes, because French, Spanish, & all other nations lie anywhere. It is their habit. They have no homes.'[13]

*

Von Zieten's I Korps had crossed the French border on 20 June and bivouacked at Beaumont. Between three and four o'clock the following afternoon, their advance guard reached Avesnes, one of the great double ribbon of star-plan citadels fortified by Marshal Vauban in the late seventeenth century to protect the French frontier. Avesnes' bastions, curtain walls, redoubts and ravelins might have withstood a lengthy siege, but just eight hours and a lucky shot brought it down. At nightfall, the Prussian howitzer bombardment, reinforced by a battery of twelve-pounders, was discontinued after prolonged shelling from seven to eight hundred paces had failed to force the defenders' submission. Von Zieten contemplated giving up, assigning a detachment to blockade the fortress and marching on with the rest of his corps. Then his artillery commander, Oberst Lehmann, requested permission to resume a limited bombardment at midnight. 'At least we should not let the enemy sleep,' he urged. Permission granted, the howitzers began to fire. Thirteen shells were hurled over the walls. The fourteenth hit the main powder magazine, causing an explosion that lit up the night sky and flattened forty of the surrounding buildings. The ensuing panic persuaded the garrison commander to surrender the town.

Avesnes had been the main supply depot of Napoleon's Armée du Nord for the advance into Belgium, and the scene of his proclamation ordering them 'to conquer or perish'. It would now serve to equip Blücher's advance on Paris. When the Prussians occupied the garrison, they took possession not only of a large stock of provisions but of forty-seven heavy cannon, 15,000 artillery rounds and a million French musket cartridges of a calibre suited to their own weapons.

Three days later, on 24 June, the fortress of Guise surrendered as the I Korps' howitzers were being deployed in front of its walls. 'It would seem that the commandant . . . was merely waiting for this to happen so that he could feel comfortable about capitulating.' There was a suspicion also that 'news of the terrible catastrophe at Avesnes played no small part in this'.[14] As well as prisoners and supplies, Guise yielded fourteen cannon, 2,500 artillery rounds, 2,850 muskets, 705,500 cartridges and 9,700 pounds of powder.

The garrison at Saint-Quentin, on the Somme, did not so much capitulate as abandon the town. A force of between five and six hundred cavalry had ridden away south to Laon on 23 June, leaving behind only National Guards, who offered no resistance when the Prussians marched in the following day. Seventy-five miles closer to Paris than Avesnes, Saint-Quentin became the army's supply depot. Blücher gave orders:

Everything in the way of men and horses that can no longer be employed is to be sent there, as are any superfluous pieces of equipment, muskets, drums, etc. Any empty waggons blocking the march of the various corps are to be sent back to St Quentin as well, where they will be loaded with provisions for the army and returned to it.[15]

The town was also established as general administrative centre for the occupied provinces, under the control of Staatsrat Friedrich von Ribbentrop, and with Oberst von Loucy in charge of police. Blücher left the French in no doubt that his was an army of conquest.

It was agreed between Blücher and Wellington, following the Prussian occupation of Saint-Quentin, that the Anglo-Allied army be responsible for capturing all other fortresses west of the Sambre, and the Prussians those on the river itself, to the east and along the Meuse.

The western fortresses of Douai, Bouchain and Lille having already capitulated without attack, Wellington delegated the investment and blockade of Le Quesnoy, Condé and Valenciennes to the Netherlands Corps, commanded by Prince Frederik. Unlike his elder brother William, Prince of Orange, Frederik had taken no part in the battle of 18 June. Stationed that day with his 10,000 troops at Halle, guarding the route westward to the Channel ports, he had presumably – like Lieutenant General Sir Charles Colville and his 6,000-strong 4th British Division at the same location – been unaware of the fighting until the following morning. The tedium of siege warfare may have been scant recompense to the Prince and his corps for their enforced idleness, forfeiture of glory, and exclusion from the most celebrated land battle of the age.

The small fortress of Le Quesnoy, the Netherlanders' first engagement, endured five days of siege and a short artillery bombardment before its commandant declared loyalty to Louis XVIII and capitulated to Prince Frederik's forces on 29 June. Valenciennes and Condé, his next objectives, would hold out considerably longer.

Wellington compensated Colville and his men for their inaction on the 18th with the honour of storming Cambrai. On the evening of 24 June, they attacked the rundown fortifications of

the town by *escalade*, the simplest and most direct of siege
tactics, barely altered since the Middle Ages. One column scaled
ladders placed in an angle of the northern gateway and curtain
wall; another placed their ladders against a low escarp up to a
ravelin on the south-west side of the town, while a third – in an
assault on the southern hornwork – forced the outer gate and
carried their ladders across two overgrown and dried-up ditches
and along the rails of a drawbridge. Unable to force the inner
gate, this third column succeeded in escalading to an unrepaired
breach in the wall. The operation was supported by three
batteries of nine-pounders, which silenced all but four of the
defenders' guns and set part of the town on fire. The attackers'
losses were 'trifling': an officer and seven rank-and-file killed;
three officers, a sergeant and twenty-five rank-and-file wounded.

The inhabitants received the British troops with joy, some
illuminating their windows in celebration,[16] although many,
according to Sergeant Wheeler, 'had forgot to wash the powder
off their lips caused by biting off the cartridges when they were
firing on us from the wall'.[17]

Only the town had been carried, however. The citadel held out,
its governor, Baron Roos, being unwilling to surrender to any
authority other than that of the French King. The stalemate lasted
twenty-four hours until, at Wellington's suggestion, Louis XVIII
dispatched a messenger to Roos requesting his capitulation.
Honour satisfied, the governor complied, and both town and
citadel were formally handed over to the King. Cambrai became
the first stop on His Majesty's royal progress back to Paris,
although it remained the headquarters of Wellington's army of
occupation for the rest of the year.

The King's requests were not always so readily acceded to. The
Morning Chronicle printed a report that at Condé, invested by
troops of Prince Frederik's Netherlands Corps, 'a French officer,
commissioned by his Majesty Louis [XVIII], to summon the town
. . . to surrender, [was] arrested and shot upon the glacis of the
fortress'. The story of this outrage, 'a thing without parallel in
the annals of the law of nations',[18] was retold in a more lurid

version by the same newspaper twelve days later: '[The messenger]
appeared with a flag of truce to summon the garrison. He was
allowed to approach, and when he was within musket shot he
was fired at and fell. His dead body was then seized and cut in
a thousand pieces.'[19]

The neighbouring fortress of Valenciennes proved likewise
resistant. The Netherlanders' bombardment began on 1 July and
lasted for three days and nights. Hot shot – iron rounds glowing
red from the brazier and fired by cannon – burned down a district
of the town together with the eastern suburb of Marly. During
this attack, royalist elements within the walls instigated a popular
rising, and at one stage the white Bourbon flag was hoisted. The
garrison commandant, however, not only succeeded in suppressing
the revolt but expelled 1,500 of the malcontents from the town.
Thereafter Valenciennes, like Condé, settled down to a lengthy
but otherwise unremarkable and uneventful siege. Both fortresses
would finally capitulate in August, within days of one another,
and not to the allies but to the King.

The fortresses that fell to the Prussians, by contrast, were
obliged to capitulate unconditionally. Maubeuge surrendered on
12 July after an eighteen-day siege, Landrecies on the 21st, having
the day before offered capitulation to Louis XVIII, an offer
rejected by the Prussians. Each garrison commandant, however,
was allowed to leave and march south beyond the Loire, a token
force of 150 troops and two cannon the only concessions to
military honour granted them in defeat. Mariembourg surrendered
on 30 July, under the same terms, as did Philippeville on
10 August, Rocroi on the 18th, Mézières on 3 September and
Montmédy on the 13th.

While the Prussian II Korps, together with the North German
Federal Army Korps, laid siege in turn to the string of fortresses
stretching across the hundred miles west to east from Landrecies
to Longwy, the rest of Blücher's army marched south. It was in
vain that communities in its path signified loyalty to Louis XVIII
by putting out white Bourbon flags – or any dirty grey rag that
might pass for one. In the near-deserted villages John Scott

passed through on his way to Paris some time later, little more than the makeshift flags and rags remained – poking from smashed windows and decayed roofs – the 'wretched broken-down tenements' plundered of everything valuable.²⁰

*

The Duke had issued a proclamation to the French people when he crossed the border on 21 June and established his headquarters at Malplaquet. He came at the head of a victorious army, not as an enemy to the French nation, but an enemy only to 'the Usurper . . . who is the enemy of human nature, and with whom no peace and no truce can be maintained'. He came as a liberator, he told them, 'to relieve you from the iron yoke, by which you are oppressed'. He also published a French translation of the order he had given to his forces the previous day:

> Troops of the nations which are at present under the command of Field-Marshal the Duke of Wellington, are desired to recollect, that their respective Sovereigns are the Allies of His Majesty the King of France, and that France therefore ought to be treated as a friendly country. It is then required that nothing should be taken either by the Officers or Soldiers, for which payment be not made.

He demanded to be informed by the civilian population 'of any one who shall presume to disobey' his orders. Two classes only were exempt from his protection:

> All those persons who shall absent themselves from their dwellings, after the entrance of this army into France, and all those who shall be found attached to the service of the Usurper, and so absent, shall be considered to be his partisans and public enemies, and their property shall be devoted to the subsistence of the forces.

Private Farmer and his comrades of the 11th Light Dragoons found an entire abandoned village near Catieaux that appeared to fall into one of the categories exempted by this ordinance and for three days took full advantage:

> As the foolish people had left all their effects behind them, we saw no reason why we should not . . . appropriate[e] them to our own use. The consequence was that our meals were not only abundant but sumptuous: – fowls, geese, turkeys, ducks, pigs, rabbits, and flour and garden-stuff in abundance, furnished forth, with wine and beer, our daily tables.[21]

Later they saw evidence of the more vindictive depredations committed by Blücher's troops, who were under no obligation from their field marshal to make nice distinctions in sparing France the conquerors' right of plunder. Farmer explored the house and grounds of a large chateau. 'The skill and industry with which [the Prussians] seemed to have carried on the work of devastation, I have no language to describe,' he recalled:

> There was not one article of furniture, from the costly pier-glass down to the common coffee-cup, which they had not smashed to atoms. The flour-mill . . . attached to the mansion was all gutted, the sacks cut to pieces, and the flour wantonly scattered over the road. Stables, cow-sheds, poultry-houses, and gardens, seemed to have been, with infinite care, rendered useless.

In a nearby deserted village likewise:

> furniture, doors, windows, and here and there roofs, all seemed to have passed through the merciless hands of the spoilers. I never beheld such a specimen of war, conducted in a spirit of ferocious hostility. I was half ashamed of the connection that subsisted between ourselves and the Prussians, when I looked upon the horrid work which they had perpetrated.[22]

Uneasy, if not ashamed, Wellington was said to have remonstrated with Blücher on the subject. 'My Lord Duke,' the old man replied simply, 'the French were never in England.'[23] Sergeant Wheeler recounted a fuller version of the argument as he heard it from the Prussian troops:

> You English know nothing of the sufferings of war as we do. England has never been overrun by French Armies as our country has, or you would act as we do. The French acted a cruel part in Prussia, destroyed our houses, violated our Mothers, our wives, our daughters, and sisters, and murdered them afterwards, they taught us a lesson we are now come to France to put into practice.[24]

Although Wellington had expressly forbidden troops under his command the plunder which Prussians regarded as their right, there were instances of his orders being flouted. Some Belgian troops were hanged for looting,[25] and only a week after the General Order 'that nothing should be taken . . . for which payment be not made',[26] a number of stragglers from a British infantry regiment were detected and arrested 'in an act of plunder under the most aggravated circumstances'. A corporal would have been hanged, but the Duke was dissuaded by 'the good conduct of the regiment' from 'making so severe an example'. The culprits were flogged and the corporal broken to private.[27]

In September, His Grace had occasion to write to the officer commanding the brigade of cavalry at Beauvais, concerning 'nightly depredations upon the passengers on the high road, and even in the towns and villages in which the troops are [quartered]'.[28] It was not only the French who were preyed on by rogue British troops. 'Recently scarcely a night has passed without some act of atrocity being committed by them,' reported the *Examiner* at the end of the year. 'A Colonel was robbed by men of his own regiment; another British Officer was stopped in the street by four English soldiers, who robbed and maltreated him; and an English Gentleman who had been to take a farewell dinner with some Officers at Montmartre, was stopped on his return, robbed of three Napoleons, and had his coat torn off his back.'[29]

In addition to the proscription on looting, Wellington had also forbidden his men 'to extort contributions' from the French populace. During the occupation of Cambrai, however, Sergeant Wheeler was quite brazen in his account of the practice, whereby extortion obviated the necessity for plunder: 'We had picked up some money in the town, or more properly speaking we had made the people hand it over to us to save us the trouble of taking it from them, so we were enabled to provide ourselves with what made us comfortable.' There was looting also in Cambrai, and with unintended and alarming consequences:

A Ser[geant] Corporal and four men fell in with a barrel of gunpowder. They being drunk took it for brandy, and [the] Corporal . . . fired into it, as he said to make a bung hole, while the others were waiting with their tin canteens to catch the supposed liquor, but it blew up and all the brandy merchants were dreadfully mutilated . . . so dreadfully scorched it is feared that four cannot recover, and the other two will not be fit for service again.[30]

Of thirty individuals recorded as tried by courts martial in occupied France between July and the end of 1815, twelve were accused of offences against the civilian population. Private Chandler of the 23rd Light Dragoons was held at Passy for 'wounding an inhabitant', but acquitted. Eleven men were accused of theft. Of these, four were acquitted. One of the remainder received 1,000 lashes, one 900, one 700, one 600, and one, Private McEvoy of the 71st Regiment of Foot, 'for having ill-used and robbed a Frenchman',[31] was hanged. Another capital atrocity was of so lurid a nature as to merit reporting in the London press. On the night of 18 December, Privates Neale and Walker, riflemen of the 95th Regiment of Foot, attempted to steal a pig from a smallholding near the village of Taverney. Hearing a noise outside, old Laurence Quedon opened his cottage door and was cut in the head by a sabre. He staggered back inside, pursued by the two soldiers. One of them attacked Quedon's wife with a glancing sabre stroke that severed her right ear. The couple's daughter was in bed and the assailants attempted to kill her where she lay, but the room was dark and she escaped with only slight wounds. Meanwhile, the old man had managed to reach his gun and shot Walker in the chest. Neale assaulted him again with his sabre, opening the scalp in two places and cutting the arm he raised to ward off the blows. Fortunately, the gunshot had brought an officer to the scene and the two men were arrested and charged with 'maliciously stabbing'. Walker survived his wound and turned king's evidence against his accomplice. Neale was hanged, with his pipe in his mouth, 'and died as he had lived, without apparently knowing or caring whether there was a God or an hereafter'.[32]

III

IN retreat from Namur, by way of Dinant, Givet, Rocroi and
Mézières, Grouchy's army – the IV Corps under his own
command, the III Corps led by General Vandamme forming the
rearguard, and the whole flanked by the cavalry detachments of
Pajol, Exelmans and General Vallin – had meanwhile been
following a route to Paris well to the east of the Prussian advance.
At Rethel, on 24 June, Grouchy received a two-day-old letter from
Marshal Davout, Minister of War, informing him of Napoleon's
abdication and ordering him to proceed, with his force, by way
of Soissons, to Paris. 'France is counting on you, on General
Vandamme . . . and on all generals and officers, at this important
time,' Davout told him. 'The arrival of your army will make a
great impression in Paris.'[1] When Grouchy reached Rheims the
following day, he received another letter informing him that
the provisional government had appointed him supreme commander
of the Armée du Nord. It would rapidly become clear to him that
this honour was a dubious one.

Meanwhile, during the week following the terrible disintegration of Napoleon's forces on 18 June, his chief of staff, Marshal
Soult, had mustered all that was left – a little over 30,000 men
– at Laon, some seventy miles north-east of Paris. However, he
was struggling to keep them there: 'they disappear . . . in all
directions at the first opportunity', he reported. 'The infantry is

totally demoralized [officers and men] and are saying the most
unbelievable things.'[2] Many lacked weapons; many of the cavalry
even lacked horses. Bonaparte's abdication, announced to the
army on 23 June, had accelerated the breakdown of discipline.
A thousand infantry of the Imperial Guard had flouted Soult's
dwindling authority and left their regiment en masse. Between
23 and 25 June, Soult ordered the remnants of General d'Erlon's
I Corps and General Reille's II Corps south to join Grouchy's
IV Corps at Soissons.

   Grouchy had misgivings that contagion from the near rabble
Soult had gathered – 'the fugitives and debris of the Emperor's
army' – would affect the morale of his own troops, 20,000
infantry and 5,000 cavalry who had not experienced the trauma
of defeat at Mont-Saint-Jean. The men Soult had brought to
Soissons were, Grouchy believed, 'less well-disposed'; writing to
Davout at eight o'clock in the morning of 26 June, he admitted
they would 'require more skilful hands than [his] own to get the
best out of'.[3] By five o'clock that afternoon, his self-deprecation
seemed well founded. 'No matter what orders I give, no matter
what measures I undertake, I cannot prevent the soldiers leaving
the colours and committing the most damaging acts,' he reported.
'The Imperial Guard continue to be worked upon by agitators
seeking to persuade them that they can best serve the Emperor's
interests by quitting their ranks and going to Paris. I have limited
means of coercion to oppose this torrent.' And lest his political
masters be in any further doubt as to the state of the army they
had entrusted to him, he went on: 'The troops in Soissons do
not appear to me to be capable of fighting [and] it is not possible
to consider using such demoralised infantry in a battle. Those
in the government saying otherwise would not, I believe, take it
upon themselves to lead these men in combat.'

   It had been a difficult day for the new supreme commander.
Marshal Soult, having joined forces with him at Soissons, promptly
resigned as chief of staff and left for Paris. Many of his bureau-
cratic staff followed, claiming 'he had authorized them to do so',
and Grouchy was left with an administrative structure entirely

inadequate to the army he was attempting to reform. 'It is scandalous and distressing,'[4] he complained, and implored the Minister of War to send him another chief of staff and more staff officers.

*

By 23 June, the day after Bonaparte abdicated and Louis XVIII crossed the border from Belgium to reclaim his throne, a provisional government had been formed and a five-man executive commission – drawn from both upper and lower legislative chambers, Peers and Representatives – elected under the presidency of Joseph Fouché, Minister of Police. The commission appointed five plenipotentiaries to sue for peace.

Since the allies had declared war not on the French nation but on the person of the Emperor alone – to place him 'absolutely beyond the possibility of raising fresh disturbances'[5] – it was argued, in the chambers of Representatives and Peers, that with Bonaparte's renunciation of power the cause of contention had passed. This argument was rejected by Blücher, who wrote to Wellington: 'We should advance on Paris without stopping, refuse all negotiations, and show this traitorous and vain nation that we know it and thus despise it.' Before he would countenance entering peace negotiations, a number of conditions would have to be met: 'Bonaparte dead or delivered alive and the surrender of all fortresses on the Meuse and Sambre'. His march on Paris would continue, he declared, 'and if the Parisians will not hand Napoleon over or kill him themselves, they will experience my revenge'. And he wrote in more explicit terms to his wife: 'unless the Parisians kill the tyrant by the time I get to Paris, then I shall kill the Parisians! It is after all a nation of traitors!'[6]

On 26 June, while Marshal Grouchy was reviewing the remains of the imperial army at Soissons, twenty miles north at Laon, the plenipotentiaries from Fouché's provisional government met Blücher's aide Graf von Nostitz to negotiate an end to hostilities. The French delegation comprised the Marquis de

La Fayette, the Comte d'Agesomn, General Sébastiani, the Comte de Pontécoulant, the Comte de la Forêt, and Benjamin Constant as secretary.

Negotiations got no further than the latest Prussian demand, for the surrender of Paris. General Sébastiani declared that he would die before he would give up the city and there was nothing more to be said. As he left the meeting, Nostitz could not resist a pleasantry: he told the Frenchmen '[that he] was entirely convinced the [Prussian] army would reach Paris before them and [he] would then be delighted to welcome them back from their journey'.[7]

*

Meanwhile, Grouchy was waiting anxiously for General Vandamme's III Corps – delayed by weather and fatigue – to catch up with him at Soissons. Because Blücher's advance and Grouchy's withdrawal were following roughly convergent routes to Paris, the closer they got to the capital, the nearer the French right flank came to the Prussian left, the more vulnerable they were to attack, and the greater the danger that their line of retreat would be cut. While Grouchy delayed his departure from Soissons to allow Vandamme time to close the gap between their forces, Blücher had established his headquarters only twenty miles away to the west. A dispatch reached Grouchy from General d'Erlon's advance guard late in the afternoon of 27 June, reporting the dangerous proximity, at Compiègne, of between four and five thousand Prussians and a column of 'considerably more' approaching from the north. 'I think there is no time to be lost', d'Erlon advised the marshal, adopting the formal third person, 'in His Excellency making his move.'[8] Vandamme had still not arrived at five in the afternoon when Grouchy left Soissons and marched to Villers-Cotterêts. From there, at half past seven, he wrote to Vandamme urging him not to lose a minute in making his way directly to Paris. Grouchy himself intended resuming his march at two in the morning, but at one o'clock, the Guard Light

Cavalry and Horse Artillery bivouacking outside Villers-Cotterêts were attacked by a division of Prussians. Taken by surprise, the French were completely routed, fleeing into the town and leaving fourteen cannon, twenty ammunition caissons and a hundred and fifty prisoners to the enemy.

*

In the days that followed Bonaparte's abdication, an unreal calm, even optimism, prevailed on the Paris boulevards. It was confidently asserted on Monday 26 June that the Prussian and Anglo-Allied armies had not even crossed the border into France because their losses on the 16th and 18th had been so great and 'they were too weak to take advantage of their success'. They trembled, some said, 'at the thought of setting their feet on the *territoire sacré de la Patrie*'. This was still believed the following day until the late afternoon, when the Ministry of War issued a bulletin, signed by Marshal Davout, announcing that the invading armies were in possession of the fortresses at Noyon, Saint-Quentin, Guise and Avesnes and that the Prussian advance guard had reached Compiègne, only forty miles north of the city. Cannon fire from the north-east could be heard at daybreak on the 28th as Prussian artillery bombarded Grouchy's headquarters in Villers-Cotterêts. The distant gunfire continued as the West Prussian Fusiliers launched an assault on the town, scattering the Guard infantry, some back to Soissons and some down the road to Paris. It continued as Grouchy rallied his forces, making a stand to the south-east, and as General Vandamme's long-awaited III Corps, marching from Soissons, joined the fighting. Sporadic gunfire could still be heard throughout the day as the remnants of Grouchy's corps retreated through Nanteuil and Dammartin to Claye; Vandamme's on a parallel route to the east, by way of La Ferté Milon, to Meaux.

That morning, the provisional government in Paris formally proclaimed a state of siege, and yet at eight o'clock in the evening the city seemed calm and John Scott's correspondent was amazed that there appeared to be so little anxiety, the Prussians being but a day's march away:

> Never . . . have I seen . . . so many genteel people on the Boulevard, from the *rue de la Paix* to the gate of *St Martin* . . . Crowds of elegant females were promenading, brought out by the critical state of public affairs, yet looking cheerfulness and confidence. Miserable remnants of half destroyed [French] regiments are passing constantly before these gay companies . . . The middle of the Boulevard is crowded with artillery, cavalry, and infantry . . . At the sides of these horrid trains of destruction, people are sitting on chairs, reading the newspapers, eating ice, sipping lemonade – examining the spectacle. Is it not more than probable that in a few hours these seats will be filled with the dead and dying? What reason have we to feel confident that Paris will not this time be sacked?

It was a concern felt by Colonel Frazer of the Royal Horse Artillery at Gonnesse three days later: 'Tomorrow may see Paris in flames,' he wrote. 'Blücher avows that he cannot be answerable for his people . . .' It was claimed that, at Louvres, Prussian soldiers plundered the very building in which their field marshal had his quarters, and, like an indulgent father, all he had to say in censure was '*Mes enfants, c'est trop.*' Frazer was marching in the wake of Blücher's army and had seen the devastation it left, the deserted villages, the gutted houses:

> Should then Paris be assaulted by these troops, what may not be expected! . . . Such is the fury of the Prussians, that I am convinced that if they enter Paris by assault, it will be impossible to check them . . . I hope and expect the British will not be suffered to enter Paris by assault. Let us keep our hands free from rapine and plunder.[9]

By contrast, less than a week later, Major William Turner, of the 13th Light Dragoons, listening to gunfire on the day of the

French capitulation, seemed sanguine at the prospect: 'We are waiting for the Prussians when that infernal city Paris will be attacked and no doubt pillaged for it is a debt we owe to the whole of Europe . . . The Prussians are . . . determined soldiers and I expect in one week Paris will be completely sacked and perhaps burned.'[10]

As the Prussian forces approached, French troops within the city sometimes appeared as great a threat to the populace as the enemy outside. Along with a flood of refugees from the outlying rural areas, 'peasants flocking in, with cartloads of furniture, cows, horses, sheep',[11] disordered bands of defeated soldiers had been arriving in the city for days, sometimes in twos, sometimes four, eight, ten at a time, demoralised malcontents who had deserted Soult's muster at Laon and fugitives from the combat at Villers-Cotterêts. An English resident of Paris, Helen Maria Williams, described the press at one of the principal northern gates of the city, the Porte Saint-Martin: 'the crowd of Parisians mingled with the peasantry and their cortège of wearied animals . . . Farther on, a portion of the remains of the imperial guard were marching along . . . thundering out "*Vive l'Empereur!*"' One of them lashed out with his sabre at an old man who had the impudence to shout '*Vive le Roi!*' and Miss Williams claimed that 'five or six persons [in one day] fell the victims of this forbidden exclamation by the hands of those pretorian [*sic*] bands'.[12] On 29 June, three people were said to have been killed 'in various parts of the Capital'[13] for the same offence, as were 'one or two men . . . in the boulevard Poissoniere' alone.[14] John Scott's correspondent reported:

The soldiers are all half drunk . . . with the ferocious expression of untameable brutes, their rage against the Royalists, the Prussians, and the English, is to the last degree ferocious . . . Everyone seems mostly to fear the French troops, and the infamous conduct of the Imperial Guard too well justifies the general terror of them.[15]

*

On 29 June, at Claye, twelve miles east of Paris, Grouchy reported to Davout on the state of his army. He had 4,000 infantry and 1,800 cavalry of the Imperial Guard, in addition to the cavalry divisions of General Jacquinot and General Piré. Also, two regiments remained from Pajol's 1st Cavalry Corps. In a skirmish at Nanteuil the day before, Pajol had lost two cannon, sixty men taken prisoner and an undisclosed number 'scattered and still to rejoin'. General d'Erlon was nine miles closer to the city, at Bondy, with a combined infantry and cavalry force Grouchy estimated at no more than 1,500. 'The troops I have here and those of the comte d'Erlon', he told the Minister of War,

> are so demoralized that they would scatter at the first gunshot
> . . . As a consequence . . . the government has only a very inad-
> equate number of men available, none of whom has shown any
> inclination to fight, and who are totally disorganised. I consider
> it my duty to inform you in all haste of this tragic situation so
> that the government does not delude itself over the forces avail-
> able for the defence of Paris that I am to lead.[16]

Grouchy marched his men out of Claye at midnight, entered Paris during the early hours of 30 June, and shortly afterwards resigned his luckless commission.

Also at midnight, the infantry of Vandamme's III Corps marched through the gates of the Château de Vincennes, Charles V's immense fourteenth-century fortress on the city's eastern outskirts. Vandamme had that day been appointed commander of all troops on the left bank of the Seine and two days later would lead the doomed defence of Paris to the south-west. Exelmans' cavalry marched on, past Vincennes and across the Seine, skirting the line of southern fortifications, to Gentilly and Montrouge.

At three o'clock the following afternoon, in his headquarters at La Villet on the northern outskirts of Paris, Marshal Davout signed a letter to the Chamber of Representatives deploring the projected reimposition of Bourbon rule. It was countersigned by seventeen of his staff, the foremost of whom being *general-en-chef*, the Comte Vandamme: 'We are in the presence of the enemy. We swear before you and the whole world that we will defend to our last breath the cause of our independence and the honour of the nation.'[17] Grouchy's signature was notably absent.

Twelve hours earlier, Miss Williams had been woken by cannon firing from the fortified high ground of Belleville on the north-eastern outskirts of the city, and from Montmartre further west. She recalled the terrifying cannonades of March the previous year, when Paris had last been under attack. She thought the present bombardment 'far less formidable'. Much of the noise was that of musketry, and even this 'slackened very sensibly at six in the morning',[18] ceasing altogether by three in the after-noon, at about the time Davout and his staff were declaring their determination to fight on.

John Scott's correspondent wrote that the guns heard on the plain of Saint-Denis, 'from two o'clock . . . 'til seven', were 'a false attack to cover a grand movement, the meaning of which [was] yet unknown'.[19] This was indeed the case. Marshal Blücher's orders for 30 June had called for 'probing' attacks by light infantry with cavalry support near Aubervilliers, on entrenchments between Saint-Denis and La Villet, and between La Villet and Pantin. The attacks were to start at one o'clock in the morning. If successful, cavalry was to 'move forward immediately on the plain between St Denis and Montmartre and spread panic'. If, however, the operation proved unsuccessful, the attacks were not to be pressed. Instead, the bulk of the army – I, III and IV Korps – was to 'prepare to march off to the right . . . as soon as possible', crossing the Seine downriver at Argenteuil, Bezons and Chatou, then sweeping round to break through the weaker defences on the south side of Paris. Prussian positions in the north were to be taken by Wellington's troops when his army arrived. The IV Korps was to mask the westward march by bombarding Saint-Denis, 'leading the enemy to believe that a serious attempt to assault that place [was] being made'. Troops were also instructed to leave their camp fires burning 'to conceal [their] march from the enemy'.[20]

Certain adjustments would be made to this strategy. Because the nearest of the Seine bridges had been destroyed by the French, first crossings were to be made by the III Korps on the still intact bridges at Saint-Germain and Maisons while a new bridge was constructed at Argenteuil. The I Korps was to follow the III Korps to Saint-Germain. Also, the IV Korps was to delay moving west until their positions in front of Saint-Denis, Le Bourget and Aubervilliers had been relieved by Wellington's advance guard, still seven miles away at Vaudherland.

The initial stages of the Prussian advance on the southern defences of Paris proceeded to plan. Saint-Germain was occupied by the III Korps and its bridgehead secured, as was Maisons further downstream. The I and IV Korps were marching west, and on 1 July, Blücher received a report that Versailles had been captured. Oberstlieutenant von Sohr had been sent with two regiments of hussars – about 650 men – in advance of the main force to reconnoitre the left bank of the river. He had seen off 'an insignificant number of [enemy] infantry [and] a few cavalry' on his approach and found the town of Versailles garrisoned by 1,200 National Guard, who promptly sent out a negotiator, 'opened the gates, declared themselves for the king and requested [Prussian] protection'. Sohr accepted the capitulation, pending Blücher's approval, disarmed most of the Guards and ordered them to remove the tricolour cockades from their hats. It was a hot day and Sohr's men took the opportunity to water their horses, to eat and rest on the place d'Armes in front of the palace, and even to replace worn saddles and other equipment from a nearby cavalry depot. They set out again at four o'clock in the afternoon. At seven, they were back at Versailles, greatly depleted in numbers, riding for their lives, and with General Exelmans' entire 2nd Cavalry Corps in pursuit: eight regiments of dragoons, with an additional six regiments of *chasseurs à cheval*, two regiments of lancers, a regiment of hussars, and several infantry battalions. Sohr's division had encountered part of this force outside the town of Villacoublay and fought a vigorous action, even achieving some measure of success, before being forced to withdraw the way they had come. Galloping through the streets of Versailles towards the gates that opened onto the road back towards Saint-Germain, they came under fire from houses either side manned by National Guards they had neglected to disarm earlier in the day. Reaching the far end of town, they found every way out defended by French infantry, while behind them Exelmans' cavalry closed in, street by street, from several directions. Major von Wins, commander of the 5th Hussars, succeeded in rallying a small number of his men, who cut their way clear. Of the 650 men of Sohr's command that had ridden into Versailles earlier in the day, 330 escaped. Seventy-four were dead, 130 wounded, the rest made prisoner. Because Sohr himself had been gravely injured, it fell to the unfortunate Wins to give Blücher the news: '[He] heard the report in growing anger and then cried out in rage. "Lord! If what you are saying is true, then I wish the devil had fetched you too!" With those words, Wins was sent off. [Blücher] was greatly outraged and shocked.'[21]

But within twenty-four hours Versailles was again in Prussian hands and Blücher had established his headquarters there. He would later demand two and a half million francs – about 100,000 pounds sterling – from the town in reparation for his two lost regiments.[22]

*

In Paris, the 'hopes of . . . patriots [were] elevated',[23] however briefly, by Exelmans' success. Captured Prussian horses were paraded in the place de la Révolution and a squadron of French cavalry galloped along the rue de Rivoli to the Tuileries palace, brandishing the two regimental standards taken in the action.

A couple of days earlier, when there had been an expectation of a major battle to the north, Miss Williams remarked on the attraction felt by fashionable ladies to military spectacle. 'Had not the Parisian women been refused egress,' she speculated, 'curiosity might perhaps have got the better of fear; they would have risked a wound in the hope that it did not disfigure their faces, and the plains of St Denis might have been strewed, not only with wrecks of cabriolets and pleasure carts, but with hats, caps, and other articles of millinery baggage.' On 2 July, as the projected theatre of conflict shifted around to the south-west, the attraction was felt again. 'Many persons went in their carriages to the bridge of [Iena], which is the passage to the field. As the carriages arrived near the bridge they were immediately put in requisition; the persons within were desired to alight, and were told . . . that their carriages were borrowed to transport the wounded.' Those who protested were told 'that if they did not withdraw [they themselves would be] requisition[ed] to attend the wounded'.[24] As fighting began in the late afternoon, civilian spectators sought elevated ground within the city walls, and until midnight, cannon fire could be both heard and seen 'from the heights of Chaillot, which were crowded by people with telescopes'.[25]

Despite the roadblock at the Pont d'Iena, 'many people left Paris to watch the fighting', according to General Gneisenau, 'and the Parisians witnessed the defeat of their troops'.[26] By half past ten that night, the Prussians had advanced westward from Versailles, through Sèvres, Bellevue, Meudon and Moulineaux and had succeeded in occupying the villages of Issy, Vanves and Châtillon, while the French forces had been pushed back on Vaugirard and Montrouge. General Vandamme's chief of staff rode out to request a ceasefire. The request was refused.

During the six days since their first attempt to arrange an armistice, at Laon, plenipotentiaries of the provisional government had made several approaches to the two allied commanders, each one rejected: politely by Wellington and with characteristic contempt by Blücher.

Wellington was insistent that an agreement for the orderly restoration of Louis XVIII to the throne of France was a prerequisite and the only guarantee of a lasting future peace in Europe.

He was equally insistent that the alternatives proposed by factions in the provisional government – such as the King's cousin Louis Philippe, Duc d'Orléans, taking his place, or Bonaparte's infant son continuing his dynasty as Emperor Napoleon II – were alike unacceptable. Blücher concurred in his abhorrence for a Bonaparte succession but was otherwise indifferent. 'It doesn't interest us whether you take back the Bourbons or restore the Republic,' General Gneisenau, speaking for his master, told one French delegation. 'You may choose any government you like, except that of Bonaparte and his family.'[27] Leaving aside the succession as a matter of little importance, Blücher maintained that the surrender and occupation of Paris was the most reliable assurance of a lasting ceasefire. For the French negotiators this was the last obstacle to agreement. Honour called for a final gesture of defiance.

At three o'clock on 3 July, twenty French guns opened fire out of the morning mist on General Zieten's forces at Issy. The bombardment was followed by an infantry attack, driven back with difficulty and heavy casualties by the Prussians. A second, stronger attack followed at 5.30, also repulsed with the aid of timely reinforcements. Then, at seven o'clock, the French artillery fell silent and Vandamme's chief of staff again rode out under a flag of truce. This time General Zieten was able to report to Blücher that the city had capitulated. Later that day, at Saint-Cloud, as he awaited the arrival of the French generals and plenipotentiaries to finalise the terms of the armistice, the Prussian field marshal wrote to his wife. He still brooded over the recent losses. 'I hope to God [they] will be the last in this war! I am sick of the killing.'[28]

Of the eighteen articles that comprised the Military Convention of Paris signed at Saint-Cloud, that of most immediate importance was the second: 'Tomorrow the French army shall commence its march, to retire behind the Loire. The total evacuation of Paris shall be effected in three days, and its movement of retiring behind the Loire shall be finished in eight days.'[29] The vast exodus, eighty miles south, to the opposite side of a stretch of the Loire linking

Bloi, Beaugency, Orléans and Gien, began a day late, on 5 July, and was completed by the 11th. The French army was allowed 'to take with it its stores, field artillery, military convoys, horses, and property of the regiments, without exception'.[30] Prussian troops, following each of the eight columns, ensured that no stragglers or potential marauders were left behind, and had orders to report any deviations taken from the main roads.

Wellington's army occupied the northern and western suburbs of Paris, including a camp for 20,000 men in the Bois de Boulogne. They also guarded the northern gates of the city, and for many tourists entering Paris through the Porte Saint-Martin or the Porte Saint-Denis during the following months, 'the singular and encouraging spectacle of a Highland soldier quietly keeping sentry'[31] might have been the first military presence they would encounter. As stipulated in Article IX of the convention, 'The interior duty of Paris . . . continue[d] to be performed by the National Guard, and by corps of municipal gendarmes.' At Wellington's suggestion, his Prussian liaison officer General Müffling was appointed military governor of the city.

Wellington denied himself 'the vain triumph of entering Paris at the head of [his] victorious troops'.[32] Not so Marshal Blücher, who insisted on the Prussian army making its presence felt in a display of overbearing strength. On 6 July, Zieten's I Korps deployed three infantry battalions, a squadron of cavalry and an artillery battery at each of the eleven gates on the south side of the city. These troops were to have the honour of entering Paris first. The following day, they took possession: the 1st Brigade occupied every bridge from the Pont Neuf to the Pont d'Austerliz, the Ile St Louis, the Ile de la Cité and the 9th Arrondissement; the 2nd Brigade took the Palais de Luxembourg; the 3rd Brigade occupied the Champ de Mars, the Hotel des Invalides and all the bridges downriver from the Pont Neuf; the 4th Brigade claimed the place de la Concorde, the Tuileries and the Louvre. Zieten's reserve cavalry and artillery bivouacked on the Champs-Élysées, his baggage trains on the Champ de Mars, and a loaded cannon was placed at either end of the Pont des

Arts and the Pont Royal. Thielemann's III Korps marched in on 8 July and Bülow's IV Korps on the 9th. An English officer in the commissariat department watched a parade of 'upwards of 50,000 men [march] through the town . . . with a full band of trumpets and bugle-horns sounding triumphal marches! The infantry had their bayonets fixed, the cavalry their swords drawn, and the artillery not only their guns loaded, but matches burning.'[33]

This show of military might was, Blücher admitted, purely 'a matter of honour'. His army had been 'greatly insulted' at not being allowed to occupy Paris the previous year, and this time, 'after it has achieved more than then', there was to be no repeat of such slighting treatment. He did not intend his men to be quartered there for long, however. Their honour appeased, 'the army will be satisfied', he assured Wellington, 'and Paris will have only a short, friendly visit'.[34] Some, however, were far from satisfied at having only their honour appeased. Article XI of the convention stipulated that 'Public property . . . shall be respected', while Article XII extended that respect to 'the property of individuals'. Sergeant Wheeler and his comrades of the 51st Regiment had 'passed three days reconing [sic] on the rich booty we should possess, if we stormed the capital'.[35] The English surgeon John Haddy James observed: 'The Prussians seem sulky that Paris was not pillaged.' Although a humane and cultivated man, he shared the desire for retribution on the French:

If it had been put to the vote, mine would have gone for [the city's] destruction, beautiful as it is. It is most provoking that the Allies seem to be doing everything in their power towards mercy for this city that deserves none, and in six months after our departure they will have forgotten that we were ever here. As it is they believe it to be owing to some mistake that they were beaten at all.[36]

Public opinion in London was inclined to agree. '[People] want . . . to pillage Paris', the MP Henry Grey Bennet wrote to Thomas

Creevey, 'and the ladies of the fashionable world to massacre its inhabitants. I assure you we are very bloody in this town, and people talk of making great examples.'[37] Such opinion would have been mightily cheered by the belligerent tone attributed to the Duke of Wellington in *The Times* of 28 June: 'It is asserted that Lord WELLINGTON has issued a proclamation that if a shot is fired against his troops, he will lay Paris in ashes.' The assertion was, however, a fabrication.

Writing home to his wife from a camp outside the city walls, Sergeant William Tennant of the 1st Foot Guards expressed the regret of the common soldier: 'It would have been glorious sport for our army if we had taken [Paris] by storm, there would have been plenty of plunder and we should all have been as rich as Jews.' But on reflection he thought it 'better as it is as many thousand would have lost their lives'.[38]

*

During the week following the armistice, as the allies took control of Paris, Louis XVIII held temporary court at Saint-Denis, and it was here, on 6 July, that Fouché was granted an audience to declare his loyalty and to be reappointed Minister of Police. Another arch-intriguer, Napoleon's former Foreign Minister, Charles Maurice de Talleyrand-Périgord, accompanied him into the royal presence, Fouché attentively supporting the crippled former bishop. 'Vice leaning on the arm of crime',[39] François de Chateaubriand observed. Both men had voted, in January 1793, for the execution of Louis XVI, and to Chateaubriand it was as if the King was now shaking the hands that had all but thrust his brother's head under the guillotine blade. Neither Fouché nor Talleyrand would remain in office long after the restoration, but for that moment it was a time for compromise and reconciliation, however distasteful.

There were other, less cynical demonstrations of loyalty as Bourbon sympathisers rode out to Saint-Denis to greet their king. They judged it advisable, however, to keep their white cockades in their pockets until well clear of the Paris barriers, to avoid molestation by the anti-royalist mobs that still held sway, 'fearless of the English or Prussian bayonets', during this interim period. A family of Miss Williams's acquaintance neglected such precautions:

> Decorated with white flowers and white cockades . . . they disdained to conceal them at their return . . . Their carriage was assailed by vollies of stones, and their ears by the cry of 'Traitorous royalists! Hang them up, à la lantern!' &c. The gentleman was already dragged from his carriage, when the national guard interposed, and saved him, his trembling wife, and daughter, from the further assaults of the populace.[40]

On 8 July, order imposed by the National Guard, the city being 'perfectly quiet', and His Majesty's safety assured, Louis XVIII entered Paris to loud acclamation and some dissenting voices. Over the following months, a series of trials would be conducted of individuals shouting 'Vive Napoleon!' in the streets. One such case of prosecution for 'seditious cries' concerned several people who had done so on the very day of the King's arrival. Counsel for the defence argued unsuccessfully that the prisoners had cried out from mere force of habit: 'par l'habitude, pas par l'intention'. The prosecution countered with the argument that this was plainly impossible, since they had had plenty of time to get used to the change of regime, the King having entered Paris 'two good hours before'.[41] Such 'seditious cries' were not the only affront to the dignity of Louis XVIII. On one occasion a large pig was dressed up to resemble the King, in a blue sash, a coat and plumed hat, and paraded along the boulevards to the accompaniment of royalist songs and shouts of 'Vive le Roi!'[42] With the re-establishment of the monarchy, continued loyalty to the Emperor was demonstrated not by the traditional tricolour cockade but by the more discreet 'red pink' – or carnation. Even these, however, could be a cause of dissension, of scuffles in the crowds thronging the Tuileries gardens, and of the occasional arrest.

*

Before midnight on 8 July, Wellington received reports that Blücher had given orders for the destruction of the Pont d'Iena. This most recent bridge over the Seine – stone heroes and horses at either end, and each side adorned with four imperial carved eagles – had been completed only two years previously. It was named in commemoration of the October 1806 battle that had effectively destroyed the Prussian army as a fighting force and led to the French occupation of Berlin. The bridge was a reminder of his country's most crushing and ignominious defeat, and Blücher's vengeful feelings were understandable. Notwithstanding Article XI of the convention signed just five days previously – that 'Public property . . . shall be respected, and the allied powers will not interfere in any manner in its management, or in its conduct'[43] – Prussian engineers were already at work removing pieces of masonry from two of the bridge's five graceful arches, and laying explosive charges to blow it up, when Wellington intervened. 'As this measure will certainly create a good deal of disturbance in the town,' he wrote to his ally, 'I take the liberty of suggesting to you to delay the destruction of the bridge . . . till I can have the pleasure of seeing you to-morrow morning.'[44] The Duke persuaded Blücher to wait until the rest of the allied powers had arrived in Paris, when a consensus could be sought and a ruling made on the matter. The demolition work was halted, although a precautionary British guard was placed on the contentious structure, to ensure the reprieve was not violated by the Prussians. 'They did not dare blow my men up,'[45] Wellington remarked privately.

Parisian anxiety about Prussian reprisals persisted, however. Blücher had demanded a hundred million francs – about four million pounds sterling – in reparation from the city, and threatened that 'the *Faubourg St Germain* would be given up to pillage' if it was not paid within three days. 'The sight of the Prussian bivouacs . . . in the place du Carousel is enough to inspire every terror,'[46] wrote the English MP and friend of Lord Byron, John Hobhouse. Prussian muskets were piled under the windows of the King's apartments in the Tuileries palace, matches smouldered by their loaded cannon and 'the interior of [Bonaparte's] triumphal arch [was used as] their slaughterhouse'.[47]

While the victorious combatants of the Belgian campaign had marched on Paris from the north-east, other armies – victorious by association with their allies rather than by feats of arms – were entering France from the south-east and east. 'A vast Russian army' of 90,000 men, including 5,000 Cossacks, came through Franconia into Lorraine, its advance guard arriving on the outskirts of Paris by 8 July.[48] An Austrian army came through the Alps, occupying first Geneva then Lyons, while another, supported by Bavarian forces, crossed from the Rhineland into Alsace. By mid-July, Paris was an international armed camp.

Then came the rulers of the four great European powers – Lord Castlereagh representing the British Prince Regent; King Frederick William III of Prussia; the Emperor Francis I of Austria; and the Russian Tsar Alexander I – with their attendant ministers and commissioners, to sit in congress on the sanctions against France. The Tsar used his influence at an early stage to ensure the preservation of the Pont d'Iena, although in deference to Prussia, the designation of the bridge was changed, taking its name from the institution directly opposite its southern extremity across the Field of Mars: the Pont d'École Militaire.

IV

DURING the previous year, thousands of foreign tourists had taken advantage of the brief interlude of peace following the first allied occupation of Paris, and Bonaparte's first abdication and exile, to visit the Louvre and view the pillaged treasures amassed by conquest from across Europe. With the second occupation and abdication, Paris was again a centre of artistic pilgrimage, the Louvre its principal shrine and fashionable promenade. 'From half past two o'clock till four the gallery is crowded,' the connoisseur Henry Milton observed:

> It is the general rendezvous of the English, and appears to supply extremely well the absence of Bond Street. The ladies sit on the benches, which are placed opposite the chief pictures, and look sideways at the gentlemen: the gentlemen walk up and down in long uncivil rows, and look full at the ladies: and of the immense crowds of visitors from England who throng the Louvre, and doubtless would all assert that they came for the express purpose of studying its contents, it is laughable to observe how very few are really attentive to the treasures that surround them.[1]

Writing from Brussels, Georgy Capel was amused by what she had heard of the French capital and its attractions: 'Shoals of English are flocking there to see every thing [and] one would think from the precipitancy with which they flew there the moment that they heard that the white flag had been hoisted, that they thought Paris would run away.'[2] Parts, however, were to do just that. The spectacular display at the Louvre, in particular, was all too transient, and within three months, areas of the museum would be 'little more than a wilderness of empty frames'.

The Prussian pictures were the first to go, along with those belonging to the neighbouring German states of Hesse, Saxony and the province west of the Rhine. Following signature of the Military Convention outside Paris on 3 July, Blücher wrote to the Louvre's director general, Dominique Vivant Denon, demanding the immediate restitution of all German artistic property. Denon had been personally responsible for many of the seizures from the German states. In October 1807, a year after the battle of Iena, he had mounted an exhibition occupying four large rooms of the Louvre, comprising just one third of a total thousand or so pieces of artistic plunder – or *Kunstraub* – resulting from the German campaign. Confronted by Blücher's demands and the prospect of surrendering these acquisitions, Denon prevaricated. By 11 July, whatever patience Blücher had was exhausted and a company of the 19th Prussian Infantry Regiment – men who had fought the French at Wavre – marched in to the museum and the work of restitution began. Blücher would later defend himself against the charge of undiplomatic behaviour, in characteristically undiplomatic terms:

As my conduct has been publicly animadverted upon, for not having allowed the property plundered from Prussia by Banditti to remain in the Museum of the Louvre, I have only to remark that . . . I pursued *thieves* who had despoiled many of the nations of Europe of their inestimable Monuments of the Fine arts; I attacked and dispersed them, and restore to my Country the Plunder they had unjustly taken . . . They may now thank Providence for our not following their base example.[3]

Catalogues on sale to visitors from hawkers at the door frequently made no secret of the provenance of works in the collection, entries for some exhibits listing the town and country, the palace, gallery, church or cathedral, from which they had been taken. Marshal Blücher is said to have walked through the Louvre with his aides, catalogue in hand, occasionally pausing in front of one masterpiece or another and consulting the relevant entry. 'From the Dresden Gallery! O yes – I recollect it – take it down.'[4] The picture would then be taken from the wall while he moved on to the next. If a French official made any objection, perhaps that the painting had not been stolen from Dresden but from some other collection, Blücher silenced him with a curt *Tais toi* – hold your tongue – or in more forceful German: *Halt maul!*[5]

Paintings by Corregio – Dresden had been particularly rich in Corregios – were seized in this way, as was a late Rubens, *The Crucifixion of St Peter,* that had been taken from the church of St Peter in Cologne. A Roman bronze statue, known as the *Ganymede of Sanssouci*, and a Roman marble, the *Girl Playing Knucklebones*, from Frederick the Great's summer palace at Potsdam, were also reclaimed. Rembrandt's *Samson Threatening his Father-in-Law* was taken down, destined for return to Cassel, along with Rubens' *Coronation of Mars by Victory*, and a marble Apollo. Another male nude in bronze – its raised arms suggesting to Helen Williams a 'Gladiator giving thanks to the gods for a victory just obtained'[6] – was crated for Berlin, as were the four bronze horses and chariot taken from the top of the Brandenburg Gate. All these works, together with 'some valuable pieces of the old German school', and a great many others, left Paris in two consignments, the first on 16 July, the second a week later.

The works claimed by Blücher 'were few in number', according to Henry Milton, 'and comparatively of little interest'. The losses had not disturbed the integrity of the Louvre's collection and for some time no further demands were made on M. Denon, who doubtless decided, as John Scott remarked:

That the best way would be to keep very quiet as to the proceedings of Prussia, – to affect to take no notice of them whatever, – hoping that silence might cause the affair to die away after the removals were over, – and that either the dull indifference or the singular good-nature of the states of Europe, might yet leave to Paris the darling boast of being the capital of the world as to Fine Art.[7]

But by the end of August, Austrian troops were reportedly stripping the walls of paintings belonging to the Emperor Francis's Italian dominions of Lombardy and Venetia, 'the vacant frames . . . left hanging . . . as if to remind the French of the humiliation to which they [were] reduced'.[8] Herr Rosa, keeper of the Imperial Gallery of Paintings in Vienna, had been sent to Paris to reclaim pictures taken from the Austrian capital in 1805 and 1809, and by late September was said to have 'already packed up 300 pictures by the first masters'.[9]

Also in September, King William I of the Netherlands, seeking the restitution of paintings and sculpture from Holland and Belgium – his 'undoubted property' – was pursuing diplomatic channels. His minister, having received satisfaction neither from Denon nor from the French government in the person of the Prince de Talleyrand, spoke to the Duke of Wellington, in his capacity as commander-in-chief of the Dutch army. Wellington advised him to write an official note to Castlereagh outlining the issue, and a copy was laid before 'the Ministers of the Allied Sovereigns assembled in Conference'. The matter was fully discussed and due consideration given to discovering 'a mode of doing justice to the [claims] without hurting the feelings of the King of France'. When no response came from the French government, the Dutch minister again approached Wellington, requesting him to employ British troops to secure the disputed works. Wellington referred the request to the Ministers of the Allied Sovereigns, and with their approval went to see Talleyrand 'and begged him to state the case to the King [of France], and to ask him . . . to point out the mode of effecting the object of the King of the Netherlands which should be least offensive to His Majesty'. Talleyrand promised him an answer by the following evening. No such answer forthcoming, Wellington again called on Talleyrand, 'at night', and was told 'that the king could give no orders upon it'; that the Duke 'might act as [he] thought proper'; and that he 'might communicate with M. Denon'. In the morning, Wellington sent his aide, Lieutenant Colonel Fremantle, to discuss the matter with Denon, who informed him 'that he had no orders to give any pictures out of the gallery, and that he could give none without the use of force'. Tiring of diplomacy, the Duke sent Fremantle to Talleyrand with an ultimatum: 'that the troops would go the next morning at twelve o'clock to take possession of the King of Netherland's pictures; and . . . that, if any disturbance resulted from this measure, the King's Ministers, and not [Wellington], were responsible'.

He later claimed that it was not, after all, necessary to send British troops, 'excepting as a working party to assist in taking [the pictures] down and packing them'.[10] But this was not how it appeared to John Scott when he visited the museum that day: 'I found a guard of 150 British riflemen drawn up outside. I asked one of the soldiers what they were there for? "Why, they tell me Sir, that they mean to take away the pictures," was his reply.' Scott went in and downstairs to the sculpture gallery. A short time later, he was distracted from contemplating the marbles by the sound of 'a sudden rushing of feet'. He reached the bottom of the main staircase in time to see 'the English guard hastily tramping up . . . a crowd of astounded French . . . in their rear, – and, from above, many of the visitors to the Gallery of Pictures . . . attempting to force their way past the ascending soldiers, catching an alarm from their sudden entrance'. There were, it was felt, good reasons for alarm. Tension in this city under occupation gave rise to 'daily reports of the probability of convulsions, massacres, insurrections'. It was further believed that the Louvre, a focus of national pride and – with its collections under threat – a simultaneous focus of national humiliation, would be a likely setting for just such an 'explosion of popular fury' as might summon 150 armed men to suppress it in a

bloody massacre. The green-uniformed troops reached the top
of the staircase and stamped on in the direction of the Grand
Galerie. Scott watched from among the nervous crowd as an
officer deployed his men, a single file along each wall. A bark
of command and the soldiers 'stopped as machines', facing
each other and at intervals from one end of this vast quarter-
mile-long perspective to its tiny extremity; then the implied
threat as they untied protective oilskins from the flintlocks of
their rifles. But nothing happened. 'The bustle, and dust, and
buz of the armed men, and of the curious, agitated crowds,
presented a marked contrast to the tranquil dignity of the
Raphaels and Titians on the walls, which . . . were the causes
of all this hurley burley.'[11]

The spectacle of English soldiers on guard in the Louvre was
nothing new. As early as mid-July, Captain Mercer had seen them
on the landing of the great staircase and 'leaning on their rifles'
all along the Grand Galerie, 'whether to preserve order or the
pictures, [he] knew not'.[12] Following Blücher's seizures, the
building had been effectively under martial law, and apart from
a nominal contingent of the French National Guard, sentry duty
was taken in turn by British and Austrian troops, 'the Prussians
[declaring] that they had done their own business for themselves,
and would not now incur odium for others'.[13] Towards the end
of September, however, because the King of the Netherlands' claim
on the Flemish paintings had been exercised on British authority
and by British force of arms, even routine guard duty appeared
as an atrocity to French pride and the odium of public opinion
fell on the Duke of Wellington. 'It has tarnished [his] laurels',
wrote Lady Malmesbury, 'and the glory of the battle of Waterloo
is effaced by the storming of the Louvre.'[14] Relations were not
improved by spurious press reports that the *Apollo Belvedere*
was being sent to London.

There had been some demonstrations of anti-English feeling
from the beginning of the occupation: 'British officers [had]
on many occasions been openly insulted in the streets by [the
citizenry]. On some they vented their spleen, by spitting on

them from the windows; others have been hissed and called names that would disgrace the [slums of the] Faubourg St Antoine.'[15] In the main, however, the English were well regarded, if only by comparison with the hated Prussians, and antagonism was of a light-hearted nature. The Théatre des Variétés presented a mildly satirical play by Charles Augustin Sewrin called *Les Anglaises pour Rire*. It provoked a minor riot when a Guards sergeant and some of his men invaded the stage one night in protest at its mockery of English women.[16] Thereafter, the French regarded it as a triumph whenever English troops attended a performance and subjected them- selves to the raillery, although they were often surprised it was taken in good part. 'Is it possible *you* can laugh at this?' a Parisienne asked of a young officer. 'Yes, madame,' he replied, 'those who win may laugh!'[17]

But with the stripping of the Louvre there was a hardening of relations, and by the time he attended the Salle Favart at the invitation of legendary soprano Angelica Catalani on Monday 2 October, Wellington was left in no doubt of the change:

He appeared about the middle of the entertainment, with a military friend, both in plain clothes, and in the King's box. His Grace's appearance . . . was instantly caught at by the sensitive audience . . . The Duke was hissed and insulted from all sides . . . The bolder among the hissers . . . found courage enough to pronounce the name of '*Milord Villinton*'. [Shouts of] '*À bas Milord Villinton*,' rained thick upon him. In a few minutes he retired . . . On his departure, cries of '*Vive le Roi!*' were repeated round the house.[18]

Louis XVIII had ordered the museum closed while the Flemish pictures were removed, 'being naturally anxious, that the public should not witness so humiliating a transaction'.[19] The closure lasted only a day, however. A Prussian officer arrived with orders from General Müffling that it be reopened immediately, as if to make it publicly clear that the pictures were being taken back 'by force, and a guard of English soldiers there for the purpose'.[20]

The French National Guardsman on duty explained his own orders and pointed to His Majesty's written injunction on a placard nailed to the door. The Prussian manhandled the guard out of the way. 'He then tore down the placard, saying that he cared no more for the orders of Louis, than he did for his Guard.' Fragments of the notice remained attached to the door for days as evidence of what had happened. Thereafter the museum stayed open to the public no matter how humiliating the stripping of its treasures. Henry Milton witnessed the removal of two paintings by Rubens, originally from Antwerp Cathedral: the *Raising of the Cross* and the *Descent from the Cross*. He made no mention of a British military presence, either as guard or working party. Instead, the pictures were taken off the wall by a gang of French workmen 'of the lowest class', apparently well paid because 'they all seemed in high spirits', and a number of them clearly drunk. A group of Belgian commissioners directed the order in which the works were to be taken down. When the huge paintings had been lowered, one of the commissioners became so excited that he danced around them as they lay side by side on the floor. It was the 'happiest day of his existence', he told everyone. He was a native of Antwerp, and 'now he could go to church in comfort'. He did not even care how soon he died once the pictures were safe at home because 'their return was the only wish of his heart'. Milton feared that between the dancing Belgian and the drunken French, some accidental damage might be done to the paintings, but 'none of them sustained any injury'.[21]

The removal of these huge pictures by Rubens – and not only those belonging to Antwerp, but also to Ghent and to Bruges and to Brussels – left behind in the Grand Galerie a distinct air of desolation. 'The sublimity of its orderly aspect [had] vanished,' observed John Scott. 'It took now the melancholy, confused, dissolute air of a large auction room after a day's sale . . . It seemed as if a nation had become ruined through improvidence, and was selling off.'[22] And Antonio Canova had not even begun to stake the claims of the Pope.

His Holiness Pius VII had sent the celebrated sculptor to Paris
on a mission to negotiate the return of 'works of art ravished
from Rome, and the several Churches, Convents, and palaces of
Italy'. Canova reportedly met with a cold reception from the
Russian minister, who declared that his master Tsar Alexander
'would not suffer a single picture or bust to be displaced, as they
belonged to the French King'.[23] The Russian Emperor's concilia-
tory policy towards Louis XVIII was in line with his earlier
intervention to save the Pont d'Iena from Prussian explosives. It
was based on the principle that the first Treaty of Paris, signed
by the allies and the French government in May 1814, had
contained no provision whatsoever for the restitution of works
of art. If such works had been the legitimate property of the
French head of state in 1814, the Tsar argued, they remained so
a year later no matter what mischief had been wrought by
Napoleon in the meantime. Whatever the legal niceties of the
case, London's *Morning Chronicle* was outraged: 'Because [Russia]
herself has lost nothing – nay, gained everything, and marched
in this last campaign her numerous armies, on a jaunt of pleasure
and profit, without spilling one drop of blood, or spending a
single rouble – She, forsooth, affects to advocate the pretensions
of France!'[24]

The validity of the Pope's claims was in fact questionable.
The Vatican plunder had come to Paris under the terms of the
1797 Treaty of Tolentino and was thereby ratified by international law. Nevertheless, in the prevailing climate of restitution, Canova had the support of the British Foreign Secretary
Lord Castlereagh, whose government supplied 100,000 francs
for the packing and transportation of the Pope's restored
treasure. But it was to Castlereagh's Under Secretary of State
for Foreign Affairs, Sir William Hamilton, that Canova would
acknowledge the greatest debt of gratitude. Sir William was
himself no stranger to plunder. In 1801, following the battle
of Alexandria, he had snatched the Rosetta Stone from the
French for the British Museum, and the following year he was
instrumental in carrying off the Parthenon marbles for Lord

Elgin. He now brought all his diplomatic skills to bear on persuading the French King to agree to the Pope's demands. At the end of September, the work began. Canova wrote happily to a friend in London:

> The cause of the Fine Arts is at length safe into port; and it is to the generous and unremitted exertions of the British Minister, Lord Castlereagh, and Mr Secretary Hamilton, that Rome will be indebted for thus triumphing in the demands I came hither to make in her name. What gratitude ought we not to feel towards the magnanimous British nation! Fully does she deserve that the arts, in return for this generous act, should join hand in hand to raise a perpetual monument to her name; but the best and the more lasting monument will be engraved in the heart of every Italian, who on beholding the sacred objects torn from their country, again restored to her, will recollect the nation that stood forth as their advocate for this restitution, and will call down upon her the blessings of Providence.[25]

In the first week of October, the noise of sawing and hammering wood for the construction of packing crates made the gallery sound like a timber yard.

While many recognised the justice in returning Europe's plunder whence it came, there were mixed feelings even so. Colonel Frazer of the Royal Horse Artillery thought the process of restitution fair but at the same time regretted it, for no other reason than that 'assemblage of so many noble paintings in one place affords a facility to their inspection'.[26] As a marble female nude was carried out feet first, a French onlooker accosted an English Peninsular veteran: 'Sir, is it not a shame of your General to sanction the removal of these exquisite models, collected by the Emperor with paternal care from every country in Europe and now so well calculated to be seen by all those nations and free of expense too?'[27]

Throughout the months of July, August and September, while the fate of the Louvre collection was being decided, Henry

Milton deplored the 'trivial sights of this gaudy city' that distracted him for even an hour from the vast treasure house. He foresaw a day – 'the contents of the Louvre . . . scattered over Europe, never again to be seen except by the rich and idle few' – when he would remember not having taken fullest advantage 'with astonishment and regret'. As the debacle gathered momentum, others felt the same hectic urgency, and 'the troop of connoisseurs enter[ed] the doors every morning in fearful expectation that some of their favourites may have disappeared'. Miss Williams arrived hoping for her last sight of a sculpture the poet James Thomson had once described as 'the statue that enchants the world', and found a vacant pedestal, with the iron rail still round it, bits of wood scattered about the floor 'and the remainder of the hay used in the packing'.[28] An old attendant spoke to her. 'Ah! Madam, she is gone, I shall never see her again!'

'Gone!' said Williams.

'Yes, madam, she set out this very morning at three o'clock, *and under escort.*' The so-called *Medici Venus* had begun its journey back to Florence. It was said that the English painter Thomas Lawrence, Canova and his fellow sculptor Francis Chantrey were present to see the statue loaded on to its cart. Chantrey and Canova were overcome with emotion; the Englishman at the beauty of the piece, the Italian from happiness that it was at last 'going home'. Both men 'burst into tears [while] a German officer who stood by laughed at them'.[29]

A couple of days later, Miss Williams saw another celebrated work being crated for Rome, surrounded by grieving French artists. 'There lay the *Apollo* [*Belvedere*] on the floor, in his coffin. The workmen were busied in preparing him for his journey, by wedging him in his shell.' One of the onlookers was making a final drawing of the face, and continued right up until the moment that a workman's trowel spread the thick protective layer of plaster of Paris across the 'divine visage'. It was a touching moment. '[Apollo's] arm was still majestically stretched out [and the] artists . . . wept over it – they pressed his hand to their lips, and bade him a last adieu.' This and the *Laocoön* were the most revered works in the collection and the most devastating losses. 'Every spectator who leaves them', wrote the Scottish advocate James Simpson, 'seems to go away to die.'[30]

Someone lost his grip on Raphael's thirteen-foot-high altarpiece of the *Transfiguration* as it was being lowered flat to the ground, causing it to fall the remaining distance with a crash. The watching artists shuddered, as the picture was known to be so worm-eaten that the boards of which it was made were in places not an eighth of an inch thick. Dust, puffed from the worm holes, radiated across the floor. 'It required some courage to inspect it,' wrote Miss Williams. 'Happily it was found not damaged.' The removal of the *Transfiguration* was a particular blow to French pride. Loosely translated, the catalogue entry had read: 'It is due to Victory that France owns this, the masterpiece destined for her.'[31]

As the task of international restitution proceeded, there was, inevitably, occasional pilferage. A Prussian officer was observed in the company of two ladies who happened to admire a couple of small paintings. '*Voulez-vous les avoir?*' he asked. 'Would you like to have them?' And so saying, he unhooked the pictures from the wall and 'each woman put one in her shawl and walked off'.[32]

By the end of November, only 256 pictures were left in the Grand Galerie. Compared with the number listed in the catalogues, it was calculated that 1,115 paintings had been removed.[33] 'So forlorn a place I never saw', wrote an English visitor. 'Fine gilt frames in heaps – bare walls – and here and there a few paintings of little value. The gallery of Statues is in a still worse condition, and there seems to be little disposition to arrange, repair, and beautify what they have left.'[34]

*

The abuse that Wellington was subjected to by Parisians at the Salle Favant on 2 October had been given added fuel by the seizure of trophies particularly dear to them only two days before. These objects were not taken from the Palais du Louvre, but from outside, and within view of its windows.

'Of all the long train of humiliations to which Paris has been forced to submit', declared Henry Milton, removal of the *Quadriga* – a team of four antique bronze horses – from the top of the triumphal arch in the place du Carousel, 'was by far the most severe'. This structure had been 'a perpetually recurring annoyance' to Milton on his daily walks to and from the Louvre:

> It is contemptible in itself and absurd in its position. The arch stands in the centre of the Place . . . The four horses . . . placed on its summit abreast, and close to each other, harnessed to a triumphal car, and led by two figures representing Victory and [France]. The horses are of the natural size, these figures [are] colossal: and with a want of judgement, and a depravity of taste, astonishing even in Paris, the car, the figures, the harness, and all the other ridiculous appendages of the bronze horses, are sumptuously gilded. To build a puny arch of fine marble is no great offence; but to crowd together on its summit the matchless Venetian horses, to hide them from observation by disproportioned figures, a cumbrous car, and gaudy discordant trappings, is a transgression not easily to be pardoned.[35]

The Emperor of Austria had claimed the *Quadriga* on behalf of his Venetian dominion, and the horses were to be returned to their rightful place on the front of St Mark's basilica. So potently symbolic of Napoleonic conquest were they that it was believed that 'the mere attempt [to remove them] would cause a universal insurrection; and that the Allies might yet have to mourn the vengeance of an enraged and insulted populace'. For this reason, and from delicacy to the national pride of the French King, whose windows in the Tuileries palace overlooked the arch, it was decided that the horses be removed under cover of darkness. The Austrians having no one competent to undertake the

engineering operation, the Duke of Wellington had appointed
Major Todd of the Royal Staff Corps to supervise it. On a night
in late September, Todd – and Lieutenant Basil Jackson, who
came along to observe – with a few other officers and some
twenty pioneers, set to with hammers and chisels, loosening the
horses' hooves from the stonework. The noise, however, attracted
the attention of a group of National Guards, who came clattering
up the staircase, burst out on top of the arch and placed the
Englishmen under arrest. 'For the first time within the memory
of man,' observed Jackson, 'a British position was carried at the
point of the bayonet.'[36] At the bottom of the arch a hooting
French crowd had gathered, delighted at the embarrassment of
their conquerors. By the morning, word had spread 'how the
English mounted to steal the horses, how they had . . . feared
to do it by day, and how nicely they had been fetched down in
the night'.[37]

Released after a couple of hours, Todd reported to Wellington.
It was decided that King Louis XVIII's feelings were to be spared
no longer and that the horses would be taken down in the glare
of day and in full public view. On the morning of 30 September,
3,000 Austrian troops assembled in the place du Carousel. Along
three sides of the square, ranked two deep, was a body of cuirassiers in white uniforms, steel breastplates, and black and gold
helmets; in front of them were two battalions of Hungarian
Guards, also dressed in white, and the whole force was flanked
by artillery, 'with lighted match, ready for instant action, had
madness prompted the mob to offer interruption to the work'.[38]
High on the side of the arch, red-coated English officers clambered
about 'like wall swallows', while on top the pioneers resumed
their previous night's work, hammering loose the masonry and
lead that secured the horses. 'Officers of all nations were upon
the Triumphal Arch,' wrote a Prussian. 'We drank like fish . . .
English Officers threw the empty bottles into the air and sang
Rule Britannia.'[39]

Down in the square, the Hungarian Guards had loaded their
rifles in plain sight of the crowd and surrounded the immediate

vicinity of the arch with an impenetrable barrier of bayonets, while the cavalry held back angry crowds in the side streets opening on the rue de Rivoli and the Quai du Louvre, dispersing protesters by striking them with the flat of their sabres. Order was maintained and 'the predicted vengeance [was] confined to scowls of deeper hatred than those which [the French] features formerly wore'.[40]

John Scott was one of the curious foreigners given precedence over the French and allowed past the Austrian cordon. He was even permitted on top of the arch while the work of removal was in progress. He assisted an English lady and her husband into the 'Car of Victory', originally intended to contain a statue of Bonaparte 'when he came back a Conqueror from his Russian expedition'. Standing with Scott and the English couple, a Prussian officer observed that 'the English have now got where [the Emperor] could not!' Then, '*Ah, pauvre Napoleon!* he added in a sneering tone.' Scott got down from the chariot and, walking to the edge of the monument, looked down at the mass of troops guarding the place du Carousel at bayonet point against 'the defeated but enraged French'. Reflecting on conquest, plunder and restitution, he stooped under the horses' bellies and stood between two of them, resting an arm on each of the ancient bronzes, 'that from Greece had been taken to Rome, to Constantinople, to Venice, to Paris, – and were now to be sent back to Venice'.[41] Meanwhile, the 'triumphal car' was being stripped of its gilded lead ornaments for souvenirs – a large 'N', a laurel crown – until the only decoration left was a great spread eagle, 'which everybody found too heavy'.[42] Lieutenant Jackson planned to carry off this prize – and even engaged a couple of the pioneers to loosen the screws holding it in place prior to having it carried to his quarters in the rue Saint-Honoré. Some Prussian officers, however, had similar designs on the relic and it 'somehow disappeared, but how, and unobserved, [Jackson] could not imagine, as the figure was very large'.[43]

As the activity on top of the arch increased, Scott went back

down to the place du Carousel and, craning his neck, watched
as the first horse, disengaged from the top of the monument,
made 'a considerable movement forward', with the scaffolding,
the block and tackle, and the ropes, pulled from below, taking
the strain. Another pull made the horse shake and moved it
further forward, the front hooves appearing beyond the parapet.
A last pull, and 'it sprung grandly off, and swung in the air'. A
cry of distress went up from the French crowd, 'arms were up,
fingers pointing, heads waving'.[44] Henry Milton was watching
from one of the windows in the Grande Galerie of the Louvre:
'All the windows . . . were crowded with mingled groups of
French and English, whose contrasted expression of countenance
was not the least interesting part of the spectacle; – these all
eager curiosity, – those sullenly and furiously attentive.' As the
first horse descended slowly to the cart waiting to receive it,
many of the French 'drew back from the windows, and quitted
the gallery, unable to suppress or disguise their feelings'. Milton
observed that 'justice, policy, and good taste, all imperiously
demanded that this ill-devised trophy should not be suffered to
exist'. Nevertheless, he added, 'it was impossible at the moment
not to feel some pity for the humiliation and misery of the
French'.[45]

Lady Edgcombe had been sent shopping by her aunt Lady
Castlereagh and arrived on the rue de Rivoli, directly opposite
the arch, in time to see another of the horses lowered. Her
coach was surrounded by a number of onlookers, who stared
at her 'with the most ferocious and villainous expressions of
countenance'. With her servants on the step behind and the
adjacent massed cavalry of the Austrian army, she felt perfectly
safe but could not help thinking of 'the bloodthirsty revolutionary mobs' and imagined them thinking: 'We should like
to pull you out, and tear you to pieces if we could.' She had
been driven through angry English crowds on numerous occasions, but they were 'mild and amiable' in comparison with
these 'French specimens, who were apparently capable of any
atrocity'.[46]

It was dark by the time the English engineers had completed their work and all four horses had been safely lowered. John Scott was dining at Verrey's in the rue de Rivoli between seven and eight that evening when he heard the rumble of wheels and the clatter of cavalry outside:

> The [Venetian Horses] were going past in military procession, lying on their sides in separate cars. First came cavalry, then infantry, then a car; – then more cavalry; more infantry, then another car, – and so on, till all the four past. The drums were beating and the standards went waving by. This was the only appearance of parade that attended any of the removals.[47]

The statues were taken to a shed in the rue d'Anjou. Here they were seen later lying on the ground with 'some coal-heavers . . . engaged in melting away half a cubic foot of lead with which [each of] the legs was soldered to the stone, by means of a coal fire kindled underneath it. The operation was already performed upon two legs, but in such a manner that not only the lead but the hoofs also were gone, and all the lower part of the leg had suffered considerably.'[48] Canova was consulted and recommended that the remaining hooves be wrapped in wet rags while the lead was being melted off them, but the coal-heavers replied that they had no rags.

Another iconic Venetian monument claimed by the Austrians suffered in the process of restitution. The 300 BC winged lion in bronze – displaced by Bonaparte from the top of its column in St Mark's Square to the top of a fountain in front of the Hôtel des Invalides – had one of its legs broken, and part of the stone basin demolished, when a rope that was lowering it snapped. Helen Williams noted a 'vindictive joy'[49] at the accident, and ironic cries of '*Vive le Roi*' were heard from the onlooking crowd.[50] Parisians had never particularly cherished this trophy. A day or so earlier, the *Journal des Débats* had expressed the wish that 'the Venetians would take with their horses, also the hideous lion of St Mark, which disfigures the fountain of the *Invalides!*'[51]

*

The so-called 'stripping of the Louvre' by the Allies, however emotive for the Parisians, was far from comprehensive. The majority of the collection – amassed by generations of French kings – was left untouched and although the pictures by Rubens had returned to Belgium, his twenty-two gigantic canvases from the Luxembourg Palace, celebrating the life of Marie de' Medici, the wife of Henri VI, more than filled the gaps they left. The restitution did not extend to works of art looted under the revolution from French churches and chapels, and from the collections of Royalist emigrés, like the Comte d'Artois, the future Charles X. The Vatican sculptures had gone but the celebrated Borghese sculptures, 'purchased' by extortion in 1807, remained. The Louvre still contains around sixty Italian paintings and well over a hundred from Northern Europe, plundered between 1797 and 1814. Provenances – often including the word 'saisi' – show them to have been seized from Bologna, Florence, Mantua, Milan, Parma, Rome, Turin, Venice and Verona; from Vienna, from the Hague, from Berlin and Stuttgart. All were seemingly overlooked in the restitution, although one, seized from Venice in 1797, would have been difficult to ignore. Nearly thirty-three feet wide and twenty-two high, the largest painting in the collection, Veronese's *Marriage at Cana* was retained in exchange for the more modestly proportioned *Christ at the House of the Pharisee* by Charles Le Brun.

The desecrated Arc du Carousel, however, continued to rankle, and for some time afterwards it was 'surrounded by the populace, in sorrowful and astonished groups'. So potent a symbol, and so galling a loss, was the Venetian *Quadriga* that Louis XVIII would later have the horses copied by François Joseph Bosio and replaced between twin figures of Victory in front of a refurbished triumphal car containing the figure of Peace, the whole monument re-dedicated to commemorate 'Restoration'.

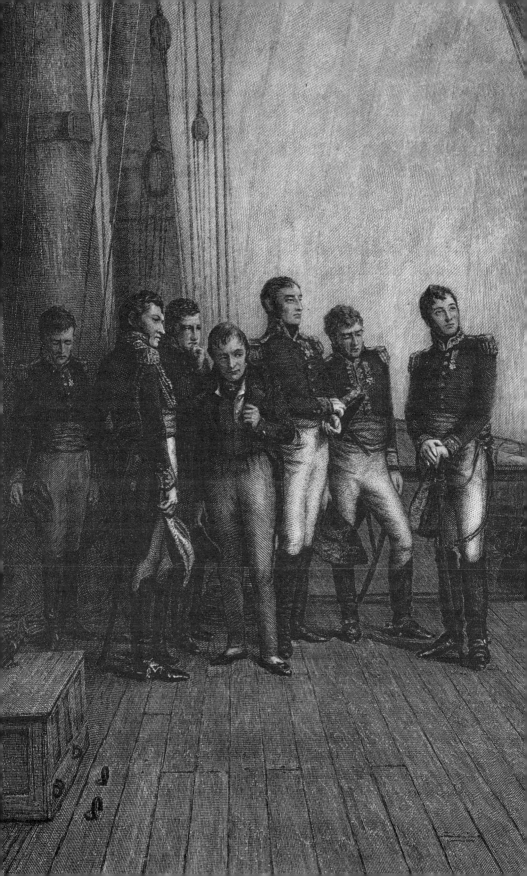

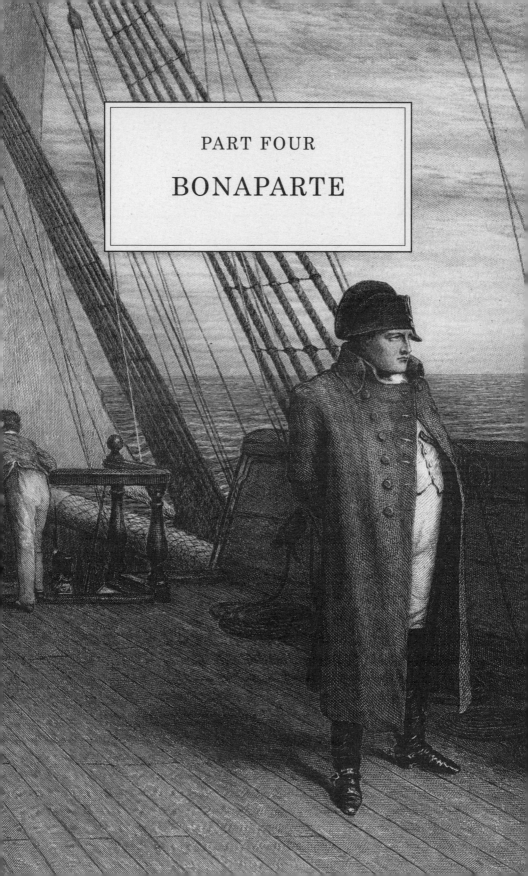

PART FOUR

BONAPARTE

I

MIDNIGHT in the centre of Genappe, choked with the seething mass of a defeated army – Sunday passing to Monday 19 June – and Napoleon realised the full extent of the disaster. He attempted to turn the tide of catastrophe, and rally his men, 'to re-establish some order . . . but his efforts were in vain . . . No voice could make itself heard above the tumult and, recognising his impotence, he gave way and let the torrent flow.'[1] It took more than an hour to force his way down the long, winding street, and it was nearly half past twelve before he was able to escape the chaos. Abandoning his now immovable campaign coach in the backed-up crush of vehicles leading to the Dyle bridge, and leaving its contents to the victorious Prussian looters, he continued on horseback in the dense, shuffling crowd of exhausted and wounded men.

In the neighbourhood of Genappe, a man of short stature wearing a grey coat and bearing 'a certain resemblance to the Emperor' was found by the Prussians wandering on foot and with sabre cuts to the head and shoulder. He was subsequently further maltreated when his disappointed captors realised he was not the prize he appeared to be. They relieved him of his ring, his pocket watch and a purse containing about forty napoleons, then stripped him of most of his clothing and dragged him away barefoot, wearing just his coat and trousers, to be shot. A victim

of mistaken identity, the eminent military surgeon Baron
Dominique Jean Larrey was spared only when he was recognised
by a Prussian medical man.[2]

Three miles beyond Genappe, at one o'clock in the morning,
Quatre Bras was ghastly under the near full moon, the battlefield
of 16 June thick with naked corpses. An incongruous cavalry
regiment still maintaining ranks and discipline and lined up in
battle formation to the left of the road – Red Lancers of the
Imperial Guard – faced the oncoming retreat. '*Voilà l'Empereur!*'
somebody whispered. In the midst of men and horses, wagons
and walking wounded, accompanied by a small group of staff
officers, dressed like himself in grey greatcoats, and followed by
four or five of his elite guard: '*Voilà l'Empereur!*' Captain Prosper
Fortuné de Brack watched him leave the herd and approach,
bright moonlight bleaching his features to a stark, livid mask.
'Never, even during the retreat from Moscow, had I seen a more
confused and unhappy expression on that majestic face.' He rode
slowly up to General Pierre Colbert Chabanais, wounded in
Friday's battle, who sat his horse with his arm in a sling:

'Who are you?'

'The Lancers of your Guard, Sire.'

'Ah yes! The Lancers of the Guard!' But confusing them with
the 6th Lancers, he asked after that regiment's divisional general:
'And where is Piré?'[3]

'Sire, we know nothing of him. He is not with us.'

'That's right . . . but Piré?'

'We know nothing of him at all.'

'But who are you . . . you?'

'Sire, I am Colbert, and here are the Lancers of your Guard.'

'Ah! yes . . . and the 6th Lancers? . . . and Piré? . . . Piré?'

Captain de Brack recalled and reported every word of this
exchange 'with a religious fidelity'.[4] Other things were then said
that he could not catch. A gunshot cracked from further back
along the road and one of his generals pulled the stricken Emperor
away.

A short distance from Quatre Bras, in a clearing of the Bois de Bossu, Lieutenant Martin of the 45th caught a passing glimpse of Napoleon by the light of a grenadier's campfire. He was 'standing still, his arms crossed, and looking back towards Waterloo'.[5] It was here that another fugitive, Major Baudus of General Soult's staff, approached and the Emperor asked if he had seen any troops who were not completely disorganised. Baudus replied that he had just passed Colonel Jacqueminot and the 5th Lancers still marching in good order. 'Go quickly', said the Emperor, 'and tell them to halt at Quatre Bras. It is already late, and when they find this point occupied, the enemy will most likely halt.'

Baudus galloped back the way he had come but found the crossroads already under enemy fire from adjacent buildings. Assuming that the 5th Lancers had now been outflanked by the Prussians, he returned to advise his master to withdraw as he could no longer be protected by any of his troops. As he spoke, Baudus was startled by the Emperor's demeanour. 'Napoleon was silently weeping for his lost army. His face was filled with an intense sadness and was as pale as wax; life had nothing more to give him, save tears.'[6] Baudus was ordered south-east to Fleurus to alert General Girard's 7th Division to the defeat and ensure they withdrew on the Sambre. The Emperor and his entourage followed the more direct route south to Charleroi. His aide-de-camp General Flahault rode close alongside him, knee to knee. 'He was so overcome by fatigue and the exertion of the preceding days, that several times he was unable to resist the drowsiness which overcame him,' recalled Flahault, 'and if I had not been there to uphold him, he would have fallen from his horse.'[7]

They reached Charleroi between four and five, Napoleon having dismounted and walked the last few miles from Gosselies. Charleroi was as congested with fugitives and wagons as Genappe had been and it took a considerable time to get through. There was another campfire halt at Marcenelle on the opposite side of the Sambre, where glasses and two bottles of wine were produced, which the Emperor shared with his officers. 'He took no other nourishment',[8] according to one account; ate 'a morsel of bread which one of his equerries had in his pocket', according to another. General Gourgaud claimed that he made another vain attempt to rally his troops but 'the men who fell into the ranks on one side slipped out at the other'.⁹ Warming himself at the fire, Napoleon turned to General Corbineau and said: 'Eh bien Monsieur, we have done a fine thing', to which inexplicable remark Corbineau saluted and replied: 'Sire, it is the utter ruin of France.' The Emperor turned away, 'shrugged his shoulders and remained absorbed for some moments. He was at this time extremely pale and haggard and much changed.'¹⁰ Dead tired, he demanded a carriage but it was explained to him that 'the roads were encumbered with vehicles, and that in a carriage he could not escape from the light horse of the enemy, which every moment [were] expected to appear'.¹¹

Before they moved on towards the French border, the Emperor's local guide, Jean-Baptiste La Coste, was allowed to return to his family. He had been at Napoleon's side – a terrified and unwilling companion – throughout the previous day's battle and the night's retreat. At no time had he been ill treated, but on the road from Quatre Bras to Charleroi the bridle of his horse had been tethered to an officer's saddle to prevent him deserting. At dawn on 19 June, his local knowledge was no longer required. The Emperor mounted a fresh horse, asked if it 'galloped well',¹² bowed slightly to La Coste and rode off. Engaging him the previous morning, Napoleon had told his guide 'that if he (Bonaparte) succeeded, his recompense should be a hundred times greater than he could imagine'. Now, instead, General Bertrand gave him 'for his services, a *single napoleon*'¹³ and left him to walk the twenty miles back to his house at La Belle Alliance.

Napoleon and his entourage took the road towards Avesnes, but hearing reports that there were enemy partisans at Beaumont, they altered their route to Philippeville. Peasants in Gerpinnes watched the Emperor ride past at eleven o'clock that morning, 'melancholy and disconcerted'. A correspondent of *The Times* reported that 'the wounded French who lined the road cried [out] as they saw him pass, "*There goes the butcher of France.*" He perfectly heard these cries, which were repeated as he passed along.'[14] They reached Philippeville around midday.[15] According to one source the gates were closed and Napoleon had to endure the humiliation of having his identity questioned by an overzealous sentry until the town governor arrived to confirm that the man waiting outside was indeed the Emperor of France.[16]

At Philippeville he wrote two letters to his brother, Prince Joseph, in Paris. One was intended to be read aloud to rally support in the Chamber of Representatives, the other was more personal but likewise defiant. 'All is not lost,' he confided, calculating that he could rely on an immediate force of 300,000 troops, made up of army, local militia – or *fédérés* – and national guards. 'I will pull the guns with carriage horses', he went on, departing phrase by phrase from reality. 'I will raise 100,000 conscripts; arm them with muskets of the royalists and of the unfit national guards; I will organise a mass levy in the Dauphiné, Lyons, Burgundy, Lorraine, Champagne; I will crush the enemy.' He was going from Philippeville to Laon, where he had no doubt of finding more people. Laon and Marshal Grouchy would furnish him with a further 50,000 men within three days – 'If [Grouchy] has not been taken prisoner, as I fear', he added. In the meantime, Joseph was to prepare the Representatives to give him their allegiance. 'At this critical moment it is their duty to rally to my side and save France.' He dictated the letter to Fleury de Chaboulon, signed it and wrote underneath: 'Courage and Strength.'

Now that they were no longer in immediate danger of being overtaken by the Prussians, a 'half broken down post-chaise'[17] was found for the Emperor, *barouches* for his staff, and they went on from Philippeville towards Laon, passing near sunset under the walls of Rocroi, whose inhabitants crowded the ramparts to cheer him.[18] Fearing they would not find fresh horses at Maubert-Fontaine, they made a detour to Mézières, arriving in the central square at half past ten. They had to wait for an hour and a half while a search was made in the environs for the necessary animals. The commander of the garrison, Commandant Traullé, the town's governor and officers of their staff stood around the carriages of the imperial party, not knowing what to do, speaking in under-tones 'as in a day of mourning'. No one alighted except for General Bertrand, who was summoned to the door of the Emperor's carriage for a murmured conference. When the little convoy set off again at midnight and approached the town gate, sentries cried out, *'Vive l'Empereur!'* repeatedly until all three carriages had passed. Traullé recalled that this cry was 'harrowing under the circumstances'.

At Maubert-Fontaine, on the morning of 20 June, the carriages stopped at the Hotel du Grand Turc, where the Emperor rested for a few hours and breakfasted on two eggs.[19] They stopped again at Rheims and at Berry au Bac.[20] They drove all day and in the evening, at Vaux, a suburb of Laon, locals gathered at the open gates of the Hotel de Poste to watch the Emperor pacing up and down the straw-covered courtyard, head bowed, arms crossed. 'It is Job on his dunghill,' someone muttered. There were a few nervous cries of *'Vive l'Empereur!'* from the onlookers. Napoleon stopped pacing, turned to face them, and raised his hat. On arrival in the centre of Laon there were more shouts of *'Vive l'Empereur!'*, shouts that Fleury de Chaboulon found painful: 'they are pleasant enough in times of prosperity; after a battle lost they tear the heart'.[21]

From varying accounts, the party left Laon between eight o'clock and nine in the evening of 20 June, or perhaps an hour or two later.[22] Noticing the dilapidated post-chaise, the prefect of Laon placed his own carriage at the Emperor's disposal and in that he set out on the final leg of the journey.[23] On the morning of the 21st he reached Paris. At the principal barrier to the city, one of the court coaches was waiting for him, sent by Caulaincourt, his Minister for Foreign Affairs, who had been informed of his approach by a courier. Napoleon preferred, however, to remain incognito and stayed in the prefect's carriage. He also ordered the driver to enter the city on the north-west side, by the less frequented Barrière du Roule.

The previous day, a group of his senior officers – Drouot, Flahaut, La Bédoyère, Dejean and Gourgaud – had discussed what the Emperor should do when he arrived in the capital. 'We all agreed that His Majesty ought . . . to go booted and travel-stained to the Chamber of [Representatives], give an account of the disaster, ask aid, and, returning to Belgium, put himself at the head of Grouchy's army.'[24] It was reasoned that even the most hostile faction among the Representatives would be unable to resist granting support to a brave commander bursting into their Chamber, clothes reeking of gun smoke and with the mud of a battlefield still on his boots. By so doing, he would gain a considerable moral, political and decidedly theatrical advantage. Instead, soon after arriving at the Elysée Palace, Napoleon took a bath.

*

'Eh bien! Caulaincourt.' Descending from his carriage at seven in the morning, he greeted the minister: 'Here is a great event! A battle lost . . . How will the nation take this defeat? Will the Chambers give me their support?' He strode into his study and threw himself on to a couch. 'All the equipment is gone. That is the greatest loss. The battle was won. The army had performed prodigies; the enemy was beaten at all points; only the English centre held. Then at the end of the day, the army was seized with a panic terror. It is inexplicable! Ney attacked like a madman . . . They destroyed my cavalry before I could use them . . . Grouchy didn't hold Bülow in check and he didn't come . . .'[25]

Then he ordered his bath to be drawn.

His breathing was laboured but he carried on talking. He intended convening a joint session of both Chambers – a *séance impériale*: 'I will inform them of the army's misfortune; I will demand of them the means of saving the country; after that I will return to the front.'

'Sire, the news of your misfortunes is already known,' Caulaincourt replied. 'It has caused great agitation; the mood among the [Representatives] seems more hostile than ever and since Your Majesty deigns to listen to me, it is my duty to tell you that it is feared they will not meet your expectations. Sire, I am sorry to see you in Paris. It would have been better had you not been separated from your army: the army is what gives you your strength, your safety.'

'I no longer have an army,' the Emperor replied. 'I have only fugitives. I will find men, but how are they to be armed? I have no guns. However, with unity all can be repaired. I trust that the [Representatives] will support me; that they will accept their responsibilities. You misjudge them I believe, misjudge their spirit. The majority are good, are French . . . A minority only do not want me, I know. They want to work for themselves . . . I will not let them. My presence here will restrain them.'

His brothers, Prince Joseph and Prince Lucien, arrived. They confirmed Caulaincourt's misgiving about the mood among the Representatives and advised Napoleon to defer calling his *séance impériale* until after his ministers had conferred.

As the Emperor lay in his bath, ministers and state officials hurried to the Elysée. There they were to be seen in clusters, eagerly questioning officers and aides-de-camp returned from the war, men for whom 'the spectacle of the army's rout and destruction was still present to their eyes; they spared no detail, carelessly throwing terror and despair into their listeners' hearts'. And while the Emperor soaked off the dust and grime of his disastrous campaign, in the antechambers of the palace 'it was said aloud that he was lost; whispered that France could only be saved by his abdication'.

His council assembled: the Emperor's brothers; Fleury de Chaboulon; Carnot, Minister of the Interior; Davout, Minister of War; Admiral Decrès, the Duc de Saint-Germain, Minister of Marine; Maret, the Duc de Bassano, Secretary of State and editor of the *Moniteur Universel*; Cambacérès, Arch-Chancellor of the Empire and president of the Chamber of Peers; Secretary of State Regnault; Gaudin, Finance Minister; Mollien, the Paymaster General; Caulaincourt; and the Minister of Police, Joseph Fouché.

Maret read aloud the Emperor's account of the battle of Mont-Saint-Jean as it would appear in the second edition of the *Moniteur* later that day. Then, flushed and revived from his bath, Napoleon addressed them:

Our disasters are great. I am come to repair them; to stimulate in the nation, in the army, a great and noble movement. If the nation rises, the enemy will be subdued. But if, instead of rising, instead of taking extraordinary measures, we argue among ourselves, all is lost. The enemy is in France. To save the country, I need to be invested with great power, with a temporary dictatorship. In the interest of the country, I could seize that power. But it would be expedient, and more to the national good, if it were conferred on me by the Chambers.[26]

Around the table everyone listened with lowered eyes. No one spoke. Then the Emperor invited Carnot's opinion and the Minister of the Interior gave his advice, 'to declare the country to be in danger, call to arms the *fédérés* and National Guards, and place Paris in a state of siege'. Should the defence of Paris fail, French forces would withdraw south of the Loire and retrench. In the meantime there was an army of between ten and twenty-seven thousand in the Vendée to the west and Marshal Brune's II Corps d'Observation at Toulon, comprising a further five to six thousand. With the recall of these forces, Carnot declared, 'we could unite and organise in sufficient strength to take the offensive and drive the enemy out of France'.

Caulaincourt did not share Carnot's optimism. He referred the meeting to the events of the previous year, maintaining that another enemy occupation of Paris would take from them for a second time the decision as to who should rule France. He said that a great effort was necessary if the nation was to preserve its independence; that the salvation of the state did not depend on taking this measure or that but on cooperation between the Chambers of Peers and Representatives, and the Emperor.

Davout disagreed:

At such times as these there should not be two powers. It takes only one, strong enough to implement all possible means of resistance and to master criminal factions and parties whose blind plots and intrigues would hinder everything. It will be necessary to prorogue the Chambers in accordance with constitutional law. It is perfectly legal. But to mitigate the effect of this measure on the minds of meticulous people it could be announced that the Chambers would assemble in some provincial town – to be identified later – for a fixed period of two or three weeks unless circumstances require further prorogation.[27]

Then Fouché spoke . . .

The Minister of Police had already been active in spreading rumours among the Representatives of just such a suspension of democratic process and the establishment of a dictatorship. He also knew that, at his instigation, the Marquis de La Fayette, a prominent republican, was about to render the current discussion at the Elysée Palace entirely futile, and ensure that the Emperor would never be granted the absolute power he demanded.

. . . Fouché spoke disingenuously. Why, he asked, should so grave a measure as the prorogation or dissolution of the Chambers be necessary at this time? After all, the Representatives would not haggle with the Emperor over giving him their dedicated support when public safety was at stake. Fouché believed, he said, that showing the Chambers trust and good faith would make them feel it was their duty to unite with the Emperor so that together, by energetic measures, they might save the honour and independence of the nation.

With the bluntness that he was known for, Admiral Decrès declared that it was useless to try to win over the Representatives by flattering them with 'trust and good faith' when they were already ill disposed and determined to take matters to the most violent extremes.

Regnault agreed. He did not believe the Representatives would be willing to support the Emperor because they were convinced he could no longer save the country. Regnault feared that a great sacrifice was now necessary . . .

The unspoken word hung in the air.

'Speak plainly,' Napoleon said. 'It is my abdication that they want, is it not?'

'Sire, however painful this is for me to say,' Regnault replied, 'it is my duty to enlighten Your Majesty as to his true position. I would add that even if Your Majesty was determined not to offer his own abdication, the Chamber would dare to demand it of him.'

Prince Lucien brushed the spectre away. He believed that the greater the crisis, the greater the energy that needed to be exerted. Fifteen years earlier, he had dissolved the upper and lower Chambers by force during the *coup d'état* of 9 and 10 November 1799 – *18 Brumaire* in the French republican calendar – and established his brother as First Consul. He now envisaged a similar measure to preserve the Empire:

> If the Chamber will not rally to the Emperor, the Emperor will do without them. The salvation of the Country is his first priority. Since the Chamber refuses to join the Emperor in saving France, he must save her himself. He must declare himself dictator; he must place the entire country in a state of siege and call all true Frenchmen to her defence.

Carnot agreed that it was essential the Emperor be given absolute power for the duration of the crisis. Then Napoleon spoke again:

> The presence of the enemy on our native soil will I hope bring the [Representatives] to a sense of their duty. The nation did not elect them to overthrow me, but to support me. I am not afraid of them. Whatever they do, I will always be the idol of the people and the army. If I give the word, they would all be thrown out. But while I have no fears for myself, I fear for France. If we quarrel among ourselves, instead of agreeing, we will suffer the same fate as the Byzantine Empire. Everything will be lost. The patriotism of the nation, their hatred of the Bourbons, their

loyalty to me, these are immense resources and our cause is far
from hopeless.

*

Meanwhile, less than a mile away, on the opposite side of the
river, behind the imposing pedimented portico of the Palais
Bourbon, the Representatives had been assembling in their great
semicircular auditorium since before midday. 'Never had the
Chamber more resembled a beehive in complete anarchy,' wrote
an eyewitness. 'All moved and buzzed, men of all kinds going in
and out, coming and going, appearing, disappearing and re-
appearing in constant agitation and with the air of having been
bitten by tarantulas.'[28] From this confusion a series of resolutions
emerged fully formed to pass quickly into law.

The session began at a quarter past twelve – an hour and
three-quarters earlier than usual – this itself a sign of the
extraordinary nature of the occasion. The deafening roar of
conversation from the crowded curving tiers of benches fell
suddenly quiet. Primed by Fouché, forewarned of the subject
under discussion at the Elysée Palace, and fired with a republican zeal to save his country from tyranny, La Fayette mounted
the steps to the speaker's tribune. He spoke for the first time
in many years, he said, 'raising a voice that the old friends of
liberty would still have recognised'. He spoke of the dangers
that the country faced, dangers that they alone – the representatives of the people – had the power to prevent. He spoke
of the need 'to rally around our ancient standard, the *tricolore*,
the flag and symbol of '89, of Liberty, Equality and Public
Order'. He spoke as 'a veteran of the sacred cause of liberty',
submitting for their consideration five resolutions, the necessity
for which he hoped they would appreciate. A transcript
published the following day in *Le Moniteur* recorded applause
as he finished speaking.

The first three resolutions were voted through without discussion, by both the Representatives and, later, the Peers. Articles I

and III seemed incontrovertible: that the independence of the nation was threatened; and that the army and National Guard deserved well of the country. But it was Article II that turned the Emperor pale with anger when the news of its passage interrupted his Council of Ministers at the Elysée Palace: 'The Chamber [of Representatives] declares itself *en permanence*. Any attempt to dissolve it is a crime of high treason; anyone guilty of that attempt will be a traitor to the country and judged as such.'

Napoleon slammed his hand on the table. 'I expected this. I should have dismissed those men before I left. It is finished. They will ruin France.' And if there was any thought of dismissing the Chamber now, Davout was quick to reject it. Davout had earlier urged the perfect legality of proroguing the Chamber indefinitely. But with the Representatives in permanent session, he, as Minister for War, would have been charged with the storming of the Palais Bourbon, and he drew back from taking that responsibility. 'The moment for action is past,' he declared. 'The Representatives' resolution may be unconstitutional but it is now an established fact. In the present circumstances we should not deceive ourselves into thinking we can relive the *18 Brumaire*. For my part I would refuse to be instrumental in such an action.'

After a moment's thought, Napoleon said: 'I see now that Regnault did not deceive me. I will abdicate if necessary.'[29] It was an incautious remark that would be repeated by his enemies both in and outside the council chamber, and before long on the Representatives' benches in the Palais Bourbon, and among the Peers in the Palais de Luxembourg. Napoleon tried to take it back. He sent Regnault to the Representatives, Carnot to the Peers, with identical messages, extenuating the military catastrophe and presenting himself as dealing with the crisis as though abdication had never been mentioned:

You are to tell them that I have returned; that I have convened my Council of Ministers; that, following a significant victory, the army fought a great battle; that all was going well; that the English were beaten; that we had captured six of the enemy's flags, when malicious elements created a panic; that now the army is rallying; that I have given orders to stop the fugitives; that I have come here to consult with my Ministers and with the Chambers; and that I am occupied at this moment with implementing all necessary measures to preserve the public safety.[30]

The two emissaries had contrasting receptions. While the Peers listened politely to what Carnot had to say, the Representatives would not even allow Regnault to read the Emperor's account of the battle, 'after he had announced that it *was not official*' and thereby prompted the inference that it was a falsehood. Empowered by their decisive action in approving La Fayette's propositions earlier in the day, the Representatives dismissed the Minister of State with instructions that the fifth of their resolutions be attended to: 'The Ministers of War, of External Affairs, of the Police and of the Interior are requested to present themselves to the Assembly immediately.' It was rumoured that 'Regnault, after his repulse, was taken ill, and carried away from the Chamber.'[31]

At six o'clock that evening, the specified ministers – Davout, Maret, Fouché and Carnot – presented themselves to the Chamber. They were accompanied by Prince Lucien, who read aloud, from the tribune, his brother's message to the Representatives, informing them that he had convened a committee of ministers 'to renew and follow up the negotiations with the Allied foreign powers in order to ascertain their real intentions, and put an end to the war, if it is compatible with the independence and honour of the nation'. The Emperor counted 'on the cooperation and the patriotism of [both] Chambers and on their attachment to [his] person'. There was uproar from the benches. As it subsided, one Henri Lacoste made himself heard. He spoke in apocalyptic terms:

The veil is torn, our sorrows are known, some of us are fearful that perhaps our disasters have not yet been fully revealed. I am not going to discuss the communication just made to us; this is not the time to demand of the Head of State an account of the blood of the fallen and the loss of national honour; but I would ask of him, in the name of public salvation, to show us the secrets of his thoughts, of his policies, of the means he is taking to close up the abyss that is opening beneath our feet. You talk to us of national independence; you talk to us of peace – ministers of Napoleon – but what new basis can you have for your negotiations [with the enemy]? What new means of communication have you in your power?

Without pausing for an answer, Lacoste delivered his conclusion with succinct but devastating logic:

You know, as well as we do, that it was on Napoleon alone that Europe declared war! Will you not then separate, henceforth, the Nation from Napoleon? For myself, I declare, that I do not see that one man should stand between ourselves and peace. Let him go and the Nation will be saved!

Lucien replied that dividing the Emperor from the nation was precisely what their enemies wanted, 'to disunite us in order to vanquish us, to plunge us again and more easily into that degradation and slavery from which his return delivered us'. He called instead for unity:

I conjure you, citizens, by the sacred name of our country, rally all of you round the chief, whom the nation has so solemnly placed at its head. Consider that our safety depends on our union, and that you cannot separate yourselves from the Emperor and abandon him to his enemies without ruining the state, without being faithless to your oaths, without tarnishing forever the national honour.

Few in the Chamber heard, few listened, as the Prince spoke against the roar of voices, some supportive, others accusatory. But it was to the last part of Lucien's discourse that La Fayette rose and responded:

You accuse us of failing in our duty towards honour and towards Napoleon. Have you forgotten all that we have done for him?

Have you forgotten that we have followed him in the sands of Africa and in the wastes of Russia, and that the bones of our children, of our brothers, lie everywhere as proof of our fidelity? We have done enough for him; our duty now is to save the country.[32]

Despite it being at the forefront of every man's mind in that vast chamber, 'none dared pronounce the word abdication', according to Fleury de Chaboulon, 'so difficult was it to conquer the respect inspired by a great man'. And after long debate the word had still not been spoken when it was agreed that two commissions – composed of five members from each Chamber – should be appointed to confer further with the Council of Ministers at the Palais du Tuileries later in the evening of that very long day.

At seven o'clock, while Prince Lucien was arguing for the preservation of his brother's throne, Napoleon summoned Benjamin Constant, author of the so-called 'Charter of 1815',[33] to the Elysée Palace. There was a twofold irony in this meeting on the eve of his abdication, of which the Emperor, as much as Constant, must have been aware: that it had been at Napoleon's invitation, on his return from Elba, that Constant had drawn up the liberal amendment to the constitution; and that it was the Chamber of Representatives, brought into being by the terms of that same constitutional amendment, that was now forcing him to abdicate. Scribbled into a notebook when he reached home, Constant distilled the Emperor's exasperated monologue from their three-hour-long conversation:

It does not concern me, it concerns France. They want me to abdicate! Have they considered the inevitable consequence of my abdication? It is around me, around my name, that the army is gathered. Take me away and the army will dissolve. If I abdicate today, in two days' time there will be no army . . . This army does not understand all your subtleties. Do you think that metaphysical axioms, declarations of rights, parliamentary speeches will stop it from disbanding? If I had been turned away when I landed at Cannes I would have understood; but abandoning me today – that I do not understand . . . When the enemy is twenty-five leagues away, you do not overthrow your government with impunity. Do they think they can turn aside the foreigners with phrases? If France had overthrown me fifteen days ago it would have taken courage . . . but I am now part of what the foreigners are attacking; I am part of what France has to defend. Surrendering me, she surrenders herself, she admits defeat, she encourages the conquerors' audacity. It is not freedom that is deposing me; it is Waterloo; it is fear – fear that will profit your enemies.

From the avenue de Marigny, running alongside the Elysée Palace, the two men could hear the Paris mob shouting 'Vive l'Empereur!' with the same savage enthusiasm, in this time of national crisis, that they brought to festivities, triumphs and riots alike. 'Vive Napoleon!' they cried, some of them attempting to climb the palace walls as though to offer him their protection, their allegiance, their love. After watching for a time in silence this display of ferocious loyalty – capable of massacring at his bidding the recalcitrant Representatives who opposed him – the Emperor turned to Constant:

You see they are not the ones I showered with honours and treasure. What have they had from me? I found them poor, I leave them poor. It is the instinct of need that animates them; the voice of the country speaks through their mouths; and if I wanted it . . . if I allowed it . . . in one hour that rebellious Chamber would no longer exist . . . But the life of one man is not worth that price. I did not return from the island of Elba to flood Paris with blood.[34]

When Lucien returned from the Palais Bourbon, he did not spare his brother the open hostility, even hatred, he had encountered among the Representatives. 'They have gone too far for there to be any hope of return,' he said. The alternatives were stark. 'Within twenty-four hours, the authority of the Emperor or that of the Chamber must cease. There is only dissolution or abdication.'[35]

Later that night, Constant wrote in his journal: 'He will abdicate tomorrow, I think.'[36]

But an alternative offered and, momentarily, was taken. That same night of 21 June, after Lucien and Constant had left the Emperor, an urgent summons brought a man called Gassicourt hurrying to the Tuileries. Gassicourt was a pharmacist. Early in June, before departing for his last campaign, and preparing his mind for 'a reverse which must not be survived, or a captivity which could not be endured', Napoleon had ordered this chemist to prepare 'a dose of infallible poison', capable of being concealed in 'the smallest possible compass'. He had carried it about his person, enclosed in a small locket, throughout the advances and retreats of the previous week, and at last, his empire crumbling about him, he had swallowed it. Either he was discovered in time, or he had himself immediately regretted the precipitancy of his action, but an antidote was called for and the terrified druggist ushered into his presence. Vomiting was induced, and prolonged by repeated and copious draughts of emetic, until the patient was out of danger.

When Napoleon died six years later, a stomach lesion suspected of being the cause, Gassicourt remained convinced it was a long-term effect of the draught he had prepared. 'Some particles of the poison cannot have been extracted, and thenceforward sooner or later death was inevitable.'[37]

II

THE Representatives assembled early, at nine o'clock on 22 June, impatient to hear an account of the discussions undertaken by their five-man commission at the Palais de Tuileries the previous night. The commission and its counterpart from the Chamber of Peers had been in conference with the Emperor's Council of Ministers from eleven o'clock and only adjourned, exhausted, at three in the morning. From the tribune of the Chamber, General Paul Grenier gave them a brief summary of the united committee's conclusions: that negotiations for peace and the preservation of national independence should be entered into with the allied powers; that negotiations should proceed from a position of strength and 'measures proper for procuring men, horses, and money' were to be taken. The Chamber was also informed that it might shortly expect a statement from the Emperor himself. Grenier had reason to believe that not only would this statement endorse the committee's proposals, but His Majesty would declare 'that if he be an invincible obstacle to the nation being admitted to treat for its independence, he will be ready to make whatever sacrifice may be demanded of him'. The mutterings of discontent that had accompanied the statement – as it became clear that after four hours of talk the Emperor still clung to power – might have hushed at 'sacrifice', the euphemism coming as close to what was in everybody's minds as delicacy would allow. But one member

of the Chamber – Antoine Louis Hippolyte Duchesne, representa-
tive for l'Isère – demanded a more explicit assurance of the
Emperor's intentions. He pointed out to Grenier and his committee
that the allied powers 'have declared that they will never treat
with you as long as you shall have the Emperor at your head'.
Without heeding the President of the Assembly, Jean Lanjuinais's
reminder – that the Chamber had just been promised a message
from the Emperor 'which will meet all its wishes' – Duchesne
pressed on with his motion: 'to engage the Emperor, in the name
of the safety of the state, in the sacred name of a suffering country,
to declare his abdication'. There must have been relief that the
word had at last been uttered aloud in the Palais Bourbon.

After further debate, it was proposed 'that a deputation of five
Members . . . be appointed to proceed to the Emperor [and]
express to His Majesty the urgency of his decision', but in order
'to preserve the honour of the Chief of the State', it was agreed
to allow him an hour to make it. A petulant exchange of threats
occurred between La Fayette and Prince Lucien:

'Tell your brother to send us his abdication or we will send
him his deposition.'

'And I will send La Bédoyère to you with a battalion of the
Guard!'[1]

There was more bad-tempered posturing at the Elysée Palace
as the Emperor appeared to renege on the decision he had been
on the point of making. He rounded on the Representatives'
delegation: 'Since you wish to violate me,' he shouted, 'I will *not*
abdicate. The Chamber is composed of none but Jacobins,
hotheads and *ambitieux*. I am going to expose them to the nation
and drive them out . . .'

'I implore you, Sire,' said Regnault, ever the one to urge unpal-
atable truths, 'do not try to fight against invincible necessity. Do
not leave the Chamber, the nation, the means to accuse you of
standing in the way of peace.'

Rage gave way to testiness. 'My intention has never been to
refuse to abdicate. But I want to be left in peace to think about
it. Tell the Chamber to wait.'

They did not have to wait long. The declaration arrived at one o'clock, and after reminding members of 'the regulation which forbid[s] any demonstration of approbation or disapprobation', Lanjuinais read the document aloud from the tribune:

FRENCHMEN! – In initiating war to maintain national independence, I relied on the union of all efforts, of all resolution, and the approval of all the national authorities. I had reason to hope for success, and I withstood all the declarations of the Powers against me. Circumstances appear to me changed. I offer myself as a sacrifice to the hatred of the enemies of France. May they prove sincere in their assurances, and harbour no enmity but against my person! My political life is terminated, and I proclaim my son, under the title Napoleon II, Emperor of the French. The present Ministers will provisionally form the Council of the Government. The interest which I take in the welfare of my son prompts me to invite the Chambers to legislate to establish the Regency without delay. I urge you all to unite to ensure public safety and to guarantee an independent nation.

NAPOLEON

Napoleon François Joseph Charles Bonaparte, Prince Imperial, King of Rome, Prince of Parma, was four years old and lived in Austria with his mother, the estranged Empress Marie-Louise. He had been proclaimed Emperor of the French only the year before, aged three, when his father abdicated for the first time. Then he retained the title Napoleon II for just a week. This time his reign would last a fortnight.

*

Shortly before Napoleon's declaration was read to the Representatives, they had been given a heartening account of the state of the army by Davout. 'Our disasters', the Minister of War told them, 'are not so considerable as we had feared.' A report from Avesnes spoke of at least 20,000 men rallied there, together with cannon, ammunition caissons, forges, and wagonloads of muskets. At Rocroi, Marshal Soult had succeeded in mustering 3,000 soldiers of the Old Guard and numerous other line detachments. Seventeen hundred cavalry were assembled at Guise, and finally, Grouchy's III and IV Corps remained in good order and barely depleted after defeating the Prussians at Wavre. In short, on the northern frontier, a French army of 60,000 men was ready to defend Paris. 'A strong barrier', Davout concluded, 'will be opposed to foreign invasion, and you will have an army sufficiently respectable to support your negotiations with an enemy, who has proved that he does not always keep his promises with fidelity.' The report was received with scepticism by some Representatives, with neither contradiction nor enthusiasm by the rest, and it was 'ordered to be inserted in the minutes'.

Two hours later, it fell to Carnot, Minister of the Interior, to read Napoleon's abdication address to the Chamber of Peers. Although the announcement was expected, 'a kind of stifled murmur' spread through the assembly as Carnot spoke. But no protest, no regret, no tribute was expressed and it was observed that 'finally they submitted to the abandonment of the Empire as they had to the yoke of the Emperor'.

No sooner had the vice president of the Peers referred the Act of Abdication to a committee for drafting into law than Carnot mounted to the tribune again and read Davout's report on the state of the army. Listening to that account detailing the enormous losses suffered by the enemy, the rallying of forces at Rocroi by Soult, and the advance of Grouchy's victorious army from Wavre, many wondered why, if the prospects were so hopeful, it had been necessary for the Emperor to abdicate at all. Before Carnot had finished speaking, another man got to his feet: 'All of this is false!'[2] he shouted. It was Marshal Ney.

Napoleon had once called him *le Brave des Braves* – the bravest of the brave.[3] To his soldiers he was *le Rougeaud*; and as he denounced Davout's testimony from the floor of the Chamber of Peers, the naturally florid complexion that gave him that sobriquet grew scarlet with excitement and fury: 'This is all delusional! You are being lied to on all sides! You are deceived . . . in everything and everywhere. The enemy is victorious at all points. I saw the disaster . . .'4 Five horses had been killed from under him on 18 June, and as the army disintegrated, he had been seen on foot trying to rally his men – any men – to fight on. Uniform torn, a ripped epaulette hanging from one shoulder, his face blackened with gun smoke, he held the hilt and shard of a broken sabre in his hand. 'Come and see how a Marshal of France can die!'5 he is said to have screamed at the remnant of an infantry brigade, before it too scattered before the allied advance and joined the flood from the field.

'I ran to the right, to the left, everywhere,' he told the silent ranks of Peers, 'wishing, with all my soul, that I could get a bullet into me.' He had seen other disasters, he said. He had commanded the rearguard on the retreat from Moscow and had 'fired the last musket shot at the Russians'. In truth, he conceded, the army was not, 'by the grace of God', so completely destroyed as it had been in 1812. But it was hopelessly dispersed:

> It is a fiction to pretend that fifty to sixty thousand men are or could be assembled at Rocroi or anywhere else. Marshal Grouchy could not have kept more than twelve or fifteen thousand men. With that and such like debris; with National Guards under orders, you are being told, to arrest fugitives; after such a débacle, with the Emperor gone, the artillery lost, how can any serious opposition to the enemy be opposed on the road to Paris?

And if Davout's report overestimated the strength of the French army, it perilously underestimated that of the invasion force:

> Wellington was at Nivelles with eighty thousand men, with artillery, with cavalry regiments intact, and more sure of victory than he has ever been. The Prussians, not so damaged from the start as we had been led to believe, and strengthened by their most recent success, are coming on with two large advance forces, without even needing to wait for other armies marching behind

and from other directions. A first wave will be at the gates of Paris within seven or eight days. You must not, in the present state, consider anything else but peace. You have been taken off guard by two formidable armies. You do not have time to recruit, to repair your equipment, to get back in action. This is not just a battlefield, this is an Empire lost . . .'[6]

A number of Peers privately reproached him for his outburst. Some thought him mad; some that so flagrant an admission of defeat amounted to treason. 'Well, gentlemen, I spoke only in the interest of the country,' he is said to have replied. 'Don't I know quite well that if Louis XVIII comes back, I will be shot!'[7] After the restoration it would be the Chamber of Peers that tried and condemned him.

*

By three o'clock on 22 June, the 'Proclamation to the French People' had been printed and plastered on walls across Paris. John Scott's correspondent wrote that there were some shouts of '*Vive le Roi!*' but a more vociferous clamour of '*Vive l'Empereur!*' from the *fédérés*, who congregated outside the Elysée Palace. General Bertrand emerged to address them. 'It is not by cries of "*Vive l'Empereur*" that you can serve the Emperor,' he shouted. 'You must serve him with weapons in your hands.' They clamoured for weapons. The National Guard made arrests. There were disturbances and more arrests in the Palais Royal, where army officers menaced passers-by into shouting '*Vive l'Empereur!*'[8]

According to the London press – appearing to play down the importance of Bonaparte to the French – such disturbances did not last. The following day, a letter to the *Morning Chronicle* reported: 'Paris is as tranquil as if profound peace prevailed all over the world. The situation and conduct of BONAPARTE are most surprising and extraordinary . . . I saw him yesterday after his abdication, walking about without the least agitation. He was with an Officer in conversation, so calm that a stranger might have passed him without taking the least notice of him.'⁹ An editorial in *The Times* suggested that this complacency reflected the degeneracy of both the fallen tyrant and his people: 'The wretch, with the blood of so many thousands on his head, seemed to carry about him all the coolness of that apathy which is part of his physical constitution: and so degraded and demoralised are the Parisian populace that they could see the butcher of their race without the least emotion.'¹⁰ Other eyewitnesses, however, recorded continued and daily demonstrations of popular feeling by the *fédérés* around the Elysée Palace, deeply disturbing to the provisional government.

Within six hours of the abdication, the Chamber of Representatives had elected a Commission du Gouvernement, consisting of Fouché, Carnot and General Grenier, supplemented by Caulaincourt and Quinette, Baron de Rochemont, from the Chamber of Peers. These five men comprised the executive committee of the provisional government of France, with Fouché its president.

Just before the Representatives cast their votes, a royalist member slyly introduced to the debate an important and, until that moment, neglected condition of Napoleon's abdication. 'You are about to name a provisional government,' he reminded members. 'I hope it will be of short duration. The revision of the constitution is first necessary, and then France will choose a Prince.' Everyone knew that one article of Benjamin Constant's 'Additional Act to the Constitutions of the Empire' would have to be struck out before the royalist faction achieved its end. Article 67 stated that, even in the case of the extinction of the imperial dynasty, the Chambers would never be entitled to propose the restoration of the Bourbons. The royalist member's intervention – and the mention of France choosing a prince – was greeted with uproar and shouts of 'He is chosen!' from the Bonapartist faction. The President called for order and informed the assembly that when he had visited the Elysée Palace earlier in the afternoon to convey the thanks of a grateful nation for his sacrifice, Napoleon had 'above all insisted on the motives which had determined his abdication, and exhorted the Chamber not to forget that he had abdicated in favour of his son'.

That evening, from half past nine until three in the morning of 23 June, the Peers debated the constitutional implications of abdication. The president of the Chamber opened the session by reiterating Napoleon's message to the Representatives. Prince Lucien said that to avoid civil war, the infant Napoleon II was to be acknowledged 'without deliberation, by a spontaneous movement'. After one emperor's abdication or death, another had to be recognised. 'All interruption is anarchy,' he declared, and swore allegiance to the former Emperor's son, asking that the Chamber follow his example. 'If a factious minority is to attack the dynasty and the constitution, it is not in the Chamber of Peers that traitors will be found, or the factious find support.'

At this point a peer questioned Lucien's entitlement to be speaking in that Chamber at all on the grounds of titles bestowed on him the year before by Pope Pius VII: Prince of Canino, Count of Apollino, and Lord of Nemori. 'Is he a Frenchman?' asked the Comte de Pontécoulant. 'I do not recognise him as such. I find him a Frenchman in sentiments, talents and services to liberty; but he who invokes the constitution has no constitutional title. He is a Roman Prince, and Rome is no longer French territory.' Also, while Pontécoulant had no objection in principle to proclaiming a dynastic successor to Napoleon, he would 'never recognise for King, a child, or for [his] Sovereign, he who does not reside in France'.

Then, for the second time that day, the Peers were thrown into uproar by the intemperate language of a soldier lately returned from battle. The twenty-nine-year-old General Charles de La Bédoyère – Bonaparte's aide-de-camp, who had communicated the lie to Ney that Grouchy had arrived, encouraging the Old Guard to destruction – dashed up the steps to the tribune. 'Napoleon abdicated in favour of his son,' he began. 'His abdication is one and indivisible. If his son is not recognised, is not crowned, I say that Napoleon did not abdicate, that his declaration should be null and void.' He surveyed the Chamber:

> I know, I see, the men who crawled at his feet during his prosperity, and the same men will now rise up against his son, a captive child, deprived of his great defender. But there are others who remain loyal to both of them. There are those in the French Chambers, impatient to see our enemies here and who will soon call them *allies*. If these men, and they are well-respected, reject Napoleon II, the Emperor has but to unsheath the sword again to surround himself with brave men who – covered with scars – will follow him once again with the cry of 'vive l'Empereur!' And when you see that, do not complain of civil war: it is you who will have caused it with your creeping treachery! And should it happen that French blood flows again; are we to go a second time under the foreign yoke? to bend our heads under a government debased by its defeat as by its victory? and show to all eyes our brave warriors drinking bitterness and humiliation, punished for their sacrifice, for their wounds and for their glory? The Emperor may be betrayed again; there are perhaps, at this moment, vile generals planning new treasons . . .

Here he looked at where Ney was seated, before venting his rage broadcast across the Chamber:

> But a curse on *every* traitor; may he be condemned to ignominy! His house razed, his family proscribed! Then no more traitors! No more of the cowardly machinations that led to our last catastrophe, the accomplices, even the perpetrators of which, are perhaps sitting here . . .

The murmur of indignation increased to a roar, and from all sides of the Chamber shouts erupted of 'Order', 'Withdraw', 'Disavow what you have said', while de La Bédoyère cried 'Hear me' from the tribune. The magisterial voice of the white-haired Marshal Massena could be heard clearly: 'Young man, you forget yourself.'

The tumult continued until the President restored calm, as tradition dictated, by putting on his hat.[11]

*

On 23 June, the Chamber of Representatives resolved that 'Napoleon II is become Emperor of the French, by the act of abdication of Napoleon I and by the power of the Constitution of the Empire.' As the resolution was adopted there were shouts of '*Vive l'Empereur!*' from the Bonapartist benches, jubilant at the preservation of the dynasty. At the Schloss Schönbrunn in Vienna, the infant Napoleon began his short reign entirely unaware of his elevation.

The Bonapartist victory was a hollow one. No regency administration was established to govern the country in Napoleon II's name. Instead a second resolution, as perfunctory as the first, was adopted: 'The two Chambers desired and meant by their decree of yesterday – in nominating a commission of provisional Government – to assure to the nation the guarantee necessary under the extraordinary circumstances in which it is placed, for its liberty and repose.' In short, power remained for the moment with the five-man commission, and primarily with its president, Joseph Fouché. Despite a further resolution, that 'Members of the Provisional Government should take an oath of obedience to the Constitutions of the Empire, and of fidelity to Napoleon II Emperor of the French',[12] the child was emperor in nothing but name; emperor until a Bourbon king was reinstated, 'Constitutions of the Empire' and fidelity of no further relevance.

*

Napoleon lingered in the Élysée Palace, to the growing unease of the provisional government. His continued presence at the centre of imperial power could only compromise peace negotiations with enemies who regarded him as the principal reason for prolonging the war. As the focus of idolatrous support from the most unruly elements of the Parisian populace, he also constituted a serious threat to public order. The *fédérés*, backed by large slum mobs, still swarmed daily in the avenue de Marigny, roaring '*Vive l'Empereur!*', and every day he showed himself to them from the terrace of the palace. Étienne-Denis Pasquier – Napoleon's former *préfect de police* in Paris, and soon to be rewarded by the restored monarchy for distancing himself from 'the usurper' – thought the ritual demeaning:

> I could not help falling prey to the deepest emotion, on seeing him reduced to coming forward and replying by repeated bows to acclamations springing from so low a source. There are few more melancholy, more touching, and more heartrending sights, than that of a man, so long the centre of so great a glory and of such prodigious power, reduced to such humiliating straits.

Pasquier was convinced that the man on the terrace felt it to be so too: 'His naturally grave physiognomy had assumed a sombre aspect; occasionally he endeavoured to smile, but the expression of his eyes reflected the sadness which pervaded his soul.'[13]

Fouché used the Chambers to persuade Napoleon to leave Paris. A motion was proposed and passed that the ex-Emperor should 'be invited, in the name of the nation to leave the capital, where his presence can only cause trouble and be a source of danger to the public'.[14] According to Chaboulon, more devious tactics were brought to bear, playing on Napoleon's fear of assassination. 'Every day officious advisers warned him, that attempts were making against his life: and to give more probability to this clumsy scheme, his guard was suddenly reinforced.' One night his entourage were roused from sleep by the commandant of Paris and warned to be vigilant as the palace was about to be attacked. Chaboulon and his companions treated the alarm with contempt and returned to their beds without even thinking it necessary to inform their master. 'Nothing, however, could have been more easy than . . . to assassinate Napoleon,' Chaboulon remarked:

His palace, which ten days before could scarcely contain the bustling crowd of ambitious men and courtiers, was now one vast solitude. All those men, destitute of faith and honour, whom power attracts, and adversity keeps at a distance, had deserted it. His guard had been reduced to a few old grenadiers; and a single sentry, scarcely in uniform, watched the door of that Napoleon, that king of kings, who lately reckoned millions of soldiers under his banners.[15]

He was fully resigned to leave but – as with his decision to abdicate – wished 'to be left in peace to think about it'. Chaboulon ascribed his inertia at this time to the trauma of his fall:

> Accustomed to see all his wishes, all his enterprises, crowned with success, he had not learned to contend against the sudden attacks of misfortune; and, notwithstanding the firmness of his character, they threw him occasionally into a state of irresolution, during which a thousand thoughts, a thousand designs, jostled each other in his mind, and deprived him of the possibility of coming to any decision.

Chaboulon called it a 'moral catalepsy'.[16]

Napoleon had decided to go first to Malmaison, the late Empress Josephine's residence, now occupied by her daughter, the Princess Hortense. But his ultimate destination remained as yet uncertain. The United States of America tempted him, and the country had much to recommend it: a republic that had until recently been at war with England. 'Several Americans, who found themselves in Paris,' Chaboulon claimed, 'wrote of their own accord to Napoleon, to offer him their services, and assure him, in the name of their fellow-citizens, that he would be received at Washington with the sentiments of respect, admiration, and devotion that were his due.'[17]

However, England exerted a surprising and apparently perverse attraction for Napoleon as a potential place of exile. 'He considered the heart of a Briton as the inviolable sanctuary of honour, generosity, and all the public and private virtues, that stamp on man loftiness and dignity.' And he seemed able to separate that idealised conception of John Bull from 'the known sentiments and principles' of the government in London. As the alternative to a future life in the United States, he envisaged the rural seclusion of an English landed gentleman. He had even weighed a choice of pseudonyms he might adopt: either Duroc, in memory of his friend, aide-de-camp and commander of the Imperial Guard, killed at Lutzen in 1813; or Muiron, a colonel who had died shielding him in 1796 at the battle of Arcola.[18] He had voiced this fantasy to Caulaincourt, who, expressing neither approval nor disapproval, advised 'that if he persisted in taking this step, to go on board a smuggling vessel', he should, 'as soon as he landed . . . present himself to the magistrate of the locality and declare that he came with confidence to invoke the protection of the English nation'.[19]

But as Napoleon made preparations to leave, he seems to have definitely decided otherwise. Late on 22 June he instructed Admiral Decrès to anchor two ships near Rochefort, provisioned for passage to America. The following day, application was made to Fouché for passports, also to America. And on the morning of the 25th, Napoleon's librarian, Barbier, was instructed to send books to Malmaison, including 'some works on America'. He was also told to bring the travelling library up to date and to ensure that it was supplemented 'by a number of works on the United States'. Finally, the main library, containing 'a complete set of the *Moniteur*, the best encyclopaedia, the best dictionaries', was to be packed up and 'consigned to an American house, which will forward it to America by le Havre'.

A necessary accompaniment to any change of regime, there was a wholesale destruction of paper at the Elysée prior to his departure. Napoleon ordered burnt the mass of addresses, petitions and letters he had received since returning to power on 20 March. It was while Chaboulon was engaged in this work that his master made him a gift to ensure his security in the uncertain times ahead. Picking up a letter that was about to be thrown into the flames, Napoleon recognised the signature of a particular nobleman and read through the ingratiating contents. He handed it to Chaboulon with a smile.

'Don't burn this,' he said, 'keep it for yourself. It will be an excellent testimonial.'

Chaboulon did not at first understand how embarrassing, and possibly incriminating, the document might be for the nobleman in question.

'This man will not fail to swear to those people [who take power after I am gone], that he has maintained his fidelity towards them inviolate; and when he knows, that you have in your hands substantial proof of his having laid himself at my feet, and that I refused both him and his services, he will be ready to quarter himself to serve you, for fear you should expose him.'

Chaboulon thought he was joking.

'No, I tell you; don't burn that letter, or any others from people like that: I give them to you for your protection.'[20]

At half past midday on 25 June, Napoleon left the Elysée for the last time. To avoid the crowds shouting '*Vive l'Empereur!*' at the front of the palace, he went through the garden at the rear and joined Bertrand in the general's two-horse carriage and departed unobserved along the Champs-Elysées. The imperial coach, drawn by six horses and accompanied by a mounted escort, contained General Gourgaud, General Montholon and the Comte de Las Cases, and set off by a different route along the rue Saint-Honoré. Safely beyond the Barrière de Chaillot, on the outskirts of Paris, Napoleon got out of Bertrand's carriage and climbed into his own for the remainder of the hour's drive to Malmaison.

*

At the chateau he was greeted by his devoted stepdaughter Hortense, and spent some time walking in the grounds with General Savary, Comte de Rovigo, who commanded the three hundred members of the Old Guard and forty dragoons responsible for protecting his person. Napoleon was shocked at how otherwise deserted Malmaison seemed. Six orderly officers arrived at dusk, and, later in the evening, two generals, 'but it was only to ask for money'.[21] One of these was General Piré, for whom the Emperor had repeatedly asked in the terrible confusion of 19 June.

Napoleon's first action on entering the chateau was to finish a proclamation he had begun writing in Paris. The declaration of 22 June announcing his abdication had been addressed to the French people. This of the 25th, at Malmaison, was to his troops:

> Soldiers! While I yield to the necessity that forces me to leave the brave French army, I take away with me the happy certainty that it will justify, by the eminent services its country expects from it, those praises, which even our enemies cannot withhold. Soldiers, I shall follow your steps, though absent. I know every Corps and none of you can win a victory over the enemy without my doing justice to the courage you display . . . Soldiers! With just a few more efforts, the coalition [of our enemies] will dissolve. Napoleon will recognise you through the blows that you strike. Save the honour, the independence of France; stay to the very end as I have known you these twenty years past, and you shall be invincible.

Some time later he would enquire how his words had been received in the ranks. This farewell to his beloved troops, however, the recalling of past glory and encouragement to continue fighting, could only be regarded as compromising by a provisional government attempting to broker peace. Unlike the more welcome announcement of his abdication, three days earlier, it was not published in the *Moniteur*. When he was told, in answer to his question, 'that the army knew nothing of it', it was observed that he displayed 'no mark of vexation or discontent' and turned the conversation to other matters.

As Napoleon finished writing his proclamation, in Paris Marshal Davout was writing an order to General Beker, Comte de Mons. Beker had been disgraced and cashiered in 1809 for unguarded remarks against the Emperor. Recently recalled from enforced retirement to serve his country at this time of crisis, he was to take command from Savary of Napoleon's guard at Malmaison. 'The honour of France demands a careful watch over the safety of his person, and a strict observance of the respect which is due to him.'[22] The national honour required something else as well: so-called 'malcontents' were to be prevented from using the Emperor's name 'in order to excite disturbance'. Beker's mission was not only to protect Napoleon but also to isolate him from elements within his circle that might encourage him to seize power. Also, as a member of the Chamber of Peers, and because he had been appointed by Davout rather than by the Emperor, Beker would be expected to report directly to the provisional government. When he arrived at Malmaison, it was at first thought that he had come to arrest the Emperor, and despite assurances to the contrary, some of the entourage continued to believe this. Princess Hortense was heard to murmur, 'O my God! Was I born to see the Emperor a prisoner of the French at Malmaison?'[23] Napoleon himself, although acceding to the arrangement, recognised the general's commission for what it was: 'a measure of *surveillance*'. Montholon was to write later: 'the captivity of Napoleon dates from this day, for after it he ceased to enjoy liberty of action'.

In Paris, during the days that followed, arrangements were made for Napoleon's departure from France. A document, signed by all five members of the Commission of Government, decreed that two frigates should be armed for the purpose of transporting 'Napoleon Bonaparte' to America. It was the first time since his abdication that the provisional government had formally referred to him in this way. He was to be provided with an escort as far as Rochefort, and General Beker was 'directed to watch over his safety'. His 'safety' would be an often-repeated reference in all the documentation arising from these arrangements. There was, however, a curious stipulation, suggesting that the intentions of the Commission of Government, perhaps especially of its presiding genius, Fouché, were not all they seemed: 'The frigates shall not leave the roadstead of Rochefort until the passes shall have

arrived.' Napoleon, it would appear, was to be given every assistance in reaching the coast, only to await delivery of the passports
that Fouché could have authorised before he set out. Whilst
hastening his departure from the Elysée and Malmaison, Fouché
was hampering his escape from France for no other reason, it
would seem, than delivering him to the enemy. That Fouché was
in communication with the Duke of Wellington at this time, as
the allied armies advanced to encircle Paris, was apparent from
assurances he gave to one of Napoleon's aides regarding the travel
arrangements:

> I will not take upon myself to let him depart without adopting
> every precaution for his safety: otherwise, I should be blamed if
> any accident were to happen to him. I will apply to Lord Wellington
> for passports for him, as it behoves me to protect my individual
> responsibility in the eyes of the nation. I should never be forgiven
> for acting without the requisite precaution.[24]

By applying to Wellington for passports, he was, of course,
informing the English commander not only of Napoleon's plan
to escape from France, but also where best to apprehend him
and prevent him from doing so. The series of dispatches that
passed from Fouché to Decrès concerning passports and frigates
was a duplicitous charade.

During these uncertain days Napoleon received visitors and
Malmaison bustled again. A number of women arrived to pay
their respects: Caulaincourt's wife, the Duchesse de Vicence;
Madame Duchatel; Madame Regnault, bringing news of conspiracy
in Paris and 'Fouché . . . at the head of the plot!' The Emperor's
former mistress, Marie Walewska, also visited. The importunate
generals, Piré and Chartran, were given notes to draw money and
hurried back to Paris to cash them, only to return the following
day disgruntled at receiving just twelve and six thousand francs
respectively. General Flahaut arrived on the 27th with de La
Bédoyère, Admiral Decrès, the Emperor's brother Joseph and
Maret, the Duc de Bassano. 'The day passed in conversation',

General Gourgaud recalled, and Bassano might well have been asked why the Emperor's last proclamation had not appeared in the *Moniteur*. Decrès would have discussed the provision of frigates at Rochefort. There was, as yet, no sign of the passports.

Finally, on 28 June, Decrès received a letter, signed by all five members of the Commission of Government, confirming the travel arrangements. 'The frigates are . . . placed at Napoleon's disposal. Nothing can any longer obstruct his departure.'[25] Decrès issued detailed orders to the commanders of the *Saale* and the *Méduse*, anchored off the Ile d'Aix near Rochefort, for the embarkation of 'the individual who was recently our Emperor', for his transportation 'with the utmost rapidity' to the United States of America, and for his disembarkation 'at Philadelphia or Boston, or any other port . . . which they might find it easiest to reach within a shorter delay'.[26] The commission's letter, hurrying Napoleon towards captivity, ended on a note of urgency: 'The interest of the state and his own well-being make it imperative that he should depart immediately.' The urgency was not misplaced.

On 28 June, with reports arriving of the Prussian advance, Gourgaud and Montholon undertook a complete survey of Malmaison's defences, and settled on the most effective placement of their little force of grenadiers. 'We were all resolved that the capture of the chateau should cost the enemy who might attack it, dear.' Scouting parties of three dragoons each were sent out in the direction of Gonesse and Saint-Germain. Beker received orders from Paris to destroy the bridge over the Seine at Chatou, less than a mile away. He and Gourgaud accomplished the sabotage with a group of guards, and later, from the chateau, it could be seen burning all night. They could also hear cannon fire from Saint-Denis.

Napoleon was to set out the following morning. Earlier on the 28th he had consulted his physician and, not apparently discouraged by his previous attempt at suicide, procured a small vial of red liquid that his valet, charged with devising a method of concealing it just inside his master's jacket, described as 'instant death'.[27] It was a wise precaution. Were he to fall into Prussian hands, his end would be summary and degrading. A letter from

Gneisenau to Müffling, written the day before Napoleon made his grim preparations, requested the liaison officer to negotiate with the Duke of Wellington 'that Bonaparte may be delivered over to *us*, with a view to his execution'. Blücher had planned both the means and the setting for sentence to be carried out. The former Emperor was to be taken to the fortress at Vincennes and shot in the south-east corner of the moat, close to the foot of the Tour de la Reine. It was the spot where, eleven years previously, a royalist martyr, the Duc d'Enghien, had been executed by firing squad on spurious charges allegedly concocted by Bonaparte, then First Consul. 'This is what eternal justice demands,' wrote Gneisenau, 'and thus the blood of our soldiers killed and mutilated on the 16th and 18th will be avenged.'[28]

*

Early on the morning of 29 June, the Prussian IV Korps received orders that an officer, with one cavalry regiment, two infantry battalions and half a battery of horse artillery, was to proceed by way of Argenteuil and Chatou to capture Bonaparte at Malmaison. 'The greatest speed is recommended and it is vital to cross the bridge at Chatou quickly.'[29] As this was the closest river crossing to their objective, it was hoped that the inhabitants might be taken by surprise.

That same morning, the day of Napoleon's departure, there were shouts from the roadway beyond the chateau walls: '*Vive l'Empereur!*', '*À bas les Bourbons!*', '*À bas les traitres!*' A division of the Imperial Army, recalled to the defence of Paris from subduing royalist rebels in La Vendée, had learnt that their Emperor was at Malmaison and demanded that he lead them. Their commander, General Brayer, craved an audience with Napoleon and explained that his troops had refused to proceed further unless their petition was heard. After a quarter of an hour, his interview at an end, Brayer returned to the head of his men and they continued to Paris, bawling out their allegiance to the Emperor and 'entertaining the hope of soon seeing him again on the field of battle'.[30]

The encounter galvanised Napoleon out of his 'moral catalepsy'. He sent for General Beker and told him that their departure for the coast would be delayed, and that the Chambers were to be informed of his willingness to resume command of the army and defend France, not in his own name but in that of the Emperor Napoleon II. Beker was sent, a reluctant messenger, to make this offer to the provisional government. The general was in an intolerable position. His instructions from the government had been to protect and accompany the former Emperor as far as his embarkation at Rochefort. Running this errand would appear to his political masters as collusion in Napoleon's quixotic enterprise. He travelled rapidly by chaise as far as the Pont de Neuilly on the western outskirts of Paris but, finding the bridge barricaded against the Prussians, he abandoned his carriage, climbed over the parapet, then, risking a plunge into the Seine, inched along the outer ledge to the opposite side of the river. There he commandeered another vehicle and drove to the Tuileries, where the Commission of Government sat in council. Fouché and his four colleagues were astonished to see Beker, whom they had thought to be well on the road to the south-west. He bowed and delivered his message:

> Gentlemen, the Emperor sends me to inform you that the situation of France, the wishes of all true patriots, and the cries of the soldiery, demand his presence to save our country. It is no longer as Emperor that he demands this, but as a General, whose name and reputation may still exercise a powerful influence over the fate of the empire. After having repulsed our enemies, he promises to retire to the United States to accomplish his destiny.[31]

He then read out the letter that Napoleon had dictated to him, outlining the efficacy of his plan. It pointed out that the 80,000 French troops in and around the city at that moment numbered 30,000 more than the force he had commanded in the campaign of 1814, a campaign that had successfully held off the combined armies of Austria, Russia and Prussia for three months; a campaign that had only failed when Paris capitulated. The letter also recalled that with 80,000 troops he would have 45,000 more than he had fifteen years earlier when, as General Bonaparte, he had crossed the Alps and conquered Italy.

As might have been predicted, Fouché declined the offer. The very last thing he wished to see was Napoleon commanding another French army. He did not even bother to consult his colleagues – who sat around the table in silence or paced despondently up and down the room – while he explained to Beker that the military prospects were not hopeful, that the Prussians were nearing Saint-Germain and Versailles, and that 'a more protracted delay will expose his Majesty to the danger of falling into the hands of the allies'.

Beker took his leave. He strode out through the antechamber, through the waiting rooms of the palace, all crowded with generals and dignitaries appalled at the news that Napoleon had not yet reached safety. 'Let him set off!' they told Beker. 'Let him go! We can undertake nothing, either for his personal advantage, or for the good of Paris.' Beker drove back to the Pont de Neuilly, crossed it in the same precarious manner as before, recovered his chaise on the other side, and in half an hour reached Malmaison.

Within an hour of the general's return, a yellow *caleche* and four was waiting at the park gates, a courier was ready to ride ahead and ensure that fresh horses were available at relay posts along the 250-mile route, and servants had assembled in the chateau's vestibule to bid Napoleon goodbye. He emerged, as Montholon recalled, 'his countenance . . . sublime from its calmness and serenity; the more so, as this calmness and serenity was that of resignation'. Memories differed as to the clothes he wore: Montholon described 'a green overcoat, azure-blue trousers, and a round hat';[32] Gourgaud specified 'a coat of maroon cloth';[33] Savary 'a plain frock[coat] without any mark of distinction'.[34]

One of the last men he spoke to at Malmaison was the Minister for Foreign Affairs, who had greeted him on his return to the Elysée Palace just eight days earlier:

All is over, Caulaincourt. In a few days hence, I must quit France for ever. I will fix my abode in the United States. In the course of some little time, the spot which I shall inhabit will be in a condition to receive the glorious wrecks of the army. All my old companions in arms will find an asylum with me. Who knows but that I may one day or other have an *hôpital des invalides* in the United States, for my veteran guards.[35]

Napoleon and Bertrand occupied the canopied rear of the *caleche*; facing them, Beker and Savary took the seats outside the canopy and open to the elements at the front, their backs to the driver and Napoleon's valet on the box above. The *caleche* itself contained no luggage and was not intended to give any indication of their embarking on a long journey. Servants and baggage occupied other carriages. General Gourgaud was to travel alone some way behind in a small two-seater with the Emperor's effects and 100,000 francs in gold. He had taken pistols and some rifles from the chateau and distributed them liberally among the other carriages. His own weapons would allow him to fire sixteen shots in defence of the gold before reloading.

The rest of the entourage – Madame Bertrand and her children; Montholon, his wife and child; Las Cases and his son; along with several orderly officers, servants and baggage – was to travel in a convoy of carriages by a separate route.

As he took his place opposite Bertrand and Napoleon, Beker handed a note he had scribbled earlier to a messenger who was to deliver it to Marshal Davout: 'I have the honour to inform you that the Emperor is on the point of entering his carriage to accomplish his destiny.' It was six o'clock in the evening. The yellow *caleche* set off 'amidst profound silence'.[36]

*

Major von Colomb of the Prussian 8th Hussars did not receive that morning's order instructing him to capture Napoleon until the afternoon. With his two infantry battalions and artillery he set out from Louvres at four o'clock and marched twenty-five miles through the night to Montesson. There, three miles from Malmaison, he received news that the bridge across the Seine at Chatou had been destroyed and Napoleon was gone.

III

ON 22 June, aboard his flagship *Chatham* in Cawsand Bay, west of Plymouth, the seventy-year-old commander of the Channel fleet, Admiral Lord Keith, ordered a salute to be fired 'in honour of the late glorious victory'.[1] Two days later, anxiety concerning the well-being of his nephews was allayed by news that, although injured in the battle, they were both out of danger. One of them, Captain James Drummond Elphinstone of the 7th Light Dragoons, had been wounded in two places and taken prisoner by the French on 17 June. Confined overnight at Genappe and throughout the following day, he had been left behind in the chaotic retreat, his guard saluting him as he left with *Mon Capitaine, je vous souhaite bonsoir* – I wish you good night.[2] When first captured, he had been brought before the Emperor for questioning and treated with great kindness. Napoleon even had occasion to reprimand the Comte de Flahault for discourtesy when his aide-de-camp expressed doubts about Captain Elphinstone's story. Admiral Keith would soon have the opportunity to convey his personal thanks to Napoleon for the consideration shown his kinsman.

In the late afternoon of 26 June, the *Chatham* received a message by telegraph: 'Buonaparte abdicated.' During the following day, Keith waited impatiently for further information and for orders from London. 'I suppose I shall be off very soon,' he wrote to Lady Keith, 'and all us sea-folks.' But no post came

on the 27th and the weather was 'too thick for telegraph'.[3] Then
a 'Private and Secret' letter arrived from Robert Saunders Dundas,
2nd Viscount Melville, the First Lord of the Admiralty, writing
from his home in Wimbledon. Intelligence had reached the government from various sources that, 'in the event of adverse fortune,
it was the intention of Bonaparte to escape to America'. Melville
thought it probable that this attempt was to be made soon, and
if by a small vessel from one of the obscurer western ports, it
would be scarcely possible to prevent. However, if Bonaparte
waited until a sloop or frigate had been fitted out for him, the
Royal Navy might 'perhaps receive information of such preparation, and may thereby be enabled to watch and intercept her'.
Keith had his orders: 'it is desirable that you should take every
precaution in your power with a view to [Bonaparte's] seizure
and detention, should he endeavour to quit France by sea'.[4]

On the night of 30 June, the British government received 'an
application from the rulers of France, for a passport and safe
conduct for Buonaparte to America'. The next day, this application 'was answered in the negative'.[5]

During the following week, Admiral Keith offered naval support
to the forces fighting for Louis XVIII's restoration. He sent transports to royalist rebel strongholds in the west of France, landing
weapons and clothing at strategic ports down the coast, from
Quiberon Bay in Brittany to as far south as the Gironde estuary.
The insurgency in Quiberon continued to 'go well', that in
Morbihan 'famous', but in La Vendée, 'things is not so well',
despite 6,000 pairs of shoes Keith had sent there on 28 June. At
the same time, he was 'seeking for Bonny on the sea', he told his
wife, using, as was his habit, this spelling instead of the more
common 'Boney'. In Plymouth, the same rumours were reaching
him as reached other newspaper readers across the country. 'It is
now said that little Nap is assassinated at Paris,' he wrote to
Lady Keith on 29 June, the day Napoleon left Malmaison for
the coast. Two days later, 'it is said Bonny is in London'. Within
a week, Napoleon was said to be even closer at hand: 'at Windsor's
Hotel, to which place all Plymouth and Dock repaired'.[6] At the

time he remarked upon this absurd rumour, Keith was clearly
unaware that Napoleon had been in Rochefort for three days.
Intelligence reaching him in Plymouth concerning developments
on the western coast of France continued to be as much as a
week out of date throughout this crisis.

On 2 July, Keith apprised Rear Admiral Sir Henry Hotham,
commanding the squadron cruising off the Breton ports of Brest
and Lorient, of Bonaparte's supposed intentions, 'furnishing them
with instructions as to the measures to be taken to intercept
him'.[7] The *Glasgow*, *Prometheus*, *Esk* and *Ferrol* were to patrol
westward of the Channel island of Ushant; *Swiftsure* to cruise
off Cape Finisterre; *Vengeur* to patrol 'in the track of the Channel'.

*

A month earlier, on 31 May, another vessel of Hotham's squadron
had arrived in the Basque Roads: the seventy-four-gun man-of-
war HMS *Bellerophon*. Beyond the channel separating the Ile de
Ré from the Ile d'Oleron – the middle and widest of three
approaches to Rochefort – the English lookouts could see, lying
between them and the entrance to the port, the small, heavily
fortified Ile d'Aix and, anchored close under its southernmost
point, a French sloop, a brig and two large frigates, the *Méduse*
and the *Saale*. For the following two months, the *Bellerophon*'s
crew, and Captain Maitland her commander, would be engaged
in the soul-destroying monotony of blockade duty – ensuring that
no French ship entered or left port and never, by day or night,
being more than three miles from the land. Despite this proximity
to France, news of the great events affecting that nation and their
own came to them surprisingly late. Not until 28 June – by which
date much of Britain was illuminated in celebration – did they
learn of Wellington's victory at Waterloo and the devastating
defeat of Napoleon.

Afterwards news arrived with greater frequency but was not
always to be relied upon. On 30 June, Maitland received an
anonymous note from Bordeaux – written on very thin paper

and rolled into the quill of a goose feather – that Napoleon had just passed through that city and was expected to be embarking from the mouth of the Gironde, or from La Teste to the south. Meanwhile, Rear Admiral Hotham was anticipating a possible embarkation much further north: from the mouth of the Loire, at Nantes. 'It is impossible to tell which information respecting Buonaparte's flight may be correct,' he told Maitland, 'but in the uncertainty, it is right to attach a certain degree of credit to all.' But on 7 July, the *Slaney* brought Maitland the latest intelligence: that Napoleon was making for Rochefort. The following day, another dispatch from Hotham expressed concern, assuming the frigates off the Ile d'Aix were to be used in the escape attempt, that Maitland would have sufficient force to stop them, 'as *Bellerophon* could only take one, if they separated, and that might not be the one [Bonaparte] would be on board of'. But Maitland had retained the *Slaney*, a twenty-gun sloop, under his command and recalled another, the *Myrmidon*, of equal strength, from patrolling off Bordeaux. These three ships – together with the *Daphne*, patrolling twenty-five miles to the south, and later the *Cyrus* – would be capable of containing the *Méduse* and the *Saale* in the Basque Roads. 'I depend on your using the best means that can be adopted', Hotham told the *Bellerophon*'s captain, 'to intercept the fugitive on whose captivity the repose of Europe appears to depend.'

*

Napoleon had arrived in Rochefort – installing himself and his fifty-strong entourage at the residence of the maritime prefect, Casimir de Bonnefoux – on the morning of 3 July. It was the same day, Montholon pointed out, 'that Paris, for the second time, opened its gates to the enemy'.[8] For the next five days they waited, making no move to board the frigates lying off the Ile d'Aix ready to receive them. The time was spent investigating alternative means of escape. They had been informed by the prefect while still on the road to Rochefort that the port was blockaded by English ships, albeit lightly at first, but with increasing strength.

General Lallemand, who had joined the company from Paris a day or so earlier, was sent south to inspect the corvette *Bayadère*, anchored in the Gironde, and returned with an assurance that its master, Captain Baudin, 'was devoted to his Majesty [and] would receive him with the highest distinction'.[9]

Another plan was for Napoleon to leave on board a ninety-ton Danish brig, the *Magdeleine*, whose captain, one Frühl d'Oppendorff, happened to be the father-in-law of a French naval officer at Rochefort, Lieutenant Besson. Las Cases drafted a complicated legal agreement between himself and Besson, comprising eight separate articles and involving 25,000 francs, a cargo of brandy and unnamed 'passengers'.[10] Not mentioned in the agreement was the concealment of Napoleon – should the ship be boarded and searched by an English patrol – inside a barrel stowed among the ballast in the hold 'with tubes so constructed as to convey air for his breathing'.[11]

A third option was that he and his people would take to the sea aboard two *chasse-marées*. Small, decked vessels rigged like an English lugger, and between twenty and thirty-five tons, they were primarily used in the coastal trade, the name itself deriving from the French term for wholesale fishmonger. A footnote in Maitland's memoir made clear the 'utter impracticability' of this plan: '[taking] into consideration the indolent habits that Buonaparte had of late years given way to; the very small space for the accommodation of himself and suite, and of the stowage of provisions, water, and other necessaries; that there was no friendly port he could have touched at, to gain supplies . . .'

Still with no decision made, Napoleon left the mainland of France at ten past five in the afternoon of 8 July, and went on board the *Saale*. No salute was fired to mark the occasion in case it attracted the premature attention of the *Bellerophon*. Apart from a brief visit the following morning to inspect the fortifications of the Ile d'Aix and receive its inhabitants' acclamations,

Napoleon would remain on the *Saale* for the next four days while negotiations were opened on his behalf with the commander of the British vessel.

*

At dawn on 10 July, a small schooner flying a flag of truce approached the English ship. On board were Savary and Las Cases bearing a letter from Marshal Bertrand:

> [The Emperor] expects a passport from the British Government, which has been promised to him, and which induces [him] to demand of you, Sir, if you have any knowledge of the above-mentioned passport, or if you think it is the intention of the British Government to throw any impediment in the way of our voyage to the United States.

Maitland would make no mention, either in his written reply or verbally to the emissaries, that to his certain knowledge, the British government had already declined the issue of passports. The captain first asked if either of his visitors understood English, and when Savary alone answered in the negative, their conversation was conducted in French. Las Cases, however, had spent some time in England and was acquainted with the language but did not admit to it, hoping to gain information from any unguarded asides Maitland might direct to his officers.

Savary and Las Cases had been instructed to make informal enquiries of their host whether – if permission were to be refused for the frigates to leave port under a French flag – Maitland intended preventing Napoleon from proceeding on his way in some neutral vessel.

Maitland replied that he could not say what his government's intentions might be. However, 'the two countries being at present in a state of war, it is impossible for me to permit any ship of war to put to sea from the port of Rochefort'. As for the proposal put to him of allowing the Emperor to travel in a neutral merchant ship, he did not have the authority 'to allow any vessel, under whatever flag she may be, to pass with a personage of such consequence'.[12]

During the two or three hours they spent on board his ship, Maitland's visitors tried to convince him that it would be in the interest of peace to allow Napoleon's passage to America. He was, they said, in wishing to leave Europe, 'actuated solely by motives of humanity; being unwilling . . . that any further effusion of blood should take place on his account'. They pointed out also that he still commanded considerable support in the centre and south of France, and that 'if he chose to protract the war, he might still give a great deal of trouble'.

At one stage of the conversation, Maitland asked: 'Supposing the British Government should be induced to grant a passport for Buonaparte's going to America, what pledge could he give that he would not return, and put England, as well as all Europe, to the same expense of blood and treasure that has just been incurred!'

'The influence he once had over the French people is past', Savary replied, 'and he could never regain the power he had over their minds. Therefore, he would prefer retiring into obscurity, where he might end his days in peace and tranquillity . . .'

It was then that Captain Maitland made a suggestion – whether casual or considered – which, in the light of future developments and decisions, was to give Napoleon grounds for accusing the English of bad faith: 'If that is the case why not ask for an asylum in England!'

Savary gave a number of reasons why not: 'The climate is too damp and cold; it is too near France; he would be . . . in the centre of every change and revolution that might take place there, and . . . be subject to suspicion . . . [and] the English [would] look upon him as a monster, without one of the virtues of a human being.'

Maitland thought the two Frenchmen were trying to give him the impression 'of Buonaparte's situation being by no means so desperate as might be supposed'. It was clear, however, that on their return to the *Saale* with news of the intractability of the English blockade, increasingly desperate measures were contemplated.

At about noon on 11 July, Maitland received reliable information that a message had been sent from the Ile d'Aix offering a large sum of money to a local pilot – the only man, it was said, who had ever succeeded in navigating a frigate through the treacherous Mamusson Passage, southernmost and narrowest out of Rochefort – to take d'Oppendorff's Danish brig to sea by the same route. Maitland took the precaution of reinforcing the *Daphne*'s patrol of that stretch of water with the *Myrmidon*. The following day he was able to telegraph to another sloop, the *Cyrus*, sighted in the offing, ordering her to take position close in with the Baleine lighthouse and thereby cover the Breton Channel, the northernmost passage from the port. The blockade of all three ways out of Rochefort was thus secured for the time being.

Escape on board the Danish brig having been abandoned, an even more drastic strategy was proposed by the *Méduse*'s Captain Ponét. It amounted to a suicide mission. Under cover of darkness, he would surprise the English man-of-war at anchor, engage in close combat his sixty guns against the *Bellerophon*'s seventy-four, and 'lash his vessel to her sides, so as to neutralise her efforts and impede her sailing'. During this fight, in which the outgunned *Méduse* 'would necessarily be destroyed', the *Saale* could take advantage of the breeze that invariably blew from the land each evening, slipping past the smaller English ships and so gaining the open sea. The heroic plan was declined, both by Captain Philibert of the *Saale* and by Napoleon himself, unwilling, it was said, 'to sacrifice a ship and her crew to his personal safety'.[13] Deprived of her bid for glory, the *Méduse* would leave Rochefort in June of the following year and sail into infamy. Commanded by an inexperienced captain, she ran aground off the coast of West Africa and 147 passengers were cast adrift on a hastily constructed raft, all but fifteen succumbing

to violence, heat, thirst and madness, the survivors feeding on
the raw flesh of the dead.

*

Over the following two days, awaiting further developments,
Maitland watched the apparent fluctuations of royalist and
Bonapartist fortunes in the port of La Rochelle to the north. On
12 July, for the first time, the white Bourbon standard was hoisted
and Maitland felt it his duty to reciprocate, flying the French
King's flag from the main topgallant masthead, and ordering a
royal salute to be fired. As though in defiance, two tricolours
continued to fly over La Rochelle throughout the afternoon and
by sunset all the white flags had been struck and replaced by
those of the revolution. The following day 'nothing of importance
occurred, except the white flag being once more hoisted all over
[La] Rochelle . . . to the entire exclusion of the tri-coloured
ensign'. But as Maitland turned his spyglass on the *Saale* and
Mèduse from a distance of about three miles, he could tell, by
the activity of boats passing between them and the Ile d'Aix; by
the arrangement of their yards and reeving of their studding sail
gear; and by 'having their sterns covered with vegetables', that
they were preparing to put to sea. He immediately signalled to
the vessels under his command that 'everything [be] kept ready
to make sail at a moment's warning'. All that night the
Bellerophon's guard boats rowed as close to the two frigates as
possible, ready to signal any indication that they were getting
under way.

Then, at dawn, the officer of the watch indicated that the same
schooner as before was approaching, once again under a flag of
truce. Las Cases and, this time, General Lallemand came aboard.
As they approached, Maitland had signalled the *Slaney*'s
commander to join him as a witness to the talks, and Captain
Sartorius arrived while they were at breakfast. Later, in the after-
cabin, Las Cases opened the second round of negotiations:

'The Emperor is so anxious to spare further effusion of human

blood that he will proceed to America in any way the British
Government chooses to sanction, either in a French ship of war
. . . a merchant vessel, or even in a British ship of war.'

Maitland replied that he still had no authority to agree to any
such arrangement; nor did he believe that his government would
consent to it.

Then . . .

'But I think I may venture to receive him into this ship, and
convey him to England. If, however, he adopts that plan, I cannot
enter into any promise as to the reception he may meet with, as,
even in the case I have mentioned, I shall be acting on my own
responsibility, and cannot be sure that it would meet with the
approbation of the British Government.'[14]

According to Las Cases, Maitland 'declared it as his private
opinion, and several [officers] who were present expressed themselves to the same effect, that there was not the least doubt of
Napoleon's meeting with all possible respect and good treatment'.
The emissaries were assured that England was not ruled by despots
and that this was reflected in the temper of its citizens: 'that there,
neither the king nor his ministers exercised the same arbitrary
authority as those of the Continent: that the English people
possessed a generosity of sentiment and liberality of opinion,
superior to sovereignty itself'. In retrospect, and even in light of
what Napoleon and his followers would subsequently regard as
the British government's betrayal of trust and confidence, Las
Cases maintained that Maitland and his colleagues behaved
honourably: 'I will do him, as well as the other officers, the justice
to believe, they were honest and sincere in the description they
gave us of the sentiments of the people of England.' When General
Lallemand, a man 'implicated in the civil dissensions of his
country',[15] enquired whether he had any reason to fear being
delivered up by England to the vengeance of France, 'Certainly
not!' Maitland replied, considering such suspicion an insult.[16]

Before leaving, Las Cases remarked to Maitland: 'Under all
circumstances, I have little doubt that you will see the Emperor
on board the *Bellerophon*.'

About seven o'clock that evening he returned, accompanied by General Gourgaud. Maitland had again ensured that he had witnesses to the meeting and Captain Sartorius was in attendance, together with the *Myrmidon*'s Captain Gambier. Las Cases handed Maitland a letter from Marshal Bertrand, informing him of His Majesty's intention to 'proceed on board your ship with the ebb tide to-morrow morning, between four and five o'clock'. It was accompanied by a list of the fifty individuals – generals, officers, women, children and domestics – who would be travelling with the Emperor. Finally, General Gourgaud declared that he was the bearer of a letter from the Emperor himself, which he had been charged to deliver personally into the hands of the Prince Regent:

> Your Royal Highness,
>
> A Victim to the factions which distract my country, and to the enmity of the greatest powers of Europe, I have terminated my political career, and I come, like Themistocles, to throw myself upon the hospitality of the British people. I put myself under the protection of their laws; which I claim from your Royal Highness, as the most powerful, the most constant, and the most generous of my enemies.

It was signed, as befitted a communication between monarchs, with the forename only: 'Napoleon'. A copy was given to Maitland to read, 'which he greatly admired', and the captains of the *Slaney* and the *Myrmidon* were allowed to make copies for themselves, to keep as souvenirs of the event.[17] Maitland was convinced that Napoleon had decided on his course of action even before that morning's negotiation, because the letter was dated 13 July, the previous day.

Gourgaud carried an additional document: a memorandum from the Emperor with which, in the event of the general being granted an audience with the Prince Regent, he was to outline the stipulations and conditions of his master's surrender:

> If HRH sees no objection to granting me passports to go to the United States, it would be my intention to go there. But I do not

desire to go to any other colony. If I cannot go to America, I wish to stay in England, assuming the name of Muiron or Duroc. In England, I would like to live in a country house about ten to twelve leagues from London, after arriving strictly incognito. I would need a house large enough for my staff. I ask to keep away from London where I do not think the Government would like me to live. If the Government intends to provide me with a super-intendent, he must not be a jailor but a man of quality and honour.[18]

Maitland gave orders for the *Slaney* to be immediately readied to take Gourgaud to England. It was explained, however, 'that he would not be allowed to land until permission was received from London, or the sanction of the Admiral at the port he might arrive at obtained'. Meanwhile, the copy of the Emperor's letter would be forwarded 'without loss of time' to His Royal Highness.

The *Slaney* sailed within the hour – Captain Sartorius waiting only for Maitland's dispatch to Sir John Barrow, the Second Secretary of the Admiralty, informing him of the momentous developments. Las Cases stayed on board the *Bellerophon*, offering advice as to the Emperor's accommodation. He was, as a matter of course, to be assigned the captain's spacious after-cabin. Maitland suggested that, as the entourage included Mme Montholon and Mme Bertrand, the cabin be divided in two and the ladies given half. 'If you allow me to give an opinion,' Las Cases replied, 'the Emperor will be better pleased to have the whole of the after-cabin to himself, as he is fond of walking about, and will by that means be able to take more exercise.' As thirty-three of the fifty passengers were to be accommodated on the *Bellerophon* – the remainder going aboard the *Myrmidon* – Maitland would be occupied until past one o'clock in the morning making the necessary arrangements.

At about ten o'clock that night, however, he was called on deck by the officer of the watch to receive information that threatened to render his preparations superfluous. A boat had come alongside bearing news that two *chasse-marées* had been sighted off La Rochelle some twelve hours earlier, and in one of them Maitland's informant had seen 'a man wrapt up in a sailor's great coat', who was pointed out to him as being Bonaparte himself. Both vessels were at that moment moored off a point of land on the north side of the Breton Channel, apparently intent on putting to sea. If this proved true, and his quarry were to escape, Maitland would be humiliated in the eyes of the naval community. The *Slaney* was out of sight and beyond recall, carrying a dispatch containing his confident promise to Sir John Barrow that Bonaparte 'is to embark on board this ship to-morrow'.

Maitland went below and confronted Las Cases, who assured him that his information must be false, as he had last seen the Emperor at four o'clock that afternoon on the Ile d'Aix, where in fact he had been since 12 July. Reassured, Maitland took no further action, despite receiving similar information of an escape attempt from another source in the early hours of the morning. He was later informed that the two *chasse-marées* had indeed been moored on the Breton Channel, 'prepared, manned, and officered . . . to be used as a last resource to attempt an escape in, in the event of Las Cases' mission to the *Bellerophon* not being successful'.

*

The man who stepped on to the deck of the *Bellerophon* at six o'clock the following morning wore 'an olive-coloured great coat over a green uniform with scarlet cape and cuffs, green lapels turned back and edged with scarlet, skirts hooked back with bugle horns embroidered in gold, plain with sugar-loaf buttons and gold epaulettes'. It was a colonel's uniform of a *chasseur à cheval* in the Imperial Guard. 'He wore the star, or grand cross of the Legion of Honour, and the small cross of that order; the Iron Crown; and the Union, appended to the button hole of his left lapel.' His outfit was completed by 'a small cocked hat, with a tri-coloured cockade; plain gold-hilted sword, military boots, and white waistcoat and breeches'.[19]

Captain Maitland had been given no instructions as to the manner in which Napoleon was to be received. The ship's guard of marines was drawn out on the poop but did not present arms. No salute was fired, nor did the crew man the yards, as would be expected when welcoming a person of high rank. Because it was not the custom on board a British man-of-war to pay these honours before the colours had been hoisted at eight o'clock in the morning, Maitland was relieved of any awkwardness regarding protocol. The earliness of the hour was sufficient excuse for withholding them.

But Napoleon gave no sign of offence, and appeared delighted by everything that was shown him. '*Une belle chambre*,' he said, when shown to his cabin. Seeing the portrait of his wife that Maitland had left hanging on the wall, he asked: '*Qui est cette jeune personne?*' Then, '*Ah! elle est très jeune et très jolie.*' It was clear to his host that Napoleon was intent on 'making a favourable impression on those with whom he conversed, by seizing every opportunity of saying what he considered would be pleasing and flattering to their feelings'. When Sir Walter Scott read the manuscript of Maitland's memoir prior to publication in 1826, he thought that 'the praise would have been bestowed even had the portrait less charm'. Nevertheless, he argued for the inclusion of the comments, however embarrassing to Mrs Maitland, on the grounds that 'everything connected with such a remarkable passage of history becomes historical'.

During breakfast, Napoleon plied Maitland with questions about the English and their customs. 'I must now learn to conform myself to them,' he said, 'as I shall probably pass the remainder of my life in England.' Maitland noticed that he ate little of the traditional English fare of coffee, tea and cold meat; learning that he was accustomed to a hot breakfast, the captain ordered his steward to allow the Emperor's *maître d'hotel* to give instructions, 'that he might invariably be served in the manner he had been used to'. Thereafter, they 'lived in the French fashion'.

HMS *Superb*, the flagship of Rear Admiral Hotham, arrived and dropped anchor close to the *Bellerophon* at about half past ten that same morning. Later in the day, Hotham, his secretary and the *Superb*'s captain came aboard to pay their respects and were received in the after-cabin, which Napoleon had made his own, surrounded by the small travelling cases of his portable library. The rear admiral and his party were invited to stay for dinner, which was served on Napoleon's plate and arranged by his *maître d'hotel*, Bonaparte having led the way into the dining room as befitted his royal status. Afterwards he invited the entire company to the after-cabin, where he took great pleasure in showing them his cunningly designed campaign bed, of which he was evidently proud. Before assembly it consisted of two small packages in leather cases. One measuring two feet long and eighteen inches in circumference contained a folded steel bedstead. The other case contained a mattress and green silk curtains. In just three minutes, Napoleon's valet erected the whole into 'a very elegant small bed, about thirty inches wide'.

The following morning, 16 July, while the crew of the *Bellerophon* made the necessary preparations for departure on the afternoon tide, Napoleon and his entourage were invited on board the *Superb* for breakfast. Maitland observed that her yards had been strung with 'man ropes', and that the tampions stoppering her guns had been removed, suggesting that Hotham intended honouring his visitor with manned yards and a salute. Worried again by the niceties of protocol, he sent an officer to enquire of the admiral whether this was so; if it were, was he to man the *Bellerophon*'s yards and fire a salute when Napoleon set out? Hotham answered 'that it was not his intention to salute, but he meant to man ship; that [Maitland] was not to do so on [Napoleon's] quitting the *Bellerophon*, but was at liberty to man yards on his return'.

Napoleon ate little of Hotham's breakfast, 'served in the English manner', but he was talkative and in good spirits. Throughout the meal, Maitland noticed that a young French officer, Lieutenant Colonel Planat, 'had tears running down his cheeks, and seemed greatly distressed at the situation of his master'. After breakfast, in the after-cabin, Napoleon raised the subject of the horses and carriages left behind at Rochefort that he wished to take with him. Maitland had been prepared to take two carriages on board the *Bellerophon*, and as many horses as she could conveniently stow. But time was pressing if she was to sail that day. So Admiral Hotham made out a passport allowing a French vessel to transport all six carriages and forty-five horses to England, which he forwarded to Captain Philibert of the *Saale*. It was the only English passport issued on Napoleon's behalf. To Maitland's knowledge, 'it was never acted upon'.

Hotham had given Maitland his orders. He was to put to sea in the *Bellerophon*, accompanied by the *Myrmidon*, 'and make the best of [his] way with Napoleon Buonaparte and his suite' to Torbay. On arrival, dispatches were to be sent to Sir John Barrow in London, and to Admiral Lord Keith at Plymouth. Maitland was then to 'await orders from the Lords Commissioners of the Admiralty, or his Lordship, for [his] further proceedings'.

As they got under way, the schooner that had taken Las Cases and his fellow negotiators to and from the *Bellerophon* during the previous week came alongside for the last time to deliver 'three or four sheep, a quantity of vegetables and other refreshments', a gift to the Emperor from the French commodore at Rochefort.

*

On the morning of 24 July, the *Bellerophon* and the *Myrmidon* dropped anchor in Brixham harbour, at the southern end of Tor Bay, Devon. The *Slaney* had arrived the day before, with General Gourgaud on board, and anchored outside the harbour, off Berry Head, flying a quarantine flag to deter the curious. Three boys, John Smart and the brothers Charlie and Dick Pudicombe, watched from the quay as officers bearing dispatch wallets were rowed ashore and post-chaises hired from the London Inn. Like many English schoolboys during the summer of 1815, they were enjoying an extra week's holiday in celebration of the recent victory over the French. That morning, they joined the local baker when he rowed out to the ships with a sack of loaves 'as a speculation and as a suggestion for further orders'. As they approached the man-of-war, they could see that other shore vessels were involved in an altercation with someone on board.

'They won't let us come alongside,' one disappointed tradesman told the baker, 'and they say as how they don't want no shore boats at all.'

'But they'll want some shore bread, I reckon,' said the baker and continued rowing. A swell of the tide carried their boat towards the vessel's stern. Above them they could see an armed sentry and an officer leaning over the rail.

'Come, sheer off; no boats are allowed here,' the officer roared.

'But I've brought you some bread,' shouted the baker and caught hold of the sill of the lower gun port with his boat hook.

'If we want bread we'll come ashore and fetch it,' said the officer, 'and if you don't let go I'll sink you.'

The sentry put down his musket, left the rail and returned holding a large cannon round shot, which he held out directly over the baker and his crew. It was heavy enough, if dropped, to hole the bottom of their boat.

'Let go, you old fool, or by the Lord I'll sink you!'

The baker rowed back to a safer distance. One of the warship's longboats approached them, containing a dozen men armed with cutlassses and commanded by an officer:

'Now, my man, you had better not get yourself into trouble; we have orders to keep off all shore boats, so you know it's no use trying.'

A tradesman's boat returned from the sloop after encountering the same embargo. The baker was indignant: 'Man and boy have I sailed on these waters, and never have I been so treated.'

The other shore boats were returning to the quay, but the baker and his young crew lingered. As the tidal current carried them along the side of the ship, John Smart noticed a sailor standing in one of the lower gun ports. He seemed to be trying to attract their attention and at the same time wishing to stay out of sight. He placed a finger to his lips. The baker rowed around the ship at a proper distance and was troubled no further

by the boat patrol. As they completed the circuit and drifted
with the tide along the line of gun ports, the sailor was still
there, standing further back in the shadows and scarcely visible,
but with his hand resting on the port sill. Smart saw a small
black object drop from the man's fingers into the water and float
away. The baker bent his strokes towards it and Smart, sitting
in the bow and trailing his hand in the water, was able to scoop
it up as it drifted by. It was a 'foreign-looking' bottle. At a
distance from the ship and masked from the sentries' view by
the broad back of the baker, the schoolboy drew out the cork.
It was slightly oily and perfumed as though the bottle had once
contained spirits. Smart unrolled the scrap of paper that he found
inside. The anonymous crewman of the *Bellerophon* gained no
advantage from his covert communication, only the relief of at
last imparting information he must have been bursting to tell
– to someone, to anyone – beyond the wooden confines of the
ship.

'We have got Bonaparte on board.'

Within a short time of the baker's boat returning to shore,
'there was not a soul in Brixham, except babies, ignorant of the
news'. By noon the quayside was swarming with people; those
possessed of boats putting out laden with sightseers; the ship
surrounded by small craft, kept at a distance by the armed patrols.
There were cries of 'Bonaparte! Bonaparte!' from the floating
crowd of several thousand, and occasional sightings of his face
in the stern windows of the ship. Then, about three o'clock in
the afternoon, Napoleon came on deck. John Smart thought 'how
little he looked, and that he was rather fat'. He took off his hat
and bowed to the crowd, as he had to the Paris mob when
showing himself from the balcony of the Élysée Palace. The English
crowd cheered him loudly and Smart recalled 'a feeling of triumph,
mixed with a natural satisfaction at seeing a wonderful sight'.
John Bowerbank, a naval lieutenant on the *Bellerophon*, was a
witness to this extraordinary reception of a man who had been
their enemy for twelve years of war, and was 'surprised at not
hearing a disrespectful or abusive word escape from anyone'.

Napoleon himself seemed nonplussed. 'How very curious these English are!' he remarked.

Hero or monster, adored or execrated, friend or enemy – it did not matter. The most famous man in the world, foremost of the age, greatest in all of history perhaps, had come to Brixham. And word spread. The following day, an extensive flotilla of boats surrounded the *Bellerophon* as the curious came from Torquay, Dartmouth, Exmouth, Teignmouth, Exeter and Plymouth. General Montholon enjoyed 'the immense and endless spectacle of beautiful and elegant women, who saluted us with their pocket-handkerchiefs and shawls, which they transformed into flags as evidences of their sympathy'. He even hoped that such acclamation was a sign 'that the national feeling would open the gates of England for our reception, or at least force the ministers to allow us to proceed to America'.[20]

Brixham's business thrived. Boatmen took more from passengers in two days than they usually did in a month. All the inns were full, and stabling for horses at a premium. When Napoleon was not on deck, the ship's crew kept the crowd informed of his activities with chalked bulletins on a board hung over the side. One of them read: 'He's gone to breakfast.'

Captain Maitland was importuned by members of the nobility and local worthies for more exclusive access. A lady sent a note, accompanied by a basket of fruit, requesting a boat be sent for her the following morning. Maitland replied that his orders would not permit him to comply with her request and 'no more fruit was sent from that quarter'. Lord Charles Bentinck and Lord Gwydir also asked to be allowed on board, 'but with no better success'.[21] Even Lady Keith had to be dissuaded by her husband from travelling from Exeter 'upon the chance of the influence of the name to get on board'.[22]

*

Lord Melville was disturbed by what he read in Hotham's and Maitland's dispatches: that HMS *Superb*, a flagship of the

Royal Navy, had honoured Bonaparte by welcoming him on board with manned yards; that he 'insists upon being treated with royal respect'; that he had invited Captain Maitland and his officers to their own table to dine with him; that 'he had been allowed to assume a great deal more state, and even authority, and had been treated with more submissiveness, than belongs to his situation as a prisoner of war, or to his rank as a General Officer, which is all that can be allowed to him in this country'.[23] He was to be addressed in future as 'General Bonaparte'. Privately, Napoleon would take particular exception to this, arguing that although the British government had never acknowledged him as Emperor of France, they should at least do so as First Consul. 'They have sent Ambassadors to me as such,' he told Maitland.[24] Lord Melville would nevertheless express satisfaction that he 'submits quietly to be unemperored'.[25]

*

On the day that *Bellerophon* dropped anchor in Brixham harbour, the South Atlantic island of St Helena was first mentioned in the London papers as Napoleon's ultimate and most likely destination. The *Morning Chronicle* provided its readers with a suitably stark sketch of the accommodation: 'One entire rock, about twenty miles in circumference, immensely steep above the sea, the waves of which dash constantly on it . . . The island is infested with rats, which commit the most dreadful destruction; otherwise it produces corn and fruit, and abounds in game.'[26] Another newspaper declared this confinement to be 'much too good a fate for such a Wretch'.[27]

The nearest land was Ascension Island, 800 miles away to the north-west. St Helena was 5,000 miles from Europe; 1,800 miles from the coast of South America; 1,200 miles from Africa. 'At such a distance and in such a place,' Lord Liverpool had written to Lord Castlereagh three days before, 'all intrigue would be impossible, and, being withdrawn so far from the European world, he would be very soon forgotten.'[28]

On board the *Bellerophon*, the French party grew anxious as the prospect of such a place of exile loomed in everyone's mind. General Gourgaud returned from the *Slaney*. Far from having been granted an audience with the Prince Regent, he had not even been allowed on shore. Since he had refused to deliver the Emperor's letter into any other hands, it remained undelivered. Napoleon's hopes of his retirement to the life of a country squire in England were receding.

*

In the early hours of 26 July, Brixham's two-day wonder came to an end. Amid fears that an attempt might be made by Napoleon's supporters to effect his escape from an anchorage exposed and open to the Channel, the *Bellerophon*, *Slaney* and *Myrmidon* received orders to proceed without delay to Plymouth. Once there, Admiral Keith ordered two frigates, the *Liffey* and the *Eurotas*, to drop anchor at a convenient distance either side of the *Bellerophon*, 'as well for the purpose of preventing the escape of Bonaparte . . . from that ship, as for restraining shore-boats and others from approaching too close'. Each frigate was to keep 'a boat manned and armed alongside, in constant readiness, as a guard boat'. No shore boats were to be allowed nearer than a cable's length* 'and no boats . . . permitted to loiter about the ship, even at that distance, either from curiosity or any other motive'.[29] The distance was increased to a cable's length and a half after 'a foreign spy [was] detected hovering around the ship, with letters addressed to BONAPARTE, and without a passport, [and] who could give no account of himself'. The suspicious individual was taken into custody.

The security provision of a larger, enclosed and heavily guarded anchorage at Plymouth had to be reconciled with increased publicity, visibility and greater accessibility by stagecoach. 'I am miserable', Keith wrote to his daughter, Margaret Elphinstone,

---

* The standard length of an anchor cable, 100 fathoms, or 600 feet.

'with all the idle people in England coming to see this man.' He estimated that every bed in every hotel in the town was taken by visitors, Windsor's Hotel alone accounting for fifty. As at Brixham, so at Plymouth, the crowd that gathered daily beyond the cordon of guard boats raised their hats and cheered the former Emperor whenever he showed himself, 'apparently', it was thought, 'with the view of soothing his fallen fortunes, and treating him with respect and consideration'. Just as at Brixham, every boat-owner was turning a profit. One entrepreneur hired the town crier to make an announcement several times daily:

O yes! O yes! O yes!
This is to give notice that the Ely pleasure boat, J. BURT, Master, will take passengers for the Sound this afternoon, from the Barbican, at one shilling and sixpence each, to see *Bonny party*.[30]

On 30 July, a Sunday, Captain Maitland counted 'upwards of a thousand [boats] collected round the ship, in each of which, on an average, there were not fewer than eight people'.[31] The following day there were 1,500 boats in the Sound, and a local newspaper estimated that '10,000 persons, at least, were supposed to be congregated'. The guard boats frequently fired musket volleys over the heads of the crowd to deter them. On occasion the *Bellerophon* kept the boats back by 'play[ing] water from an engine on the starboard quarter', causing 'groans, hisses and shouts [from] the enraged multitude'. For the most part, however, the ship's crew encouraged the sightseers and continued their chalked bulletins of Napoleon's activities: 'At Breakfast', 'In the cabin with Captain Maitland', or 'Going to Dinner.' At least once a day there would be a buzz of anticipation with the chalking up of 'Coming upon deck.'

Privileges of kin, as well as rank, were shamelessly – if vainly – exploited to get within the security cordon. 'Here is among others my niece Anne,' wrote Keith, 'with "dear friends" she never saw before, arrived from Exmouth! Sir J. Hippisley and Sir H. McLean and family – [other] people all the way from Birmingham.'[32] Lady

Keith was allowed aboard the *Eurotas* on 28 July – the day that
her husband had his first meeting with Bonaparte – but as they
remained in the after-cabin for the duration of the interview, she
got no better view of him than did the crowd, to whom 'indescrib-
able disappointment was occasioned'.[33] Captain Maitland's wife
was more fortunate. Joined in her boat by Sir Richard and Lady
Strachan, and Lady Duckworth, she managed to get close enough
to have conversation with Napoleon. He invited Mrs Maitland on
board, and when it was explained that Admiral Keith's orders
forbade it, he said to her: '*Milord Keith est un peu trop sevère,
n'est-ce pas, Madame?*' He also observed to the captain that the
portrait in his cabin did not do her justice.[34] For his part, Keith
was becoming increasingly exasperated with the situation: 'I am
worried to death with idle folk coming, even from Glasgow, to see
him; there is no nation so foolish as we are!'

There was a rival attraction in town whenever Napoleon's
linen – 'exceedingly fine in texture' – was sent ashore to be laun-
dered. 'Many individuals', it was reported, 'have temporarily put
on one of his shirts, or waistcoats, or neck cloths, merely for the
purpose of saying that they had worn his clothes.' The laundress
who indulged this 'blind infatuation' doubtless did so for a price.
The 'exquisite cambric' bed sheets were closely examined. It was
noted that some were decorated in the corners with a letter 'L'
embroidered in red silk and surmounted by a flat crown. These
were assumed to have been left behind at the Tuileries by Louis
XVIII when he fled Paris. Others were embroidered with a red
letter 'N' and a much taller crown.[35]

*

At ten o'clock in the morning of 31 July, Admiral Lord Keith
and Major General Sir Henry Bunbury, Under-Secretary for War,
went on board the *Bellerophon* to formally break the news to
'General Bonaparte' of the British government's intentions.
Melville had anticipated that this would be a painful meeting
and for that reason suggested Bunbury be present. As he explained

to Keith, 'it will probably be more agreeable to you that some person should accompany you at the conference which it will be necessary for you to have'. The two men were shown into the after-cabin, where they found Napoleon, with Bertrand in attendance. Following the usual civilities, Keith began to read aloud the letter Melville had sent him:

It would be inconsistent with our duty to this country and to his Majesty's allies if we were to leave to General Buonaparte the means or opportunity of again disturbing the peace of Europe and renewing all the calamities of war.

Melville had not thought fit to provide a French translation of this document and Keith had not proceeded far in his reading before Napoleon interrupted and requested him to translate it as he went along. Keith's French being inadequate, Bunbury, who had a better command of the language, was asked to continue:

It is therefore unavoidable that he should be restrained in his personal liberty to whatever extent may be necessary to secure our first and paramount object.

Napoleon knew what was coming next, not only from references that had appeared in the English press over the previous week, but because Captain Maitland had acquainted him with the main drift before Keith and Bunbury arrived:

The island of St Helena has been selected for his future residence. The climate is healthy, and the local situation will admit of his being treated with more indulgence than would be compatible with an adequate security elsewhere . . .

Most of Bunbury's lengthy report of the meeting, written for his superior, Lord Bathurst, was devoted to Napoleon's protests, arguments and appeals, which, rambling and repetitious, were delivered at considerable length, with few gestures, and without interruption. In his report to Lord Melville, Keith was able to summarise the monologue more succinctly:

> That [Napoleon] had no power; that he could do no harm; that he would give his word of honour to hold no communication with France; that he could have remained there with the Army [had he wished]; that it was not an act of necessity, but of choice, which induced him to throw himself for protection into the hands of the English; and that he now claimed that protection out of justice and humanity.

On the subject of his proposed future domicile, he remained adamant: 'Go to St Helena – no! – no! I prefer death.' Often he appealed personally to his listeners, asking what they would do under the same circumstances. Several times Keith attempted to bring the meeting to a close and withdraw, but 'the General continu[ed] to urge to the last the same style of argument'.

As Napoleon spoke on, Bunbury was able to study him closely, and even had time to make descriptive notes for his future memoirs:

> bald about the temples and the hair on the upper part of his head is very thin, but long and ragged, looking as if it were seldom brushed . . . eyes are grey, the pupils large, his eyebrows thin . . . his complexion pallid, his flesh rather puffy. His nose is well-shaped, the lower lip short, a good mouth, but teeth bad and dirty; he shows them very little.

As for his expression and demeanour, Bunbury thought him 'serious and almost melancholy', and despite the injustices he felt were being done to him, 'showed no sign of anger or strong emotion'.

The two men eventually succeeded in terminating the interview and retired to the quarterdeck, only for Keith to be immediately recalled for further talk. He returned to the after-cabin alone. Napoleon asked for his advice:

'Is there any Tribunal to which I can apply?'

'I am no lawyer, but I believe none,' replied the Admiral. He could only repeat the official line: 'I am satisfied there is every disposition on the part of the British Government to render your situation as consistent with prudence.'

Napoleon became briefly animated. Snatching up the government papers that still lay on the table, he flourished them: 'How so! St Helena?'

'Sir, it is surely preferable to being confined in a smaller space in England, or being sent to France, or perhaps to Russia.'

'Russia! *Dieu garde!*' he replied. 'God forbid!' And the admiral took his leave.

During the days that followed, Napoleon would repeat his protests both verbally and in writing.

After concluding their talks with 'General Bonaparte', Keith and Bunbury visited the fore-cabin, where the members of his immediate circle had assembled to learn their fate. Of the company of fifty who had come with Napoleon from Rochefort, only twelve domestics were to be allowed to join him on St Helena, together with three senior officers of his choice, Generals Savary and Lallemand excepted. Neither of these two men had wished to be included, but, having both been recently proscribed by the restored King, they were alarmed at the prospect of being returned to face French justice and a probable French firing squad. Lallemand had been given Maitland's assurance that a rendition of this nature was out of the question, and the *Bellerophon*'s captain would later appeal directly to Lord Melville on the grounds that his honour as an English officer would be compromised were it to prove otherwise.

Keith suspected that fewer than half even of the limited number permitted would be willing to follow Napoleon into exile. 'No one but Bertrand has offered,'[36] he told his daughter. The marshal's wife, however, was not of the same mind as her husband, and begged the admiral to use his influence with the government to forbid him from going as well. That night, after Keith and Bunbury had left the ship, the highly strung Mme Bertrand attempted to drown herself, and was halfway out of the first lieutenant's cabin window before she could be dragged back inside and laid on her bed 'in strong hysterics, at intervals abusing the English nation and its Government, in the most vehement and unmeasured terms'. She was of Irish extraction and raged sometimes in English, sometimes in French.[37]

*

Meanwhile, the clamour to catch sight of the notorious captive and the congestion of vessels around the *Bellerophon* became critical: 'The crush was so great as to render it quite impossible for the guard-boats to keep them off; though a boat belonging to one of the frigates made use of very violent means to effect it, frequently running against small boats, containing women, with such force as nearly to upset them, and alarming the ladies extremely.'[38] Inevitably some capsized. One containing three gentlemen, a woman and child was run down by a guard boat and sank. The mother and child were rescued by members of the *Bellerophon*'s crew, but one of the gentlemen was drowned, 'leaving a wife and four little children to deplore his loss'.[39] The following evening a boat 'was cut *into two pieces* by a man of war's launch'. John Boynes, a thirty-five-year-old stonemason from Plymouth dockyard, was drowned, 'his wife and three children happily escaping'.[40]

According to a report in *The Times*, it was 'the concourse of boats in Plymouth Sound and the loss of some lives which had already taken place [that] induced the Government to remove the *Bellerophon* to a greater distance'.[41] There were, however, other considerations governing the ship's departure on 4 August, not least of which was the dubious legal status of Napoleon's captivity.

*

If Mr Capel Lofft had been so distressed by news of the French defeat at Waterloo as to consider deserting his dinner guests at the mere mention of the catastrophe, he was equally appalled by the fate the British government appeared to have in store for the former Emperor: 'The intelligence that the great Napoleon . . . is to be sent perhaps to St Helena is almost overwhelming to me.' In a letter to the *Morning Chronicle* that appeared on 2 August, the radical barrister outlined the relevant tenets of constitutional law. '*All* persons within the Realm of *England*, which includes the adjoining *seas*,' he pointed out, 'are temporary subjects if *aliens*, or *permanent* if *natural born*.' By dint of his location on board one of His Majesty's ships presently at anchor within English territorial waters, and regardless of his nationality, Napoleon was a 'temporary' English subject, and 'though not on the British soil he [was] within the protection of the *British law*'. This meant that he was also protected by the ancient statute of habeas corpus and could not legally be held without trial, nor sent against his will to St Helena or anywhere else. '*Deportation*, or *transportation*, or *relegation*', declared Lofft, 'cannot legally exist in *this* country, except where the *law* expressly *provides* it on trial and sentence.' A writ of habeas corpus, being 'the legal mode of investigating, as to all persons, whether their liberty be *legally* or *illegally* restrained', would necessitate either Napoleon's appearance in a court of law or his release.

According to Montholon, General Savary 'succeeded in establishing secret communications with an English lawyer, who sent him a variety of notes and documents, in order to guide us in the adoption of a course, which . . . would place the Emperor under the protection of the English law'. No details were given as to how the channel of 'secret communications' was effected, apart from mention of a sailor from the *Bellerophon* 'who was a good swimmer'.[42] However, if the helpful legal authority was Mr Capel Lofft, and the 'notes and documents' related to the law of habeas corpus, both his and the swimmer's efforts were in vain.

Habeas corpus was not applicable in time of war, nor was a prisoner of war protected by it. The French prisoners on Dartmoor and in the Solway hulks would never be brought to trial, but on conclusion of a peace treaty between France and England, they would be set free. Such would also be the case with Napoleon if he were regarded as an ordinary prisoner of war. That eventuality threatened, however, not only the national security of Great Britain but also the future security and peace of Europe. A legal nicety was required to permanently remove the former Emperor from posing any such threat. After due deliberation, Lord Eldon, the Lord Chancellor, ruled that Napoleon was to be considered a sovereign with whom England was at war; that the war could only be terminated by a peace treaty between England and himself; that it rested with England to conclude, or refrain from concluding, such a treaty; and that until it was concluded, England had the legal right to continue his detention as a prisoner of war.[43] In short, he would remain imprisoned without trial, the sole combatant of a war that would cease only with his death.

And the place of his imprisonment had been selected with care. The moment he set foot on St Helena, Napoleon would be even further disqualified from the safeguard of English law by the anomalous territorial peculiarity of the island itself. Since 1657, this isolated volcanic rock had been the property of the East India Company, and although afforded the protection of the Royal Navy, it was neither ruled by the British Crown, nor was it under the jurisdiction of the English courts. Two centuries after the decision was made to send Napoleon to St Helena, the transportation of prisoners to legally ambivalent destinations for the supposed preservation of national security would be termed 'extraordinary rendition'.[44]

Following Lofft's intervention, government ministers braced themselves for a challenge. Lord Melville wrote to Admiral Keith:

> In some of the newspapers a notion is held out that [Bonaparte] may be brought out of the ship by a writ of habeas corpus. The serious public inconvenience and danger which would arise from such an occurrence . . . renders it indispensably our duty to prevent it . . . If we were to receive an intimation of any such proceeding going forward here, we should order the *Bellerophon* to sea.[45]

Some such intimation must have been received, because two days later, in the early hours of Friday 4 August, a courier arrived in Plymouth with news that a 'lawyer' was on his way from London to serve a writ, either on Napoleon or on any one of his keepers. Keith ordered Maitland to 'make preparations to be under weigh at a moment's notice'.⁴⁶ That day would prove an ordeal for Keith, the writ server chasing him from his home and from ship to ship throughout the morning and into the afternoon. The man who pursued him was not in fact a lawyer and the paper he carried not a writ of habeas corpus. It could, however, have considerably delayed Napoleon's deportation and attracted unwelcome publicity to what was being done to him, thereby creating severe embarrassment to the British government. The document which that importunate individual would try so hard to serve on Admiral Keith was a subpoena summoning the former Emperor of the French to testify at a trial for criminal libel.

In August of the previous year, a pamphlet had been published purporting to be the 'Secret Memoirs' of three members of the Cochrane family. It included 'an Account of the Circumstances which led to the Discovery of the Conspiracy of Lord Cochrane and others to Defraud the Stock Exchange'. The conspiracy in question had been perpetrated the previous February. A false report of Napoleon's death – in which it was said he had been captured and hacked to pieces by a band of Cossacks – caused a steep hike in the price of government stock, greatly enriching, among others, it was alleged, the Member of Parliament and naval commander Charles, Lord Cochrane, and his uncle, Mr Andrew Cochrane-Johnstone. Both men had been tried and convicted in June 1814, fined £1,000 and imprisoned for twelve months. Lord Cochrane had also been sentenced to stand for an hour in the pillory opposite the Royal Exchange.⁴⁷

The third target of the pamphlet, however, had played no part in the Stock Exchange conspiracy. Cochrane-Johnstone's elder brother, Vice Admiral Sir Alexander Forrester Cochrane, was charged in the 'Secret Memoirs' with misconduct while he was commander-in-chief of the Leeward Islands. His accuser, and author of the pamphlet, was a Mr Anthony McKenrot,⁴⁸ employed between 1803 and 1813 as a translator to a naval agent on the Caribbean island of Tortola, where he had conceived a deranged animosity towards the vice admiral.

McKenrot claimed that Cochrane had smuggled mules from Halifax, Nova Scotia, and sold them in Tortola 'for his own profit' without entering them at the custom house; that he had defrauded the navy victualling board by purchasing 'a quantity of duck' on his own account, using bills of exchange 'purporting to be for fresh beef supplied to his Majesty's ships'; that he had 'fraudulently appropriated to himself about 200 prize negroes' and transported them to 'a sugar plantation of his own at Trinidad'. But the allegation that was to bring McKenrot to Plymouth in early August 1815 was as follows:

> That [Cochrane] was guilty of cowardice, when he was Commander in Chief of the Leeward Islands station on 6th July [1806] in not making the necessary preparations to fight the French squadron under Admiral Willaumez and Jérome Bonaparte [captain of the seventy-four-gun *Vétéran*], off the island of Tortola and St Thomas, &c.

There was in all probability as little truth in this charge as there was in any of the other three. Nevertheless, as a defendant in the libel suit Cochrane had brought against him in June, McKenrot was entitled to call witnesses in support of his case. He had accordingly obtained a subpoena commanding the appearance in the King's Bench Court, 'on Friday the tenth of November by nine of the clock in the forenoon of the same day', not only of Willaumez and Captain Bonaparte, but also of the Emperor himself, 'to testify the truth according to [their] knowledge'. On the day this document was issued, 14 June 1815 – with Napoleon approaching the Belgian border at the head of a 90,000-strong invasion force – there must have seemed scant prospect of his being available to testify in an English court of law. Seven weeks later, with the former Emperor a prisoner in English territorial waters, McKenrot saw his chance and hurried to Plymouth.

Arriving at Keith's residence on the morning of the 4th, he was told by James Meek, the admiral's secretary, that his lordship was away from home. After perusing the writ, Meek directed McKenrot to the office of Sir John Duckworth, Plymouth's naval commander-in-chief, before writing an urgent note to Keith on board HMS *Tonnant*, warning him to expect the visitor. Duckworth also examined McKenrot's writ and suggested where he might find Keith. By the time McKenrot had hired a boat and been rowed to the *Tonnant*, Keith was on his way from that ship to the *Eurotas*. Then, just as his pursuer's boat touched the landward side of the *Eurotas*, the nimble Keith clambered down the opposite side into a twelve-oared launch. Easily out-rowing the other boat, the admiral's crew pulled towards the Rame peninsula, west of Plymouth. He landed at the little village of Cawsand – still followed by the implacable McKenrot – and made his way out to the point, where he was at last able to shake off his pursuer by going aboard the *Prometheus*, lying at anchor off Rame Head. By sunset, he was back where he started, his flag flying once more from HMS *Tonnant*.

Meanwhile, on board the *Bellerophon*, Maitland had been making urgent preparations to sail since dawn. He replied to anxious enquiries from his French passengers that his orders were to meet HMS *Northumberland*, expected from Portsmouth, to which larger and more seaworthy vessel Napoleon was to be transferred for the long voyage to St Helena. '*L'Empereur n'ira pas à St Hélène*,' General Bertrand declared: 'The Emperor will not go to St Helena.'

At half past nine they weighed anchor, but with the flood tide against them and a light breeze blowing towards land, it took a considerable time to clear the Sound. Maitland ordered the guard boats forward to tow, but progress was protracted and the ship still some way from the open sea when he caught sight of 'a suspicious-looking person in a boat approaching'. McKenrot, returning from Cawsand to Plymouth, and frustrated in his attempt to serve his writ on Admiral Keith, saw in the slowly departing *Bellerophon* his final opportunity. He caught sight of

Napoleon's face at one of the stern windows, stood up in the boat and waved his paper, as though offering to serve the subpoena personally there and then. At the very least he could serve it on the ship's captain. Maitland, however, had ordered one of the guard boats to leave off towing and keep under the ship's stern – 'and not allow any shore boat, under any pretext, to come near'. When McKenrot persisted, the officer of the guard threatened to shoot him.

That night in his room at the King's Arms Tavern, Plymouth Dock, the disappointed McKenrot wrote to Admiral Keith:

> I humbly entreat your Lordship to consider that an evasion to give due facility to the execution of any process would amount to a high contempt against that Honourable Court from whence it issued and that under the continuance of such circumstances I shall be under the painful necessity of making my return accordingly. Leaving the issue to your Lordship's discretion, I shall remain here until tomorrow night.[49]

He received no reply. None of the witnesses mentioned in the subpoena appeared in his defence at the King's Bench Court, and he was never tried for libel. In an entirely unconnected case, McKenrot would be indicted in January 1816 for 'forging and uttering a bill of exchange for £800'. He would plead insanity. After several witnesses were called to testify that he had exhibited 'acts of absolute madness', that he had 'thrown his cat on the fire', and that he had 'gone to Plymouth to subpoena Bonaparte', he was acquitted and confined to Bedlam.[50]

As HMS *Bellerophon* laboured out of the becalmed Sound that afternoon, Maitland watched two well-dressed ladies in a boat – the last of the Plymouth spectators – following as close to the ship as the guards would allow, 'and, whenever Buonaparte appeared at the stern window, [they] stood up and waved their handkerchiefs'.[51]

*

As the *Bellerophon* and the *Tonnant* approached Torbay from the east, another ship came into view ahead of them. HMS *Northumberland*, flying the flag of Admiral Sir George Cockburn, had sailed from Portsmouth two days earlier with orders to meet the *Bellerophon* and relieve her of her prisoner. It was Sunday 6 August.

Lord Bathurst had sent detailed instructions to Admiral Cockburn regarding Napoleon's reception aboard the *Northumberland*, his transhipment to St Helena, and the security measures that were to be taken in order to keep him there. Before embarkation, a complete inventory of Napoleon's property and that of his companions was to be drawn up. He would be allowed to take with him to St Helena any 'Articles of Furniture, Books, and Wine' that he had brought from France. His plate and other silverware was to be included under the heading of furniture, 'provided it be not to such an amount as to bespeak it to be rather an article of convertible property than of domestic use'. However, 'His Money, Diamonds, and Negotiable Bills of every description [were] to be given up'. Cockburn was to explain to him the reason for this stipulation: 'It is by no means the intention of the British Government to confiscate His Property, but simply to take the Administration of these Effects into their own Hands for the purpose of preventing their being converted by him into an Instrument of Escape.'[52]

The three senior officers chosen by Bonaparte to accompany him were General Gourgaud, General Montholon, with his wife and child, and General Bertrand. There had been some doubt as to whether Bertrand was to be included because of the volatile character of his wife, but at last Napoleon agreed and Fanny Bertrand, reconciled to the voyage, joined the party with her three children. When Dr Maingault, Napoleon's physician and personal secretary, baulked at the prospect of a life in the tropics, the *Bellerophon*'s surgeon, Barry O'Meara, agreed to go in his place. Las Cases came in the capacity of private secretary and was joined by his fourteen-year-old son, acting as pageboy.

The redundant fifteen or so domestic staff, together with the surgeon, Maingault, remained aboard the *Bellerophon* and were taken to Portsmouth, whence they were transported to Cherbourg. Savary, Lallemand and another six officers – including Lieutenant Colonel Planat, who had wept through breakfast aboard the *Superb* – were transferred to the *Eurotas* and shipped to Fort Manoel on Malta as prisoners. A sixteen-year-old subaltern by the name of Sainte-Catherine – said to be a nephew of the Empress Josephine – was a native of Martinique, and was returned to that island aboard a sloop of war.

At midday on 7 August, Napoleon and his retinue, including the chosen domestics, went on board the *Northumberland*.

Two more lives were lost to curiosity before England saw the last of him. A boat from Torquay containing a gentleman, three ladies, a child and a servant went out to watch the former Emperor cross from one ship to the other. Rounding one of the vessels, their boat was run down by a cutter and capsized. The first lieutenant of the *Northumberland* jumped into the water and succeeded in rescuing Mrs Harris and the child. The husband of this lady was saved by his own exertions and dragged into the cutter, along with the servant and two boatmen. But the other two ladies 'sank to rise no more'.[53] They were an aunt and her niece, both of them young.

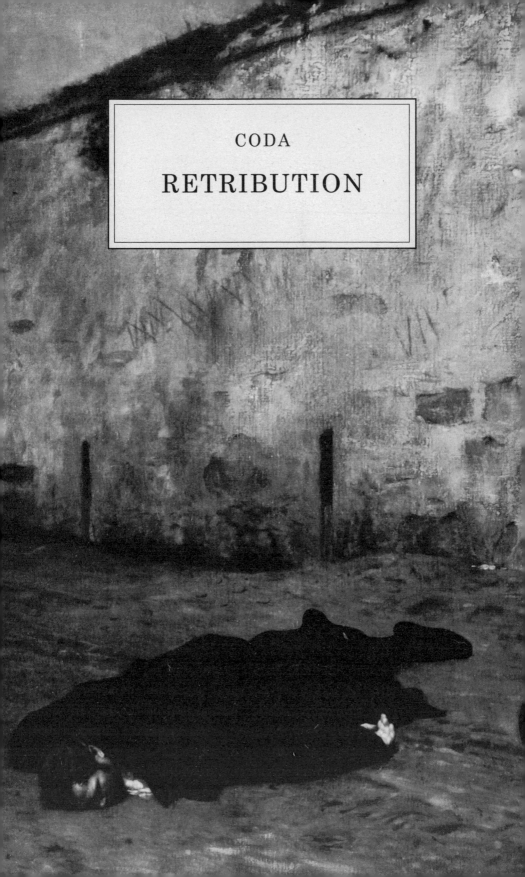

CODA

RETRIBUTION

NAPOLEON stepped aboard HMS *Northumberland* exactly fifty days after the battle of Waterloo. The following day, 8 August, news of the battle and its outcome reached the island of Guadeloupe, the most distant outpost of Bonapartist rule, a tricolour still flying above its governor's residence. The news was accompanied by a British invasion fleet of eight warships, fifty-five sail of gunboats, bomb vessels, troop ships and transports, a corps of field artillery and a land force of 5,000 infantry.

The first landing, of 850 Royal York Rangers, was made at a cove called Saint-Sauveur on the eastern coast of Basse-Terre, after HMS *Chanticleer*'s guns had swept the beach of its 500 or so defenders. The second landing, at Grand Anse, further south, was more strongly contested by an artillery battery and a much larger body of troops commanded by the island's two rebel leaders: the governor, Admiral Linois, and General Boyer. A line of three British ships, the *Barbadoes*, the *Columbia* and the *Fairy*, raked the shore with cannon fire so effective as to dismantle all but one of the enemy guns and drive the rebel forces inland. Two thousand British troops were safely landed, although a gunboat was lost in the mountainous surf. It was the hurricane season, and the invaders bivouacked for the night in high wind and torrential rain. After another heavy cannonade from the sea at daybreak on 9 August, the third and final landing was accomplished on the lee of the island at Baillif, north of the capital. Minimal casualties were reported by the invasion force in the fighting that followed: a sergeant and fifteen men killed; four officers, two sergeants and forty-five men wounded. Two hundred rebels were killed.

By the end of the following day the fighting was over, all tricolours struck and the British standard run up in their place. A proclamation was posted in Basse-Terre:

> Inhabitants of Guadaloupe! – The misrepresentations and artifices which have been employed to deceive you with regard to the true situation of Europe, the principles resulting at the same time from despotism and anarchy by which your revolutionary chiefs have conducted you to the brink of the precipice on which you stand, can no longer prevail. The veil is torn – your eyes are opened . . . Buonaparte has been defeated by the Duke of Wellington and Prince Blücher in a great and decisive battle, fought on the 18th of June – his army annihilated, and all his artillery and baggage taken. The usurper fled with some of his perjured generals, and reached Paris, where, knowing how desperate was his situation, he abdicated the pretended Imperial Crown.

Writing to Lord Bathurst, General Sir James Leith, 'Commander of His Britannic Majesty's land forces', declared that the invasion had been notably fortunate; had it not been accomplished in so timely a fashion, 'every sanguinary measure had been devised, and . . . the worst scenes of the revolution were to be recommenced'. Leith claimed that, less than a week later, Bonaparte's birthday on 15 August was to have been celebrated by the execution of royalist prisoners held by the rebels; that 'the slaves had been called to arms, and many were wrought up to such a pitch of sanguinary frenzy, [as] threaten[ed] the immediate destruction of the colony'. But as the result of the intervention of His Majesty's forces, 'the flag of the most unprovoked rebellion . . . has disappeared from the American archipelago'.

The ceasefire terms included a demand that 'All the eagles, tri-coloured flags, the public treasure, archives, plans, everything which appertains to the administration, civil and military, the magazines of every description, arms of all kind, [were to] be immediately given up.' Sir James Leith declared himself commander-in-chief and governor of the island 'for the time being'. The former governor, Rear Admiral the Comte de Linois, his second in command, General Boyer, and all rebel troops of the line, along with members of the military administration, were sent to the Duke of Wellington in France as prisoners of war.

Meanwhile, however, the insurgency continued and 'bands of revolutionary coloured people' who had retreated into the jungle made 'depredations' upon British troops until the end of August, when they attacked a company of the 6th West India regiment and succeeded in killing eighteen grenadiers. A considerable military force was sent in pursuit. Three hundred and fifty-five of the 'brigands' were captured and immediately shipped off to the plantations of America.[1]

Linois and Boyer were tried by French courts martial for treason. Boyer claimed, in his defence, 'to have had no motives other than to save the colony for France, to preserve it from bloody revolution and civil war, and to protect the person of the governor'. He also argued that by abandoning France and fleeing to Ghent, Louis XVIII had in effect terminated his own oath of service to his country. Boyer concluded that even if this did not entirely absolve his subjects from their oath of loyalty, it should at least permit them to yield, as His Majesty had done, to changing circumstances. The remark 'that the King himself, in removing from his capital, had given [them] an example of his submission to the power of the Usurper'[2] elicited a slight murmur in the courtroom. Admiral Linois was asked, on his 'soul and conscience', who had been the instigator of the rebellion on Guadeloupe. There was a moment's silence. 'There is no doubt it was M. Boyer,' he replied. 'He acted, he said, only with a view of saving the colony and me.' Linois was acquitted, Boyer found guilty and condemned to death. The King, however, exercised clemency and the capital sentence was commuted to twenty years' confinement in a state prison.

*

At Cambrai on 28 June, ten days before he reached Paris, Louis XVIII had issued a proclamation in which he promised to pardon 'misled Frenchmen' all that had happened since the day he left them 'amidst many tears' until the day he returned 'amidst so many acclamations'. But he went on:

> The blood of my people has flowed in consequence of a treason of which the annals of the world present no example. That treason has summoned foreigners into the heart of France. Every day reveals to me a new disaster. I owe it, then, to the dignity of my crown, to the interest of my people, to the repose of Europe, to except from pardon the instigators and authors of this horrible plot.[3]

In short, those who had withdrawn their loyalty to the king before he left France on 23 March would be subject to the rigour of law. A list of fifty-seven individuals exempted from the general amnesty was drawn up and published in the *Moniteur* on 26 July. There were two categories. Thirty-eight civilian and military figures who had rallied to Bonaparte during the Hundred Days, either in public statements or by taking up arms after the King's departure from France on 23 March, were ordered to leave Paris within three days and placed under surveillance in the provinces pending a decision by the legislature. The fate of the other nineteen was to be more clear-cut. With a single exception, these were high-ranking military figures who had actively participated in the violent over-throw of royal authority before 23 March, and were to be tried for treason. The names of Marshal Ney and General de La Bédoyère headed this exclusive list of the proscribed.

De La Bédoyère was court-martialled, and executed on 19 August. Refusing a blindfold, he claimed the right of giving their final orders to the soldiers appointed to kill him. He walked forward to within five paces of their muskets, shouted 'Ready! Present! Fire!' and dropped to the crashing detonations.[4]

Challenging the competence of a military tribunal to judge him, Ney elected to be tried by the Chamber of Peers, and was found guilty. The bullets he had sought in vain on 18 June found him on 7 December in a secluded corner of the Luxembourg Gardens, but fired from the muskets of a French execution squad: six to the chest, three to the head, one each through the right arm and throat. A twelfth went high, striking the wall behind him – one of the veterans being loath to shoot *le Rougeaud*.

The only civilian among the nineteen – the Comte de Lavalette, Bonaparte's Director General of Posts – was condemned to the guillotine for having taken command of the central post office in the name of the Emperor on 20 March. He had, it was alleged, been privy to the usurper's plans, because at four thirty on the same day he had issued a circular to the directors of posts in every *département* of France: 'The Emperor will be in Paris in two hours, and perhaps sooner; the capital is in the greatest enthusiasm: all is tranquil, and whatever some may say, there will be no civil war anywhere – *Vive l'Empereur!*'[5] Following the passing of sentence, and the rejection of his appeal, Madame de Lavalette approached the King on her husband's behalf. She received the reply: 'I am very sorry madam that my clemency cannot accord with my duty.'[6] She was, however, granted unlimited and unsupervised access to the condemned man during the time left to him. Two days after his wife's plea had been rejected by the King, Lavalette walked out of the Conciergerie wearing her clothes and accompanied by their eleven-year-old daughter. By the time a turnkey entered the condemned cell to find the redoubtable Madame de Lavalette sitting in an armchair wrapped in his cloak, the former Director General of Posts was free and clear. The conspiracy to smuggle him out of Paris and across the Belgian frontier disguised as a Guards officer, then for him to settle in Bavaria, was masterminded by the English clubman and adventurer Sir Robert Wilson, the 'bird of ill-omen' of Brooks's. Wilson and his two companions in the plot were later arrested by the French authorities, tried and sentenced to three months' confinement in La Force prison.

On 9 January, a curious ceremony occurred on the place de Grève, 'the common place of execution', when the sentence of the court that had condemned Lavalette 'to the pains of death' was carried out *par contumace* – by default – in his absence: 'A gibbet was erected [and to it] was affixed, by the hangman, a tablet, containing the name, surname, and qualities of the culprit, and the cause of his sentence. The exhibition, which was superintended by gens d'armes, lasted two hours.'[7] A fortnight after her husband's symbolic execution, Madame de Lavalette was released from the Conciergerie on bail. Charges against her of assisting the escape were dropped the following March.

Apart from Ney, de La Bédoyère, and General Mouton-Duvernet – shot at Lyons on 27 July 1816 – none of the nineteen proscribed for treason paid with their lives. General Drouet d'Erlon had taken refuge in Munich, a number of others in the United States. Bertrand, a voluntary exile with his Emperor on St Helena, was likewise unreachable, as were Savary and Lallemand, interned by the British on Malta. All were tried and condemned to death *par contumace* although there are no further reports of ceremonial execution against 'name, surname, and qualities'.

*

In the south of France there were numerous cases of retribution being exacted outside the royal ordinance's jurisdiction. Twin brothers César and Constantin Faucher were retired generals who had fought royalist rebels in the Vendée uprising during the mid-1790s. On 29 July, they were arrested in Bordeaux and charged with possessing a small cache of somewhat antiquated weapons, in supposed contravention of Article 93 of the Penal Code. They were tried, condemned and shot. Facing the firing party hand in hand, one of them gave the order to fire. César was killed outright. Constantin still breathed as he lay on the ground looking tenderly at his brother, until a sergeant administered the *coup de grâce*, a pistol shot into the ear.[8]

The name of Guillaume-Marie-Anne Brune, Marshal of France and former commandant of the citadel at Toulon, did not appear on either of the lists published in the *Moniteur*. He was travelling north to Paris when, on 11 August, his coach halted in the place de la Comédie in Avignon to change horses. He was recognised, and the inexplicable rumour spread through this fiercely royalist town that twenty-three years earlier he had carried the head of the Princess Marie Louise of Savoy on the end of a pike. An angry crowd gathered and the marshal took refuge in the Hotel du Palais Royal. It was here, in Room 3 on the first floor, while besieged by a baying mob, that Brune was assassinated, allegedly by a group of national guards. An inquest was convened on the still-warm body. Despite evidence that he had been shot with a musket from behind, the ball entering obliquely between the shoulder blades and emerging on the right side of his neck, rupturing the carotid artery, it was given out that he had shot himself with a pistol. A burial in the cemetery of Saint-Roch was hastily authorised and the corpse placed on a bier to be carried there. But the crowd, cheated of injuring the marshal when he was alive, was determined to vent its fury on his corpse. On the pretext that a suicide was not worthy to rest in sanctified ground, they dragged it by the feet from the bier and dropped it into the Rhône from the middle of a wooden bridge. In a mockery of military last rites, a salute of fifty gunshots was fired into the body as it floated below. Someone chalked the words '*C'est ici la cimetière du maréchal Brune*' on a beam above the third arch of the bridge, along with the date.[9] It was later scratched into the wood and remained visible long afterwards.

In Toulouse, on 15 August – the Feast of the Assumption – another amnestied Bonapartist fell victim to irregular royalist vengeance. The town was celebrating and there was dancing in the place des Carmes when General Ramel left his Italian mistress at eight in the evening and walked towards his lodgings. As he crossed the square he was recognised and followed by a crowd

of thirty or forty men shouting '*À bas Ramel!*' and '*Vive le Roi!*'
As he neared his own door, he enlisted the protection of a sentry,
who flourished his bayonet at the approaching assailants while
the general drew his sword. The sentry was stabbed, a pistol fired
and Ramel doubled over with a bullet to the lower stomach. The
gunshot momentarily stopped the dancing. While the crowd gathered and grew outside, the general's secretary and valet managed
to get him upstairs to his apartment on the first floor and then
went out to fetch medical help and military protection. Left alone,
Ramel could hear the mob hammering on the door below and
staggered to the second floor to ask a neighbour for shelter – but
was refused. He crawled to the top of the building, other neighbours unwilling to compromise themselves by assisting him. Half
an hour later his servants returned with a surgeon and some
national guards, followed the trail of blood and found him face
down and unconscious in an attic. They carried him back downstairs, where his wound was dressed and he was put to bed. But
no effective guard was mounted on the house and later in the
night the mob broke in and found the general helpless and unde-
fended. When they left, the blood-drenched bed looked like a
butcher's stall: the victim's nose was sliced in half, the frontal
bone of his skull broken, his arms fractured in ten places. The
little finger of his right hand hung by a shred of skin and an eye
was displaced from its socket. General Ramel lived until the
following day.[10]

Although the royalist backlash that followed Napoleon's fall
extended, to varying degrees, across the entire south of France, it
was at its most savage in the south-eastern *département* of the
Gard. On 17 July, at Nîmes, a force of militia massacred two
hundred unarmed Bonapartist soldiers trapped in their barracks.
But it was Calvinist civilians who suffered most under the 'White
Terror' that followed. This traditionally industrious class had
prospered under Napoleon. It had benefited not only from freedom
of public worship, but from municipal and judicial appointments
and the commercial opportunities resulting from them. Protestants
constituted a third of the population in Nîmes but commanded

sufficient political power to challenge and prohibit the Catholic majority's right to hold religious parades in the city streets. With the return of the King, it was a time for the settlement of scores, and the Protestant community became dangerously vulnerable to the lowest elements of the royalist, Catholic majority. Wealthy Protestant houses on the outskirts were pillaged and destroyed, as were poor artisan workshops producing silk stockings. On Sundays, especially, Protestants who ventured out in public were in danger of insult, hounding and worse. A particularly sadistic form of retribution was meted out to as many as forty women: their skirts raised behind, they were beaten with planks of wood studded with nails in a *fleur-de-lis* pattern. Two or more are said to have perished under this treatment.[11]

In the *département* of the Gard, around a hundred civilians were assassinated by royalist gangs during July and August, the majority of them in Nîmes. On 1 August, twelve were killed, most shot on their doorsteps. In the town of Uzés, on 4 August, twenty houses were torched and nine Protestants killed. On the night before departmental elections that would invest the royalist *ultras* with overall political control, fifteen Protestants were murdered, five of them hacked to death with sabres.[12] The persecution had a disastrous effect on the region's prosperity. It was estimated that between July and October, 2,500 men fled from Nîmes and its environs: 400 employers, 1,500 formerly employed workers, and 600 agricultural labourers. 'The largest manufactories are shut up', reported an English observer, 'and the silk trade, [once] so prosperous . . . is entirely ruined.'[13]

*

In May 1816, a Washington newspaper carried the report of a public entertainment and dinner given in the Philadelphia Masonic Hall to honour 'those illustrious chiefs' Marshal Grouchy, General Clausel and General Lefebvre-Desnouettes. A toast was drunk to 'the French citizens of Philadelphia, excellent members of an exemplary community'.[14] During the following years, American letters to the European press carried frequent reference to the activities of these and other émigrés. Napoleon's brother and former King of Spain 'Mr Joseph Buonaparte' divided his time between New York City and Philadelphia 'without any great show'. He had 'laid aside all titles, dignities, and orders, and his servants [went] without livery', and yet he was 'extremely liberal to every man who [had] any claim upon him for assistance in obtaining a settlement, which his great wealth enable[d] him easily to do'.[15]

Following their release from Fort Manoel, Generals Savary and Lallemand took ship to Smyrna. Savary made his way by a circuitous route to England, Lallemand to the United States, arriving in Philadelphia during the early spring of 1817. During the rest of that year and for part of the next, he commanded an expedition into the Spanish territory of West Texas, bordering on the former French colony of Louisiana. The Generals Clausel and Vandamme were also mentioned in connection with this enterprise. A French banker and naturalised American, Stephen Girard, had subscribed 50,000 dollars and 'Joseph Bonaparte, Marshal Grouchy, and others contributed largely'. By early 1818, a small colony of 400 settlers had been founded, and an encampment laid out and fortified, on the Trinity River, fifty miles north of Galveston. It was called *Champ d'Asile* – the Field of Asylum – and 'only Frenchmen or military men who ha[d] served in the French army'[16] were to be admitted. It might have been just that American asylum for 'the glorious wrecks of the army' Napoleon had envisaged to Caulaincourt before he left Malmaison. A declaration appeared in the *New Orleans Gazette* signed by General Lallemand's brother Henri, a man also under sentence of death *par contumace*: 'that the French colonists, who have gone to settle on the river Trinity, have no other object than the choice of productive lands, and look for no other advantages than those to be derived from a rich soil'.[17] Doubts were cast on the sincerity of the declaration by a number of English newspapers: 'Such men as Clausel, Grouchy, Vandamme are unable to direct agricultural or commercial pursuits; they are men of war simply, and some of them not famed for gentleness or humanity among cultivated nations, even in that sanguinary trade.'[18]

It was rumoured that their ultimate objective was to take possession of the entire province of Texas, drive the Spanish out of Mexico, and 'raise an American throne for King Joseph'.[19] Such warlike preparations may have prompted a visit Grouchy paid in March 1818 to Victor Dupont's extensive gunpowder mills at Brandywine, Delaware. His visit coincided with a widely reported disaster, when an explosion in the factory killed thirty people and wounded ten more. The roof, windows and some floors of Dupont's house were blown away, and Grouchy was said to have 'exerted himself greatly, but in vain' during the salvage operation. 'The only article saved', according to one newspaper, 'was a portrait of Napoleon Buonaparte.'[20]

The Trinity River adventure failed in July 1818 with the approach of a Spanish military force mistrustful of the French colonists' intentions. Champ d'Asile was abandoned and the settlers evacuated by ship from Galveston. Lallemand took up residence in New Orleans, purchased a plantation and by 1820 was the owner of fifteen slaves. He is said to have been part of a conspiracy to liberate the prisoner on St Helena, a conspiracy rendered superfluous by Napoleon's death on 5 May 1821.

By then many émigrés had gone back to France, having first gained assurances of amnesty from Louis XVIII. General Savary crossed from England in December 1819 and was retried and acquitted. Grouchy arrived in Paris the following June and was restored the titles and honours he had enjoyed before March 1815. He would, however, have to wait until another revolution and the ascension of Louis Philippe, the 'Citizen King', for the return of his marshal's baton and place in the Chamber of Peers. General Lefebvre-Desnouettes was given permission to return in 1822 but was drowned off the southern coast of Ireland when the *Albion* packet out of New York that was bringing him home was wrecked with the loss of all but two of her passengers.

General Lallemand returned to France after the July revolution of 1830. His last posting was the military governorship of Corsica.

*

France paid a high price for Napoleon's last adventure. Article IV of the Treaty of Paris, signed on 20 November 1815, ruled that an indemnity of 700 million francs was to be distributed among the allied powers over the following five years. In addition, the armies of Wellington and Blücher were each to receive a gratuity of twenty-five million francs for their exertions. 'A statement of the Rank and Numbers of the Officers, Non-Commissioned Officers and Privates of the British army [the Netherlands army, and the Nassau, Hanoverian and Brunswick troops] entitled to participate in the Prize Money granted for the Battle of Waterloo and Capture of Paris' was drawn up and certified by the Duke of Wellington on 19 June 1817.[21]

Twenty-five million francs – after cash paid for legal opinion, loss on currency exchange, and agency percentage had been deducted – converted to £978,850.15s.4d. For the purposes of fair distribution, this sum was divided into sixteen equal shares of £61,178.3s.5½d. Four shares were divided between the 95,323 surviving rank-and-file, giving each the sum of £2.11s.4d. Two shares were divided between 6,367 sergeants, giving each £19.4s.4d. Another two shares disbursed £34.14s.9d each to 3,522 subalterns, while a further two shares gave £90.7s.3d each to 1,354 captains. Five hundred and sixty-five field officers were given £433.2s.4d each from four shares, while a single share gave each of forty-eight general officers £1,274.10s.10d. As commander-in-chief, the Duke of Wellington received a single share of £61,178.3s.5½d.*

*

Less than two years after watching HMS *Northumberland* bear the 'Reptile' Bonaparte out of sight – if not out of mind – Admiral Keith found his family ties seriously strained by his eldest daughter's choice of husband. On 19 June 1817, a day after the second

---

* The relative worth of the private soldier's share of prize money – using the retail price index – would today be approximately £142; that of the Duke of Wellington's £3,360,000.

anniversary of the battle of Waterloo, Margaret Elphinstone married the émigré General Charles-Joseph le Comte de Flahault, Napoleon's former aide-de-camp. By an ironic chance of war, not only had Flahault been present at Genappe when his future wife's cousin, Captain James Drummond Elphinstone, was interrogated in the presence of Napoleon, but he had earned a rebuke from the Emperor for suggesting the young officer might have been lying. The wedding, at St Andrew's Church in Edinburgh, was in defiance of Admiral Keith's wishes, and for some time he refused to receive the couple. Eventually he relented, but only towards his daughter, and it was some years before he would agree to meet the Frenchman. 'Flahault's tact and charm of manner', his grandson wrote, 'eventually triumphed . . . and he was at length admitted into the Admiral's home circle, if not to his affections.'[22]

Having played her part in the capture of Napoleon, HMS *Bellerophon* – like the French frigate *Méduse* – was to have a far from illustrious subsequent career. Relieved of her prisoner by the *Northumberland* in early August, she was ordered to the Sheerness dockyard at the mouth of the river Medway. Here her crew was paid off, her guns disembarked, and her spars stripped of rigging. By September 1816, a dismasted hulk, iron gratings bolted across her seventy-four gun ports, her gun decks filled with cages, she was ready to receive other, less celebrated prisoners. She was moored close to another hulk that had once – as HMS *Edgar* – been Admiral Keith's flagship, but had now been renamed *Retribution*, in recognition of her penitentiary function. The *Bellerophon* remained a prison ship on the Medway for the next ten years, until she was refitted for towing to Plymouth, where she would serve out the remainder of her days in the same ignominious capacity. When she arrived at her final mooring on 8 June 1826, those who had seen her in the summer of 1815 – the cynosure of a thousand little boats – would not have recognised her, least of all by the new name this Trafalgar veteran had been given: *Captivity*.

ENDNOTES

PRELUDE: BEGUN AND WON

1 Combes-Brassard, *Notice sur la bataille de Mont St Jean*, published in *Souvenirs et correspondance sur la bataille de Waterloo* (Paris: Teissedre, 2000), p.15; quoted Field, p.43.
2 Grouchy, *Marshal Grouchy's Own Account*, p.11.
3 Leeke, Vol. I, pp.10–11, 1866.
4 See Merode-Westerloo, Vol. I, p.349.
5 De Lancey, p.48.
6 Mercer, Vol. I, pp.242–3.
7 Ibid., pp.161–2.
8 Anglesey, *Capel Letters*, pp.111–13.
9 Letter to M d'Arblay, 15–19 June 1815: Burney, Vol. VIII, p.213.
10 Heeley, p.107.
11 Glover, *Waterloo Archive*, Vol. I, p.226.
12 Creevey, *Papers*, p.230.
13 Booth, Vol. I, pp.16–17.
14 Burney, Vol. VIII, pp.430–1.
15 Jackson, pp.16–17.
16 Bell, *Letters*, p.242.
17 Eaton, p.94.
18 Mercer, Vol. I, pp.247–9.
19 Ibid., p.233.
20 Eaton, pp.56–62.
21 Elizabeth Ord's account: Glover, *Waterloo Archive*, Vol. I, p.226.
22 Eaton, p.66.
23 Elizabeth Ord's account: Glover, *Waterloo Archive*, Vol. I, p.226.

24 Creevey, *Life and Times*, p.87.
25 Eaton, pp.62–6.
26 Letter from Col. Samuel Rudyerd, 6 May 1838: Siborne, *Waterloo Letters*, p.231.
27 Lemonnier-Delafosse, p.189.
28 Clarke, p.255.
29 Weltman, p.99.
30 Uffindell, p.104.
31 Barral, p.163.
32 Hofschröer, *Wellington*, p.286.
33 Weltman, p.99.
34 Coignet, p.284.
35 Uffindell, pp.109–10.
36 See Barral, p.112.
37 Simpson, *Visit to Flanders*, p.46.
38 Mercer, Vol. I, p.260.
39 Mercer was convinced this 'single horseman' was Napoleon, citing General Gourgaud's account of the Emperor's impatiently leading his advance guard against the retreating enemy. See Gourgaud, *Campaign of MDCCCXV*, pp.81–2.
40 Mercer, Vol. I, pp.268–70.
41 Morris, pp.140–1.
42 Lieutenant Donald Mackensie, 1st Battalion 42nd Foot: Glover, *Waterloo Archive*, Vol. I, p.185.
43 Hope, p.240.
44 Major General H.T. Siborne, p.337.
45 Glover, *Waterloo Archive*, Vol. I, p.167.
46 Lieutenant Mackensie: Glover, *Waterloo Archive*, Vol. I, p.185.
47 Hope, p.240.
48 Wheeler, p.170.
49 Barral, p.112.
50 Booth, Vol. I, p.15.
51 Simpson, *Paris After Waterloo*, p.18.
52 *The Times*, 21 June 1815.
53 Creevey, *Life and Times*, pp.77–8.
54 Simpson, *Paris After Waterloo*, p.20.
55 Eaton, p.101.
56 Merode-Westerloo, Vol. I, pp.350–1.
57 Burney, Vol. VIII, pp.214–15.
58 Ibid., p.435.
59 Creevey, *Life and Times*, p.86.
60 Glover, *Waterloo Archive*, Vol. I, p.228.
61 Creevey, *Life and Times*, p.78.

62 Chateaubriand, tome II, 3ème Partie, livre 6ème, Chap. 16, p.605.

63 Hope, p.301.

64 De Lancey, p.108, n.14. See also Southey's notes to *The Poet's Pilgrimage*, p.206.

65 Leeke, Vol. 1, pp.10–11.

66 *Mémoires pour server à l'histoires* (107), quoted Houssaye, *1815 Waterloo*, Book II, Chap. IV, n.21.

67 Chateaubriand, tome II, 3ème Partie, livre 6ème, Chaps 16 and 17, pp.606–7.

68 Creevey, *Papers*, p.232.

69 Heeley, p.112.

70 Houssaye, *1815 Waterloo*, Book III, Chap. II, n.40.

71 Ibid., p.256.

72 Grouchy, *Le Maréchal de Grouchy*, pp.113–14.

73 Biot, p.250.

74 Barail, Vol. III, p.185. Houssaye (*1815 Waterloo*, p.460), however, insists the incident is entirely apocryphal, because Gérard and Exelmans were not in the same place at any time on 18 June.

75 See Houssaye, *1815 Waterloo*, p.452.

76 Eaton, p.138.

77 Booth, Vol. I, pp.17–18.

78 De Lancey, pp.48–50.

79 Creevey, *Life and Times*, p.79.

80 Burney, Vol. VIII, pp.214–15.

81 Glover, *Waterloo Archive*, Vol. I, p.228.

82 Anglesey, *Capel Letters*, p.115.

83 Mauduit, Vol. II, p.400.

84 Field, pp.186–7.

85 Pontécoulant, p.328.

86 Mauduit, Vol. II, p.425 footnote.

87 Pontécoulant, p.328.

88 Martin, pp.296–7.

89 See Hofschröer, *German Victory*, p.145; Dörk, p.134.

90 W. Hyde Kelly, p.124.

91 Sir J. Leith to Earl Bathurst, 10 June 1815: Southey, *Chronological History of West Indies*, Vol. III, p.591.

92 Boyer-Peyreleau, p.349.

93 Anon., *Procès du Contre-Amiral le Comte Durand de Linois*, p.8.

94 Southey, *Chronological History of West Indies*, Vol. III, p.594.

95 Anon., *Procès de M. le Comte Durand de Linois*, p.69.

96 Anon., *Procès du Contre-Amiral le Comte Durand de Linois*, p.42.

97 Anon., *Procès de M. le Comte Durand de Linois*, p.37.

98 Anon., *Procès du Contre-Amiral le Comte Durand de Linois*, pp.43–4.
99 Boyer-Peyreleau, pp.363–4.
100 Anon., *Procès du Contre-Amiral le Comte Durand de Linois*, p.78.

PART ONE: SHAMBLES

I

1   Mercer, Vol. I, pp.334–5.
2   Ibid., p. 327.
3   Mercer to H. M. Leathes: Glover, *Waterloo Archive*, Vol. I, p.109.
4   Major General H.T. Siborne, p.222.
5   Sir Harry Smith, p.275.
6   Morris, p.157.
7   Mercer, Vol. I, p.333.
8   Ibid., pp.338–9.
9   Sergeant D. Robertson, 'What the Gordons did at Waterloo': Low, p.164.
10 Leach, pp.394–5.
11 Howell, pp.225–6.
12 Morris, p.163.
13 William A. Scott, p.220.
14 Barbero (p.312) suggests a figure fewer than the combined Anglo-Allied and Prussian losses; Adkin (p.73) suggests 30,600.
15 Hamilton, 2nd Line Battalion, King's German Legion, to his wife, 21 July 1815, Paris: National Army Museum Archive: 2002-07-179.
16 Pattison, p.36.
17 *United Services Journal*, reprinted in *The Kaleidoscope; or Literary and Scientific Mirror*, no. 447, Vol. IX, Liverpool, Tuesday 20 January 1829.
18 Southey, *Tour in the Netherlands*, pp.88–9.
19 Pattison, p.36.
20 Smithers, p.242.
21 Christopher Kelly, p.99.
22 Mercer, Vol. I, pp.335–6.
23 Ibid., p.336.
24 Hope, p.276.
25 Kincaid, p.359.
26 Lawrence, p.213.
27 Jackson, p.69.
28 *Pall Mall Gazette*, 15 February 1865.

29   Ross-Lewin, pp.282–3.
30   Ibid., p.285.
31   Adkin, p.404.
32   Hay, p.201.
33   Robertson, p.161.
34   Ibid., pp.161–2.
35   Mercer, Vol. I, p.342.

II

1   Tomkinson, p.314.
2   Evans, pp.455–6.
3   O'Neil, pp.250–1.
4   Mercer, Vol. I, p.340.
5   William A. Scott, pp.219–21.
6   Eaton, p.281.
7   Simpson, *Visit to Flanders*, p.142.
8   Booth, Vol. I, pp.43–4.
9   Simpson, *Paris After Waterloo*, p.47.
10   John Scott, *Paris Revisited*, p.208.
11   Simpson, *Visit to Flanders*, p.142 footnote.
12   Walter Scott, *Paul's Letters*, Letter IX, p.199.
13   Simpson, *Paris After Waterloo*, p.47.
14   Booth, Vol. I, p.44.
15   Rev. Mr James Rudge, *The Peace-Offering: a Sermon on the Peace*, 1815, quoted in Evans, p.444 footnote.
16   Gleig, *The Subaltern*, p.184.
17   Tomkinson, p.314.
18   Smithers, p.249.
19   Croker, Vol. I, pp.73–4.
20   Ompteda, p.313.
21   Cooper, Vol. I, pp.401–2.
22   Ibid., p.418.
23   Ibid., pp.414–15.
24   *United Services Journal*, reprinted in *The Kaleidoscope; or Literary and Scientific Mirror*, no. 447, Vol. IX, Liverpool, Tuesday 20 January 1829.
25   Cooper, Vol. I, p.417.
26   *Quarterly Review* (March 1843), p.547.
27   Ibid.
28   *Pall Mall Gazette*, 15 February 1865, p.6.
29   Hay, p.202.

30 Walter Scott, *Paul's Letters*, Letter IX, p.205.
31 Cotton, pp.271–2.
32 Tomkinson, p.317.
33 Leeke, Vol. I, pp.75–7.
34 Anon., 'Operation of the Fifth, or Picton's Division in the Campaign of Waterloo', *United Service Journal*, June 1841, pp.189–90.
35 Gleig, *Light Dragoon*, Vol. II, pp.89–90.
36 Colonel Sir Horace Semour KCH: Major General H.T. Siborne, p.19.
37 Wheeler, p.173.
38 See Glover, *Waterloo Archive*, Vol. II, pp.78–88.
39 Howell, p.222.
40 See Christopher Kelly, p.93, and Simpson, *Paris After Waterloo*, pp.279–81, Appendix 1, 'Sufferings of Sir Wm. Ponsonby on the Field'.
41 Anglesey, *Capel Letters*, p.124.
42 Hay, p.212.
43 Croker, Vol. I, p.73.
44 Southey, *Journal of a Tour in the Netherlands*, pp.89–90.
45 Evans, p.456.
46 See George Finlayson, Hospital Assistant, *c*.26 June: Glover, *Waterloo Archive*, Vol. III, p.222.
47 Booth, Vol. II, p.122.
48 Heeley, p.38.
49 Daniel, p.437.
50 Heeley, p.38. See also Southey, *Journal of a Tour in the Netherlands*, p.88.
51 Jackson, p.75.
52 Hay, p.212.
53 Ibid., pp.200–11.
54 Jackson, pp.74–5.
55 Booth, Vol. II, p.122.
56 Croker, Vol. I, p.71.
57 John Scott, *Paris Revisited*, p.219.
58 Glover, *Waterloo Archive*, Vol. III, p.200.
59 Frye, p.27.
60 Evans, p.446.
61 Eaton, pp.287–8.
62 George Finlayson, Hospital Assistant, *c*.26 June: Glover, *Waterloo Archive*, Vol. III, p.222.
63 Anglesey, *Capel Letters*, p.128.
64 Booth, Vol. II, p.122.
65 Walter Scott, *Paul's Letters*, Letter IX, p.205.

66   Thomson, p.5.
67   Georgy to Lady Uxbridge: Anglesey, *Capel Letters*, pp.119–20.

III

1   Vansittart, pp.35–6.
2   To Richard James Esq., Dumbleton, nr. Evesham, Worcs., Brussels, 29 June 1815: Glover, *Waterloo Archive*, Vol. I, p.223.
3   Bell, *Letters*, p.247.
4   Thomson, pp.8–9.
5   Glover, *Waterloo Archive*, Vol. I, p.219.
6   Simmons, pp.367–8.
7   Ibid., p.369.
8   Guthrie, *Surgery of the War*, p.96.
9   Simmons, pp.370–1.
10   Thomson, pp.26–51.
11   Bell, *Letters*, p.230.
12   Thomson, p.28.
13   Hay, pp.198–204.
14   Simpson, *Paris After Waterloo*, Appendix I, p.281.
15   De Lancey, pp.56–70.
16   Hennen, p.255.
17   Guthrie, *Surgery of the War*, p.76.
18   Glover, *Waterloo Archive*, Vol. II, pp.168–9.
19   See Gregory, pp.414–15.
20   Glover, *Waterloo Archive*, Vol. I, pp.214–15.
21   Anglesey, *One-Leg*, p.150.
22   Glover, *Waterloo Archive*, Vol. I, p.215.
23   Hennen, p.255.
24   Guthrie, *Surgery of the War*, p.73.
25   Glover, *Waterloo Archive*, Vol. I, p.221.
26   Hennen, p.255.
27   O'Neil, pp.254–5.
28   Heeley, p.36.
29   Eaton, p.239.
30   Simpson, *Visit to Flanders*, pp.34–41.
31   Hay, p.209.
32   Thomson, pp.22–3.
33   Bell, *Letters*, p.231.
34   Hennen, p.239.
35   Creevey, *Papers*, p.239.
36   Frye, p.28.

37   Creevey, *Papers*, p.239.
38   *The Times*, 25 July 1815.
39   Hennen, p.240 footnote.
40   Bell, *Letters*, pp.241–2.
41   Ibid., p.246.
42   Hennen, p.241.
43   Ibid., pp.241–2.
44   Ibid., p.242.
45   Thomson, p.10.
46   Hennen, p.241.
47   Simpson, *Visit to Flanders*, p.21.
48   Ibid., pp.28–9.
49   Hope, pp.271–3.

IV

1   Mercer, Vol. I, p.346.
2   Eaton, p.160.
3   Jackson, pp.74–5.
4   Creevey, *Papers*, p.238.
5   Frye, pp.27–8.
6   John Scott, *Paris Revisited*, pp.166–7.
7   Simpson, *Visit to Flanders*, p.54.
8   Eaton, p.246.
9   Lady Charlotte, 3 July 1815: Glover, *Waterloo Archive*, Vol. III, p.15.
10   Lady Charlotte, 27 June 1815: ibid., p.9.
11   Lady Charlotte, [28?] June 1815: ibid., p.13.
12   Henry Paget, 24 June 1815: ibid., p.5.
13   Lady Charlotte, 3 July 1815: ibid., p.15.
14   Eaton, pp.270–1.
15   Cole, pp.147–8.
16   Anglesey, *Capel Letters*, p.128.
17   See Croker, *Papers*, Vol. I, p.72.
18   Eaton, p.260.
19   Simpson, *Visit to Flanders*, p.69.
20   Haydon, *Correspondence*, Vol. I, p.288.
21   Southey, *Journal of a Tour in the Netherlands*, pp.92–3.
22   Eaton, pp.263–70.
23   Anglesey, *Capel Letters*, pp.137–8.
24   Southey, *Journal of a Tour in the Netherlands*, p.91.
25   Evans, p.442.
26   Southey, *Journal of a Tour in the Netherlands*, pp.85–6.

27 Eaton, p.295.

28 Ibid., pp.295–6.

29 Haydon, *Correspondence*, Vol. I, pp.287–8.

30 Croker, *Papers*, Vol. I, p.73.

31 Simpson, *Visit to Flanders*, pp.53–4.

32 Ibid., p.143.

33 Croker, *Papers*, Vol. I, p.73.

34 John Scott, *Journal of a Tour of Waterloo and Paris*, p.46.

35 See Walter Scott, *Paul's Letters*, Letter IX, p.208.

36 Eaton, p.284.

37 Walter Scott, *Paul's Letters*, Letter IX, p.209.

38 Evans, pp.448–9.

39 Ibid., pp.449–50.

40 MS *Tour of Waterloo*, quoted by Longford, *Pillar of State*, p.9, where it is cited as belonging to the Naval and Military Club. The archivist of the Naval and Military Club has to date been unable to locate it.

41 Walter Scott, *The Field of Waterloo*, p.16.

42 'Epigram on Scott's Waterloo', *Monthly Repository of Theology and General Literature* 11 (March 1816), p.174.

43 Southey, *The Poet's Pilgrimage to Waterloo*, p.68.

44 Ibid., p.62.

45 Ibid., p.73.

46 Ibid., pp.79–80.

47 Letter to John Cam Hobhouse, 16 May 1816: Byron, p.76.

48 *The Field of Waterloo from the Picton Tree* was auctioned at Sotheby's, London, on Wednesday 4 July 2007: 'Important Turner Watercolours from the Guy and Myriam Ullens Collection'.

49 J. M. W. Turner, *The Field of Waterloo*, Fitzwilliam Museum, Cambridge.

50 J. M. W. Turner, *The Field of Waterloo*, Tate Britain.

51 Canto III, Verse XXVIII.

52 Wordsworth, p.29.

PART TWO: DISPATCHES

I

1 *Royal Cornwall Gazette, Falmouth Packet & Plymouth Journal*, 24 June 1815; *Morning Chronicle*, 21 June 1815; *Trewman's Exeter Flying Post or Plymouth and Cornish Advertiser*, 22 June 1815.

2   21 June 1815.

3   *Morning Post*, 21 June 1815.

4   'Private Correspondence, London, June 16, half past seven p.m.'
     Quoted *Caledonian Mercury*, 19 June 1815.

5   *Quarterly Review*, June 1845, pp.221–3.

6   Wynn, p.166.

7   Sir Harry Smith, Vol. I, p.291.

8   Longford, *Years of the Sword*, p.484.

9   Quoted ibid., pp.484–5.

10   *Morning Post*, 21 June 1815.

11   Lennox, p.218 (quoted from a lecture on the character of the Duke
     of Wellington, delivered at Wells, September 1852, by Montague
     Gore).

12   Anglesey, *Capel Letters*, p.122.

13   Charlotte to Caroline, 26 June 1815: Glover, *Waterloo Archive*,
     Vol. III, p.6.

14   *London Gazette*, 24 June 1815.

15   *London Gazette Extraordinary*, 21 June 1815.

16   See Chateaubriand, tome II, 3ème partie, livre 6ème, Chap. 17,
     pp.607–8.

17   Stanhope, pp.122 and 173.

18   Ibid., p.122.

19   *Morning Post*, 22 June 1815.

20   'Private Correspondence, London, June 21, half past seven p.m.'
     Quoted *Caledonian Mercury*, 24 June 1815.

21   Stanhope, p.122

22   Colby, p.20.

23   *Notes and Queries*, 4th Series, Vol. II, 19 September 1868,
     p.283.

24   *The Christian Miscellany and Family Visitor*, 1865, p.115; Frederick
     Martin, *Stories of Banks and Bankers*, 1865, p.74; Henry Christmas,
     The Money Market: What it is, what it does, and how it is managed,
     1866, p.191.

25   Croker, *Papers*, Vol. I, p.60.

26   Letter from Benjamin Cohen's granddaughter, Lady Colyer-
     Fergusson, *Daily Telegraph*, 9 November 1962 (quoted Rothschild,
     p.37).

27   Rothschild, p.39.

28   *Sun*, 21 June 1815 (quoted *Royal Cornwall Gazette, Falmouth
     Packet & Plymouth Journal*, 24 June 1815).

29   *The Times*, 22 June 1815. The value of stock continued to rise

after the victory was officially announced on Thursday morning, and on Friday: 'Omnium reached 9(5/8) prem[ium] . . . and left off at about 9¼. Consols rose in proportion' (*The Times*, 24 June 1815).

30 Raikes, p.46 (Stanhope, p.122, puts him, mistakenly, at White's).

31 See Evans, p.278. Also quoted in William A. Scott, pp.127-8, dated 17 June.

32 Translation in Christopher Kelly, pp.37-8.

33 Quoted Hofschröer, *Wellington*, p.332.

34 Wellington, *Dispatches*, pp.394-6.

35 Caulaincourt, *Mémoires*, Vol. I, pp.195-6.

36 *Journal de Paris*, 21 June 1815.

37 Caulaincourt, *Napoleon and his Times*, Vol. II, p.156.

38 'Journal kept by a Gentleman in Paris of the daily events and rumours, that agitated the capital from June 20th to July 8th, inclusive': John Scott, *A Visit to Paris in 1814*, pp.xliii-iv.

39 Reprinted *Caledonian Mercury*, 29 June 1815.

40 Raikes, pp.46-7.

41 Thomas Boys, 'Waterloo, arrival in London, and first reading of the Duke's Dispatch', *Notes and Queries*, 1858, 2nd Series, Vol. VI, No. 448.

42 See Southey, *Journal of a Tour in the Netherlands*, p.5.

43 Quoted *Derby Mercury*, 29 June 1815.

44 Thomas Boys, 'Waterloo, arrival in London, and first reading of the Duke's Dispatch', *Notes and Queries*, 1858, 2nd Series, Vol. VI, No. 448.

45 Stanhope, p.173.

46 Thomas Boys, 'Waterloo, arrival in London, and first reading of the Duke's Dispatch', *Notes and Queries*, 1858, 2nd Series, Vol. VI, No. 448.

47 Shelley, p.87.

48 Hon. H. Bennet to Creevey, July 1815: Creevey, *Papers*, pp.240-1.

49 Young, pp.213-15.

50 Brownlow, pp.118-19. Her brother, the Hon. Ernest A. Edgcombe, was unscathed.

51 Young, p.214.

52 Berry, Vol. III, p.61.

53 Brownlow, p.120.

54 See Wynn, p.168.

II

1 Haydon, *Correspondence*, Vol. II, p.272.
2 Haydon, *Diary*, Vol. I, pp.457–8.
3 *Examiner*, 25 June 1815.
4 Haydon, *Life*, Vol. I, p.281.
5 Haydon, *Correspondence*, Vol. II, pp.271–2.
6 Hutchinson, p.82.
7 Thomas De Quincey, 'Dr Parr and His Contemporaries', *Blackwood's Edinburgh Magazine*, June 1831.
8 *Morning Post*, 24 June 1815.
9 *Morning Post*, 23 June 1815.
10 *Morning Post*, 14 June 1814.
11 *Morning Post*, 24 June 1815.
12 *Morning Post*, 24 June 1815.
13 Ballard, pp.116–20.
14 *Morning Chronicle*, 30 June 1815.
15 *Morning Chronicle*, 24 June 1815.
16 *Morning Post*, 26 June 1815.
17 *London Gazette*, 24 June 1815.
18 *The Times*, 24 June 1815.
19 Reported *Morning Chronicle*, 23 June 1815.
20 *Morning Post*, 26 June 1815.
21 *Morning Post*, 29 June 1815.
22 *Morning Chronicle*, 27 June 1815.
23 *Morning Post*, 12 July 1815.
24 *Morning Post*, 17 August 1815.
25 *Morning Post*, 27 June 1815.
26 *Morning Post*, 30 June 1815.

III

1 Irving to Brevoort, 5 July 1815: Irving, p.331.
2 *Leeds Mercury*, 24 June 1815.
3 To Mrs Clarkson, 28 June 1815.
4 *Caledonian Mercury*, 26 June 1815.
5 *Caledonian Mercury*, 26 June 1815.
6 James Pagan, *Glasgow, Past and Present* (Glasgow: 1851), Vol. II, p.113.
7 See 'The mail coach brings the news of Waterloo to Beaminster', at rupertwilloughby.co.uk.

8   De Quincey, p.240.

9   *Edinburgh Advertiser*, 30 June 1815.

10   *Leeds Mercury*, 1 July 1815.

11   *Liverpool Mercury* (quoted from the *Globe*), 30 June 1815.

12   *Morning Chronicle*, 28 June 1815.

13   *Royal Cornwall Gazette* (Truro), 1 July 1815.

14   *The Times*, 7 July 1815.

15   *Morning Post*, 7 July 1815.

16   *Morning Chronicle*, 7 July 1815.

17   *Morning Post*, 7 July 1815.

18   Irving, pp.331–2.

19   Ballard, p.146.

20   Reported *Caledonian Mercury*, 27 July 1815.

21   *Morning Post*, 25 July 1815.

22   Anglesey, *Capel Letters*, pp.130–3.

23   Haydon, *Correspondence*, Vol. I, p.287.

24   *Trewman's Exeter Flying Post or Plymouth and Cornish Advertiser*, 6 July 1815.

25   See Constable, Vol. I, p.128.

26   *Derby Mercury*, 10 August 1815.

27   *Kelso Mail*, 3 July 1815.

28   *Cumberland Pacquet*, 22 August 1815.

29   *Westmorland Advertiser*, 9 September 1815.

30   *Carlisle Patriot*, 26 August 1815.

31   *Carlisle Patriot*, 26 August 1815.

32   *Cumberland Pacquet*, 22 August 1815.

33   Southey to Grosvenor Charles Bedford, 14 August 1815 (Bodleian Library, MS Eng. Lett. C. 25).

34   *Cumberland Pacquet*, 22 August 1815.

35   *Cumberland Pacquet*, 29 August 1815.

36   Southey to Henry Herbert Southey, 23 August 1815 (Bodleian Library, Don. D. 3).

37   Mrs Coleridge to Thomas Poole, 20 September 1815: Coleridge, pp.38–9.

38   *Derby Mercury*, 7 September 1815.

39   Southey to Grosvenor Charles Bedford, 22 August 1815 (Bodleian Library, MS Eng. Lett. C. 25).

40   Southey to Henry Herbert Southey, 23 August 1815 (Bodleian Library, Don. D. 3).

41   Ibid.

42   *Derby Mercury*, 7 September 1815.

43   *Cumberland Pacquet*, 5 September 1815.

PART THREE: DEBACLE

I

1   Grouchy, *Le Maréchal de Grouchy*, p.73.
2   François, Vol. II, p.889.
3   Ibid., p.890. François translated the German as: '*Venez avec nous, braves Français, vous n'avez plus d'armée, Napoleon est mort.*'
4   He is usually, and more correctly, referred to as von Pirch I to distinguish him from his brother, Major General von Pirch II, who commanded the 2nd Infantry Brigade of the I Korps and did not arrive at Waterloo in time to see any action.
5   Gottschalck, p.102.
6   Houssaye, *1815 Waterloo*, p.262.
7   Pajol, p.239.
8   Houssaye, *1815 Waterloo*, p.262.
9   Pajol, p.240; Vandamme to Simon Lorière, 10 May 1830: quoted by Houssaye, *1815 Waterloo*, p.450, n.54.
10   Based on Mann's translation in the 1900 English edition of Houssaye's *1815 Waterloo*, p.263.
11   Martin, p.298.
12   Ross-Lewin, p.282.
13   Fleury de Chaboulon, p.152.
14   Mauduit, pp.471-2.
15   Fleury de Chaboulon, p.152.
16   Coignet, p.288.
17   Mauduit, pp.470, 479.
18   Müffling, *Sketch*, pp.xlvi and xlviii.
19   Southey, *Journal of a Tour in the Netherlands*, p.102.
20   Booth, Vol. II, p.93.
21   'Report of Prussian Officer': ibid., p.100.
22   Lieutenant Golz, 2nd Squadron Brandenburg Uhlans: quoted Hofschröer, *German Victory*, p.152.
23   Booth, Vol. II, pp.99-101.
24   Ibid., Vol. I, p.156.
25   Now the official home of the Belgian royal family.
26   Evans, p.197.
27   Frazer, p.572.
28   'Letter from an Officer of high Rank in the Prussian Army. Genappe sur Oise, near Guise, June 24, 1815': Booth, Vol. I, pp.98-9.
29   Wellington, *Dispatches*, p.552.
30   *The Times*, 29 June 1815.

31 Anon., *Journal of the Three Days of the Battle of Waterloo*, p.64.
32 'From an Officer to his Father (written on the field of battle) dated Les Quatre Bras, 19th June, 1815': Booth, Vol. I, p.71.
33 Lt James Johnstone, Inniskilling Dragoons, to his mother, 11 July 1815: Glover, *Waterloo Archive*, Vol. III, p.52.
34 *The Times*, 29 June 1815.
35 Evans, p.287.
36 Wheatley, pp.75-6.
37 'Extract of a Letter from Charleroi, June 20th, in the morning': Booth, Vol. I, p.83.
38 Müffling, *Sketch*, pp.il-l.
39 Mauduit, p.489.
40 'Extract of a Letter from Charleroi, June 20th, in the morning': Booth, Vol. I, p.84. See also Zieten letter, 20 June at Baumont: ibid., p.226.
41 *Sun*, 20 June 1815.

II

1   Biot, pp.260-1.
2   Quoted Hofschröer, *German Victory*, p.195.
3   Biot, p.263.
4   Fantin des Odoards, pp.438-9.
5   Quoted Uffindell and Corum, p.313.
6   Fantin des Odoards, pp.438-9.
7   John Scott, *A Visit to Paris in 1814*, pp.li-liv.
8   Quoted Hofschröer, *German Victory*, p.190.
9   Blücher to Knesebeck, quoted Houssaye, *1815 Waterloo*, p.242.
10 Blücher to Müffling, quoted Hofschröer, *German Victory*, p.187.
11 Nostitz, quoted ibid., p.190.
12 Müffling, *Passages from my Life*, p.250.
13 Haydon, *Diary*, Vol. IV, p.586.
14 Quoted Hofschröer, *German Victory*, p.207.
15 Ibid., p.209.
16 Arthur Hill to Creevey, 25 June: Creevey, *Papers*, p.239.
17 Wheeler, p.175.
18 *Morning Chronicle*, 13 July 1815.
19 *Morning Chronicle*, 25 July 1815.
20 John Scott, *Paris Revisited in 1815*, pp.246-7.
21 Gleig, *Light Dragoon*, Vol. II, p.103.
22 Ibid., pp.112-13.
23 Quoted Hofschröer, *German Victory*, p.203.
24 Wheeler, pp.179-80.

25 See Frazer, p.586.
26 20 June 1815: Wellington, *Dispatches*, p.494.
27 28 June 1815, 'Adjutant-General to the Officer commanding the — Foot': Wellington, *Supplementary Dispatches*, p.564.
28 'Paris 27 Sept., 1815': Wellington, *Dispatches*, p.647.
29 *Examiner*, 31 December 1815.
30 Wheeler, p.176.
31 *Morning Post*, 18 December 1815.
32 *Morning Chronicle*, 6 January 1816.

III

1   Quoted Hofschröer, *German Victory*, p.215.
2   Quoted ibid., p.216.
3   Grouchy to Davout, 8 a.m., 26 June, Soissons: Grouchy, *Relation Succincte*, 3ème serie, p.106; quoted Hofschröer, *German Victory*, pp.217–18.
4   Grouchy to Davout, 5 p.m., 26 June, Soissons: Grouchy, *Relation Succincte*, 3ème serie, pp.109–10.
5   Article III of treaty executed at Vienna, 25 March 1815, between Great Britain, Austria, Russia and Prussia: Markham, Appendix III, pp.144–5.
6   Unger, Vol. II, pp.310–12.
7   Quoted Hofschröer, *German Victory*, p.222.
8   D'Erlon to Grouchy, 'sur les hauteurs de Gelocourt', 3 p.m., 27 June 1815: *Grouchy, Relation Succincte*, 3ème serie, p.138.
9   Frazer, pp.590 and 591.
10 Copy of letter from Major William Turner, dated 3 July 1815: National Army Museum, Dept. Archives. Acc. No. 7509–62.
11 John Scott, *A Visit to Paris in 1814*, p.lv.
12 Williams, pp.148–9.
13 John Scott, *A Visit to Paris in 1814*, pp.vii–viii.
14 Hobhouse diary, p.145.
15 John Scott, *A Visit to Paris in 1814*, pp.lviii–lix.
16 Grouchy to Davout, 29 June, Claye: *Grouchy, Relation Succincte*, 3ème serie, pp.151–2.
17 Vandamme, p.573.
18 Williams, p.233.
19 John Scott, *A Visit to Paris in 1814*, p.lviii.
20 Hofschröer, *German Victory*, pp.244, 245 and 248.
21 Nostitz, quoted ibid., p.261.
22 *Morning Chronicle*, 17 July 1815.

23 Hobhouse, *Some Letters*, Vol. II, p.117.
24 Williams, pp.239 and 243–4.
25 Hobhouse, *Some Letters*, Vol. II, p.120.
26 Gneisenau to Wellington, quoted Hofschröer, *German Victory*, p.272.
27 Henry Lachouque, *The Last Days of Napoleon's Empire*, p.142, quoted Markham, p.55.
28 Unger, Vol. II, p.319.
29 Reprinted Markham, Appendix VIII.
30 Article III.
31 Simpson, *Paris After Waterloo*, p.101.
32 Wellington, *Dispatches*, p.526.
33 Daniel, p.455.
34 Quoted Hofschröer, *German Victory*, pp.276–7.
35 Wheeler, p.177.
36 James to Fuller, 15 July 1815, Rueil, near Paris: Vansittart, pp.48–9.
37 Creevey, *Papers*, p.241.
38 'Letters of Sergeant William Tennant', Paris, 12 July 1815: Glover, *Waterloo Archive*, Vol. III, p.96.
39 Chateaubriand, tome II, 3ème partie, livre 6ème, Chap. 20, p.628.
40 Williams, pp.262–3.
41 *The Times*, 13 September 1815.
42 Thomas Sydenham to Ben Sydenham, Paris, 11 August 1815: Owen, p.36.
43 Markham, Appendix VIII, p.155.
44 Wellington, *Dispatches*, p.549.
45 Hobhouse diary, p.277.
46 Ibid., p.276.
47 Hobhouse, *Some Letters*, Vol. II, p.173.
48 See *Hull Packet*, 11 July, and *Morning Chronicle*, 13 July 1815.

IV

1 Milton, pp.27–8.
2 Anglesey, *Capel Letters*, p.123.
3 Blücher to Müffling, 19 October 1815, Paris: *Morning Chronicle*, 4 November 1815.
4 *Jackson's Oxford Journal*, 29 July 1815.
5 Walter Scott, *Paul's Letters*, p.328.
6 Williams seems to have conflated and confused this piece with the *Ganymede of Sanssouci*.

7   John Scott, *Paris Revisited in 1815*, p.317.
8   *Morning Post*, 28 August 1815.
9   'Vienna, Sept 24': *Examiner*, 15 October.
10 Wellington to Castlereagh, 'Paris, 23rd Sept., 1815': Wellington, *Dispatches*, pp.642–3.
11 John Scott, *Paris Revisited in 1815*, p.328.
12 Mercer, Vol. II, p.281.
13 John Scott, *Paris Revisited in 1815*, p.329.
14 Cole, p.179.
15 Hope, p.290.
16 See Gronow, pp.92–3.
17 Stanhope, p.217.
18 *Bury and Norwich Post*, 18 October 1815.
19 Milton, p.94.
20 Cole, p.179.
21 Milton, p.97.
22 John Scott, *Paris Revisited in 1815*, p.328.
23 *Morning Chronicle*, 12 September 1815.
24 *Morning Chronicle*, 16 September 1815.
25 Letter from Canova, 'Paris, Sept. 31 [*sic*]': *Morning Chronicle*, 16 October 1815.
26 Frazer, p.602.
27 Quoted Longford, *Pillar of State*, p.26.
28 'From the Rhenish Mercury': *Morning Chronicle*, 18 October 1815.
29 *Leeds Mercury*, 7 October 1815.
30 Simpson, *Paris After Waterloo*, p.268.
31 '*C'est à la Victoire que la France doit ce chef-d'oeuvre, qui lui était destiné*': see Milton, p.96.
32 Cole, p.180.
33 *New Monthly Magazine*, Vol. 7, 1 May 1817, p.307. John Scott, however, put the figure remaining at 274 out of 1,500, and the number removed at 1,226: see *Paris Revisited in 1815*, pp.337–8.
34 Private letter from Paris, 26 November: *Morning Post*, 30 November 1815.
35 Milton, pp.175–6.
36 Jackson, p.107.
37 'Brussels and Frankfurt Papers and Rhenish Mercuries': *Morning Chronicle*, 13 November 1815.
38 Jackson, p.109.
39 'Brussels and Frankfurt Papers and Rhenish Mercuries': *Morning Chronicle*, 13 November 1815.
40 Milton, pp.176–7.
41 John Scott, *Paris Revisited in 1815*, p.350.

NOTES TO PAGES 234–247 353

42 'Brussels and Frankfurt Papers and Rhenish Mercuries': *Morning Chronicle*, 13 November 1815.
43 Jackson, p.110.
44 John Scott, *Paris Revisited in 1815*, pp.349–51.
45 Milton, p.180.
46 Brownlow, pp.170–1.
47 John Scott, *Paris Revisited in 1815*, p.352.
48 *New Monthly Magazine*, Vol. 7, 1 May 1817, p.307.
49 Williams, p.348.
50 'Brussels and Frankfurt Papers and Rhenish Mercuries': *Morning Chronicle*, 13 November 1815.
51 *York Herald, and General Advertiser*, 7 October 1815.

PART FOUR: BONAPARTE

I

1   Coignet, p.288.
2   Larrey, pp.10–13.
3   Comte Hippolyte Marie Guillame Piré.
4   Brack, p.35.
5   Martin, pp.300–1.
6   Notes of Colonel Baudus, recounted by Houssaye, *1815 Waterloo*, p.245.
7   Flahault, p.131.
8   'La Coste's Narrative': Evans, p.402.
9   Gourgaud, *Talks of Napoleon*, p.1.
10 Low, p.185.
11 Gourgaud, *Talks of Napoleon*, p.1.
12 Low, p.185.
13 'La Coste's Narrative': Evans, pp.399 and 402.
14 *The Times*, 29 June 1815.
15 Coignet (p.288) says 10.00.
16 See Anon., *Relation Circonstanciée*, p.99.
17 Fleury de Chaboulon, p.156.
18 Anon., *Relation Circonstanciée*, p.100.
19 Houssaye, *1815 Waterloo*, pp.441–2, n.57.
20 Gourgaud, *Talks of Napoleon*, pp.2–3.
21 Fleury de Chaboulon, p.159.
22 Houssaye, *1815 Waterloo*, p.442, n.60.
23 Saint-Denis, p.136.
24 Gourgaud, *Talks of Napoleon*, p.3.

25 Caulaincourt, *Mémoires*, p.196.
26 Fleury de Chaboulon, pp.166–7.
27 Houssaye, *Seconde Abdication*, pp.17–20.
28 Thiébault, *Mémoires*, Vol. V, p.359.
29 Quoted by Houssaye, *Seconde Abdication*, p.31.
30 Fleury de Chaboulon, pp.171–2.
31 John Scott, *Visit to Paris in 1814*, p.xlv.
32 Fleury de Chaboulon, pp.174–6.
33 More correctly, the 'Additional Act to the Constitutions of the Empire'.
34 Constant, pp.284–5.
35 Houssaye, *Seconde Abdication*, p.46.
36 Constant, p.283 footnote.
37 Thiébault, *Mémoires*, Vol. I, p.424.

II

1   Houssaye, *Seconde Abdication*, p.56.
2   Villemain, pp.308–9.
3   Atteridge, p.229.
4   Villemain, pp.309–10.
5   Atteridge, pp.327–8.
6   Villemain, pp.310–12.
7   Atteridge, p.331.
8   John Scott, *Visit to Paris in 1814*, p.xlvii.
9   *Morning Chronicle*, 28 June 1815.
10 30 June 1815.
11 *Morning Chronicle*, 28 June 1815.
12 *Leeds Mercury*, 1 July 1815.
13 Pasquier, p.281.
14 Martineau, p.41.
15 Fleury de Chaboulon, p.200.
16 Ibid., p.202.
17 Ibid., p.209.
18 See O'Meara, Vol. I, p.125.
19 Fleury de Chaboulon, p.208.
20 Ibid., p.201.
21 Gourgaud, *Talks of Napoleon*, p.5.
22 Montholon, Vol. I, p.30.
23 Fleury de Chaboulon, p.211.
24 Savary, p.117.
25 Ibid., p.130.

26 Markham, Appendix VII, pp.152–3.
27 Marchand, pp.267–8.
28 Müffling, *Passages from My Life*, p.272.
29 Hofschröer, *German Victory*, p.240.
30 Montholon, Vol. I, p.48.
31 Ibid., pp.49–50.
32 Ibid., p.55.
33 Gourgaud, *Talks of Napoleon*, p.7.
34 Savary, p.135.
35 Caulaincourt, *Napoleon and His Times*, Vol. II, p.194.
36 Montholon, Vol. I, p.55.

III

1   Flahault, p.143.
2   Ibid., p.144, n.1.
3   Keith to Lady Keith: ibid., pp.144–5.
4   27 June 1815: ibid., p.145.
5   Maitland, p.16.
6   Flahault, pp.146–8.
7   Ibid., p.147.
8   Montholon, Vol. I, p.66.
9   Ibid., p.69.
10 Ibid., pp.70–2.
11 Maitland, p.45.
12 Ibid., pp.30–1.
13 Montholon, Vol. I, pp.82–3.
14 Maitland, p.42.
15 Las Cases, pp.29–30.
16 Maitland, p.45; Las Cases, p.29.
17 Las Cases, p.31.
18 Duhamel, p.41.
19 Maitland, p.68.
20 Montholon, p.101.
21 Maitland, p.115.
22 Keith to Miss Elphinstone, 25 July 1815: Flahault, p.155.
23 Melville to Keith, 25 July 1815: ibid., pp.157–8.
24 Maitland, p.141.
25 Melville to Keith, 29 July 1815: Flahault, p.161.
26 24 July 1815.
27 *Morning Post*, 3 August 1815.
28 Liverpool to Castlereagh, 21 July 1815: Thornton, p.63.

29 Keith to commanders of *Liffey* and *Eurotas*, 26 July 1815: Maitland, pp.125–6.
30 *Morning Post* (from the *Plymouth Telegraph*), 8 August 1815.
31 Maitland, p.135.
32 Keith to Miss Elphinstone, 1–3 August 1815: Flahault, p.167.
33 *Morning Post* (from the *Plymouth Telegraph*), 8 August 1815.
34 Maitland, p.132.
35 *Leeds Mercury*, 12 August 1815 (from *Congdon's Plymouth Telegraph*).
36 Keith to Miss Elphinstone, 1 August 1815: Flahault, p.167.
37 Maitland, p.150.
38 Ibid., p.136.
39 *Star*, 5 August 1815.
40 *Morning Post*, 5 and 8 August 1815.
41 11 August 1815.
42 Montholon, p.104.
43 See Yonge, p.175.
44 The parallel was made by Norman MacKenzie in an article in *History Today* (Vol. 60, Issue 5, 2010). See also his book, *Fallen Eagle*.
45 Thornton, pp.156–7.
46 Maitland, p.161.
47 He was spared this humiliation because of government fears of riot.
48 He was variously referred to subsequently as Andrew and Alexander. There was similar confusion about the surname, which included the variants Mackenrot and Mackernot.
49 Thornton, p.176.
50 *Bury and Norwich Post*, 17 January 1816.
51 Maitland, pp.167–8.
52 Duhamel, p.95.
53 *Star*, 10 August 1815.

CODA: RETRIBUTION

1 Southey, *Chronological History of the West Indies*, pp.594–605.
2 *The Times*, 13 March 1816.
3 *The Times*, 4 July 1815.
4 *Morning Chronicle*, 30 August 1815.
5 *The Times*, 25 November 1815.
6 *The Times*, 26 December 1815.
7 *Morning Post*, 15 January 1816.

8   See Houssaye, *Seconde Abdication*, pp.512–18.
9   Conchard, p.86.
10   See Houssaye, *Seconde Abdication*, pp.476–9.
11   See Resnick, p.52.
12   See Gwynn Lewis, 'The White Terror of 1815 in the Department of the Gard: Counter-Revolution, Continuity and the Individual', *Past & Present*, No. 58 (February 1973), pp.108–35.
13   Quoted Resnick, p.55.
14   *The Times*, 13 July 1816.
15   *The Times*, 8 August 1816.
16   Hartmann and Millard, p.47.
17   Reported *Liverpool Mercury*, 5 June 1818.
18   *Leeds Mercury*, 1 November 1817.
19   *Liverpool Mercury*, 5 June 1818.
20   *Royal Cornwall Gazette*, 16 May 1818.
21   National Army Museum 7001/11.
22   Flahault, p.178.

SELECT BIBLIOGRAPHY

Primary Sources

Anglesey, George Charles Henry Victor Paget, Marquess of (ed.), *The Capel Letters* (London: 1955)

Anglesey, George Charles Henry Victor Paget, Marquess of, *One-Leg: The Life and Letters of Henry William Paget* (London: 1961)

Anon., *Journal of the Three Days of the Battle of Waterloo* (London: 1816)

Anon., *Procès de M. le Comte Durand de Linois, Contre-Amiral et de Monsieur le baron Boyer de Peyreleau* (Paris: 1816)

Anon., *Procès du Contre-Amiral le Comte Durand de Linois, Gouveneur de la Guadeloupe, et de l'Adjutant-Commandant Baron Boyer de Peyreleau, Commandante de la meme colonie . . .* (Paris: 1816)

Anon., *Relation circonstanciée de la dernière Campagne de Buonaparte, terminée par la bataille de Mont-Saint-Jean, dite de Waterloo ou de la Belle Alliance* (Paris: 1816)

Bagot, Mrs Charles, *Links with the Past* (London: 1901)

Ballard, Joseph, *England in 1815* (Boston & New York: 1913)

Barail, François Charles du, *Mes Souvenirs*, Vol. III, 8th edn (Paris: 1898)

Barral, Georges, *L'épopée de Waterloo; narration nouvelle des cent jours et de la campagne de Belgique en 1815 composée d'apres les documents inédits et les souvenirs de mes deux grand-pères, officiers de la grande armée, combattants de Waterloo* (Paris: 1895)

Bell, Charles, *A Dissertation on Gun-Shot Wounds* (London: 1814)

Bell, Charles, *Letters of Sir Charles Bell* (London: 1870)

Berry, [Mary], *Extracts of the Journals and Correspondence of Miss Berry*, ed. Lady Theresa Lewis, 3 vols (London: 1865)

Biot, Hubert François, *Souvenirs Anecdotiques et Militaires* (Paris: 1901)

[Booth, John], *The Battle of Waterloo*, 10th edn, enlarged and corrected (London: 1817)

Boyer-Peyreleau, Eugene-Edouard, *Les Antilles Françaises, particulierement La Guadeloupe*, Vol. III (Paris: 1826)

Brack, Général de, 'Recit inedit d'un combattant', *Carnet de la Sabretache, Revue militaire retrospective* (Paris: 1901). Reprinted as *Waterloo: Récits de Combattants* (Paris: 1999)

Brownlow, Emma Sophia, Countess, *Slight Reminiscences of a Septuagenarian from 1802 to 1815*, 3rd edn (London: 1868)

Burney, Fanny, *The Journals and Letters of Fanny Burney*, ed. Joyce Hemlow, Curtis D. Cecil, Althea Douglas, Patricia Boutilier, Edward A. Bloom, Lillian D. Bloom, Peter Hughes, Patricia Hawkins and Warren Derry, 12 vols (Oxford: 1972–84)

Byron, George Gordon, *Byron's Letters and Journals*, ed. Leslie A. Marchand, Vol. V (London: 1976)

Caulaincourt, Duke of Vicenza, *Napoleon and His Times*, 2 vols (Philadelphia: 1838)

Caulaincourt, Géneral de, Duc de Vicence, *Mémoires*, Vol. I (Paris: 1933)

Chateaubriand, François de, *Mémoires d'Outre-Tombe*, Edition du centenaire intégrale et critique en partie inédite établie par Maurice Levaillant (Paris: [1947])

Coignet, Jean-Roche, *Cahiers (1799–1815)*, nouvelle édition revue et corrigée (Paris: 1909)

Cole, Sir Lowry, *Memoirs of Sir Lowry Cole*, ed. Maud Lowry Cole and Stephen Gwynn (London: 1934)

Coleridge, Mrs S.T., *Minnow among Tritons: Mrs S.T. Coleridge's Letters to Thomas Poole*, ed. Stephen Potter (London: 1934)

Conchard, Vermeil de, *L'Assassinet du Maréchal Brune* (Paris: 1887)

Constable, John, *Correspondence*, ed. R. B. Beckett, 6 vols (Ipswich: 1962–8)

Cotton, Edward, *A Voice from Waterloo*, 6th edn, revised and enlarged (London: 1862)

Cooper, Bransby Blake, *The Life of Sir Astley Cooper, Bart*, 2 vols (London: 1843)

Constant, Benjamin, 'Memoirs sur les Cent-Jours', *Oeuvres Complètes*, ed. Kurt Klooche and André Cabanis, Vol. XIV (Tubingen: 1993)

Creevey, Thomas, *The Creevey Papers*, ed. the Right Hon. Sir Herbert Maxwell (New York: 1904)

Creevey, Thomas, *Creevey's Life and Times: a further selection from the correspondence of Thomas Creevey*, ed. John Gore (London: 1934)

Croker, John Wilson, *The Croker Papers*, ed. Louis J. Jennings, 3 vols (London: 1884)

Damitz, Karl von, *Histoire de la Campagne de 1815*, traduite d'allemand par Léon Griffon (Paris: 1840)

[Daniel, John Edgecombe], *Journal of an Officer in the Commissariat Department of the Army* (London: 1820)

De Lancey, Magdalene, *A Week at Waterloo*, ed. Major B.R. Ward (London: 1906)

De Quincey, Thomas, 'The English Mail Coach', *Confessions of an English Opium-Eater and Other Writings*, ed. Barry Milligan (London: 2003)

Dörk, E.M., *Das Koniglich Preussische 15 Infanterie-Regiment . . . in Kriegsjahren 1813, 1814 und 1815* (Eisleben: 1844)

Drouet, [Jean Baptist], Maréchal, Comte d'Erlon, *Vie Militaire* (Paris: 1844)

[Eaton, Charlotte Anne, née Waldie], *Narrative of a Residence in Belgium* (London: 1817)

Evans, John, *Battle of Waterloo; or A Faithful and Interesting History of the Unparalleled Events connected therewith . . .* (New York: 1819)

Fantin des Odoards, Louis Florimond, *Journal du General Fantin des Odoards* (Paris: 1895)

Flahault, *The First Napoleon, Some Unpublished Documents from the Bowood Papers*, ed. Henry William Edmund Patty FitzMaurice, Earl of Kerry (London: 1925)

Fleury de Chaboulon, Pierre Antoine Édouard, *Mémoires*, Zèine partie (Paris: 1901)

François, Charles-François, *Journal du Capitaine François 1792–1830*, ed. Charles Grolleau, 2 vols (Paris: 1903–4)

Frazer, Augustus Simon, *Letters of Colonel Augustus Simon Frazer written during the Peninsular and Waterloo Campaigns*, ed. Major General Edward Sabine (London: 1859)

Frye, Major W.E., *After Waterloo: Reminiscences of European Travel 1815–1819* (London: 1908)

Gérard, Étienne Maurice, *Quelques Documents sur la Bataille de Waterloo* (Paris: 1829)

Gibney, the Late Dr, *Eighty Years Ago, or the Recollections of an Old Army Doctor* (London: 1896)

Gleig, G.R., *The Subaltern* (London: 1825)

Gleig, G.R. (ed.), *The Light Dragoon*, 2 vols (London: 1844)

Gleig, G.R., *The Story of the Battle of Waterloo* (New York: 1847)

Glover, Gareth (ed.), *Letters from the Field of Waterloo* (London: 2004)

Glover, Gareth (ed.), *The Waterloo Archive*, 4 vols (Barnsley: 2010–13)

Gomm, Sir William Maynard, *Letters and Journals* (London: 1881)

Gourgaud, Gaspard, *The Campaign of MDCCCXV* (London: 1818)

Gourgaud, Gaspard, *Talks of Napoleon at St Helena*, trans. Elizabeth Wormeley Latimer (Chicago: 1903)

Gregory, James, *Additional Memorial to the Managers of the Royal Infirmary* (Edinburgh: 1803)

Gronow, [Rees Howell], *Reminiscences and Recollections*, 2 vols (London: 1900)

Grouchy, Emmanuel de, *Fragments Historiques relatifs à la Campagne de 1815 et à la Bataille de Waterloo* (Paris: 1829)

[Grouchy, Emmanuel de], *Relation Succincte de la Campagne de 1815 en Belgique* (Paris: 1845)

Grouchy, Emmanuel de, *Le Maréchal de Grouchy du 16 au 19 Juin 1815* (Paris: 1864)

Grouchy, Emmanuel de, *Marshal Grouchy's Own Account of the Battle of Waterloo* (St Louis, MO: 1915)

Guthrie, George, *A Treatise on Gun-Shot Wounds*, 3rd edn (London: 1827)

Guthrie, George, *Surgery of the War*, 6th edn (Philadelphia: 1862)

Hartmann and Millard, *Le Texas, ou Notice Historique sur le Champ d'Asile* (Paris: 1819)

Hay, William, *Reminiscences 1808–1815 Under Wellington*, ed. his daughter, Mrs S. C. I. Wood (London: 1901)

Haydon, Benjamin Robert, *Life of Benjamin Robert Haydon, Historical painter, from his Autobiography and Journals*, ed. Tom Taylor, 3 vols (London: 1853)

Haydon, Benjamin Robert, *Correspondence and Table-Talk*, ed. Frederic Wordsworth Haydon, 2 vols (London: 1876)

Haydon, Benjamin Robert, *Diary*, ed. Willard Bissell Pope, 5 vols (Cambridge, Mass.: 1960–3)

Heeley, Edward, 'Journal of Edward Heeley', *Journal of the Society for Army Historical Research*, Vol. 64, Summer and Autumn 1986, Nos 258–9

Hennen, John, *Principles of Military Surgery*, 3rd edn (London: 1829)

Hobhouse, John Cam, *The Substance of Some Letters . . . during the Last Reign of the Emperor Napoleon*, 2 vols (London: 1816)

Hobhouse, John Cam, *Diary*, petercochran.files.wordpress.co/2009/12/17-hundreddays.pdf

[Hope, James], *Letters from Portugal, Spain, and France, during the Memorable Campaigns of 1811, 1812, & 1813; and from Belgium and France in the year 1815 by a British Officer* (London: 1819)

[Howell, Thomas], *Journal of a Soldier of the 71st or Glasgow Regiment, Highland Light Infantry, from 1806 to 1815* (Edinburgh: 1819)

Hutchinson, Sarah, *Letters of Sarah Hutchinson from 1800–1835*, ed. Kathleen Coburn (London: 1954)

Irving, Washington, *Life and Letters*, ed. Pierre M. Irving, 4 vols (London: 1862–4)

Jackson, Lieutenant Colonel Basil, *Notes and Reminiscences of a Staff Officer, chiefly relating to the Waterloo Campaign and to St Helena matters during the captivity of Napoleon*, ed. R. C. Seaton MA (London: 1903)

Kelly, Christopher, *A Full and Circumstantial Account of the Memorable Battle of Waterloo* (London: 1817)

Kennedy, General Sir James Shaw, *Notes on the Battle of Waterloo* (London: 1865)

Kincaid, John, *Adventures in the Rifle Brigade*, 3rd edn (London: 1847)

Larrey, Dominique Jean, Baron, *Relation Médicale de Campagnes et Voyages de 1815 à 1840* (Paris: 1841)

Las Cases, Comte Emmanuel de, *The Life, Exile, and Conversations of the Emperor Napoleon* (Edinburgh: 1835)

Lawrence, William, *Autobiography of Sergeant William Lawrence* (London: 1886)

Leach, Jonathan, *Rough Sketches of the Life of an Old Soldier* (London: 1831)

Leeke, William, *Lord Seaton's Regiment . . . at the Battle of Waterloo*, 2 vols (London: 1866)

Leith, Sir James, *Memoirs* (London: 1818)

Lemonnier-Delafosse, Marie Jean Baptiste, *Campagnes de 1810–1815 Souvenirs Militaires* (Havre: 1850)

[Lennox], *Three Years with the Duke of Wellington in Private Life* (London: 1853)

Low, Edward, *With Napoleon at Waterloo and other Unpublished Documents* (London: 1911)

Maitland, Sir Frederick Lewis, *The Surrender of Napoleon*, a new edition (Edinburgh & London: 1904)

Marchand, Louis-Joseph, *In Napoleon's Shadow. Being the First English language Edition of the Memoirs of Louis-Joseph Marchand, Valet and Friend of the Emperor 1811–1821* (San Francisco: 1998)

[Martin, Jacques-François], *Souvenirs d'un Ex-Officier* (Paris: 1867)

Mauduit, Hippolyte de, *Derniers Jours de la Grande Armée*, Vol. 2 (Paris: 1848)

Mercer, Cavalié, *Journal of the Waterloo Campaign*, 2 vols (Edinburgh and London: 1870)

Merode-Westerloo, Henri Marie Ghislain, Comte de, *Souvenirs du Comte de Merode-Westerloo, Senateur du royaume, ancient envoyé extraordinaire . . .* , 2 vols (Paris: 1864)

Milton, Henry, *Letters of the Fine Arts, written from Paris in the year 1815* (London: 1816)

Montholon, Charles Jean François Tristan de, *History of the Captivity of Napoleon at St Helena*, 2 vols (London: 1846)

Morris, Thomas, *Recollections of Military Service* (London: 1845)

Müffling, Friedrich Carl Ferdinand von, *History of the Campaign . . . in the Year 1815* (London: 1816)

Müffling, Friedrich Carl Ferdinand von, *Sketch of the Battle of Waterloo* (Brussels: 1833)

Müffling, Friedrich Carl Ferdinand von, *Passages from my Life*, ed. with notes by Colonel Philip Yorke, 2nd edn revised (London: 1853)

O'Meara, Barry E., *Napoleon in Exile, or A Voice from St Helena*, 2 vols, 4th edn (London: 1922)

Ompteda, Ludwig Friedrich Christian Carl von, *Hanoverian-English Officer a hundred years ago: Memoirs of Baron Ompteda*, ed. L. von Ompteda (London: 1892)

O'Neil, Charles, *Military Adventures of Charles O'Neil* (Worcester, MA: 1851)

Ord, Elizabeth, 'Memoir', in Glover, *Waterloo Archive*, Vol. 1 (Barnsley, South Yorkshire: 2010)

Owen, Edward (ed.), *The Waterloo Papers: 1815 and Beyond* (Tavistock: 1997)

Pajol, Charles Victor, *Pajol: Général en Chef*, Vol. III (Paris: 1874)

Pasquier, Etienne-Denis, *Memoirs*, ed. Duc d'Audiffret-Pasquier, trans. Charles E. Roche, Vol. III (London: 1894)

Pattison, Frederick Hope, *Personal Recollections of the Waterloo Campaign* (Glasgow: 1870)

Peyrusse, Guillaume Joseph Roux, *Mémorial et Archives* (Carcassonne: 1869)

[Pontécoulant, Count Louis Gustave le Doulcet de], *Napoleon à Waterloo* (Paris: 1866)

Raikes, Thomas, *Reminiscences of Social and Political Life in London and Paris*, Vol. III (London: 1857)

Robertson, David, *Journal of Sergeant D. Robertson, late 92nd Foot: comprising the different campaigns, between the years 1794 and 1818, in Egypt, Walcheren, Denmark, Sweden, Portugal, Spain, France, and Belgium* (Perth: 1842)

Ross-Lewin, Henry, *With the 'Thirty-Second in the Peninsular and Other Campaigns . . .*, ed. J. Wardell (Dublin: 1904)

Saint-Denis, Louis Etienne, *Napoleon from the Tuileries to St Helena; personal recollections of the emperor's second mameluke and valet, Louis Etienne St Denis (known as Ali)*, trans. Frank Hunter Potter (New York and London: 1922)

Savary, Anne Jean Marie René, Duc de Rovigo, *Memoirs*, Vol. IV, Parts I and II (London: 1828)

Scott, John, *A Visit to Paris in 1814*, 2nd edn (London: 1815)

Scott, John, *Paris Revisited in 1815 by way of Brussels, including a walk over the Field of Waterloo* (London: 1815)

Scott, John, *Journal of a Tour of Waterloo and Paris* (London: 1842)

Scott, Walter, *The Field of Waterloo, a Poem* (Edinburgh: 1815)

[Scott, Walter], *Paul's Letters to his Kinsfolk* (Edinburgh: 1816)

Scott, William A., *Battle of Waterloo, or Correct Narrative of the Late Sanguinary Conflict* (London: 1815)

Shelley, Frances, Lady, *Diary of Frances Lady Shelley*, ed. her grandson, Richard Edgcumbe (London: 1913)

Shorter, Clement (ed.), *Napoleon and his Fellow Travellers* (London: 1908)

Siborne, Major General H.T. (ed.), *Waterloo Letters* (London: 1891)

Simmons, George, *A British Rifle Man: Journals and Correspondence*, ed. Lieutenant Colonel Willoughby Verner (London: 1899)

Simpson, James, *Visit to Flanders in July, 1815* (Edinburgh: 1816)

Simpson, James, *Paris After Waterloo* (Edinburgh: 1853)

Smith, Sir Harry, *Autobiography of Lieutenant-General Sir Harry Smith* (London: 1901)

Smithers, Henry, *Observations made during a residence in Brussels* (Brussels: 1820)

Southey, Robert, *Collected Letters of Robert Southey*, ed. Ian Packer and Lynda Pratt, Part Four (1810–15), available online; original MSS in the Bodleian Library

Southey, Robert, *The Poet's Pilgrimage to Waterloo* (London: 1816)

Southey, Robert, *Journal of a Tour in the Netherlands in the Autumn of 1815* (Boston and New York: 1902)

Southey, Thomas, *A Chronological History of West Indies*, Vol. III (London: 1827)

Stanhope, Philip Henry, *Notes of Conversations with the Duke of Wellington*, 3rd edn (London: 1889)

Thiébault, Paul Charles François Adrien Henri Dieudonne, *Mémoires*, publiés sous les auspices de sa fille, Mlle Claire Thiébault, d'après le manuscript original, tomes I–V (Paris: 1893–95)

Thiébault, Paul Charles François Adrien Henri Dieudonne, *Memoirs*, trans. and condensed by Arthur John Butler, 2 vols (London: 1896)

Thomson, J., *Report of Observations made in the British Military Hospitals in Belgium after the Battle of Waterloo; with some remarks on Amputation* (Edinburgh: 1816)

Tomkinson, William, *The Diary of a Cavalry Officer* (London: 1895)

Vandamme, *Le Général Vandamme et sa Correspondance*, ed. A. du Casse, Vol. II (Paris: 1870)

Vansittart, Jane (ed.), *Surgeon [Haddy] James's Journal* (London: 1964)

Villemain, Abel François, *Souvenirs Contemporains d'Histoire et de Littérature*, 3ème partie (Paris: 1855)

Wellington, Arthur Wellesley, Duke of, *Dispatches . . . 1799 to 1815*, Vol. 12 (London: 1838)

Wellington, Arthur Wellesley, Duke of, *Supplementary Dispatches, Correspondence and Memoranda*, Vol. 14 (London: 1872)

Weltman, Hans, *Geschichte des Infanterie-Regiments von Horn (3-tes Rheinisches) N. 29, im Auftfrage des Regiments* (Triers: 1894)

Wheatley, Edmund, *The Wheatley Diary: A Journal and Sketchbook Kept during the Peninsular War and the Waterloo Campaign*, ed. Christopher Hibbert (London: 1964)

Wheeler, William, *The Letters of Private Wheeler*, ed. B. H. Liddell Hart (London: 1951)

Williams, Helen Maria, *A Narrative of the Events which have taken place in France from the Landing of Napoleon Bonaparte . . . till the Restoration of Louis XVIII* (Cambridge: 1894)

Wordsworth, Dorothy, *Journals of Dorothy Wordsworth*, ed. E. de Selincourt, Vol. II (London: 1944)

Wynn, Frances Williams, *Diaries of a Lady of Quality*, ed. A. Hayward, 2nd edn (London: 1864)

Young, Julian Charles, *A Memoir of Charles Mayne Young, Tragedian* (London and New York: 1871)

Secondary Sources

Adkin, Mark, *The Waterloo Companion* (London, 2001)

Atteridge, A. Hilliard, *The Bravest of the Brave: Michel Ney, Marshal of France, Duke of Elchingen, Prince of the Moscowa 1769–1815* (London: 1912)

Barbero, Alessandro, *The Battle: a New History of the Battle of Waterloo* (London: 2005)

Black, Jeremy, *The Battle of Waterloo: a New History* (London: 2010)

Clarke, Hewson, *History of the War from the Commencement of the French Revolution to the Present Time*, Vol. III (London: 1816)

Colby, Reginald, *The Waterloo Dispatch* (London: 1965)

Cordingly, David, *Billy Ruffian: the Bellerophon and the Downfall of Napoleon* (London: 2003)

Crumplin, Michael, *Men of Steel: Surgery in the Napoleonic Wars* (Wykey: 2007)

Crumplin, Michael, *The Bloody Fields of Waterloo: Medical Support at Wellington's Greatest Battle* (Huntingdon: 2013)

Crumplin, M.K.H., and P. Starling, *A Surgical Artist at War: the Paintings and Sketches of Sir Charles Bell 1809–1815* (Edinburgh: 2005)

Dalton, Charles, *The Waterloo Roll Call*, 2nd edn, revised and enlarged (London: 1904)

Duhamel, Jean, *The Fifty Days: Napoleon in England* (London: 1969)

Field, Andrew W., *Waterloo: the French Perspective* (Barnsley: 2012)

Foulkes, Nick, *Dancing into Battle: a Social History of Waterloo* (London: 2006)

Giles, Frank, *Napoleon Bonaparte England's Prisoner: the Emperor in Exile, 1816–21* (London: 2001)

Glover, Michael, *A Very Slippery Fellow: the Life of Sir Robert Wilson* (Oxford: 1978)

Gottschalck, Max, *Geschichte des 1. Thüringischen Infanterie-Regiments Nr.31* (Berlin: 1894)

Hamilton-Williams, David, *Waterloo New Perspectives* (London: 1993)

Hamilton-Williams, David, *The Fall of Napoleon: the Final Betrayal* (London: 1994)

Hofschröer, Peter, *1815 The Waterloo Campaign – Wellington, His German Allies and the Battles of Ligny and Quatre Bras* (London: 1998)

Hofschröer, Peter, *1815 The Waterloo Campaign – The German Victory: From Waterloo to the Fall of Napoleon* (London: 1999)

Houssaye, Henry, *1815 Waterloo*, trans. Arthur Emile Mann (London: 1900)

Houssaye, Henry, *1815: La Seconde Abdication – La Terreur Blanche*, 4th edn (Paris: 1905)

Howarth, David, *A Near Run Thing: the Day of Waterloo* (London: 1968)

Jorricks, Raymond J., *In Flight with the Eagle: A Guide to Napoleon's Elite* (Tunbridge Wells: 1988)

Kaufman, Mathew H., *Musket-Ball and Sabre Injuries from the First Half of the Nineteenth Century* (Edinburgh: 2003)

Keegan, John, *The Face of Battle* (London: 1976)

Kelly, W. Hyde, *The Battle of Wavre and Grouchy's Retreat* (London: 1905)

Longford, Elizabeth, *Wellington: The Years of the Sword* (London: 1969)

Longford, Elizabeth, *Wellington: Pillar of State* (London: 1972)

MacKenzie, Norman, *Fallen Eagle: How the Royal Navy Captured Napoleon* (Lewes: 2009)

Markham, David J., *The Road to St Helena: Napoleon after Waterloo* (Barnsley: 2008)

Martineau, Gilbert, *Napoleon Surrenders* (London: 1971)

Resnick, Daniel P., *The White Terror and the Political Reaction after Waterloo* (Harvard, MA: 1966)

Robbe, Emilie, and François Lagrange (eds), *Napoléon et L'Europe* (Paris: 2013)

Roberts, Andrew, *Waterloo: Napoleon's Last Gamble* (London: 2005)

Rothschild, Nathaniel Mayer Victor, Baron, *The Shadow of a Great Man* (London: 1982)

Samuel, Ian, *An Astonishing Fellow: the life of General Sir Robert Wilson* (Abbotsbrook, Bourne End, Bucks.: 1985)

Siborne, William, *History of the War in France and Belgium in 1815 . . .* (London: 1844)

Smith, Digby, *The Napoleonic Data Book* (London: 1998)

Thornton, Michael John, *Napoleon after Waterloo: England and the St Helena Decision* (Stanford, CA: 1968)

Uffindell, Andrew, *The Eagle's Last Triumph: Napoleon's Victory at Ligny, June 1815* (London: 2006)

Uffindell, Andrew, and Michael Corum, *On the Fields of Glory: the Battlefields of the 1815 Campaign* (London: 1996)

Unger, W. von, *Blücher*, Vol. II (Berlin: 1908)

Yonge, Charles Duke, *The Constitutional History of England from 1760 to 1860* (London: 1882)

ACKNOWLEDGEMENTS

I am grateful to the Society of Authors for the award of a travel grant that enabled me to visit the battlefield of Waterloo for the first time in February 2013. Thanks also to John Mackinson of Discovery Travel for accompanying me on the trip, for driving me along the route of Napoleon's advance and retreat, and for exploring with me the battle sites of Quatre Bras, Ligny and Wavre, as well as the bars and restaurants of Brussels.

Thanks also to the staff of the wonderful London Library, the British Library, Liverpool University Library, Liverpool Central Library, the John Rylands Library, Manchester, the National Library of Scotland, the Fellow's Library of the Surgeon's Hall, Edinburgh, and the library of the National War Museum at Edinburgh Castle; and to the staff of the National Archives, the Tate Britain Archive, and the archive of the National Army Museum in Chelsea. Thanks to Johanna Cook at Abbotsford for showing me Sir Walter Scott's Waterloo relics; to Julie Lawson for arranging the visit; and to Jim Lawson for driving us there. Thanks to Ian S. Wood for reading the Prelude of this book in manuscript, and for late-night discussions of military matters over drams. Thanks to Gordon Whiteman for help with French translation, Waltraud Boxall and Eberhard Bort for German and Mike Wrigglesford for Dutch. Thanks also to Leonie Stedman at the Victoria Gallery and Museum, Liverpool, for showing me a fine collection of 'Waterloo Teeth' and to Helen Swan at Apsley House for allowing me to view the Duke of Wellington's own set outside of opening hours. Thanks to Carys and Julian McCarthy for hospitality in New Malden. Thanks to David Blayney Brown of Tate Britain for pointing me towards Turner's Waterloo sketchbook; to Justin Cavernelis-Frost, Archivist of the Rothschild Foundation, for answering my queries about Nathan Rothschild; to Owen Connolly for material about the Waterloo Monument on Peniel Heugh Hill; to Graham Snell, secretary of Brooks's, for an inconclusive search of the club's 'betting book' for wagers made on the night of 21 June 1815. I was privileged to spend a happy couple of hours discussing Waterloo with the Marquess of Anglesey at Plas Newydd, the year before he died. Dr Michael V. Leggiere of the University of North Texas and Professor Christine Haynes of the University of North Carolina provided me with useful information at the King's College London conference, 'Waterloo: The Battle that Forged a Century', in September 2013.

I owe a great debt of gratitude to Michael Crumplin FRCS for his generous help, advice and encouragement in lending me precious source material from his collection, sharing his surgical knowledge and skill, and reading the 'Shambles' section in manuscript.

As ever, my thanks and love for so many things go to my partner Sian Hughes, who has lived with this subject matter of this book for the last four years and with whom I climbed to the top of Peniel Heugh and its tower late on an August afternoon.

Thanks to my agent Bill Hamilton; to my publisher at the Bodley Head, Stuart Williams; to my copy-editor Jane Selley, to Julia Connolly for a stunning jacket design and to Katherine Ailes for her patience and efficiency in navigating the book through production to publication.

I do not know whether other authors write with a particular reader in mind – a reader they know will be fascinated, amused, or gripped by the same subjects, the same humour, the same ways of telling a story, as they are themselves. When that reader is also the author's editor the writing of a book is a less lonely occupation and becomes instead an immensely rewarding collaboration. I have been fortunate, for nearly twenty-five years, to have Will Sulkin as my particular reader, editor, collaborator and friend. To him this book is dedicated.

LIST OF ILLUSTRATIONS

Prelude: 'Übersichtskarte für den 18 Juni' from *Napoleons Untergang 1815* by von Lettow-Vorbeck (Berlin: 1904)

Shambles: engraving of J. M. W. Turner's *Field of Waterloo from the Picton Tree* © Tate, London 2014

Dispatches: engraving of David Wilkie's *Chelsea Pensioners reading the Waterloo Dispatch* © The Trustees of the British Museum

Debacle: engraving of George Cruikshank's *Return of the Paris Diligence* © The Trustees of the British Museum

Bonaparte: engraving of William Orchardson's *Napoleon on board the Bellerophon* © The Trustees of the British Museum

Retribution: engraving of Jean-Léon Gérôme's *Execution of Marshal Ney* © Museums Sheffield

INDEX

French army: and Waterloo
campaign, 3–5, 12–15, 21–3,
25–8, 31–5; battalion size, 169;
retreat from Waterloo, 175–89;
wounded arrive in Paris,
189–90; disintegration, 201–3;
defeated by Prussians in
skirmish outside Villers-
Cotterêts, 204–5; causes trouble
in Paris, 207; ongoing morale
problems, 208–9; prepares for
defence of Paris, 208–9; chiefs
protest against Bourbon
reinstatement, 208–9; Exelmans
beats Prussians at Villacoublay
and Versailles, 210–11; defends
Paris, 212; forced to retire
behind Loire, 213–14; Davout
and Ney report to Chambers
on state of, 261–4; Napoleon's
farewell proclamation to, 273;
lingering links with Napoleon,
277–9
French prisoners: medical
treatment of wounded, 85–8,
89–90; conditions on Medway
hulks, 123, 176; Grouchy
considers trying to rescue those
in Brussels, 174; Prussian
treatment of, 176; legal status
of, 309–10; *Bellerophon* fitted
out as hulk, 333
Fromentin, Captain, 38–9
Frye, Major W. E., 92
Fuller, John, 147

Gambier, Captain, 292
gangrene, 82, 86–8
Gassicourt (pharmacist), 258
Gaudin, Michel, Duc de Gaëta
(French Finance Minister), 248
Genappe, 177–80, 241–2
George Augustus Frederick,
Prince Regent (later George IV,
King of England): attends
entertainment at Boehms'

house, 127–8; Waterloo
dispatch is brought to, 134,
135; goes into mourning, 145;
and fundraising for veterans
and families, 148; announces
Wellington's capture of Paris,
156; fifty-third birthday, 160;
Prussians give him a pair of
Napoleon's spurs, 180;
Napoleon writes to him to ask
for sanctuary, 292–3; letters
never delivered, 302
Gérard, General, 22, 23, 28, 174
Géricault, Théodore (painter),
140–1
Germany *see* Prussia; Prussian
army
Gerpinnes, 244
Ghent, 21, 23–4, 117–18
Girard, General, 243
Girard, Stephen (banker), 330
Glasgow, 152
Glasgow, HMS, 284
Gneisenau, General Graf von, 14,
180–1, 212, 213, 276–7
Gordon, Lieutenant-Colonel Sir
Alexander, 113, 114, 116
Gordon, Theodore (hospital
superintendent), 86
Gourgaud, General: accompanies
Napoleon from battlefield, 244,
246–7; accompanies him to
Malmaison, 272, 275–6;
surveys Malmaison's defences,
276; on Napoleon's clothes
when leaving Malmaison, 279;
follows Napoleon to coast,
280; sails to England with
letters for Prince Regent from
Napoleon, 292–3; arrives in
England but not allowed to
disembark, 297, 302; returns
to Napoleon's entourage, 302;
accompanies Napoleon to St
Helena, 315
Grantham, Lady, 127

Chart of Basque Roads
and the
Three entrances to the Port of
Rochefort.

La Rochelle

Les Baraig

Fort

La Digue

Pointe de l'Aiguillon

F

Les Tour

Rade de la Basque Police

Vergeron

S. Blanceau

Port

ISLE
DE
RE

Madame de la Faute

S. Martin

Pointe Sablon

Rade de S. Martin

St. Martre

Les Dun

Longitude west from Greenwich

PERTUIS BRETON

PERTUIS D'ANTIOCHE

La Charente

Chatelaillon

Rochers de Saumonards

C

Les Sables d'Olonne

N

S